Parnell in Perspective

Parnell in Perspective

Edited by
D. George Boyce
and
Alan O'Day

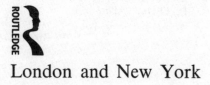

London and New York

First published 1991
by Routledge
11 New Fetter Lane, London EC4P 4EE

Simultaneously published in the USA and Canada
by Routledge,
a division of Routledge, Chapman and Hall, Inc.
29 West 35th Street, New York, NY 10001

Typeset in 10/12pt Times by
Intype, London
Printed in Great Britain by
Clays Ltd, St. Ives plc

British Library Cataloguing in Publication Data
Parnell in perspective.
  1. Ireland. Politics
  I. Boyce, D. G. (David George) II. O'Day, Alan
  941.5081092

Library of Congress Cataloging in Publication Data
Parnell in perspective / edited by D. George Boyce and Alan O'Day.
      p. cm.
    Includes bibliographical references and index.
    1. Parnell, Charles Stewart, 1846–1891. 2. Ireland—Politics and
government—19th century. 3. Nationalists—Ireland—Biography.
4. Politicians—Ireland—Biography. 5. Home rule (Ireland)
I. Boyce, David George, 1942-   . II. O'Day, Alan.
DA958.P2P43 1991
941.5081'092—dc20   91–10043

ISBN 0–415–06722–7
ISBN 0–415–06723–5 pbk

Contents

vi *Contents*

Chronology of key dates in Parnell's life

1846 (27 June) Born of John Henry and Delia Stewart Parnell, at Avondale, County Wicklow
1853 Went to school in England
1859 Death of father – made ward of chancery and received Avondale
1865 Matriculated at Magdalene College, Cambridge
1869 Sent down from Cambridge
1871 Visited the United States
1872 Returned home from his American trip
1873 High sheriff, Wicklow; ineligible to stand at the general election, early 1874
1874 (March) Stood for and lost County Dublin parliamentary by-election
1874 Co-opted onto Executive Committee of Home Rule League
1875 (April) Contested and won Meath by-election
1875 (26 April) Made maiden speech in House of Commons
1876 Joined Joseph Biggar in parliamentary obstruction
1876 (November) Visited the United States with John O'Connor Power for the celebration of the Independence centenary
1877 (August) Elected president of the Home Rule Confederation of Great Britain
1878 (October) John Devoy offered conditional support of Fenians to Parnell
1879 (April) First meeting of Devoy and Michael Davitt with Parnell in Dublin
1879 (5 May) Death of Isaac Butt. William Shaw replaced Butt as chairman of the home rule party
1879 (8 June) Spoke at Westport, Mayo, land meeting
1879 (July) His candidate successful at Ennis by-election

1879 (October) Irish National Land League founded. Parnell accepted its presidency

1880 (January–March) Fundraising tour of the United States and Canada

1880 (April) Parnell returned for Meath, Cork City and Mayo at general election. He chose to sit for Cork

1880 (May) Parnell elected chairman of the Irish parliamentary party

1880 (July) Parnell first made acquaintance with Mrs Katharine O'Shea

1880 (August) Compensation for Disturbances Bill defeated in House of Lords

1880 (19 September) Spoke at Ennis, advocating 'moral Coventry'

1880 (December) Prosecuted by the government. Trial collapsed in January 1881 when jury failed to reach a verdict

1881 (February–April) Government introduced a number of coercion measures and the Land Bill. Michael Davitt's ticket of leave was withdrawn

1881 (2 February) Irish parliamentary party considered and rejected withdrawal from Westminster

1881 (September) National Conference determined, on Parnell's advice, to 'test' the Land Act

1881 (9 October) Parnell spoke at Wexford in reply to Gladstone's 'resources and civilization' speech at Leeds

1881 (13 October) Parnell arrested and confined in Kilmainham jail. Remained imprisoned until May 1882

1881 (18 October) No-Rent Manifesto issued from Kilmainham jail

1882 (April) Parnell set out conditions of 'Treaty' with government

1882 (2 May) Parnell released from prison as cabinet accepted Kilmainham Treaty

1882 (6 May) Lord Frederick Cavendish and Thomas Burke, the Irish chief secretary and under-secretary respectively, murdered in Phoenix Park, Dublin. In aftermath the police watched Parnell. His association with Mrs O'Shea came to the general attention of the cabinet

1882 (October) Irish National League founded with Parnell as president

1883 (October) Irish National League of Great Britain founded with T. P. O'Connor as president, replacing Parnell who had remained nominal head of the earlier organization since first being elected in 1877

1883 (December) Parnell received cheque for over £37,000 as testimonial at public meeting

1884 (27 November) William Henry O'Shea gave Chamberlain note purporting to be Parnell's views on Crimes Act and local government reform

1885 (21 January) Parnell spoke at Cork on 'ne plus ultra'

1885 (June) Resignation of Gladstone's government; Salisbury became prime minister

1885 (25 August; 1 September) In major addresses in Dublin Parnell defined the position for the coming general election

1885 (5 October) Parnell spoke at the first nominating convention held at Wicklow

1885 (30 October) Katharine O'Shea sent Gladstone draft by Parnell of home rule constitution of Ireland

1885 (November–December) General election. Eighty-five Irish constituencies returned nationalists, plus T. P. O'Connor's triumph for the Scotland Division, Liverpool, giving Parnell the 86 of 1886, a number which exactly equalled the difference between the two British parties

1885 (17 December) Gladstone's conversion to home rule disclosed by his son

1886 (January) Salisbury resigned

1886 (1 February) Gladstone prime minister

1886 (10 February) Galway by-election: Parnell overcame opposition to W. H. O'Shea's candidature

1886 (8 April) Gladstone introduced Home Rule Bill

1886 (17 April) John Morley introduced Land Purchase Bill; later withdrawn

1886 (8 June) Government of Ireland Bill defeated in the House of Commons

1886 (July) Coalition of Conservatives and Liberal Unionists gained a majority at the general election

1886 (December) Plan of Campaign begun

1887 (April) *The Times* published letters purported to be Parnell's, apparently justifying Phoenix Park murders. Coercion Bill passed through Parliament

1888 (20 July) Parnell spoke at the National Liberal Club

1888 (13 August) Special Commission established

1889 (February) Forgery by Pigott of the Parnell letters exposed

1889 (8 May) Parnell spoke at the Eighty Club, London

1889 (22 November) Conclusion of Special Commission

1889 (18–19 December) Parnell visited Gladstone at Hawarden

1889 (24 December) Captain O'Shea filed a divorce petition against his wife naming Parnell as co-respondent

1890 (13 February) Report of Special Commission

1890 (17 November) O'Shea received a decree nisi in his successful divorce petition

1890 (20–1 November) National Liberal Federation expressed strong feelings privately against Parnell

1890 (25 November) Parnell re-elected chairman of Irish party

1890 (28 November) Parnell issued manifesto 'To the people of Ireland' (published in morning press on 29 November)

1890 (1–6 December) Second party meeting in Committee Room 15 began 'split' when a majority of MPs left to convene a further meeting under the chairmanship of Justin McCarthy

1890 (3 December) Catholic Episcopal Standing Committee denounced Parnell

1890 (10 December) Parnell arrived in Dublin for a hero's welcome

1890 (22 December) Anti-Parnellite candidate won Kilkenny by-election

1891 (February) Boulogne negotiations between Parnell, John Dillon and William O'Brien broken off

1891 (April) Anti-Parnellite won North Sligo by-election

1891 (25 June) Marriage of Parnell and Mrs O'Shea

1891 (July) Anti-Parnellite won Carlow by-election

1891 (27 September) Parnell's last speech at Creggs, Roscommon

1891 (6 October) Death of The Chief at Brighton

1891 (11 October) Funeral, burial in Glasnevin

Notes on contributors

Paul Bew is a Reader in the Department of Political Science at The Queen's University of Belfast. His many publications include *Land and the National Question in Ireland; C. S. Parnell*; and *Conflict and Conciliation in Ireland*.

D. George Boyce is a Professor in the Department of Political Theory and Government at the University College of Swansea. Among his publications are *Englishmen and Irish Troubles; Nationalism in Ireland; The Irish Question in British Politics*; and *Nineteenth-Century Ireland*.

Philip Bull is Senior Lecturer in the Department of History at La Trobe University, Melbourne. He has written several articles including recent contributions to *Irish Historical Studies* and *The Revolution in Ireland* edited by D. George Boyce.

Anthony Claydon is a Fellow of the Institute of Historical Research. He is completing a Ph.D. at University College, London.

Sally Warwick-Haller is a Senior Lecturer in History at Kingston Polytechnic. Her *William O'Brien and the Irish Land War* was published in 1990.

Michael Hurst is a Fellow at St John's College, Oxford. His many books have been on varied topics. His contributions to Irish history include *Joseph Chamberlain and the Liberal Reunion; Parnell and Irish Nationalism*; and *Maria Edgeworth and the Public Scene*.

John Kelly is a Fellow in English at St John's College, Oxford. He is Editor of *The Collected Letters of W. B. Yeats*, Vol. I, Vol. II will appear shortly.

Liam Kennedy is a Lecturer in the Department of Economic and

Social History at The Queen's University of Belfast. He has published widely in academic journals and co-edited *An Economic History of Ulster*.

James Loughlin is a Lecturer in History, University of Ulster. He has written several articles and is the author of *Gladstone, Home Rule and the Ulster Question*.

Alan O'Day is a Senior Lecturer in History at the Polytechnic of North London and Visiting Professor at Concordia University, Montreal. His many writings include *The English Face of Irish Nationalism*; and *Parnell and the First Home Rule Episode*. He edited *A Survey of the Irish in England (1872)* which was published in 1990.

C. J. Woods is a part-time Lecturer in History at St Patrick's College, Maynooth. He has published several articles including a contribution to *Ireland Under the Union* edited by F. S. L. Lyons and R. A. J. Hawkins, and is working on an edition of Thomas Russell's journals.

Introduction

D. George Boyce
and
Alan O'Day

Charles Stewart Parnell (1846–91) stands between Daniel O'Connell and Eamon de Valera in the triumvirate whose careers coincided with, and helped shape, the formation of modern Irish nationalism; but he towers above them in popular perception; and, unlike his great predecessor and successor, he became a focus for those whose concerns were as much literary as political. He was enveloped in a kind of mystique usually reserved in Ireland for the martyred dead – an accolade not normally accorded to politicians in the constitutional tradition. Parnell mounted no scaffold and spent merely a brief time in prison, a confinement passed in relative comfort. He differed from other heroes in the nationalist Pantheon in being the universally recognized leader of the Irish 'race'. O'Connell and de Valera cast no similar net which covered those outside Ireland as well as the people at home.

Parnell's lofty standing is at first sight surprising. He had few of the popular gifts of O'Connell, nor de Valera's baptism of fire in the cauldron of armed insurrection. O'Connell made his way to the political leadership of Catholic Ireland in adverse circumstances. He was a Catholic in an age when his co-religionists were trying to advance from a century of powerlessness and degradation. Although he achieved much, his reputation remains the object of criticism and he is regarded with ambivalence: was he not the Catholic who promised that, if Ireland was governed well, then her people of all religious persuasions would be content to become 'West Britons'? De Valera steered his country to the brink of total sovereign independence and yet – father of his people though he might claim to be – he never achieved that romantic and enduring fame that made Parnell an influential figure posthumously as he was in life. Neither O'Connell or de Valera has been the subject of a Hollywood film or BBC mini-series: Parnell has featured in both media.

2 D. George Boyce and Alan O'Day

On the face of it Parnell seems an unlikely candidate for political canonization. He was fundamentally a West Briton. Parnell was reserved and spoke with a polite, unmistakable English voice. Moreover he was a Protestant landlord who sought to take Ireland not towards a bucolic Gaelic future, like some of the later Sinn Feiners, but a leader more concerned to industrialize and modernize Irish society. O'Connell, the Catholic landlord, trained as a lawyer, had to fight his way to the top; de Valera, a teacher, was typical of his 'revolutionary generation', but owed his rise to a dry, but passionate, style and an ability to learn from his mistakes and then to claim that he had never made any. He and O'Connell were able political organizers who never neglected the structures of power. Parnell, in contrast, entered politics from the top. As a landlord, a political career was always open to him – it was what people of his class did. But they rarely entered politics on the nationalist side; it was even more rare to find them heading popular causes. And his rise was remarkably quick: in 1874 he was an unknown and unsuccessful parliamentary aspirant; in 1875 he was returned to the House of Commons for Meath; within two years he was a promising newcomer; by 1880 he had become the master of a small and as yet insecure home rule party. Yet also by 1880 he had won the recognition of rural Ireland because he did what no other leading home ruler would: he placed himself at the head of a widespread, and frequently illegal, agrarian radical movement, the Land League. Parnell, however, was never driven by the hatred of landlordism which motivated many of his supporters and his championship of home rule contained a cerebral quality usually absent in those who followed him. He was 'uncrowned king' of a country, the object of a popular veneration of a people who shared few of his opinions on the proper order of society.

Historians have been aware of the need to study Parnell and also of the problems of assessing him. F. S. L. Lyons caught both the fascination and dilemma of portraying 'one of the most elusive and shadowy figures in the modern history of Ireland'.[1] Despite massive documentation for the era, Parnell himself has remained a problem for study because he left no significant body of personal papers, kept no diary, was naturally reserved, even mysterious, in his relationships – and notably in his contacts with his newer, less gentlemanly colleagues in the Irish party. Much of what is known about Parnell is second-hand information – chiefly the later memories of people who knew him – or his own words delivered in numerous parliamentary and public speeches. Yet, there is little of a private or intimate nature which sheds light on Parnell's inner thoughts or motivations.

In spite of, or perhaps because of, his ambiguity Parnell is one Irish figure whose place has remained unchallenged. Opinions concerning his affair with Mrs O'Shea, or the attempt to retain the leadership in 1890–1, differ but no aspersion has been cast on the genuineness of Parnell's commitment to the aim of Irish self-government. O'Connell's credentials as a popular nationalist and democrat are suspect, de Valera's record of government soiled his repute among posterity, but Parnell's standing as the man who, but for the treachery of colleagues and bigotry of the clergy, would have secured home rule remains unsullied. O'Connell and de Valera were defeated by the efforts of Britain and their own limitations – Parnell's failure was due to the treason of his own people. His success in the 1880s has seemed the lesson of national unity, the disaster of the fall, a parable on the defects of the Irish. In reality, as modern writers have recognized, Parnell's views were more complex, his actions less than totally self-sacrificing. It was the land question which catapulted him into being the 'uncrowned king', but from the shelter of Kilmainham jail he confessed to Mrs O'Shea that 'Politically it is a fortunate thing for me that I have been arrested, as the movement is breaking fast, and all will be quiet in a few months, when I shall be released'. In February 1882 he reported to her,

> At least I am very glad that the days of platform speeches have gone by and are not likely to return. I cannot describe to you the disgust I always felt with these meetings, knowing as I did how hollow and wanting in solidarity everything connected with the movement was.[2]

If academics have come to explore Parnell's ideas and intentions with critical scrutiny, little of this has seeped through to the wider public. Hugh Leonard's 'Parnell and the Englishwoman' simply repeats and confirms the old uncritically admiring version of the Parnell myth.

While Parnell's most concrete achievement was to win legislation and change attitudes on Irish land ultimately culminating in making the country's farmers owners of the soil they worked, his lasting recognition arose from Gladstone's adoption of home rule for Ireland. Parnell's role and his vision have been the subjects of intense analysis but little has happened to blur the near triumph. The unity he forged among the nationalist majority in Ireland, his apparent influence on British leaders, the sense of strength which Parnell imparted, were lasting legacies which time has not blotted out. Parnell's era remains the only time when Irishmen seemed capable of dictating to Britain's leaders. O'Connell turned tail and ran at the sight of British resistance; the Free State, or at least its form and extent, was forced upon the Irish people by a prime minister of Britain. De Valera might talk tough about the Treaty but it was he who declined to face the lion in his den – Parnell not only did so but bearded him in it as well.

Throughout the 1880s The Chief moved from strength to strength. After the tribulations of the years 1880 to 1885 he formed a working alliance with a great English political movement. The attempt by *The Times* to link him with agrarian crime collapsed in humiliating defeat with the revelation that Richard Pigott had forged the letters which purported to reveal Parnell's sympathy for the Phoenix Park murders. By 1890 he seemed to be an omnipotent figure, but the revelations of the divorce court, where he did not contest the allegations of Captain O'Shea, suddenly cast Parnell from his pedestal. The manner of his fall, the last campaign with its appeal to the 'hillside men', the marginal people at the bottom of the heap in Ireland, his tragic death, and the subsequent weakness of the national movement, reinforced the Parnell legend and, in fact, added new dimensions to it. Neither O'Connell or de Valera found fresh sources of support in their respective demises. O'Connell's death was an anticlimax; de Valera, though a much beloved elder statesman, had become a political embarrassment to a country anxious to move in different economic and political directions from his. Parnell's vision has never come to seem so dated. His movement and the ideals which animated it have remained germane to successive generations. This is because it has been possible to see him from so many angles. Even Parnell's Protestantism, something he wore very lightly himself, has proved a bonus. To have a Protestant head of a popular movement has made it possible to equate nationalism with something more and nobler than simply being coterminous with Catholicism, and also has reflected a tolerance which the Irish people have aspired to rather than the sectarianism which too often has been characteristic of the island. Parnell's significance has been neatly expressed by two people, one a great leader in his own right, de Valera, the other a popular American novelist, Thomas Flanagan. The former, speaking at Creggs, Roscommon, the scene of Parnell's final speech, in 1946, linked him to the onward march of the nation but also paid tribute to his contribution to land reform and 'on the very ground on which we stand, came to an end a long period of devoted service – a period of leadership which brought our people from the slough of despair to the firm hope of a final victory'.[3] Parnell had, de Valera declaimed, taught the Irish to 'set aside the futility of expecting a voluntary change of heart in imperial masters and to rely confidently on themselves'. Equally pertinently, a character in Flanagan's novel, *The Tenants of Time*, observes that Parnell was 'in life what he is now is memory – an outline, a shape into which we had poured our hopes'.[4]

This volume marks the centenary of Parnell's death and serves as a salute to his continued impress upon the active memory not merely of Ireland and the Irish 'race' but of the wider world. His significance seems as compelling now, even after critical academic reassessment, as it was a hundred years ago. Yet, the contributions show that there is still no consensus on precisely what made up Parnell's mystique, influence and policy. Passage of time has added new dimensions to understanding The Chief without rendering a final verdict. Two broad themes weave the chapters together – analyses of the contexts of power and the ideas and images he evoked. In the first section essays examine Parnell's relations with the Catholic church, with colleagues such as Michael Davitt and William O'Brien, where he fits in the spectrum of nationalisms, his impact on British politics and the political content of the last campaign. In the second section chapters consider Parnell's political and economic ideology, the factors which made him a charismatic figure, and how he came to be treated in literature and biography. In short, the volume deals with the man and the myth.

Readers will find themes, incidents and facts which are familiar along with those which are less well known. Also, they quickly will be aware that the individual contributors interpret facets of Parnell's life differently and even at times in quite contradictory ways, thus emphasizing the variety of possibilities opened up by his life. The chapters do not make a biography in the usual sense but confirm and advance existing studies of Parnell and his times, providing meat for future interpretations. Although the volume does not purport to be a collective biography, it will be evident that the pictures of R. Barry O'Brien and F. S. L. Lyons are shaded now in distinctively fresh colours. In an age of revisionist history, it is notable that the chapters do not make Parnell seem smaller than he appeared to his contemporaries; but, rather, by exploring the complexity of the political world in which he lived, they explain more clearly his significance. And not just his political significance narrowly construed. For those who stray into this volume from the BBC series 'Parnell and the Englishwoman',[5] a quite different sort of person unfolds before their eyes. Still, the series, for all its manifold factual misrepresentations and interpretative simplicities, reveals both the special power and the fascination of The Chief. That quality inspired James Joyce to write one of the most moving passages in modern Irish literature:[6]

> Mr Casey, freeing his arms from his holders, suddenly bowed his head on his hands with a sob of pain.
> - Poor Parnell! he cried loudly. My dead king!
> He sobbed loudly and bitterly.
> Stephen, raising his terror-stricken face, saw that his father's eyes were full of tears.

NOTES

1 F. S. L. Lyons, review of Conor Cruise O'Brien, *Parnell and his Party, 1880–90, Irish Historical Studies*, 11, 1958–9, pp. 64–9.
2 Katharine O'Shea, *Charles Stewart Parnell: his Love Story and Political Life*, London, 1914, vol. I, pp. 207, 235–6.
3 Quoted in Maurice Moynihan (ed.), *Speeches and Statements by Eamon de Valera, 1917–73*, Dublin 1980, p. 492.
4 Thomas Flanagan, *The Tenants of Time*, London, 1988, p. 313.
5 'Parnell and the Englishwoman', BBC television series. Published as: Hugh Leonard, *Parnell and the Englishwoman*, London, 1991.
6 James Joyce, *A Portrait of the Artist as a Young Man*, London, 1964 edn, p. 40.

Part I
Contexts of power

1 Parnell and the Catholic church

C. J. Woods

Parnell's Protestantism was purely social. As a boy he questioned religion and as squire of Avondale he never read the lesson in church. Tolerant of the religious beliefs of others, he was himself an unbeliever.[1] His lack of concern for Protestant interests does at least help to explain how Parnell found it possible to co-operate with Catholic ecclesiastics and to promote their objectives; it helps also to explain the willingness of the ecclesiastics to co-operate with Parnell. Why Parnell and the Catholic church should have found it desirable to work together remains to be seen.

I

When the young Charles Stewart Parnell sought to enter Parliament in 1875 as one of the representatives for County Meath he was careful to secure the support of the parish priest of Rathdrum in County Wicklow, where he was the landlord, as well as of local Meath priests and of the Bishop of Meath, Thomas Nulty.[2] The choice of constituency was a good one, considering the course Parnell's political career was to take, for Nulty was one of the very few bishops at that time not beholden to Cardinal Cullen (who detested the Fenians) and he was the only one to be already an active promoter of agrarian reform.[3]

Once elected, Parnell showed little interest in ecclesiastical issues. His concerns were ones that were likely to endear him to the Fenians rather than to the priests. Quickly he rose to prominence in Butt's home rule party as a leading member, and then as head, of a small group of 'obstructionists', who defied custom and decorum as a means of focusing attention on the home rule question. Three other members of the group were Fenians: Joseph Biggar (its founder), John O'Connor Power and Frank Hugh O'Donnell.[4]

Parnell caused a sensation in the House of Commons in 1876 by a spirited defence of the 'Manchester martyrs'. Inside and outside Parliament he campaigned for an amnesty for the remaining Fenian prisoners.[5] He became a member of a political prisoners visiting committee formed in April 1877 at the instigation of Michael Davitt, then still imprisoned in Dartmoor; he was one of the first to meet Davitt after his release in December 1877; and he was one of the few non-Fenians on the reception committee that organized a rapturous welcome home a month later to the last of the liberated Fenian prisoners – probably the largest Fenian-organized demonstration in Dublin since the McManus funeral in 1861. Parnell's association with Fenians went deeper in March 1878 when he and two other 'active' members of Butt's party attended a secret meeting of Fenians in London to discuss mutual co-operation.[6] In August 1879 Parnell had been elected President of the Home Rule Confederation of Great Britain, a body much more under Fenian influence than the Irish parent-body, the Home Rule League, which the Parnellites had already penetrated.[7]

Parnell's espousal, in the closing weeks of 1879, of the cause of agrarian reform in the west of Ireland likewise had little to do with the Catholic church. It was the beginning of the 'new departure' in Irish politics – a combination of 'active' parliamentarians and Fenians or ex-Fenians with local leaders to form the Land League. The initiatives were taken locally in County Mayo by James Daly of Castlebar (editor of the *Connaught Telegraph*), John James Louden of Westport (a barrister and farmer) and Matthew Harris of Ballinasloe (a builder and member of the supreme council of the Irish Republican Brotherhood (IRB), the Fenian organization in Ireland). In the spring of 1879, Daly called the famous Irishtown meeting. He was assisted by some local farmers and by some Connaught Fenians including Davitt.[8] Parnell was consulted by Davitt and, though he was not present, he did attend and address (speaking after Davitt and two other well-known Fenians) a similar but better publicized meeting at Westport on 8 June. It is the Westport meeting that best illustrates Parnell's involvement in the land agitation at this time and his relations with the Catholic church. It was held in the face of episcopal opposition, a letter having appeared in the Nationalist daily, the *Freeman's Journal*, above the name of the popular Archbishop of Tuam, John MacHale, denouncing the agitation as 'directly tending to impiety and disorder in church and society'. Davitt considered Parnell's refusal to be deterred by the archbishop's letter as 'the most courageously wise act of his whole career'.[9] The only flicker of support from the Catholic clergy was a public letter from two priests of MacHale's diocese.[10]

At the meetings at Irishtown, Westport and elsewhere in the summer of 1879 the absence of priests was as evident as the presence of Fenians. One meeting, that held at Claremorris on 13 July, was different in this respect and a closer examination reveals something of the delicate nature of relations between the emerging agrarian movement and the local clergy. On the platform together were Fenians and priests as well as other local organizers (merchants from the town and tenant-farmers from the countryside). The parish priest of Claremorris, Ulick Joseph Bourke, presided.[11] Bourke must at least have had a sneaking sympathy for Fenianism, for as president in the 1860s of St Jarlath's, the diocesan college at Tuam, he had been the mentor of a number of young men belonging to the IRB; he was moreover a firm believer in peasant proprietorship.[12] 'For the past six months', he stated from the chair, 'the Catholic clergy have not, owing to some misunderstanding, been on the same platform with the people. Today, however, the priests and people of Mayo are as one.'[13] This unity was more apparent than real. John Devoy, emissary of the American Fenians who was behind the scenes (attending a meeting of Mayo Fenians in a Claremorris public house), recalled how Bourke arrived early to find awaiting him letters and telegrams from the archbishop's secretary (and nephew), Thomas MacHale,

> insisting that the resolutions must include one for Catholic education and another in favour of the temporal power of the pope. He was told that this was to be a land meeting . . . and . . . there must be nothing sectarian in the resolutions.[14]

The clergy stayed away from the meeting on 16 August at Daly's Hotel, Castlebar, to form the Land League of Mayo; so did Parnell.[15] Why Parnell did not take any prominent part in the agitation between the Westport meeting on 8 June and a farmers' meeting at Limerick on 21 August has not been satisfactorily explained. Davitt was to recall how Parnell, questioning him afterwards about the Irishtown meeting, 'was intensely interested, especially about the clerical opposition, and this hostility may perhaps have been one reason why he showed some disinclination for a time to become identified with the movement'.[16] Parnell was involved in the summer months in what must then have seemed a mere sideshow to the great land meetings even if with hindsight it can be seen as a highly significant event in the history of his relations with the Catholic church: the Ennis by-election. In opposition to the candidate of the Home Rule League, the *Freeman's Journal* and the local clergy, Parnell nominated one of his own disciples, James Lysaght Finigan, an anticlerical who had served in the French Foreign Legion. Finigan won by six votes. Later Parnell confided: 'I would have retired from public life if Ennis had been lost, for it would have satisfied me that the priests were supreme in Irish politics.'[17] When the proprietor of the *Freeman*, Edmund Dwyer Gray, accused Parnell of using the expression 'papist rats' to describe opponents of a university bill, the archbishop of Cashel, Thomas William Croke, intervened to reconcile the two antagonists.

The role of Croke in relations between Parnell and the Catholic church was to prove pivotal. From that time on Croke took every opportunity to intervene in politics, almost always in support of Parnell, on whom he bestowed the most lavish praise – he referred to him publicly in June 1881 as 'the immortal Parnell'.[18] Parnell for his part made use of Croke at about this time by approaching him and obtaining his support for the agrarian agitation. In a speech made at Holycross on 1 June 1881, Croke stated:

Mr Parnell, in Dublin, more than two years ago, when this movement first commenced, waited upon me in the hotel in which we stop in Dublin and, to use a common expression, he literally went upon his knees to me . . . to use all my influence to have the priests join the movement, because, said he, without the priests it cannot succeed and with them it cannot be a failure.[19]

The existence of this encounter is mentioned by MacHale's biographer, Bernard O'Reilly, who recalled hearing both Croke and Parnell refer to it at a meeting at Kildare in mid October 1885.[20] The date Croke gave at Holycross for his meeting with Parnell in 1879 is earlier than the date of the Westport meeting. A later date is more plausible. It was on 21 September 1879 that he wrote the first of his many public letters in Parnell's support.[21] But it is difficult to reconcile Croke's Holycross speech or this public letter with a private letter he wrote on 21 November 1879 to an Irish ecclesiastic in Rome in reply to a charge that he had given his 'public support and approbation to a politician known to be a violent man' (presumed to be Parnell):

I have never spoken a word to Mr Parnell but once and that casually; nor have I ever mentioned his name in any public document . . . but once and then I referred to him because of a mischievous contention that had arisen between himself and Mr Gray . . . and solely in the interest of peace and charity. At *that* time he had held no meeting and made no pronouncement on the land question; nor did I know anything whatever about his views on the subject.[22]

The archbishop did sometimes speak with tongue in cheek. It is safe to state that Parnell solicited Croke's support in 1879. The two men had much in common. Both came from well-to-do families, had powerful personalities, were firm disciplinarians, held extreme political opinions and had a penchant for dramatic gestures.

In September 1879, on agreeing to join Davitt in putting the Land League on a national basis, Parnell invited some ninety public men to a meeting in Dublin on 21 October. Most agreed to join the proposed committee. Among them were fourteen priests. Two of these, both curates, Eugene Sheehy of Kilmallock (in the Limerick diocese) and John Behan (Dublin), were present; eight sent letters of support, among them Ulick Bourke of Westport (Tuam diocese), William Quirke (who was Dean of Cashel and an intimate of Croke) and Thomas Lynch and Michael Tormey (both of Painestown in Nulty's Meath diocese).[23] Parnell's invitation to members of the Catholic clergy to participate in the Land League was another new departure. What motivated Parnell and how he drew up his list of invitations are matters for speculation. It would seem reasonable to suppose that, despite his association with the Fenians and his defiance of the local clergy at Westport and Ennis, Parnell never lost sight of the usefulness to politicians of the traditional role of priests in the countryside; he was therefore trying to draw priests into the movement by inviting those he had reason to believe were both willing and able to join, something he was better able to do after getting Archbishop Croke on his side. What is most significant about this episode in Parnell's relations with the Catholic church is that the clergy did not join the new movement until it was already firmly in existence and then by Parnell's invitation and on his terms. The priests on the national committee became only sleeping partners, power being vested in the executive and day-to-day business being conducted by a triumvirate of Davitt, Thomas Brennan and Patrick Egan – all Fenians.[24]

Parnell was not to get the universal support of the Catholic church until four more years had passed. In the general election of 1880, Parnellites stood in only a handful of constituencies; some received clerical support, others clerical opposition. Parnell himself

again had the backing of the Catholic church in Meath: a prominent
Navan priest acted as his agent and Bishop Nulty ordered a collection to be taken at chapel doors to defray his expenses.[25] But in
Cork city, where he was also a candidate (a successful one, as it
proved), only two priests, John O'Mahony and Denis McCarthy,
braved the hostility of the bishop, William Delany (who called
Parnell 'a self-elected dictator'), by electioneering on his behalf.[26]
In the Cork county constituency, after encountering much clerical
opposition and causing several ugly scenes, Parnell narrowly failed
to secure the election of a prominent member of the Land League,
Andrew Kettle.[27] The significance of the election of 1880 was that
in consequence Parnell was elected chairman of the Irish party in
the House of Commons and so was in future able to exercise to
the full his great capacity for leadership, which he did by imposing
a tighter discipline on the party and allying it firmly with the more
militant elements of Irish society represented in the Land League,
thus making the party both more effective and more popular – and
so irresistible to those ecclesiastics who had misgivings about him.

In the course of 1880 and 1881 the diocesan clergy became, if
their bishops would allow it, more and more involved in the agitation of the Land League, with its associated boycotting and violence, partly because they sympathized with the tenant-farmers (with
whom they had family as well as social and economic ties) and
partly because they considered it their duty to exert a moderating,
if not a controlling, influence to offset the influences of Fenians
and others whom they mistrusted. Only a handful stood aloof or
were hostile. With Parnell on the platform at Ennis from which he
made his 'moral Coventry' speech advocating boycotting were as
many as eight priests.[28] One priest, Eugene Sheehy (one of those
on the national committee), was imprisoned for some months in
1881 for his activities. Several others were also convicted of offences
connected with the agitation.[29]

The agitation was therefore a subject of utmost concern to the
Irish Catholic bishops, more especially as the Vatican began to take
note of the increasing clerical involvement in political affairs in
Ireland and to attempt to exert an influence of its own.[30] But if the
diocesan clergy were throwing themselves into the agrarian agitation, the episcopate was seriously divided. The death of Cullen
in October 1878 had removed the discipline and unanimity that had
characterized the episcopate during the long office of that stern
martinet as papal legate. Some bishops, most notably Croke of
Cashel and Nulty of Meath, now favoured Parnell; others, especially

Edward McCabe of Dublin and Delany of Cork, were vehemently opposed; the largest number kept to the middle ground. In 1880 McCabe issued two pastorals hostile to the Land League, the second of them on the eve of the trial of Parnell and thirteen other Land Leaguers on charges connected with the agitation; from Rome, where they were on an official visit, Croke of Cashel, Butler of Limerick, Fitzgerald of Ross and McCormack of Cloyne (all proven Parnellites) reacted by sending contributions to the Parnell defence fund. McCabe wrote privately to an agent in Rome lamenting that their action could 'be distorted into a sort of papal sanction' and 'an endorsement of Mr Parnell's policy which brought the country face to face with revolutionary and communistic doctrines'.[31]

The next clash was more open, more unseemly, more damaging. In March 1881 two bishops, Bartholomew Woodlock of Armagh and McCabe of Dublin, publicly denounced the Ladies' Land League and by implication the whole agrarian agitation. McCabe used language that was, in the opinion of one episcopal colleague, 'severe and unmeasured'.[32] The meeting of all the Irish bishops on 15 March (called to consider Gladstone's new land bill) was stormy.[33] The bishops' disagreement deepened when Croke wrote a letter to a layman (immediately published) denouncing McCabe in contemptuous terms. It needed discreet intervention by Cardinal Simeoni for Croke to apologize.[34]

McCabe's star rose in the months that followed. Parnell's credit with those bishops normally sympathetic towards him appeared to fall when he stomped the country employing his rhetoric against Gladstone's land measure (which the bishops generally approved) and, after being held in preventive detention under emergency legislation with a grand total of nine hundred and fifty-five other Land Leaguers, issued a manifesto urging tenant-farmers to pay no more rent until they were released (a manifesto which even Croke denounced). Archbishop McCabe's elevation to the cardinalate, news of which broke on 9 March when Parnell and the others were still in detention, was rightly interpreted as a success for George Errington, a dissident member of the Irish party who had been opposing Parnell's leadership by bringing to bear in the right quarters in Rome (where he regularly wintered) the influence he possessed as a well-connected Catholic gentleman and as a person trusted by Gladstone's foreign secretary, Lord Granville.[35] Probably under McCabe's influence, the Irish bishops at their annual meeting on 10 June 1882 agreed to prohibit clergy from attending public meetings without the consent of the local parish priest.[36] This restricted clerical participation in politics at national level, as McCabe kept a tight discipline over the parish priests in Dublin.

II

But Parnell's political decline was more apparent than real. His outspokenness on the subject of Gladstone's land measure was intended only to propitiate his Fenian and Irish-American supporters, who could not accept that anything good could come from a British government; privately, like most tenant-farmers and the priests, he saw the measure as a success for the Land League and as a means of improving landlord-tenant relations. The problem was to resolve the conflict of interest that existed, throughout 1881, between the different groups constituting the Land League: the Fenians, who were the 'organization men', both at national level and in the small towns of Connaught; the Irish-Americans, who were the financiers; the farmers at the grass roots; and the priests who were the reliable agents in the countryside. Parnell's stay in Kilmainham jail (13 October 1881 till 2 May 1882), where he had great leisure to confer with his lieutenants, gave him respite from his difficulty and the opportunity to plan ahead. In the autumn of 1882 he formed a new organization, the Irish National League, on the ruins of the banned Land League. The new body was very much under the control of Parnell and his parliamentary colleagues, some of whom were firm moderates; the Fenian triumvirate was no more.[37] The Irish National League both strengthened Parnell's hand and made him more acceptable to the Catholic church. Thus Parnell was breaking with his Fenian past and espousing Catholic politics.

An episode that occurred in the spring of 1883 reveals much about Parnell's relations with the Catholic church at this time. A subscription was opened in County Wicklow, on the initiative of the Avoca branch of the Irish National League (some members of which would have depended on Parnell for a livelihood), 'to help pay off the inherited mortgage on his estate'.[38] The parish priest of the town of Kildare, James Kavanagh, proposed that it should become a Parnell testimonial fund; on St Patrick's Day Archbishop Croke sent a cheque for £50, declaring that the amount each person subscribed would be regarded as a measure of his patriotism.[39] Soon, many members of the clergy and about one-third of the episcopate had become associated with the testimonial. Other bishops (notably McCabe, Moran of Ossory and Walshe of Kildare and Leighlin) refused.[40] The new Archbishop of Tuam, John McEvilly, told his diocesan clergy of his determination not to subscribe but did not forbid them to do so. He afterwards explained his attitude to his agent in Rome:

> I myself can never pardon Parnell his putting in a worthless Presbyterian minister to represent Catholic Mayo and many other slights offered to the clergy, not to speak of his alleged association with French reds and atheists.[41]

The explanation sent by a County Kilkenny curate, Michael Corcoran, with the sum collected by his parishioners is one that most country priests would have endorsed in the aftermath of Gladstone's second Irish Land Act: 'we feel that we owe a deep debt of gratitude to Mr Parnell. He found the Irish farmer the slave and serf of a tyrant; thank God, he has uplifted him and given him high hopes of a bright future'.[42] It was in the diocese of Cashel that ecclesiastics did most to relieve Parnell: Archbishop Croke, a member of the national committee for promoting the testimonial, ordered collections to be made in every parish and the proceeds to be forwarded to him within three weeks; his priests responded with great enthusiasm.[43] Of the £7,688 collected nationally by 11 May, £2,500 came from the Cashel diocese.[44]

All of a sudden Croke was summoned to Rome where on 11 May he was humiliatingly reprimanded by Pope Leo XIII for his role in Irish politics;[45] on the same day the Sacred Congregation of Propaganda Fide (which regulated the Irish church) issued a rescript holding that 'the collection called the "Parnell testimonial fund" cannot be approved . . . and consequently it cannot be tolerated that any ecclesiastic, much less a bishop, should take any part whatever in recommending it'.[46] The reaction of Parnell's friends in Ireland, lay and clerical alike, was to assert that the rescript was based on misrepresentation by Errington at the behest of the government.[47] When the Irish bishops met as a body on 5 July they issued a statement that made no mention of the papal rescript but blamed the government for the economic distress of the Irish farmer.[48] Parnell, far from suffering as a consequence of the Vatican's condemnation, gained even greater popularity: the fund increased rapidly to a total of £37,000. Though ecclesiastics generally ceased to be associated with it, they did so only for appearances' sake, resentful, even jealous, of Errington's success at the Vatican and foreseeing the benefit Parnell would obtain from the episode. At the presentation banquet in Dublin on 11 December 1883, nearly forty priests were present (chiefly from the dioceses of Cashel and Meath); Fr Kavanagh of Kildare said grace but the plan for Eugene Sheehy and Croke's administrator at Cashel, James Cantwell, to speak was dropped.[49]

In 1883, Charles Stewart Parnell made two gestures to endear himself further to his Catholic supporters and to disarm or even win over his Catholic opponents. One was to take a stance against Charles Bradlaugh, the well-known atheist who had been elected to serve as Member of Parliament for Northampton but was not permitted to take his seat in the House of Commons. In June 1880, Parnell had spoken strongly in Bradlaugh's favour when he was threatened with arrest for refusing to leave the chamber; he and five other Irish members were among the seven who voted against arrest; and Parnell and four colleagues visited Bradlaugh in the office of the sergeant-at-arms to tender sympathy. Such behaviour conformed with Parnell's association with Fenian and democratic causes in the 1870s, for Bradlaugh too had had Fenian associations, like Parnell he had spoken up for the 'Manchester martyrs' and both men were vice-presidents of the Democratic League of Great Britain and Ireland. But some Irish members hotly disagreed with Parnell over the Bradlaugh affair, while in Ireland Catholic opinion, lay and clerical alike, was generally very hostile to Bradlaugh.[50] Parnell kept silent on the affair until the spring of 1883 when he veered publicly into the anti-Bradlaugh camp by opposing a government Bill to allow any member to affirm instead of swearing.[51] One explanation of Parnell's volte-face is that he now sought at least to respect the wishes of the Catholic bishops, every one of whom had signed a petition against the affirmation Bill.[52] It is likely that he recognized the political expediency of deferring to Catholic opinion with regard to an issue on which it was so sensitive and so unanimous and which affected the Irish issues of home rule and land reform so little.

Parnell's second gesture was to speak in the House of Commons against the annual vote for the Queen's Colleges when other members failed to do so.[53] These colleges, at Belfast, Cork and Galway, secular in inspiration and religiously mixed, had been, ever since their inception in 1845, a source of grievance to the Catholic bishops, who had founded their own rival university in Dublin in 1854. Despite an episcopal resolution and the dispatch of letters to individual Catholic members urging them to attend the debate on the Queen's Colleges in August 1883, only one did so.[54] 'So far as I know', wrote one senior ecclesiastic with special responsibility for higher education in February 1884,

Parnell was not spoken to or communicated with at all. I carefully avoided meeting him. . . . Yet, with his usual skill, he seized the opportunity and in the absence of everyone else (except Colonel Colthurst) made a Parnellite stand against the queen's colleges. This is the sort of thing that is throwing the whole country into the hands of him and his followers.[55]

Parnell had previously, in 1878 and 1879, promoted the bishops' views in Parliament by calling for equality of funding for the Catholic university.[56] Yet privately, as late as 1885, he questioned the need for a Catholic university.[57] Why then did he take up an issue that was controversial among his supporters (the American Fenians were dismissive of it) and had nothing to do with home rule or land reform? As F. S. L. Lyons put it, Parnell realized that, as a Protestant, he 'would have to identify himself positively with those causes which were most relevant to the needs and desires of Irish Catholicism'.[58]

The other side of the rapprochement between Parnell and the Catholic bishops was the movement of the episcopal bench towards Parnell's position, the result partly of change in its leadership, partly of a change in its attitude. Early in 1883, Cardinal McCabe became ill and was at death's door; he made a recovery but seems never again to have been in robust health before his death on 11 February 1885.[59] Therefore it was not McCabe but Daniel McGettigan, the Archbishop of Armagh, who presided at the episcopal meetings that followed the papal rescript condemning the Parnell testimonial; at those held in July and October 1883 it was not even mentioned. Belonging neither to the McCabe nor the Croke camp, McGettigan was no doubt in a good position to assess the general mood of his colleagues. The rescript, to judge from the bishops' correspondence, weighed on their minds and seems to have brought despair at what they considered to be undue interference by Rome based on misrepresentation.[60] A long letter, really a memorandum, dated 26 March 1884, from Bishop Higgins of Kerry to Cardinal McCabe (to whose camp he belonged) is indicative of a consequent change of episcopal attitudes: the reception of the rescript in the country, said Higgins, showed the depth of popular sympathy for Parnell and his movement; Parnell's political power was so strong that the clergy could not be counted on to challenge it; with the extension of the franchise to small farmers and artisans it would soon be even greater; the bishops had therefore to reach an understanding with

Parnell; such an understanding could be advantageous as Parnell would press their educational demands.[61]

It was another issue, the threat perceived as being presented by the Italian government to the property of the Sacred Congregation of Propaganda Fide, that the Irish bishops at their next meeting, in July 1884, urged 'the Irish members of parliament, of all political parties', to take up with the British government.[62] The member who responded most satisfactorily was Parnell. His party at a private meeting discussed the matter and decided that he should bring it to the attention of Parliament. Before he could do so Cardinal Manning, who had his ear closer to the ground than any Irish bishop, approached him and expressed the view that as none of the Catholic powers had acted it would be inexpedient for England to do so. Parnell therefore let the matter drop. But an Irish member no longer belonging to Parnell's party (despite his Fenian past), a noisy Catholic and political maverick, Frank Hugh O'Donnell, pressed it upon the House of Commons, forcing a division in which only twenty-six members 'backed the pope'.[63] The discipline of Parnell's party must have created a more favourable impression on the Irish bishops than O'Donnell's independence.

But what brought final approval of the Parnellite party by the Irish hierarchy was a matter that became of public moment out of the blue. In the summer of 1882 all but one of a family named Joyce living at Maamtrasna in County Mayo were murdered. The suspected culprits were arrested, tried and convicted; three of them were hanged the following December, one, Myles Joyce, protesting his innocence on the scaffold. The crime seems to have had no political connotations.[64] On 7 August 1884, when Archbishop McEvilly was administering confirmation at the chapel at Cappaghduff, not far from the scene of the crime, Thomas Casey, a prosecution witness, publicly confessed that he had falsely sworn against Myles Joyce and against four men who had been imprisoned for complicity. Casey said that a Crown solicitor, George Bolton, had compelled him to perjure himself under threat of being tried for murder as a fourth man.[65] McEvilly was convinced by Casey and publicly put blame on the government, calling for the release of the imprisoned men and restitution to Myles Joyce's family.[66] The correspondence that ensued between McEvilly and Dublin Castle proved most unsatisfactory to the archbishop, who was rebuffed and snubbed.[67] Two of Parnell's lieutenants, William O'Brien and Timothy Harrington, plunged the House of Commons into a heated debate on the Maamtrasna affair on the night of 11–12 August.[68]

The affair aroused deep passions among Catholic Irishmen, because (like the papal rescript) it challenged their religious allegiance. Feelings were all the stronger as Bolton was plaintiff in a libel action pending against the Parnellite newspaper, *United Ireland*, which had accused him of homosexual practices. The lord lieutenant, Lord Spencer, was singled out for popular opprobrium.[69] The effect the affair had on McEvilly was to make him join the Croke camp, with momentous consequences.

When the bishops met on 1 October, it was McEvilly who seconded a resolution moved by Croke calling upon 'the Irish parliamentary party . . . to urge generally upon the government the hitherto unsatisfied claims of Catholic Ireland in all branches of the education question'.[70] Thus Parnell's followers alone were accredited as the Irish Catholic church's agency for promoting the political cause it had for so long considered supremely important. The conversion of such 'Castle bishops' as McEvilly, Higgins and Gillooly (secretary of the hierarchy's education committee) was the culmination of the process of rapprochement begun by Parnell after he left Kilmainham jail. McEvilly explained the bishops' action in a letter to a correspondent in Rome: 'the fact is many of the bishops who, like myself, never joined the Irish party feel that there is no other possible way of gaining our rights from a government that will give Catholics nothing from love'.[71]

In all Parnell's political career no development was more significant in his relations with the Catholic church than the decision taken by the episcopate on 1 October 1884. The decision came as a result of greater discipline and solidarity on the part of the Irish bishops to match the exemplary discipline and solidarity that Parnell had made the hallmarks of his parliamentary party. Among its consequences it fatally weakened the still numerous dissident or independent Irish home rule Members of Parliament (men like Errington and O'Donnell); it guaranteed the support of all ecclesiastics but the most incorrigibly hostile. Professor Emmet Larkin goes as far as to see 'the concluding of the clerical-nationalist alliance' in 1884 as 'the fundamental turning point' in the process of making the Catholic church the state church in independent Ireland.[72] Certainly, clerical-nationalist relations were from October 1884 until November 1890 on a plateau of almost perfect harmony unprecedented since O'Connell's day and came to be regarded, after the reunion of the divided party in 1900, as model.

There emerged in 1885 an ecclesiastic who was to personify as much as Parnell himself the new alliance, a man who in his wide, practical knowledge, his level-headedness and his ability to get things done had much in common with 'the uncrowned king'. This was William Joseph Walsh, who became Archbishop of Dublin in the summer of that year after a contest in which he received the support of the large majority of the Dublin diocesan clergy and of the episcopal bench and the opposition of the Errington circle and of the British government. Walsh was more astute than his predecessor, McCabe, as well as more popular. Like Croke, he had a high opinion of Parnell. The advantage to Parnell of having such a bishop in Dublin, where affairs were centralized, was appreciable. On his return from his consecration in Rome he presciently stated his belief in home rule by pleading for Ireland's right 'to have her own laws made here upon Irish soil and by the legally and constitutionally chosen representatives of the Irish people'.[73]

An early opportunity for co-operation between Parnell and Walsh came with the calling of a general election towards the end of the year. The constitution of the Irish National League, set up by Parnell in 1882, provided for county conventions intended to secure the adoption as candidates of the men he wanted to have in his parliamentary party; Walsh secured the attendance of the clergy at the Wicklow convention to be held in his extensive diocese on 5 October 1885. In confidential instructions to them he laid down certain principles: to favour the two candidates (one for each seat) of most satisfactory antecedents; to block surprise candidates; failing that, to try and secure an adjournment or, if that failed, to withdraw in a body from the proceedings.[74] The other bishops, at the regular episcopal meeting in October, approved his action.[75] The different conventions, made up in the ratio three to one of Irish National League delegates and Catholic priests, met in two sessions, one private, the other public. The private session was presided over by a Member of Parliament sent by Parnell's election committee with written instructions, 'the first of which was to get the man through who had been chosen by the committee in Dublin'.[76] Normally the committee got its way. T. P. O'Connor maintained afterwards that if Parnell's committee got wind of an undesirable coming forward it would arrange for his nomination by a tame priest who would, after listening to the arguments, rise and announce that the name was withdrawn. The public session, usually chaired by a priest, did little more than present the agreed candidates. The order of the day was harmony. There is, concludes Dr Conor Cruise O'Brien, 'no real evidence of a conflict of interest or policy between the clergy and the party managers at this date'.

Rather, the managers used the clergy to secure reliable candidates and to eliminate undesirable ones.[77]

The general public knew little of what was happening, for Walsh had persuaded the proprietor of the *Freeman's Journal*, Gray, to suppress all news of dissent. As the chief telegraphist explained in a very private letter to the lord lieutenant's secretary:

> Previous to the conventions a conspiracy of silence was organized by which the names to be submitted to them were kept in the dark. Under no circumstances were the intended nominees' names to be published in the *Freeman*, *United Ireland* or other national papers lest it might provoke criticism and discussion . . . Then came Dr Walsh's pronouncement that his clergy had received instructions which amounted in short to this – that unless the names submitted to the convention were adopted, if any other names were sprung on the convention, the priests were to withdraw . . . Not a few important and influential letters were sent to the *Freeman* protesting against this 'gagging', but the word was given that the letters were not to be published and they were not. This is how the 'harmony' has been secured.[78]

Gray seems to have received some favour from Walsh in being nominated (despite Parnell's disapproval) for a prestigious Dublin constituency; a pious Catholic, he was seeking papal permission (not easily obtained) for a private oratory in which to keep the blessed sacrament; after the elections he asked Walsh to use his influence at Rome for him.[79] As for *United Ireland*, it was very much Parnell's own mouthpiece, having been started by him as such with his lieutenant, William O'Brien, as its editor. When, therefore, J. J. Louden, who had been one of the organizers of the Irishtown meeting of 1879 but was now disapproved by Parnell as an inveterate Land Leaguer and general trouble-maker, wrote complaining how Parnell as chairman of the county convention for Mayo had prevented him from being adopted as a candidate, it was to the Conservative *Irish Times* that he addressed himself.[80]

The contrast between the universal and overwhelming support churchmen gave Parnell in 1885 and the localized or hesitant support given in 1879 was striking. No less striking was the extent of Parnell's electoral victory: every seat (except Trinity College Dublin's two) in Connaught, Munster and Leinster fell to his party and a majority of those in Ulster (85 altogether, compared to about 30 seats held by Parnellites at the dissolution); no longer in the House of Commons were there dissident home rulers and independent

Irish Catholics unbeholden to him, the greatly enlarged Parnellite party was tightly disciplined, its members remunerated by the party organization and pledged in advance to vote together – a formidable group in any parliament and a powerful one in that of 1885–6 where neither of the main parties had an overall majority. The Catholic church's support for Parnell in 1885 was not, however, the main reason for his stupendous victory, for a Parnellite victory was already foreseeable in 1883 and it was in anticipation of such a victory that many ecclesiastics finally turned to him in 1884.

Gladstone's conversion to home rule and the introduction (albeit unsuccessful) of a home rule Bill on 8 April 1886 strengthened Parnell's alliance with the Catholic church, for Parnell's ability to achieve results was made more manifest and the hierarchy were heartened at the prospect of the granting of their educational demands, either by a future Liberal government dependent for its majority in the House of Commons on the Irish party or by an Irish parliament in Dublin with a permanent Catholic majority. But home rule soon ceased to be a current issue and land reform caught the public imagination again.

In October 1886 there began a new phase of agrarian agitation, known as the Plan of Campaign.[81] There were similarities with the Land League campaign of 1879–82, but dissimilarities too. The initiatives were taken locally by disaffected farmers rather than by sympathetic townsmen. There was help from national politicians, amongst them veterans of the Land League like John Dillon and William O'Brien. A few leading campaigners had connections with Fenianism, in particular David Sheehy (brother of Fr Eugene Sheehy) who had been in the IRB and Daniel Crilly and Joseph Richard Cox who were members at the time; but on the whole the Fenian presence was minimal.[82] There were priests galore; Archbishop Croke was again enthusiastic and supportive. The Plan of Campaign was accompanied by intimidation and violence which brought counter-measures by the government, some campaigners finding themselves in prison in consequence (O'Brien three times).

It was the dissimilarities between the two phases of agitation that affected, in the long run, Parnell's relationship with the Catholic church. They were determining factors in the breakdown of the accord and the party split that occurred four years later. The role Catholic priests played in the Plan of Campaign was much greater than it had been in the Land League. Dr Laurence Geary goes so far as to state that 'the local leadership . . . was drawn almost exclusively from the ranks of the Catholic clergy'.[83] The reason for the major role of the clergy lay in the nature of the agitation: tenants demanding an abatement of rent would combine and hand over to persons they trusted the amounts they were prepared to pay pending a satisfactory agreement with their landlord; the most trustworthy person was often the local priest, accustomed as he was to handling parish funds and unlikely to peculate or abscond. As Croke told a Cashel diocesan curate facing arrest for his part in the agitation, 'if you were not a priest, the people would never have entrusted you with either their confidence or their cash'.[84] On many of the 203 or more estates where the Plan of Campaign was operative it was a priest who was entrusted with the rents.[85] And priests also chaired meetings, wrote letters and did all those things they had done during the Land League campaign.[86] But the priests were participants in the Plan of Campaign from the beginning and by virtue of their special position in the farming community, not at a later stage and by the invitation of organizers based in nearby towns. Many of the farmers in dispute, the large majority on some estates, were leaseholders, unprotected by the 1881 Act;[87] they were the 'strong' farmers who formed the important class of countrymen to which the clergy belonged.[88] There were twenty-three cases of priests being prosecuted under the new emergency legislation, passed in July 1887, for their part in the agitation; as many as fifteen priests were imprisoned (four of them twice), thus becoming martyrs to the cause.[89] The law-breaking priest was subject to surveillance by the police as much as any local Fenian.[90] Bishops approved, indeed recommended and justified, the Plan of Campaign from the beginning, most influentially Archbishop Walsh who made an impressive defence of it in an interview with the *Pall Mall Gazette* published on 2 December 1886.[91] The participation of churchmen did not significantly diminish even when, in April 1888, the Plan of Campaign was condemned by the pope in the most explicit terms.

The role of Charles Stewart Parnell in the Plan of Campaign was minimal. He seems privately to have had serious misgivings about the agitation, fearing that it would damage the alliance between the Irish party and Gladstone's Liberals.[92] He was reluctant to lend his name and seldom spoke of it in public. In contrast to his behaviour in the years 1878–81, Parnell never campaigned in the disaffected districts in Ireland. During the period 1886–90 he lived in seclusion with his mistress in a London suburb, going to Avondale only for the grouse season.[93] In a real sense he ceased to lead the party in the country.[94] The one occasion when he did speak of the Plan of Campaign at any length, in a speech to Liberals at the Eighty Club on 8 May 1888, was in the aftermath of the papal condemnation. Parnell was depreciative of both the plan and the Holy Office decree and left it to his Catholic colleagues to deal with the matter. Professor Emmet Larkin argues that Parnell's response to the papal intervention was masterly: he foresaw that the Catholic Members of Parliament would rebuff the pope, thus placing on the bishops, due to meet shortly, 'the responsibility for maintaining or weakening the clerical-nationalist alliance'.[95] But Parnell's evasiveness, his unwillingness to become involved in the agrarian agitation and his preference for high politics in London during a lengthy period when the local elites in the Irish country-side, particularly the clergy, were battling, at great cost, against British authority were in the long run to contribute to his ruin.

III

The view, still widespread, that Parnell's fall in 1890, after the public hearing in November of the O'Shea divorce petition, was due to pressure from the Catholic church has been shown, in the several studies of the subject,[96] to be oversimplified. Clerics and laymen reacted alike in disbelieving what had been said about Parnell and hesitating to speak out against him until he could clear his name. It was Gladstone's intervention that precipitated the split. Few would disagree, however, with Professor Larkin that 'when all is said and done, it was the bishops and their clergy who did most to depose him as the leader of the Irish people' and that the anti-Parnellite campaign in 1891 'was only made possible because the Roman Catholic hierarchy and their clergy fought a determined holding action until the party was able to regroup and organize. The bishops and priests had also made heavy contributions in man-power and money'.[97]

I will confine myself here to the thesis that Parnell – his party split and the churchmen in the hostile camp – attempted to revert to the type of politician he had been before 1882, appealing to the Fenian and democratic elements in society over the heads of the bishops and priests; he failed, however, to recover the political power of his earlier days because the bishops and priests, collaborat-ing with some of his most dynamic lieutenants and foot-soldiers in promoting the Plan of Campaign, had seized his power base in the countryside.

Parnell rallied to himself the Fenians, the physical-force men, the working classes and urban elements generally. His denunciation of Gladstone and the Liberals for dictating to the Irish party and for their alleged unreliability on the home rule issue had inherent appeal for advanced nationalists. In the ten months between the split and his death, Parnell peppered his speeches with cliches of a republican or physical-force tendency, in particular calling (as he had done in the 1870s) for the release of Fenian prisoners.[98] The old Fenian chiefs James Stephens and John O'Leary soon came out in his support, and in America John Devoy became one of his most influential promoters. The personnel of the Parnell Leadership Committee that came into existence in December 1890 was substantially Fenian; a member of its executive, John Wyse Power of Naas, and the chairman of its Belfast branch, Robert Johnston, were members of the supreme council of the IRB.[99] It was Johnston who in the summer of 1891 led a team of northern Fenians to the scene of the Carlow by-election to join (in the words of a police report) 'men from Tipperary, south Cork, Clare, Waterford and Dublin, all Fenians and advanced nationalists, assisting the Parnell party'.[100] At Bodenstown in County Kildare, on 21 June, at what was to be the first of the annual demonstrations at the grave of the famous Irish republican of the French revolutionary era, Theobald Wolfe Tone, there was another coming together of Parnellites and Fenians.[101]

Parnell's appeal was answered, too, by the leadership and rank and file of the Gaelic Athletic Association (GAA). Never purely a sporting body, the association was in 1890 largely under the control of Fenians: priests had been forced out of most branches and about half the county committee men were members of the IRB. When Parnell returned to Ireland on 10 December 1890 among those to greet him on the quay-side were delegates from the GAA headed by J. K. Bracken, a man prominent also in the IRB. Sympathy for Parnell quickly spread through the several hundred GAA clubs, which consequently bombarded him with letters, telegrams and resolutions of support and, wherever he went in the early months of 1891, local clubs presented him with addresses of welcome.[102]

The GAA, like the IRB, drew its membership very largely from the lower classes. It had been formed in 1884 to provide sporting opportunities (in the words of one founder-member, Maurice Davin) 'especially for the humble and hard-working who seem now to be born into no other inheritance than an everlasting round of labour'. It attracted clerks, artisans, shop assistants and labourers, classes of men who would have been refused admission to the middle-class clubs of the Irish Amateur Athletic Association.[103] It is hardly surprising therefore to find evidence also of mutual attraction between Parnell and the labour movement. On 12 December 1890, after arriving in Cork and meeting delegates from the Irish Democratic Labour Federation, Parnell made his first appeal to labour.[104] He was the guest-speaker on 15 March 1891 at a well-attended conference in Dublin of trade unionists (mainly general labourers) which had on its agenda, and largely endorsed, an imposing programme of reform (including nationalization of the land), to which he gave his 'general and practical agreement'.[105] At the May Day rally in Phoenix Park, attended by over ten thousand workers, both skilled and unskilled, some of the speeches were of a markedly Parnellite tenor.[106] A month later Parnell himself made a speech nearby at Inchicore in which he predicted 'the future is undoubtedly with the working classes'.[107]

Parnellism became very much an urban phenomenon. Dublin was its stronghold. In medium-sized towns like Kilkenny and Waterford the Parnellites were the majority. In the small country towns this was more often than not the case, as has been shown in two local studies.[108] One reason that Parnell did not have more support in the city of Cork, which had returned him to Parliament since 1880, was that he grossly neglected labour interests there.[109]

The extent to which Parnell threw in his lot with the Fenians and the lower classes generally is vividly illustrated by an account of his funeral in Dublin on 11 October 1891:

> There must have been nearly 100,000 people out. They were out in defiance of the priests, who at the chapels dissuaded the people from attending. . . . Parnell dead has done what Parnell living could not do – he has struck a staggering blow at priestly domination. . . . The Fenians are triumphant. The organization of the mob yesterday was theirs and it was most creditable to them. There was no disorder whatever. . . . The most striking feature of the demonstration to my mind was the fact that it was so entirely composed and controlled by the lower classes. Special trains ran from all parts of the country and yet there were few if any farmers present. Townspeople and labourers – and Fenians – composed the multitude. . . . Not a single priest was to be seen.[110]

Bishop Brownrigg in Kilkenny noted only a few days after the split that 'the lowest dregs of the people, the Fenian element and the working classes are all to a man with Parnell'.[111] Archbishop Croke commented in January how 'the lower stratum of society in Ireland is almost entirely for him'.[112] The new Fenian dimension to Parnellism helps to explain a renewed concern about 'secret societies' expressed by some bishops in their Lenten pastorals;[113] it was a concern evident in advice not to attend Parnellite meetings given by Bishops Woodlock of Armagh and Lynch of Kildare a few months later and in the threat made on 6 June by the Bishop of Down and Connor, Patrick MacAllister, to excommunicate members of the Belfast Parnell Leadership Committee.[114] The presence in the Parnellite camp of large numbers of enthusiastic, athletic young men under Fenian influence and discipline could only have aroused the hostility of Catholic churchmen, alarmed at a revival of Fenianism in new guises. And any urbanization of Irish politics would have put 'the fear of the modern' into them.[115]

Parnell failed to regain the position he had held before 1882. After the split he had no effective support whatever from the Catholic clergy, for even the handful of priests who spoke up for him[116] were prevented from lending any practical support by their bishops, who were united against him. So many of those who had aided him before 1882 became his enemies, e.g. the Cork priest John O'Mahony, who in 1880 as a curate had incurred the wrath of his bishop by supporting Parnell's candidature, in 1890 as administrator of Cork cathedral led twenty-five local priests in publicly testifying their loss of confidence in him, an example that was soon followed by groups of clergy all over Ireland.[117] O'Mahony became the scourge of Parnellism in Cork and surely contributed to its defeat there in the by-election that followed Parnell's death.[118] Other examples can be given of ecclesiastics who fervently supported Parnell in Land League times (when it was not always prudent to do so) and turned against him after the split: John Behan, Eugene Sheehy, Thomas Doyle of Ramsgrange and (one of many such Cashel priests) David Humphreys of Tipperary,[119] not to mention the egregious Archbishop Croke.

Perhaps Parnell's most serious weakness was the generation-gap between him and the priests of the Plan of Campaign. Whilst he had remained aloof from that phase of agrarian agitation, many priests had been deeply involved, sometimes heroically, thereby securing the trust and confidence of the tenant-farmers, as Parnell had done formerly. One example is Canon Keller of Youghal, who led the tenants on the Ponsonby estate, wrote a pamphlet on the subject and spent some time in Kilmainham jail; after the split he stated 'so far as we are concerned Parnell is dead'.[120] The influence the priests brought to bear against Parnell was reinforced by many of his former lieutenants who were also veterans of the Plan of Campaign; nearly all veterans became anti-Parnellites, some of them (like David Sheehy) despite their Fenian antecedents. One such lieutenant, O'Brien, afterwards attributed the defeat of Parnellism in Munster (where the agitation was most protracted) at the general election of 1892 to 'the popularity of a few priests who had signalized themselves as leaders in the Plan of Campaign'.[121] In County Tipperary, at least, Parnell's apathy to the plight of farmers in dispute with their landlords as a result of the Plan of Campaign was shared by his followers; the farmers and their friends, the priests, were together in the anti-Parnellite camp.[122] This may partly explain why in 1892 the Parnellites failed to get even one-third of the combined nationalist vote in any of the nineteen rural constituencies in Munster (excluding County Clare, beyond the Shannon).[123] It was not so much that the clergy influenced the farmers in the way they voted as that both groups were part of a rural consensus, connected by family ties and sharing the same values.[124]

IV

Why did Parnell, after leaving Kilmainham in 1882, turn his back so largely (if not entirely) on his Fenian and democratic followers in order to curry favour with prelates and priests? Probing questions about Parnell are hard to answer: he did not keep a journal; his letters were brief and businesslike; he was aloof from his colleagues and reserved even with his few friends. It is likely that in Kilmainham jail he was alarmed at the course the Land League was taking, its leaders nearly all in prison, agrarian outrages still common and many farmers prepared to settle for what was being offered by the government led by Gladstone (a popular figure in Ireland). To change course meant allying firmly with the Catholic church. Such an alliance had many attractions to Parnell, who, being unaffected by religious feeling (he never attended church away from home) or abstract theories of government (he seldom, if ever, read a book) and having learnt from the practical experience of life (as an entrepreneur he prospered for a while), saw the Catholic clergy, because of their peasant origin, social and economic position and ability to manage men and money, as indispensable agents of social control. As an elite the Catholic clergy were much more numerous and influential than the Catholic gentry and bourgeoisie, two groups who similarly mistrusted the Fenians and the minor professional, artisanal and shopkeeping classes to which they belonged and from which Parnell wished to distance himself.

For their part, the lower clergy (like the peasantry) already recognized Parnell's capacity for leadership, seeing him as an achiever, who had helped tenant-farmers obtain some political 'clout' and who was the true author of Gladstone's Land Act. Those members of the episcopate who did not share this view of Parnell had only to be won over by his distancing himself from men like Bradlaugh and voicing more loudly their demands for state funding of Catholic schools. What particularly endeared Parnell to senior churchmen was the discipline he imposed on his party; he was therefore a politician with whom they could deal in confidence and from whom they could expect results.

Parnell's irregular relationship with Katharine O'Shea was unquestionably, to the mind of nearly every Irish ecclesiastic, an irremovable disqualification for leadership. But after that relationship came to public notice, it was only when doubt was cast on the ability of Parnell to achieve home rule, and party discipline began to break down, that churchmen generally deserted him. The Fenian and 'modern' elements that so quickly found a home in Parnellism after the split clearly came to cause serious alarm among leading churchmen; it was an alarm that reinforced their opposition and prolonged it beyond the death of the man whose moral transgression was the initial cause.

After the split Parnell was in the unusual position, for an Irish parliamentarian, of leading a party made up of Catholics that was vilified and obstructed by the heads of the Catholic church. 'Parnell did break', comments Dr Paul Bew, 'with what might be called Catholic nationalism – as opposed to a broader, non-sectarian conception which has always coexisted uneasily with it.'[125] It is difficult to avoid the conclusion that this break was disastrous for Parnell. It is also difficult to see that the non-sectarianism of the Parnellites had any permanence. After the union of the Parnellite and anti-Parnellite factions, eight years after Parnell's death, church and party once again had a relationship that was close and mutual, a renewal of the *entente* that Parnell had skilfully concluded in 1884 and maintained until the split.[126] His successors too realized that collaboration with the Catholic church was advantageous: it kept the wilder men under control and provided a broader political base.[127]

32   C. J. Woods

NOTES

1 J. H. Parnell, *Charles Stewart Parnell: a Memoir*, London, 1916, p. 28; R. F. Foster, *Charles Stewart Parnell: the Man and his Family*, Hassocks, 1979, p. 318; Katharine O'Shea, *Charles Stewart Parnell: his Love Story and Political Life*, 2 vols, London, 1914, vol. II, pp. 246–7; William O'Brien, *The Parnell of Real Life*, London, 1926, pp. 46–7.

2 F. S. L. Lyons, *Charles Stewart Parnell*, London, 1977, pp. 45, 47, 49–50; Foster, *Parnell*, pp. 140–5.

3 For an account by Nulty of his early relations with Parnell, see *United Ireland*, 6 October 1888. For Nulty as an agrarian reformer, see Gabriel Flynn, 'Bishop Thomas Nulty and the Irish land question', *Riocht na Midhe*, VII (3), 1984, pp. 14–28; (4), 1985–6, pp. 93–110.

4 The Fenian dimension of Parnell's early career is effectively portrayed in T. W. Moody, *Davitt and Irish Revolution, 1846–82*, Oxford, 1981, pp. 130–3.

5 Ibid., p. 177.

6 Ibid., pp. 205–6.

7 David Thornley, *Isaac Butt and Home Rule*, London, 1964, pp. 141, 157, 291–4, 330–45, 370.

8 Sam Clark, 'The social composition of the Land League', *Irish Historical Studies*, XVII (68), September 1971, pp. 458–9; Moody, *Davitt*, pp. 284–5; Donald Jordan, 'Merchants, "strong farmers" and Fenians: the post-Famine political elite and the Irish Land War', in C. H. E. Philpin (ed.), *Nationalism and Popular Protest in Ireland*, Cambridge, 1987, pp. 320–48.

9 Michael Davitt, *The Fall of Feudalism in Ireland*, London, 1904, p. 154.

10 *Connaught Telegraph*, 14 June 1879.

11 *Freeman's Journal*, 19 June, 14 July 1879.

12 Moody, *Davitt*, pp.45–6, 309–10.

13 *Freeman's Journal*, 14 July 1879.

14 John Devoy, 'Davitt's career', *Gaelic American*, 3 November 1906.

15 *Nation*, 23 August 1879.

16 Davitt, *Fall of Feudalism*, p. 151.

17 R. Barry O'Brien, *The Life of Charles Stewart Parnell, 1846–91*, 2 vols, London, 1893–4, I, p. 101; William O'Brien, *Recollections*, London, 1905, p. 222.

18 Mark Tierney, *Croke of Cashel: the Life of Archbishop Thomas William Croke, 1823–1902*, Dublin, 1976, *passim*, esp. p.125.

19 *Freeman's Journal*, 2 June 1881. Cf. Croke's much later recollection in an interview published in 'Archbishop Croke', *Review of Reviews*, 14 September 1895, pp. 204–16; Parnell is said here to have gone to the archbishop's seat at Thurles on his own initiative and pleaded for his support.

20 Bernard O'Reilly, *John MacHale, Archbishop of Tuam*, 2 vols, New York, 1890, vol. II, pp. 670–1. A meeting at Kildare on 10 October 1885 addressed by Croke and Parnell was reported in *Freeman's Journal*, 12 October, and *Leinster Leader*, 17 October 1885; the reports

state that Croke spoke of the role of priests in politics but do not give the detail given by O'Reilly. Croke also visited Kildare in March 1882 but the report of the visit in *Freeman's Journal*, 21 March 1882, does not confirm O'Reilly's statement.

21 Tierney, *Croke*, p. 100.
22 Archbishop Croke to Mgr Tobias Kirby, 21 November 1879 (Irish College, Rome, Kirby papers).
23 Moody, *Davitt*, pp. 300–1, 325, 334.
24 Ibid., p. 343.
25 *Freeman's Journal*, 6, 19 April 1880.
26 Ibid., *passim*; J. J. Horgan, *Parnell to Pearse: Some Recollections and Reflections*, Dublin, 1948, p. 21; A. J. Kettle, *Material for Victory; Being the Memoirs of Andrew J. Kettle*, Dublin, 1958, p. 27.
27 *Freeman's Journal*, 7, 9, 10, 12, 13 April 1880; Kettle, *Material for Victory*, p. 31.
28 *Freeman's Journal*, 20 September 1880.
29 C. J. Woods, 'The Catholic church and Irish politics, 1879–92', unpublished Ph.D. thesis, University of Nottingham, 1968, pp. 84–6.
30 C. J. Woods, 'Ireland and Anglo-papal relations, 1880–85', *Irish Historical Studies*, XVIII (69), March 1972, pp. 29–60.
31 C. J. Woods, 'The politics of Cardinal McCabe, archbishop of Dublin, 1879–85', *Dublin Historical Record*, XXVI (3), June 1973, p. 103.
32 Bp John Power to Mgr Tobias Kirby, 29 March 1881 (Irish College, Rome, Kirby papers).
33 Emmet Larkin, *The Roman Catholic Church and the Creation of the Modern Irish State, 1878–1886*, Philadelphia, 1975, pp. 98–101.
34 Ibid., p. 106.
35 Woods, 'McCabe', pp. 105–6.
36 *Freeman's Journal*, 18 July 1882.
37 Conor Cruise O'Brien, *Parnell and his Party, 1880–90*, Oxford, 1964, pp. 126–8.
38 *United Ireland*, 10 February 1883.
39 *The Times*, 27 February 1883; *Freeman's Journal*, 19 March 1883.
40 *United Ireland*, 14 April 1883 et passim.
41 Archbishop McEvilly to Mgr Tobias Kirby, 30 May 1883 (Kirby papers). The allusion is to a visit by Parnell to Paris in February 1881, one of several he made.
42 *Freeman's Journal*, 12 May 1883.
43 *United Ireland*, 7 April 1883; James O'Shea, *Priest, Politics and Society in Post-Famine Ireland: a Study of County Tipperary, 1850–1891*, Dublin, 1983, pp. 215–17.
44 *The Times*, 14 May 1883.
45 George Errington to Lord Granville, 11, 18 May 1883 (PRO, FO 800/237/118, 119, 120); W. S. Blunt, *The Land War in Ireland*, London, 1912, p. 195; William O'Brien, *Evening Memories*, Dublin, 1920, pp. 50–2.
46 *The Times*, 15 May 1883.
47 *United Ireland*, passim.
48 *Freeman's Journal*, 6 July 1883.

34 *C. J. Woods*

49 Ibid., 12 December 1883; *United Ireland*, 15 December 1883; O'Shea, *Priest, Politics and Society*, p. 217.
50 W. L. Arnstein, 'Parnell and the Bradlaugh case', *Irish Historical Studies*, XIII (51), March 1963, pp. 217–19.
51 Ibid., p. 222.
52 Ibid., p. 231.
53 *Hansard*, 3rd series, vol. cclxxxiii, cols 1061–4, 1078, 17 August 1883.
54 Lyons, *Parnell*, p. 254.
55 Revd W. J. Walsh to Cardinal McCabe, 12 February 1884 (Dublin Diocesan Archives, McCabe papers), cited in Lyons, *Parnell*, pp. 253–4.
56 *Hansard*, 3rd series, ccxli, cols 1538–9, 15 July 1878; vol. ccxliv, cols 865–6, 13 March 1879; vol. ccxlviii, cols 1947–8, 2 August 1879; vol. ccxlix, col. 276, 5 August 1879.
57 O'Brien, *Parnell*, vol. II, p. 65.
58 Lyons, *Parnell*, p. 253.
59 Woods, 'McCabe', p. 106; Emmet Larkin, *The Roman Catholic Church and the Creation of the Modern Irish State, 1878–1886*, 1975, pp. 182–3.
60 See various letters in Larkin, *Modern Irish State*, and P. J. Corish (ed.), 'Irish College, Rome: Kirby papers. 1862–1883', *Archivium Hibernicum*, xxx, 1972, pp. 112–14.
61 Bishop Andrew Higgins to Cardinal McCabe, 26 March 1884 (Dublin Diocesan Archives, McCabe papers), quoted in Larkin, *Modern Irish State*, pp. 237–8, and Lyons, *Parnell*, pp. 254–5.
62 Larkin, *Modern Irish State*, pp. 239–40.
63 *United Ireland*, 9 August 1884; *Hansard*, 3rd series, vol. ccxci, cols 1634–40, 4 August 1884; Lyons, *Parnell*, p. 254; Larkin, *Modern Irish State*, pp. 240, 243. But Larkin may be mistaken in seeing O'Donnell as acting for Parnell's party.
64 There are brief references to the Maamtrasna affair in *United Ireland*, 26 August, 18 November, 16 December 1882.
65 *Ballinrobe Chronicle*, 9 August 1884; *United Ireland*, 9 August 1884.
66 *Freeman's Journal*, 12 August 1884.
67 *United Ireland*, 6 September 1884.
68 *Hansard*, 3rd series, vol. ccxcii, cols 537–81; *Freeman's Journal*, 13 August 1884.
69 For an example of this, see Stephen Gwynn and Gertrude Tuckwell, *Life of Sir Charles Dilke*, 2 vols, London, 1917, vol. II, p. 139.
70 *Cork Examiner*, 2 October 1884; *United Ireland*, 4 October 1884.
71 Archbishop McEvilly to Mgr Tobias Kirby, 26 October 1884 (Kirby papers), quoted in Larkin, *Modern Irish State*, p. 245.
72 Emmet Larkin, *The Roman Catholic Church and the Plan of Campaign in Ireland, 1886–1888*, Cork, 1978, p. 318.
73 *United Ireland*, 12 September 1885.
74 C. C. O'Brien, *Parnell and his Party*, p. 129.
75 Larkin, *Modern Irish State*, p. 335.
76 C. C. O'Brien, *Parnell and his Party*, p. 131. It is from this work that the two quotations from T. P. O'Connor, *Memoirs of an Old Parliamentarian*. 2 vols, London, 1929, II, pp. 14, 16, are taken.
77 Ibid., pp. 157–8.

78 M. O'Toole to H. Rochefort, 26 October 1885 (PRO, Carnarvon papers, 30/6/66), quoted in Larkin, *Modern Irish State*, pp. 337–8.
79 Larkin, *Modern Irish State*, pp. 341–2, 351, 354, 375–6.
80 C. C. O'Brien, *Parnell and his Party*, pp. 131–2.
81 The standard work on the subject is Laurence M. Geary, *The Plan of Campaign, 1886–1891*, Cork, 1986.
82 Ibid., pp. 26–7 *et passim*.
83 Ibid., p. 27. See also pp. 34, 127–8.
84 Archbishop Croke to Revd Matthew Ryan, 21 March 1887 (Cashel Diocesan Archives, Croke papers).
85 Two early examples are Lord de Freyne's estate at Kilfree in County Sligo and Lord Dillon's near Ballaghaderreen (*United Ireland*, 11, 18 December 1886). The total of 203 is taken from Geary, *Plan of Campaign*, p. 41 and app. 2.
86 *United Ireland, passim.*
87 James S. Donnelly, jr, *The Land and the People of Nineteenth-century Cork*, London, 1975, pp. 334–5. Geary, in his *Plan of Campaign*, which is wider in geographical scope, is not explicit on this point.
88 The close ties between priests and stronger farmers are meticulously examined in O'Shea, *Priest, Politics and Society*, ch. 1. See also K. T. Hoppen, *Elections, Politics and Society in Ireland, 1832–1885*, Oxford, 1984, pp. 173–85.
89 These figures are worked out from *United Ireland*, 18 September 1886 to 8 March 1890; T. C. Harrington, *A Diary of Coercion: a List of the Cases Tried under the Criminal Law and Procedure Act*, 3 vols, Dublin, 1888–90; Blanche E. C. Dugdale, *Arthur James Balfour*, 2 vols, London, 1936, vol. i, 167.
90 *United Ireland*, 24 May, 21 June 1890.
91 P. J. Walsh, *William J. Walsh, Archbishop of Dublin*, Dublin, 1928, pp. 237–41.
92 Lyons, *Parnell*, pp. 362–8.
93 Foster, *Parnell*, p. 150.
94 This view was put by Dr Laurence M. Geary in his paper on Parnell and the Plan of Campaign read at a conference at Avondale on 15 October 1989.
95 Larkin, *Plan of Campaign*, pp. 211, 219, 233.
96 Esp. F. S. L. Lyons, *The Fall of Parnell*, London, 1962.
97 Emmet Larkin, *The Roman Catholic Church in Ireland and the Fall of Parnell, 1888–1891*, Liverpool, 1979, pp. 234, 263.
98 *United Ireland*, 11 April, 19 September 1891; Lyons, *Fall of Parnell*, pp.169–70; Paul Bew, *Conflict and Conciliation in Ireland, 1890–1910: Parnellites and Radical Agrarianism*, Oxford, 1987, p. 19.
99 Marcus Bourke, *John O'Leary: a Study in Irish Separatism*, Tralee, 1967, pp. 202–7.
100 SPO, CSO, Crime Branch Special papers, 1890–91, file 2267, quoted in Bourke, *O'Leary*, pp. 205, 244.
101 *United Ireland*, 27 June 1891; C. J. Woods, 'Tone's grave at Bodenstown: memorials and commemorations, 1798–1913', in Dorothea Siegmund-Schultze (ed.), *Irland: Kultur und Gesellschaft VI*, Halle, 1989, p. 146.

102 Tom Garvin, *The Evolution of Irish Nationalist Politics*, Dublin, 1981, pp. 65–8; W. F. Mandle, *The Gaelic Athletic Association and Irish Nationalist Politics, 1884–1924*, London, 1987, esp. pp. 81–3.

103 Mandler, *Gaelic Athletic*, pp. 2, 5, 8, 24–5.

104 *The Times*, 13 December 1890.

105 Lyons, *Parnell*, p. 580; J. W. Boyle, *The Irish Labor Movement in the Nineteenth Century*, Washington, 1988, pp. 135–6.

106 Boyle, *Irish Labor Movement*, pp. 136–7.

107 Lyons, *Parnell*, p. 581.

108 O'Shea, *Priest, Politics and Society*, pp. 220–1; A. C. Murray, 'Nationality and local politics in late nineteenth-century Ireland: the case of County Westmeath', *Irish Historical Studies*, xxv (98), November 1986, pp. 151–5.

109 Maura Murphy, 'Fenianism, Parnellism and the Cork trades, 1860–1900', *Saothar*, v, 1979, pp. 33–4.

110 Sir Joseph West Ridgeway to A. J. Balfour, 12 October 1891 (BL, Balfour papers, Add. MS 49812), quoted in Larkin, *Fall of Parnell*, pp. 285–6.

111 Brownrigg to Archbishop Walsh, 10 December 1890 (Dublin Diocesan Archives, Walsh papers), quoted in Lyons, *Parnell*, p. 543.

112 Archbishop Croke to Mgr Tobias Kirby, 29 January 1891 (quoted in Mark Tierney (ed.), 'Dr Croke, the Irish bishops and the Parnell crisis', *Collectanea Hibernica*, (11) 1968, p. 139). See also Bishop McCarthy of Cloyne to Kirby, 26 December, and Bishop O'Callaghan of Cork to same, 27 December 1890 (ibid., pp. 125, 127).

113 *Irish Catholic*, 14 February 1891.

114 Bourke, *O'Leary*, p. 205. See also *Irish Catholic*, 9 May, 13 June, 1 August 1891.

115 The expression is in Tom Garvin, *Nationalist Revolutionaries in Ireland, 1858–1928*, Oxford, 1987, p. 58. See also ibid., pp. 58–66.

116 For these *rarae aves*, Parnellite priests, see *United Ireland, passim*; Emmet Larkin, 'Launching the counterattack: part II of the Roman Catholic hierarchy and the destruction of Parnellism', *Review of Politics*, xxviii, 1966, pp. 361–5, 382; O'Shea, *Priest, Politics and Society*, pp. 218–19, 223.

117 Woods, 'Catholic church and Irish politics', pp. 67–70, 368, 375–6.

118 Ibid., pp. 394–5; Lyons, *Parnell*, pp. 576–7.

119 For Humphreys, see D. G. Marnane, 'Fr David Humphreys and New Tipperary', in William Nolan (ed.), *Tipperary, History and Society* Dublin, 1985, pp. 367–78.

120 Woods, 'Catholic church and Irish politics', pp. 242, 251–3, 376. Keller's words are in a letter to William O'Brien, 19 December 1890 (NLI, Gill papers).

121 William O'Brien, *An Olive Branch in Ireland*, London, 1910, pp. 23–4. The plan began in Munster, 75 of the 203 affected estates were in that province, and it dragged on there after the split (Geary, *Plan of Campaign*, p. 41, app. 2 *et passim*).

122 O'Shea, *Priest, Politics and Society*, pp. 226–7.

123 C. J. Woods, 'The general election of 1892: the Catholic clergy and the defeat of the Parnellites', in F. S. L. Lyons and Richard Hawkins

(eds), *Ireland under the Union . . . : Essays in Honour of T. W. Moody*, Oxford, 1980, pp. 293, 309. In both Clare constituencies the Parnellites were the majority, a phenomenon that has still to be explained.

124 This thesis is developed in Frank Callanan, ' "Clerical dictation": reflections on the Catholic church and the Parnell split', *Archivium Hibernicum*, XLV, 1990, pp. 64–75.

125 Paul Bew, *C. S. Parnell*, Dublin, 1980, p. 127.

126 This relationship is a theme of David W. Miller's major study of Catholic politics during a slightly later period, *Church State and Nation in Ireland, 1898–1921*, Dublin, 1973.

127 I am grateful to the Revd Prof. Donal Kerr and Prof. R. V. Comerford for their comments on an earlier draft of this paper.

2   Parnell and Davitt

Paul Bew

> Parnell is completely in the hands of Davitt, although he does not see where Davitt is leading him.[1]

> Right through the heart of the nationalist fight, Parnell was always held back by a strain of sympathy for the landlords.[2]

The relationship between Charles Stewart Parnell and Michael Davitt in the 1880s illuminates not only the differing personalities of the two men but two contrasting philosophies of Irish development. Parnell's conservative vision of an Ireland reconciled to the leadership of the gentry contrasted dramatically with Davitt's socially radical peasant-based vision. Davitt, too, has always been considered a serious thinker on social matters, whilst Parnell has been more narrowly defined as a technician of power. Yet fifteen years after Parnell's death and on the eve of his own, Michael Davitt began to raise fundamental critical questions about the progress of the Irish revolution – a revolution in which he had played a key role. As the era opened up by the Irish revolution of 1879 to 1923 draws to a close, it may be worth reflecting on the differing legacies of Parnell and Davitt.

At first sight Parnell and Davitt had little in common. Consider their lives before they began to work together politically in 1879. Davitt, born in 1846, had known nothing but life's harshest experiences: an evicted Catholic cottier's son; a poverty-stricken emigration to Lancashire; a factory accident which deprived him of an arm; a long prison sentence following an imprudent involvement with Fenianism. A recent commentator, Margaret O'Callaghan, has shrewdly summarized:

> Davitt locked in the bitter romance of his own family's history was the victim of an industrialism which affected millions of

English workers. Yet imaginatively, he still remained wedded to the image of a family on the roadside near Straide thirty years before.[3]

Parnell, born also in 1846, was a child with a privileged Protestant gentry background. There is little in his early life of that sense of earnest striving and suffering which characterized Michael Davitt; instead there was a decent cricketing competence and a reasonably serious attempt to win an American heiress. His Cambridge career ended prematurely and without credit following a boozy incident. He probably entered politics in the mid 1870s, at least partly in an effort to relieve his boredom. Yet by 1891 Parnell was dead; excoriated by the bitter public exposure of his private commitment to Mrs Katharine O'Shea. Davitt lived on, however, until 1906, his life characterized by no public crisis or humiliation – rather, his reputation as a reformist thinker and writer grew steadily – buttressed by a string of six significant books from his pen.

Davitt was not without compulsive and neurotic aspects to his personality. For a long time he was deeply, even obsessively, afraid of alcohol; it was William O'Brien who persuaded him that he might be able to make moderate use of the drug. But this was as nothing compared to Parnell's foibles. Parnell had an extraordinary superstitious horror of the number thirteen and would never dine thirteen at a table. In the summer of 1883, at a by-election in Monaghan, he rushed out of the room assigned him at his hotel, pointing to the door, which bore the number thirteen. He had to get another room. When he was imprisoned in Kilmainham, Maurice Healy visited him there to consult about the nationalist Bill to amend the Land Act of 1881. Parnell counted the clauses and then threw the papers on the table as if he had been stung. 'What is the matter?' asked the solicitor Healy in alarm. 'There are thirteen clauses,' said Parnell. 'We can't have thirteen clauses. What Bill with thirteen clauses would have any chance? It would be horribly unlucky.'[4] The problem of the thirteen clauses was got over by the addition of another one, which Parnell had at first opposed. It is hard to imagine anything more removed from Davitt's nationalist and theoretical approach to the problem of land reform.

Because of the O'Shea divorce crisis Parnell's biographers have always been aware of the ambiguous aspect of the Wicklow squire's character. Davitt's later respectability has rather encouraged a more deferential, uncritical approach towards the great progressive. Writing in 1953, T. W. Moody spoke enthusiastically of Davitt's 'robust faith in the common man'[5] – in fact, in common with the bulk of humanity, Davitt's faith in the common man was not unwavering. In 1887, W. S. Blunt reported how

> he [Davitt] has altered his views of late about education, and he was beginning to see it had its disadvantages for Ireland as well as its advantages. Every post brought him requests from farmers' sons for places as clerks or pressmen and the labouring population was getting too proud to dig. If this was to be the result of education for Ireland, the education he was inclined to wish for was a manual one.[6]

More profoundly, in the same classic article, T. W. Moody speaks of Davitt's 'abhorrence' of sectarianism, stressing the benign influence of a Wesleyan schoolteacher. For Davitt, the division of the Irish populace along sectarian lines was an unpleasant mystery. But there are some sharp questions which need to be asked. Was there anything in Davitt's own political strategy which might have exacerbated sectarian tension in Ireland? Despite all the stress in the literature on Davitt's purity of intention, was he in fact quite so innocent? To answer these questions, it is necessary to turn to the Land League crisis of 1879–82, the scene of Parnell and Davitt's early co-operation.

In its classic phase, from 1858 to 1867, Irish Fenianism had committed itself to the destruction of the Irish landlord system and the large-scale redistribution of Irish land.[7] This agrarian radical outcome was, however, to be the end-product of a successful military insurrection against British rule. Exploitation of land hunger was not to be a part of the immediate strategy of Fenianism, which was instead focused on militarism. Yet, in a military sense, Fenianism was a proven failure by the end of 1867. Hence a certain casting around in the 1870s for new paths of development by the activists – still a numerous body – whose enthusiasm for Irish independence survived the débâcle of the 1867 Rising. This 'new thinking' led to a reconsideration of the role of the land question in political strategy. Associated with this was a reconsideration by revolutionaries of the role of constitutional politicians – in particular, that vociferous minority of militant home rule MPs led by Charles Stewart Parnell who had emerged in the late 1870s.

The Irish-American Fenian leader, John Devoy, later claimed that, after some inconclusive discussions, he and Michael Davitt, 'speaking for large bodies of Fenians', although not official representatives, reached an agreement with Parnell on 1 June 1879.

The agreement, while utterly ignoring details, was clear, definite and precise as far as vital political principles were concerned. It had four main points:

1 In the conduct of the public movement, as far as Parnell and Davitt were able to influence it, there should not be anything said or done to impair the vitality of the Fenian movement or to discredit its ideal of complete national independence to be secured by the eventual use of physical force.
2 The demand for self-government should not for the present be publicly defined, but nothing short of a national parliament with power over all vital national interests and an executive responsible to it should be accepted.
3 The settlement of the land question to be demanded should be the establishment of a peasant proprietary to be reached by compulsory purchase.
4 The Irish Members of Parliament elected through the public movement should form an absolutely independent party, asking and accepting no places, salaried or honorary, under the British government, either for themselves, their constituents or anyone else.

The full political meaning of this agreement, for Devoy at any rate, can only be deduced from his comment on this last plank:

> Parnell was already acting on it and it was his own policy. Davitt was not bothering himself much at that time about what might be done in Parliament. His mind was filled with the work to be done on the soil of Ireland and among the Irish in America. He and I agreed to the plank as a necessity of the situation *but Davitt seemed to me at that time to be as strongly as I was myself in favour of a policy looking to an eventual withdrawal from parliament.*(My italics)[8]

The strategic thinking of neo-Fenianism is here very clear. It was still felt – and this is the absolutely critical point – that the land question was the 'material for victory' in the sense that the British Parliament's likely refusal of the full Irish demand for land reform would create the condition for a possible Irish withdrawal from the House of Commons: a withdrawal which would then raise the issue of Irish political independence. Of course, John Devoy and other neo-Fenians considered the possibility of other outcomes to the Land League crisis, but they preferred to concentrate on the notion of an obdurate British refusal to meet Irish peasant demands because it created the apparent basis for a new popular mass-based nationalist strategy. After all, even in the event of successful government sponsored reform – as, in effect, the Land Acts of 1881 to 1909 turned out to provide – a new generation of peasants with good reason to be grateful to nationalist political leadership would be created.

This exposition of Devoy's political position is a necessary preliminary to a discussion of his claim that a definite agreement was reached at the meeting on 1 June. Both Davitt and Parnell later strongly denied it. Parnell's evidence before the Special Commission was designed to protect his image of the late 1880s as a constitutional politician; it is certainly misleading on certain points as to the nature of his relationship with 'extreme men' in the late 1870s. Nevertheless, it has been felt unlikely that Parnell would compromise himself by such a compact. There are, however, hints in *Devoy's Post-Bag* which suggest that such an agreement may have existed or, at least, that Parnell may have connived at creating the appearance that such an agreement existed.[9] But it is certain that Parnell did not accept the 'spirit' of the compact as outlined in Devoy's supplementary remarks, for he did not share the Clan na Gael's view of the relationship between the land and the national question. Parnell's view on this relationship was to emerge with a rare (for him) and unambiguous clarity in the course of the agitation. It is therefore clear that any agreement on 1 June could not have had a substantial basis.

Though he made substantial concessions to Fenianism, Parnell's own priorities lay elsewhere. He aspired to satisfy the tenantry on terms which were not disadvantageous to the landlords – the whole process to be subsidized by a generous contribution from the British Treasury. Parnell hoped that this would open the way for landlord acquiescence (or perhaps even co-operation) in the nationalist project. Parnell did not think in this way because of any excessive regard for the susceptibilities of his own class; he often spoke of them in dry and unemotional terms. He once told William O'Brien: 'The only good thing the Irish landlords have to show for themselves are their hounds and perhaps in the Roscommon country their horses.'[10] Rather, as F. S. L. Lyons has acknowledged, 'Parnell's favourite nostrum in these critical years was to bring the younger and more progressive landlords into the Home Rule movement so as to give it sufficient cachet to convince British legislators in London.'[11] Thus, he was willing to contemplate a struggle which, in his words at New Ross in September 1880, would be 'short, sharp and decisive' as the 'best way of bringing' the 'landlords' into the 'national ranks'.[12] By ending all the troublesome disputes over the level of rents Parnell hoped to open up a new and better future for the Irish landlords.

> With a suitable solution of the land question we should gladly welcome the continued presence of these gentlemen in Ireland (hear, hear). We should gladly see them taking their part for which they are fitted in the future social regeneration of this country, in the future direction of its affairs and in the future national life of Ireland.[13]

Davitt equally was determined in later years to protect his image as a compassionate Christian reformer, and there is no doubt that he both suppressed the extent of his Fenian commitments (he was involved, for example, in gun-running in the first hectic days of the Land League), while exaggerating his involvement in the land question by the claim that he had largely evolved the Land League plan during his jail sentence. In fact Davitt's interest in the land question was relatively undeveloped on his release, although under the stimulus of Irish-American radicalism combined with the depression in Ireland his position was soon altered. There is little doubt from the surviving letters that Davitt at least was bound to an agreement as Devoy suggested. 'Mr Davitt's idea was greater than the land question when he first organized the Land League,' said Devoy in 1881. 'He believed in separation and the Land League was only a stepping-stone to it.'[14] There is no doubt also that leading Clan na Gael cadres accepted the existence of this agreement, and this was to be of decisive importance.

It is very important to draw attention to these political calculations which surround the formation of the Land League in 1879. Professor Moody has written that the 'Land League was an emergency organization with exclusively agrarian purposes – the immediate defence of the tenant farmers threatened with mass eviction and then eventual conversion into peasant proprietors'.[15] Such an exclusive emphasis on social objectives fits perfectly with Davitt's later rewriting of his own history in such a way as to downplay his connections with violent conspiracy. But it has to be pointed out that the stress on the Land League as an emergency organization arising out of a spontaneous reaction to the distress of 1879 has to be modified in the light of the fact that an organized (organized, that is, by neo-Fenians) agitation predated the onset of severe economic distress in 1879 by some months.

It is perfectly true to say that the objectives of the Land League were attainable, and were eventually attained, within the structure of the United Kingdom. However, in 1879 hardly anyone of any political consequence on either side of the Irish Sea would have accepted this view. It is a consequence of the immense revolution achieved by the Land League that it later came to be so widely held. In 1879 the neo-Fenian leadership of the Land League certainly believed that the abolition of Irish landlordism and the creation of a peasant proprietary could be achieved only when the British link was broken. In other words, the connections between the New Departure and the Land League, which Professor Moody allows, cannot be reduced to the matter of Devoy's probably sincerely held belief that Parnell was committed to the original New Departure. It lay at the very heart of the radical Land League leadership's conception of the role of their movement – to smash landlordism, certainly, but, by so doing, also to smash the British link. A land league of some kind is conceivable without the New Departure background, but it would have been a very different movement – characterized by an entirely different relationship between leadership and followers.[16]

It is possible to expand this argument. According to Professor Moody's magisterial but kindly biography, Davitt devoted his energies

> after 1877 to persuading and inspiring his countrymen to combine in a disciplined organization to effect a social revolution by nonviolent means. Insisting that the demands of the tenantry were founded on a morality and national justice, he counselled them to refrain from violence, which could weaken their cause in the eyes of an awakened public opinion.[17]

There is no question that Davitt hated the typical forms of Irish agrarian violence – 'damned petty outrages' – and regarded such outbreaks as likely to discredit his cause. But the balance of evidence still strongly suggests that he remained committed to the traditional Fenian ideal – which saw a role for physical force in bringing about Irish independence – until his arrest in early 1881.

On 14 December 1880 Davitt issued a memorandum to the organizers and officers of the league which stated: 'Evidence is not wanting that numbers of men have formed and are joining the League who gave but a half-hearted allegiance to the League programme . . . men who denounced the programme of the League but six months ago.'[18] On 16 December, he wrote to John Devoy:

There is a danger, however, of this class and the priests coalescing and ousting the advanced men or gaining control of the whole thing and turning it against us. I am taking every precaution, however, against this Whig dodge. Already I have carried a neat constitution by a *coup de main* and on Tuesday next I intend to carry the election of an executive council of fifteen in whose hands the entire government will be placed. The Council will consist of six or seven MPs, and the remainder, men like Brennan, Egan and myself. . . . If we could carry on this movement for another year without being interfered with we could do almost anything we pleased in this country. The courage of the people is magnificent. All classes are purchasing Arms openly.[19]

This is a letter which reeks of the world of the manipulator and conspirator. It was unavailable to Moody when he constructed his noble portrait of Davitt in 1953, but he had to deal with it in his later 1982 biography. Clearly highly embarrassed, Moody speaks of Davitt undergoing 'excessive mental stimulation'[20] at the time. Another possible explanation for this letter exists, one which would save the picture of Davitt in 1880 as essentially a social reformer. Davitt, knowing full well that the Land League was not capable of playing its envisaged role in separatist strategy, might have intended to keep John Devoy (and Irish American nationalism generally) sweet by muttering revolutionary phrases in his letters. Against this interpretation lies the fact that we have to explain not just Davitt's phrases but his public actions in this period, including the 14 December statement and the organizational *coup de main*. More important, it is worth pointing out that it was Davitt who opposed the thesis of Thomas Sexton and other members of the Land League leadership that the movement should be prosecuted in the north as purely a social movement.[21] In late 1880, the land reform movement had demonstrated a substantial appeal in the north-east, as Irish Chief Secretary Forster told Gladstone: 'No Ulster Liberal has a chance of return who does not pledge himself to it and even the Orangemen cry out.'[22] It was Davitt who insisted (against Sexton's advice) that nationalist emblems should be carried at Land League meetings thus giving the terrified Ulster Tory aristocracy a chance to fight back. Lord Enniskillen was now able to proclaim with some effect: 'The Land League is essentially a disloyal organization and although landlordism may be the immediate object of its attack, the ultimate separation of the two countries is its aim.'[23] In short, Davitt's abhorrence of sectarianism, whilst entirely genuine, was not so great as to force him to take the practical step (a downplaying of nationalism) which would have limited its operation in Irish politics.

In 1953, T. W. Moody felt able to argue – almost unproblematically – that an important part of Davitt's life work was to demonstrate the common nature of the struggle of the British working man and that of the Irish peasant. From the writings of Karl Marx on Ireland to that of Erich Strauss in his seminal *Irish Nationalism and British Democracy* (1951), this has been a much reiterated theme of left-wing commentators on Ireland. But this notion has always depended – amongst other things – on a rather undifferentiated and sentimentalized view of the nature of the Irish peasantry. To be fair to Davitt, he grappled with the problem in a serious way – Davitt saw the Land League primarily as an agency for protecting the poorest and most oppressed sections of the Irish peasantry. Those who benefited most in the end were the richest and strongest. Davitt turned in disgust from the spectacle and explicitly espoused land nationalization and the ideals of Henry George after 1882. The peasants – all sections, rich and poor – had the whiff of property in their noses and tossed out the idea of state ownership of land; by the mid 1880s Davitt himself was watering it down.

The foundation of the United Irish League in 1898 allowed Davitt the chance to redeem his radical reputation. It was specifically designed to help those small farmers left out of the Land League settlement. Davitt joined in enthusiastically, even threateningly, but at the same time was rather inconsistent. Whilst he stirred up hostility against graziers, he also cooled it down in one specific case – that of a Catholic and nationalist friend Bernard Daly. He also evinced an inability to see that the Protestant Ascendancy was now a fading force. When the British government took the decisive step of passing the Wyndham Act in 1903, Davitt was reluctant to believe the evidence that the end of the landlord system was in sight. He continued to maintain a hostile attitude, not just towards diehard landlords but also towards very much more conciliatory unionists. Davitt was never really at home with the new movements of the 1900s which attempted to break the sectarian moulds of Irish politics. Then suddenly, when he seemed set into a terminal rut of nationalist conformism, Davitt spoke out in an unexpected and unsettling way.

Following the Liberal landslide of 1906, there was much pressure to reconsider the restrictions on Canadian cattle importation into the United Kingdom. Davitt believed that in the long run the case for cheap food for the labouring masses in England would prove irresistible. Nevertheless, the Irish party, both in 1906 and later in 1908, felt compelled to oppose any change which might harm the Irish cattle trade. Davitt insisted that the underlying problem lay with Irish farming practices, in particular, the neglect of tillage.

The present system of using every available acre of land for cattle raising, is a deadly injury to the country. Land purchase is not stopping this pernicious practice. Quite the contrary. It has increased it, so far; which means that the rights won for the peasant proprietors of the future at enormous sacrifices to the nation of our day, are in no way helping to solve the industrial problem, nor to materially lessen the disastrous effects of emigration. The tendency among large numbers of tenants who have recently bought their holdings is to turn more land into grass, and thus to narrow still more the opportunities of employment for labour. This is a most serious national concern, and cannot be ignored much longer without our conniving at the slow, but certain and inevitable, ruin of the towns and villages that can only subsist economically upon an industrial population.[24]

Many contemporary commentators had made similar points about Irish agriculture. Michael Davitt's remarks had, however, a very particular significance. The sponsor of the Irish agrarian revolution was here admitting publicly that the programme was not working according to plan. It was an honest admission of a serious problem: more explicit than anything to be found in his major work, *Fall of Feudalism*, published in 1904. Davitt, it is true, reacted by trying to spruce up the old doctrine. William O'Brien had already decided that this was a pointless task and was instead trying to develop a new politics based self-consciously on old Parnellite principles.

The ambiguity of Davitt's career is the ambiguity at the heart of Irish radical nationalism. It can mobilize broad masses with astonishing effectiveness but it cannot deliver its material promises to this constituency: notably an end to emigration, successful industrialization and land redistribution. When Davitt produced his cry of pain in 1906 he concluded by calling for a reinvigoration of the traditional virtues. Shortly after his death, the experience of the Irish ranch war was to demonstrate the futility of such an argument. Again and again agrarian radicalism ran into stiff opposition from mainstream nationalists – embarrassingly, too, many who took the radical course against the 'ranching system' were revealed to have ranching interests themselves. In 1932, a Fianna Fail government was elected which was formally committed to the Davitt programme of 1906 – but by this time Robert Davitt, Davitt's son, was quite prepared that the Davitt name and prestige should be thrown against the old policies. It is hardly surprising: as early as 1898 his father had been prepared to abandon basic principles in Mayo in the case of Bernard Daly.

Parnell had always offered an alternative to the Davitt vision. The Parnell tradition as it existed in his own lifetime – and as it was developed in different ways by John Redmond and William O'Brien – had certain key characteristics. It was explicitly pragmatic about the role of agrarian radicalism. It tended not to put radical democratic considerations into the forefront. Most dramatically in 1886, Parnell and Gladstone – at the height of the home rule crisis – were agreed on the need to preserve a key role for landlords in the political life of the 'new Ireland'.[25] Instead, it laid heavy emphasis on the notion of conciliation between creeds and classes.

From 1858, with the founding of the IRB, to 1958, Davitt's views always lay closer to the heart of the mainstream Irish nationalist project or, at least, its formal rhetoric. His views fitted more neatly the broad notion of the historically dispossessed coming into their rightful inheritance. Few openly disputed Davitt's ideals though many quietly and privately disavowed them. In 1958, the Whitaker Report formally shattered this conceptual order and the Irish generation which has grown up since its collapse – in a world where international capital and the dominance of grassland production are freely accepted – has perhaps a reason for looking with renewed sympathy at the themes of Parnellism, themes which were eclipsed by a pious, if often empty, adherence to Davitt's theory for much of this century. Parnell, who was himself partly descended from Ulster Protestant stock – as Redmond pointedly insisted – even managed to extend his conciliatory approach, at the least, to the northern question. Speaking in Belfast in 1891 he declared: 'It is undoubtedly true that until the . . . prejudices of the minority whether reasonable or unreasonable are conciliated . . . Ireland can never enjoy perfect freedom, Ireland can never be united.'[26]

During the third home rule crisis of 1912–14, Parnell became again a central figure for nationalist reference. To justifiably nervous home rulers, even his fear of the number thirteen seemed to have a certain relevance. The *County Cork Eagle* on 24 February 1912 drily observed,

> It is well known that the date just fixed for the reassembling of Parliament this week was February 13, and that it was changed on representations to the Government that the number 13 was unlucky and an ill omen for the commencement of a Home Rule session.

More seriously, John Redmond invoked Parnell's name against the spirits of separatism. Speaking at Kilkenny on 18 October 1914, he argued:

> What is the theory of Home Rule? What is the basic theory of the whole constitutional movement for the last century in Ireland? The theory all through the century, put forward by Daniel O'Connell, put forward by Isaac Butt, put forward by Parnell (applause), put forward by us since Parnell's death with the unanimous consent of Nationalist Ireland – the theory of that constitutional movement has been, that we in this country claim to become an autonomous nation within the Empire, O'Connell stated it, Parnell stated it, Butt stated it, I stated it – every responsible leader of the constitutional movement for the last quarter of a century has stated it over and over again to England, that if that were done, if Ireland were brought into the Empire as an . . . autonomous nation within the Empire that Ireland was quite willing, while taking any advantages that might flow from her connection with the Empire, to manfully and honestly bear her share of the burdens that that Empire cast upon all the nations comprised within its organization (applause).[27]

The *Freeman's Journal* in commenting favourably upon this speech was especially determined to insist that Redmond was following Parnellite principles. 'Parnell said at Wolverhampton in the Gladstonian days before Home Rule what Mr Redmond is saying now.' In the most recent phase of the Irish troubles, the current leader of constitutional nationalism in Ulster, John Hume, has likewise been keen indeed to insist that he, too, is following Parnellite principles. Speaking to the SDLP conference in 1984 he repeated enthusiastically the words of Parnell's Belfast speech of 1891. There is inevitably an element of the utilitarian and pragmatic involved when an active politician today resurrects the language of a nineteenth-century speech. John Vincent's *Disraeli* (1990) has decisively demonstrated that much of the current Tory utilization of the 'one nation' theme is based on a profound misrecognition. Nevertheless, it is perhaps ironic that whilst the impulse of Davitt's agrarian social theory seems to have lost all relevance in modern Ireland, some of the themes of the somewhat less intellectual Parnell – an intensely superstitious man who rarely read, let alone wrote, books – still play a significant role in the public discourse of key figures of modern Irish nationalism.[28]

NOTES

1 Mitchell Henry to O'Neill Daunt, National Library of Ireland, Daunt papers, ms 11446.
2 Harold Spender, 'John Redmond: an impression', *Contemporary Review*, 113, April 1918, p. 376.
3 Margaret O'Callaghan, 'Crime, nationality and the law: the politics of land in late Victorian Ireland', unpublished dissertation, Cambridge, Ph.D., 1989, p. 135.
4 T. M. Healy, *Letters and Leaders of My Day*, London, 1928, vol. I, p. 153.
5 T. W. Moody, 'Michael Davitt and the British labour movement 1882–1906', *Transactions of the Royal Historical Society*, series 5, iii, 1953.
6 W. S. Blunt, quoted in J. P. Loughlin, *Gladstone, Ulster and the Home Rule Question*, Dublin, 1986, p. 105.
7 On the subject matter, see now the concise summary by J. S. Donnelly, jr, 'The land question in nationalist politics', in T. E. Hachey and L. J. McCaffrey (eds), *Perspectives in Irish Nationalism*, Lexington, 1989.
8 *Gaelic American*, 29 September 1906.
9 T. N. Brown, *Irish American Nationalism 1870–90*, Philadelphia, Pa, 1966, ch. 5.
10 W. O'Brien, *Recollections*, London, 1905, p. 202.
11 F. S. L. Lyons, 'The Land War', *Irish Times*, 12 May 1979.
12 *Freeman's Journal*, 27 September 1880.
13 Quoted in Paul Bew, *C. S. Parnell*, Dublin, 1980, p. 33.
14 See Paul Bew, *Land and the National Question in Ireland 1858–82*, Dublin, 1978, p. 54.
15 T. W. Moody, in *Irish American Nationalism*, xv (60), September 1967, pp. 444–5.
16 Bew, *Land and the National Question*, ch. 3.
17 T. W. Moody, *Davitt and Irish Revolution 1846–82*, Oxford, 1982, p. 553.
18 *Weekly Freeman*, 18 December 1880.
19 W. O'Brien and D. Ryan (eds), *Devoy's Post-Bag 1878–1928*, 2 vols, Dublin, 1948–53, vol. 2, pp. 20–5, Davitt to Devoy, 16 December 1880.
20 Moody, *Davitt and Irish Revolution*, pp. 440–2.
21 *Weekly Freeman*, 18 December 1880.
22 Quoted in O'Callaghan, 'Crime, nationality and the law', p. 96.
23 *Fermanagh Times*, 20 January 1881.

24 See Paul Bew, *Conflict and Conciliation in Ireland*, Oxford, 1987, p. 127.
25 See Bew, *Parnell*, Loughlin, *Gladstone*, and Alan O'Day, *Parnell and the First Home Rule Episode*, Dublin, 1986.
26 *Northern Whig*, 23 May 1891.
27 *Weekly Freeman's Journal*, 24 October 1914.
28 In particular, John Hume, the leader of the SDLP in Northern Ireland, has formally invoked Parnell's ideas at many points in the current crisis. See Barry White's slightly pious *John Hume: Statesman of the Troubles*, Belfast, 1984.

3   Parnell and William O'Brien

Partners and friends – from consensus to conflict in the Land War

Sally Warwick-Haller

It was the Land War that brought Parnell and William O'Brien together.[1] Parnell was a very private man, but O'Brien was one of the few people who managed to become close to him and whom Parnell really liked.[2] In 1924, a former Land Leaguer, J. M. Wall, reminded O'Brien of their pastimes during their days in Kilmainham jail in the early 1880s and how Parnell 'had favoured your companionship' at chess 'most of all'.[3] O'Brien became one of Parnell's most devoted and loyal supporters. During his imprisonment in 1891 in Galway jail for his activities with the Plan of Campaign, O'Brien reflected on the sad state of affairs which had overtaken Ireland. In his letters to his wife, Sophie, he made no secret of the pain he felt at the way Parnell was being vilified: 'the new line of attack on P. is infamously unjust', and he could not be a party to it. Yet he blamed Parnell and his faction for their determination to prolong the feud with their bitter recriminations. He despaired of a solution, for 'the extremists on both sides are so envenomed'.[4] In the end, on his release from prison just two months before Parnell's death, O'Brien joined forces with the anti-Parnellites, but more to thwart Tim Healy's ambitions than to fight his former leader. It must have been with a heavy heart that he took such a decision.

It could be argued, and with good reason, that O'Brien's eventual stand was a natural outcome of the strained relations that had existed between him and Parnell over the Plan of Campaign: O'Brien found it hard to accept his leader's disapproval of the renewed agrarian agitation. This, however, overlooks the way they had worked together in the first phase of the Land War, when Parnell offered the young O'Brien the editorship of *United Ireland* – an invitation that was to have such far-reaching consequences for O'Brien's own career. The characters of the two men were very different, and their views on tactics and priorities often diverged; Parnell once gently chided O'Brien for his approach: 'My dear O'Brien,' he was reported to have said, 'your spectacles ought to be coloured rose. You expect too much from human nature.'[5] But overall they complemented one another, and were a good team in the first half of the 1880s, when Parnell had a distinct role for O'Brien to play in the movement.

O'Brien first met Parnell in 1878 when, as a 26-year-old reporter for the *Freeman's Journal*, he accompanied him on the journey back to Dublin after a land meeting at Tralee which Parnell had addressed. O'Brien's account in his diary gives some insight into their relationship, for he had somehow managed to penetrate Parnell's customary reserve. Their conversation was intimate as they 'exchanged no end of confidences', and O'Brien quickly fell under Parnell's spell:

> He has captured me, heart and soul, and is bound to go on capturing. A sweet seriousness *au fond*, any amount of nervous courage, a delicate reserve, without the smallest suspicion of hauteur; strangest of all, humour; above everything else, simplicity; as quietly at home with the girls in Mallow as with his turbulent audience in Tralee. . . . As romantic as Lord Edward [Fitzgerald], but not to be shaken from prosier methods.

'In any case,' he concluded in his diary, 'a man one could suffer with proudly.'[6] Nearly fifty years later O'Brien's admiration for Parnell was just as strong.

Their respect was mutual, for Parnell swiftly recognized the young journalist's extensive abilities, and he retained an affection for O'Brien throughout his life. In the task of building up the Irish parliamentary party, O'Brien became Parnell's main 'lieutenant' and it was to him that Parnell turned when, in 1886, he needed to defuse the impatience of Irish-Americans and to discourage them from turning to violence, which would do irreparable harm to the prospects for home rule and the Irish party's new relationship with the Liberals. 'I am most anxious', he wrote to O'Brien, 'that you should attend the Convention at Chicago . . . as you would be better able than anybody else to smooth over the existing jealousies in America.'[7] O'Brien's role as a mediator or conciliator had already proved itself during the crisis over Captain O'Shea's candidature at the Galway by-election; he was the key factor in preventing a mutiny in the party, though his loyalty to Parnell had been put under considerable strain on this occasion. O'Brien once again played the part of the peace-maker in the abortive negotiations with Parnell at Boulogne in early 1891. Parnell's proposal that O'Brien should replace him as chairman of the party can be seen as proof of the esteem with which the Land War campaigner was held by his leader, as can Parnell's letter to O'Brien when the peace talks collapsed. In this Parnell expressed his admiration for O'Brien's courage and devotion to the cause and how deeply he felt:

> the kindness and gentleness of spirit which you have shown me throughout these negotiations. . . . I know you have forgiven much roughness and asperity upon my part and have made allowances for some unreasonable conduct from me, which, to anybody gifted with less patience and conciliation than yourself, would have been most difficult.[8]

O'Brien's role as a conciliator was not one that is usually identified with the earlier phases of his career. Subsequently, he did assume that function, for it was O'Brien who engineered the reunification of the party in 1900 through his organization, the United Irish League, and, of course, he took his famous stand in 1903 as an ardent and sincere champion of the conciliation of landlords. In the late 1870s and throughout the 1880s, he was generally seen as the scourge of landlords, as he waged war on them and the whole system from the columns of the press and through the Plan of Campaign.

One of the qualities which O'Brien so admired in Parnell was, to use O'Brien's own words, 'the supreme gift, so rarely to be found in Ireland, of knowing when it was wisdom to be moderate and when it was wisdom to be extreme'.[9] O'Brien did not always share such a trait, and at times Parnell had to restrain his impetuous colleague from rash action. Such an instance occurred in 1882, when, to force the government to relax coercion and concede further land reforms, O'Brien devised a plan to kidnap the viceroy (Lord Spencer) and his chief secretary and hold them hostage in the Wicklow mountains. However, O'Brien's ability to support moderate policies with militant-sounding language was to be put to effective use by Parnell, and this was one of the reasons he invited O'Brien to edit his new mouthpiece for the Land War, *United Ireland*.

The main purpose behind the launching of *United Ireland* was to use it to heal the rift that was threatening to disrupt the political movement Parnell was endeavouring to build up. The general elec-

tion of 1880 had brought supporters of Parnell into political prominence for the first time. They made up nearly 40 per cent of those
MPs who were committed to home rule, and this was enough to
give him the chairmanship of the parliamentary party. Though a
keen participant in the Land League, the leadership of which he
shared with Davitt, Parnell's long-term aim, which he pursued for
the next five years, was to win over the remaining Irish MPs and
to transform the party into an effective fighting-force at Westminster. He was fully aware that if the party was to be successful, it
must be reinforced by a strong movement throughout the country,
which would involve nationalists of all hues from moderates to
Fenians; he also recognized the importance of Irish-American support. Thus, one of the most delicate tasks Parnell faced was to
keep the right and left wings of his movement together, and particularly to avoid the defection of radical agrarians like Davitt and
Dillon. Parnell's notorious speech at Ennis in September 1880, in
which he urged the boycotting of land-grabbers, had been designed
to appeal to extremists and keep the allegiance of Dillon who had
himself, the previous month, delivered the fiery speech which
brought him fame and in which he had recommended the withhold-
ing of rents. Similarly, Parnell's use of obstructionist tactics in
Parliament in early 1881 was really aimed at keeping the extremists
happy, for the imposition of coercion had divided the movement,
with calls from the militant wing for secession from Parliament and
a no-rent strike. Parnell, essentially a constitutionalist, rejected such
revolutionary steps, and obstruction was a useful ploy to dress up
a moderate policy in extremist garb.

The most threatening strain on the uneasy alliance came with the
new Land Bill which the Liberal government presented in early
1881. The radical agrarians were totally opposed to considering any
land legislation, however beneficial, while coercion was in force.
On the other hand, the proposed legislation did offer some major
concessions to Ireland, and no one of moderate persuasion in Ireland could have accepted a policy of wrecking the Bill. Parnell's
temporary solution was to advise the Irish MPs to abstain on the
second reading; the other course – to have allowed a free vote –
would, in Parnell's view, have resulted in 'a still more serious
division of opinion and much less unanimity', and 'would practically
destroy the usefulness of the party by showing that it could not be
relied upon to act as a body at any important juncture'.[10] Even this
compromise did not placate the moderates, backed by the *Freeman's Journal*, the *Nation*, and the Archbishop of Cashel, Dr

Croke, who openly denounced Parnell's policy and supported the Bill. The extremists were furious, and the division within the Irish parliamentary movement was clear for all to see. Moreover, Parnell was particularly disturbed by the fact that the nationalist press had refused to endorse his strategy of abstention. Thus his solution to these problems was to form his own 'Irish National Newspaper and Publishing Company', purchase the three papers owned by Richard Pigott, and convert one of them into *United Ireland*.

William O'Brien was an obvious choice for the editorship. He had established himself as the most brilliant member of the *Freeman* staff, becoming well known as a result of his numerous articles on the land question – 'Christmas on the Galtees' series – and subsequently as the 'Special Commissioner' sent by the *Freeman* to investigate the plight of the tenant-farmers of the west of Ireland, about whose position he wrote with a passionate anger. The sufferings that he had witnessed helped to convert him into an implacable opponent of landlordism. His descriptions were graphic, and the tone of his writing was often militant. He had all the attributes which would have endeared him to the extremists in the Parnell movement, while the fact he had been such a respected journalist for the *Freeman* might have helped assuage the fears of the moderates if *United Ireland* seemed too outrageous.

Parnell had already acknowledged O'Brien's abilities some eighteen months before when he asked him to join Dillon and himself on an American tour. O'Brien was unable to accept, as his mother, the sole surviving member of his family, had succumbed to the fatal consumption which the previous winter had claimed the lives of his brothers and sister.[11] In July 1881, however, O'Brien would find it hard to decline this second approach from Parnell, who made it clear from the outset that he was not prepared to consider an alternative for the editorship. He impressed on O'Brien that he was 'very anxious' that he should accept 'as I feel sure from your well-known ability and great experience, you would conduct the undertaking to success'.[12] Parnell's opinion was reinforced by letters and telegrams from leading Parnellites, including Patrick Egan, T. P. O'Connor and James O'Kelly. O'Brien's response was not one of joy; he greeted Parnell's 'summons' as a 'death-bell'. He was not enamoured of any contact with Pigott, who was already suspected of shady dealings; but what probably influenced him more was his memory of the off-hand way Pigott had rejected the 16-year-old O'Brien's offerings to his paper. He was also unwilling to give offence to the *Freeman*'s owner, Edmund Dwyer Gray, for though he did not sympathize with his more conservative leanings, he had 'been like a brother to me'. O'Brien's most serious misgivings, however, stemmed from Dillon's hostile response. The letter he sent O'Brien from Kilmainham jail (where he was serving his sentence under the Coercion Act) came as a 'bombshell'; until then O'Brien had not realized how wide the rift was among the Parnellites.[13] The main explanation for Dillon's attitude was his opposition to Parnell's tactics over the Land Bill; if he approved of *United Ireland* and thus allowed his name to be identified with the new paper, this could be misinterpreted as acceptance of Parnell's policy. For Parnell's choice of editor, however, Dillon had nothing but praise.[14]

In attempting to reassure O'Brien, Parnell impressed on him his need 'to conciliate all sections of opinion comprised in the movement'. He also indicated that O'Brien's task would be to manage the paper on 'straightforward' *but* 'advanced' lines; once the radical agrarians learned of its true nature, *United Ireland* 'would have the entire support of the Land League'. Of one thing O'Brien was quite clear: Parnell would not abandon the venture.[15] O'Brien was seen as an instrument of unity in the movement; he would, in *United Ireland*, speak for and appeal to the extremists, for the paper was to have a fighting tone. O'Brien subsequently recalled how he had warned Parnell 'that if the object is to preach moderation or to save the paper from the Castle, I am the last man to be placed at the helm'.[16] *United Ireland* quickly became known for its full coverage of Land League activities, for its defiance of the government policy of coercion, and for the violence and outspokenness of its tone. The chief secretary's daughter commented in her diary that the paper used language against her father that was 'worthy of Billingsgate'. O'Brien immediately proved his value to Parnell for *United Ireland* became the imprisoned Land League leaders' favourite paper.[17] With the left wing appeased, Parnell could then be free to concentrate on action through Parliament rather than direct action in Ireland. The fears of moderates would thus also be calmed. In addition, *United Ireland* would be a means of communicating to extremists, in language that sounded militant, Parnell's more moderate plans, for although Parnell had promised that he would not interfere in the running of the paper, and that O'Brien could go as far as he pleased, short of getting either of them hanged,[18] he could be confident of O'Brien's basic loyalty to him.

The next four years saw O'Brien playing the role of the radical agrarian, while at the same time reinforcing Parnell in his commit-

ment to a constitutional approach, and in his aim to consolidate
his leadership over the party. O'Brien's function was swiftly put to
the test when, a week after the opening issue of *United Ireland*,
the Land Bill became law. Parnell resolved his dilemma of being
caught between the demands of moderates and extremists for
acceptance or outright rejection respectively, by suggesting that the
Act should first be 'tested' – through certain selected cases – before
tenants could be recommended to use the Land Courts set up by
the legislation. This ambiguity and his attempt to please both sides
were echoed in *United Ireland*: O'Brien was opposed to rejecting
the Act, for it did bring some improvements, and these should be
seen as steps towards the ultimate goal of a peasant proprietorship;
at the same time, he highlighted the weaknesses. He warned tenants
against rushing into the courts, and he denounced the veteran
campaigner on behalf of tenant right, Charles Gavan Duffy, for his
demand that the Act be given a fair trial. O'Brien told his readers
to focus their energies on the Land League and on combating
landlordism. His inflammatory language, which was full of the military metaphors which are so associated with his style of writing
(possibly attributable to his favourite pastime as a child of playing
with his toy army), gave all the appearance of fighting the Land
War with full vigour. O'Brien was skilful at balancing the moderate
and extreme views. The week before he attacked Duffy, he had
included an interview given by a supporter of the Land Act, the
Archbishop of Cashel, who was also O'Brien's close friend. O'Bri-
en's true position of upholding Parnell's policy became clear when
he urged the crucial National Convention meeting to back Parnell's
policy of testing the Act, and his stress on the apparent harmony
that had prevailed at this convention was very much an attempt to
heal the fundamental disagreements which had simmered just below
the surface. Yet O'Brien ended the article, in which he had recommended Parnell's approach, with words that were highly pro-
vocative:

> And it may as well be frankly proclaimed once for all that the
> Irish race will show landlordism no more mercy now, than in the
> days of its insolence it showed to the millions whom it hunted
> to death like vermin when the millions were weak and hungry.
> Impoverish it and manacle it in the Land Courts, if that be
> possible; and if not, or whether or not, hunt it down steadily,
> patiently, remorselessly – to the death.

When Parnell's plan failed to work, for tenants ignored his advice and flocked to the courts to obtain judicially fixed rents, O'Brien was ready with cogent explanations. He neglected, however, to mention the confusion in Ireland as to what policy the tenants should follow after the issuing from Kilmainham jail of the No-Rent Manifesto and Parnell's seeming change of direction in favour of more extreme action.[19]

O'Brien is usually seen as the author of this manifesto, but other Land League leaders (including Parnell) were also involved in its production. This abortive call for a general strike against rent was a tactic that O'Brien, unlike Parnell, had supported for some weeks, and in fact he was the one who successfully put pressure on Dillon to add his signature. Now Parnell, according to O'Brien's version, was 'the most resolute' of them all in his support of this ploy. At the time of its appearance, both Parnell and O'Brien were in agreement that this was the right policy for the moment,[20] but as far as Parnell was concerned, with the Land League on the verge of disintegration, this gave him the chance to *appear* to be extreme, and thus keep the militant critics quiet, when a rent strike could have little hope of success and would largely serve to strengthen the wisdom of moderate action.

The seeds of a potential divergence between Parnell and O'Brien were sown by the so-called 'Kilmainham Treaty' of May 1882 and the setting up, some five months later, of the Irish National League which replaced the defunct Land League. These two events made it clear to O'Brien that Parnell was not only a constitutionalist at heart, but, of more significance to O'Brien, now placed home rule above land law reform as the main goal. Parnell was no longer a participant in the Land War, and had drifted away from his hitherto declared view that 'the land question has to be settled. If the land question were settled every other question would, I think, settle itself'.[21] One of the creeds to which O'Brien remained adamantly faithful throughout his career was that the solving of Ireland's agrarian problems must take pride of place. However, it can still be argued that, for the time being, Parnell and O'Brien continued to work as a team, with O'Brien reinforcing his leader's policies.

Though Parnell may have abandoned the land agitation, O'Brien and *United Ireland*'s main concern between 1882 and 1885 was to continue to fight the Land War, for this was an issue which would have far more appeal to the Irish people than home rule would have. O'Brien's role was two-fold. His efforts would help to keep alive the political awareness in rural Ireland that the Land League had stimulated, and thus he was of fundamental importance to

Parnell, for a strong party at Westminster would be rendered ineffective if it was not backed by an equally strong movement throughout Ireland. He would also continue to conciliate the more militant
members of the movement, while at the same time supporting
Parnell's plans. A few examples can be cited to illustrate these
points.

In May 1882 O'Brien (and *United Ireland*) approved Parnell's
discussions with the Liberal government and defended them from
the extremists' attacks. O'Brien's capacity to steer a middle course
between the two wings of the movement was revealed in the paper's
key editorial of 6 May. The language was moderate, the author
was hopeful of positive action from Gladstone, especially over the
rent arrears issue; but there was no explicit reference to the negotiations with the Liberals and the 'Kilmainham Treaty', and the
Liberal prime minister was still denounced for refusing to remedy
their other grievances with the 1881 Land Act.

O'Brien did not want to see the Irish National League as primarily an electioneering agency, which would consolidate the position
of the parliamentary party in Ireland – Parnell's aim for this new
organization. Yet his portrayal of it in *United Ireland* – as a means
of pursuing a 'vigorous agitation for the amendment of the Land
Act as a preliminary to the abolition of landlordism by purchase
and the substitution of an occupying proprietary' – was useful in
providing an explanation of the National League that extremists
could approve.[22] Moreover, O'Brien did what he could to make the
new league a success; he was on the organizing committee from
the outset, and when not at Westminster he toured Ireland to build
up its support. O'Brien's skills as a public orator were beginning
to manifest themselves, especially in his incursions into Ulster,
where the Parnellites were endeavouring to establish the party. The
agrarian question, rather than that of home rule, would clearly have
more appeal there. In his (and other Parnellites') speeches, and
in some of his editorials in *United Ireland* intended for northern
consumption, the emphasis was on those issues – like denunciation
of landlords – which could enhance the links, instead of the differences, with the rest of Ireland.

In the summer of 1884, the Central Branch of the National
League commended O'Brien for his 'triumphant vindication of the
cause of morality and freedom of the press', and his courage in
standing out and battling single-handedly against Dublin Castle.
O'Brien was already known as a man who had defied government
coercion during his imprisonment in Kilmainham, when *United Ire-*

land had, with the help of the Ladies' Land League and a few articles smuggled out of prison, proved insuppressible. This reputation was boosted still further by his sustained exposure in *United Ireland* of corruption, vice and serious immorality among named officials of the Dublin Castle administration. These allegations were not at all unfounded, though O'Brien's treatment of them was vicious. However, his attacks on the honour of the lord lieutenant, Lord Spencer, and his chief secretary, Trevelyan, were most reprehensible; O'Brien himself subsequently recanted his charges against Spencer. This onslaught on the Liberal regime in Ireland must have appealed to the extreme Parnellites, as well as the Irish-Americans, and may also have helped Parnell in the tactic, which he briefly employed in the mid 1880s, of asserting the independence of the Irish party in Parliament.

Two men who were often ready to defy Parnell over his moderate policies were Dillon and Davitt. O'Brien's role as 'the restorer of harmony' showed itself when the tension between Dillon and Parnell, which had been heightened by the 'Kilmainham Treaty', of which Dillon disapproved, finally erupted in September 1882 with Dillon's resignation. O'Brien firmly pointed out in *United Ireland* that there was 'no shadow of division' between Dillon and his leader, and that poor health was the *sole* reason for his action. (Dillon did, in fact, have tuberculosis.) O'Brien claimed the same for Davitt, that there was no difference of opinion between the founder of the Land League and Parnell. There were several occasions when O'Brien had to give replies to those who rejoiced in signs of a split between Parnell and Davitt. Though neither he nor Parnell could share Davitt's advocacy of land nationalization, in his editorial in *United Ireland* O'Brien implied some approval and even praise for Davitt's schemes, which did not really obstruct the movement's basic aim to lower rents and create a peasant proprietorship. He selected for particular comment Davitt's words which emphasized the natural right the people had to own the land. The key issue in Davitt's speech was, according to O'Brien, 'National Autonomy': 'Nationalization of the land, Mr Davitt makes perfectly clear must go hand-in-hand with the Nationalization of the Government'. O'Brien had thus in his carefully worded article moved the focus away from their basic differences over the land question to the theme of home rule, over which Parnell and Davitt were in agreement.[23] There was one time, however, when O'Brien made no secret of his support for Parnell against Davitt's position: when Davitt condemned Parnell's Land Purchase Migration Company, which was a short-lived attempt to deal with the acute poverty of the west through purchasing estates for resale, O'Brien came firmly to Parnell's defence, and gave full approval to Parnell's project.[24] A decade later, O'Brien himself was to pursue similar ventures in his work with the Congested Districts Board.[25]

O'Brien was at his most fulfilled when he was working to improve the conditions of rural Ireland, but unlike many of his colleagues in the Parnell movement, and particularly unlike Parnell after 1881, he saw that his main sphere of operation was in Ireland. Though he received praise from many quarters as a brilliant orator in the House of Commons, he did not enjoy his participation at Westminster, and his rejoicing was loud when, in the mid 1890s, he was declared a bankrupt and forced to resign. Parnell had had to be fairly persuasive in 1882 to convince O'Brien that he had to stand for Parliament when a by-election was pending for O'Brien's birthplace, Mallow: 'It is of the greatest importance', he wrote to him, 'that we should get men of your stamp into the representation' – these words are evidence of the value Parnell placed on O'Brien.[26]

As the 1880s unfolded, Parnell was becoming more preoccupied with action in Parliament, and with home rule and the forging of the 'Liberal alliance'; he was also becoming increasingly detached from Ireland – all this must have widened any differences that might have existed between him and O'Brien. However, though Parnell disapproved of further direct agrarian action in Ireland, in the form of the Plan of Campaign, it was to O'Brien that he turned in his attempt to calm the agitation. This was, of course, a recognition of the leading role O'Brien played in initiating and spreading the Plan of Campaign, but it also reflected the relationship between them and O'Brien's record of loyalty to his leader. He could have sent for Dillon, who was, at least, of equal significance in the activities of the plan.

The main reason Parnell objected to the plan was his fear that such extreme tactics would harm the 'Union of Hearts' with the Liberals that he was so carefully developing, and with it the prospects for home rule. Parnell had good reason for this view, for John Morley was warning him that the effect on English public opinion was 'wholly bad'.[27] In addition, Parnell did not believe that the plan could succeed; it would be an unnecessary drain, in terms of time and money, on the movement. His hostility to the plan did not lessen throughout its existence, and he resisted O'Brien's attempts to involve him. Moreover, he did not conceal his attitude from the public – the most notable instance being his famous Eighty

Club speech in May 1888. Parnell's response undoubtedly encouraged other members of the party to remain aloof, a factor which O'Brien continually lamented: 'It seems a terrible pity that P. wont [*sic*] come upon the scene and say something which could justify vigorous action by the party without compromising himself.'[28] These words, which he wrote to Harrington in November 1887, also show that O'Brien had some appreciation of the difficulties of Parnell's position.

It is possible that Parnell's good will had been lost at the outset by O'Brien's apparent failure to discuss the plan with him before its publication, or so Parnell claimed, and Tim Healy and Davitt have stressed how much he had been offended by this omission. However, the evidence points to the fact that O'Brien *did* consult Parnell about the possibility of renewed agrarian agitation – though it is doubtful that he showed him the actual text of the plan before it appeared in *United Ireland*. Indeed, O'Brien's version implies that Parnell had not been unsympathetic to the prospect of another land war, as long as Gladstone was not compromised by illegal and violent action. If that occurred, Parnell made it plain to his colleague, he himself could not take part – a stand to which the Irish leader stuck steadfastly.[29] As far as the relationship between O'Brien and Parnell was concerned, the important point is that O'Brien had naturally assumed that the line they had evolved together, earlier in the decade, would be continued.

It must have been with this hope that O'Brien came to the famous secret interview with Parnell behind the Greenwich Observatory in December 1886, which he has described so graphically:

In Greenwich Park I found myself . . . in a clammy December mist that froze one to the bone, and left little visible except the ugly carcase of the Observatory. After groping around helplessly before even discovering the river-side of the monster, I suddenly came upon Parnell's figure emerging from the gloom in a guise so strange and with a face so ghastly that the effect could scarcely have been more startling if it was his ghost I had met wandering in the eternal shades. He wore a costume that could not well have looked more bizarre in a dreary London park if the object had been to attract, and not to escape observation. But the overpowering fascination lay in the unearthly, half-extinguished eyes flickering mournfully out of their deep caverns, the complexion of dead clay, the overgrown fair beard, and the locks rolling down behind almost to the shoulders. It was the apparition of a poet plunged in some divine anguish, or a mad scientist mourning over the fate of some forlorn invention.[30]

This meeting can be interpreted as an attempt to find common ground rather than Parnell trying to exert his authority. He accepted that the Plan of Campaign had to continue, but O'Brien agreed that it should be calmed down and confined to about ten estates. Whether or not the session had been an amicable one is not so easy to establish. Once again the evidence produces conflicting versions. According to Katharine O'Shea and, to a lesser extent, John Morley, relations had been strained, with Parnell denouncing the plan and O'Brien persisting in defending it. However, Parnell's comment to Mrs O'Shea, that he would 'let O'Brien run it by himself', does not sound so different from his policy over *United Ireland*.[31]

O'Brien's recollections imply that harmony had prevailed and that they had been on friendly terms. The fact that later that day they were able to engage in a long dinner together in the French room of the Criterion Restaurant supports O'Brien's view. They apparently talked for nearly four hours, and were able to avoid any mention of the plan. Reminiscent of their first meeting, Parnell shared some of his innermost thoughts with O'Brien, and they conversed with more intimacy and openness than O'Brien had ever encountered before with Parnell, who spoke in 'gentle and caressing tones'. They discussed a wide range of topics: the need for the friendship of a woman (O'Brien had not yet met Sophie Raffalovich), Parnell's early life and his family, religion, astronomy, Parnell's superstition – his fear of magpies, the colour green, the number thirteen (he had a horror of travelling in a railway compartment which had that number or any multiple of it). He even talked a little about his illness, but he made no complaints and did not go into any detail. The whole incident, as told by O'Brien, underlined Parnell's loneliness, which O'Brien had – for a brief time – been able to relieve. It also gives considerable insight into their close relations, which disagreements over the plan had not yet succeeded in undermining.[32] Moreover, O'Brien's commitment to Parnell's leadership had not been shaken by the encounter at Greenwich, for a fortnight later, on Christmas Eve, O'Brien wrote to Tim Healy that Parnell was 'the cornerstone of our Cause, and that the moment I would feel bound to renounce a frank allegiance to him would be my last in public life'.[33]

Parnell had had some influence over O'Brien. In a number of

his speeches in early 1887 O'Brien did stress that tenants should refrain from acts of outrage and violence; also, he was now only too aware of the awkwardness and delicacy of Parnell's relationship with the Liberals, and from now on he would often include in his words praise of Gladstone and his party, thus glorifying the 'Union of Hearts' with the Liberals. The Plan of Campaign was indeed limited to about ten estates; O'Brien kept that part of his promise to Parnell; but on the troubled estates he did not, in practice, 'calm down' the agitation and call off meetings.

For his part, O'Brien had failed to persuade his leader to become involved, and Parnell remained ominously silent for some time on the subject of the plan, thereby implying to the public his disapproval. Dillon and O'Brien had always believed that Parnell would step in to help them if things went badly. Such an occasion presented itself with O'Brien's imprisonment in Tullamore in late 1887, when it became clear that Balfour and the Conservative government were determined to suppress the plan. Their hopes were dashed, and both were bitter; O'Brien began to express his sense of personal betrayal. While he was in prison he managed to see a copy of an interview Parnell had given the *Freeman* in late November, in which he stated that he refused to approve the management of the plan. O'Brien's response was heartfelt. Parnell's words have '*deeply depressed* me. I cannot tell what I feel', he wrote to Harrington; 'I have almost made up my mind to resign *U.I.* Of all men I least deserved it.'[34]

However, in this interview Parnell had also refrained from criticizing the perpetrators of the plan. Such a stand was renounced the following May (1888) at the Eighty Club in London. Parnell's speech on this occasion was mainly directed at his Liberal audience, to reassure them that the Irish nationalist party's *main* preoccupations were still home rule and the 'Liberal alliance'. It was also an attempt to divert attention away from the very recent condemnation of the plan by the papacy – the papal rescript, he declared, was irrelevant. On the topic of the plan, Parnell's position was quite unequivocal. He did not support it: if he had not been ill when it started, and if O'Brien and Dillon had not already been under arrest when he learnt of it in early 1887, he would have endeavoured to have it stopped. Parnell's memory was playing a strange trick here, for he certainly knew of the plan in mid December 1886, the time of his interview with O'Brien at Greenwich, and this was *before* the government had attempted to secure the conviction of either O'Brien or Dillon.[35]

O'Brien's immediate reaction to the speech, which took the form of an article intended for publication in *United Ireland*, was revealing. At first his words expressed anger against Parnell for cutting away the 'moral strength' of their position. On the other hand, knowing that Parnell's disapproval stemmed mainly from fear of offending English public opinion, his anger was replaced by a gentle statement about the differences in their outlook. O'Brien had always had a lot of respect for Parnell's authority, and to this he seemed, in the final count, prepared to abandon the plan. Thus the article can be seen, not so much as a protest, but as an act of submission from a very discouraged O'Brien who decided that:

> We cannot endorse Mr Parnell's reasoning; we loyally and finally bow to his authoritative judgment. He is the only man living who has the right or power to wound the Plan of Campaign in a fatal spot. May the new policy which he foreshadows prove to be as strong an armour for oppressed Irishmen and as redoubtable a terror for their foe.

Dillon, however, was so disturbed by the tone of O'Brien's article – 'had it been published', he wrote to O'Brien, 'it would have utterly ruined our movement and driven me and others out of public life' – that he joined forces with Harrington to suppress it. O'Brien did not resist, and cabled to Dillon: 'Do as you desire.'[36]

The Eighty Club speech had put O'Brien's loyalty to a severe test, and his relationship with Parnell would never be quite the same; six weeks after this speech O'Brien was commenting to Dillon that 'relations between P. and myself are still strained to the point of frigidity and I see no good reason for altering them'. In retrospect, O'Brien admitted that this was the first and last time that he had really been angry with Parnell, and he had told him so in London. There is evidence, however, that they did struggle to preserve their friendship. In discussions with Parnell, O'Brien came under his spell once again, as the Irish leader responded with 'the charm and tolerance' which were always present in their private sessions. They had a frank exchange of views in these talks and seemed to come to an understanding, though not before Parnell had tried to entice O'Brien away from active agrarian agitation with the tempting offer of the editorship of the *Freeman's Journal*, a suggestion which O'Brien politely, but resolutely, rejected. O'Brien was hopeful, and by mid July he wrote to Dillon that 'late troubles have thrown the Chief and myself very intimately together again. He thinks he recognizes now his mistake in attempting to crush us', and on 4 August he was able to report: 'P. and I are on the old terms.' O'Brien's optimism was misplaced – a point which he refused to concede in his recollections, where he still claimed that he had won the day, but Dillon recorded in his diary for 5 November 1888 a conversation he had had with O'Brien:

> William came in at 8.00 and sat for two hours. We both agreed that if P. maintains attitude he has for the last year, we would not see how it would be possible for us to maintain the fight over another year. The situation is doubtless one of tremendous difficulty.[37]

Matters next came to a head between Parnell and O'Brien in the summer of 1889 over the Tipperary struggle. The involvement of Parnell and members of the parliamentary party became crucial with the stiffening of landlord resistance to the plan through the Smith-Barry-led landlord syndicate, Dillon's prolonged absence in Australia, a prison sentence looming for O'Brien, and, above all, the severe financial problems the plan was encountering. In their interview at Greenwich, Parnell had put his finger on this last factor as the weak spot in the plan. Parnell's lack of support was giving too much encouragement to the landlords, who believed the proponents of the plan had been 'abandoned' by their leader. Parnell and O'Brien were once again able to discuss the problems, and this time O'Brien did seem to gain the upper hand. He threatened to advise mass capitulation on the part of all the tenants involved in the plan throughout Ireland, and the responsibility for this, O'Brien warned, would fall on Parnell, who agreed that such a surrender would be 'fatal' to their cause.

Parnell was thus cajoled into giving some support to the Land War, not directly to the plan, but through a new organization: the Tenants Defence Association. The main object of this body was to raise money, and it was made clear that its appearance was 'the official Act of the whole Irish Party'.[38] However, O'Brien's victory was a limited one; Parnell argued that the association did not exist to aid the plan – a view shared by Davitt and Thomas Sexton. This was in direct conflict with O'Brien's argument that it had 'no *raison d'être* at all except to fight out our campaign battles. Its one business is to raise a Fund of £30,000'. Further discussions with Parnell ensued in an attempt to win him round to this interpretation, and, above all, to get him to declare publicly that he was fighting the tenants' cause, and to support a series of county conventions and parish collections to raise the money. O'Brien had no influence over Parnell on these occasions. On 14 August he sent Dillon a highly emotional letter in which he spoke frankly about his relationship with Parnell, and his words were full of reproach towards his leader:

Things have reached a crisis between Parnell and myself. Having started the new Tenants' Defence League, with the assurance that it would be used in support of the Plan, he now flatly refuses to take any effective steps to put life in it. He first allows us to announce that he will throw himself into the fight and now he says he cannot see his way to starting any new movement and will not do anything himself. I am aware this will not surprise you, but I confess that until last night I did not believe him capable of taking advantage of our difficulties to deliberately make the situation intolerable.

From this letter it appears that, in a meeting between Parnell and O'Brien the previous evening, Parnell had flatly refused to help. O'Brien was so hurt that he talked of resigning and applying for the Chiltern Hundreds; but Dillon's absence persuaded him to carry on.[39]

Parnell's hand was eventually forced when O'Brien put an alternative plan into action: to ensure that the prosecution for a speech he had given in June resulted in a substantial imprisonment:

We will thus force upon him [Parnell] the responsibility of getting himself out of the responsibility for the new League. I am confident the result will be that Parnell and the rest [of the party] will be coerced into activity and that the result will be a big Fund which cannot possibly be used for any purpose except the support of the Campaigners. In that way, I calculate the struggle can in no way suffer pending your [Dillon's] return and Parnell and Co. will be forced to bestir themselves and to recognize that we are not quite such helpless victims in their hands as they imagine.[40]

Thus O'Brien refused to give a guarantee to the court of good behaviour – and was awarded a four-, rather than a two-month, prison sentence. The plan apparently worked, and two letters O'Brien sent to Dillon from Galway jail had none of the despair of his previous communications:

The outlook upon the whole was never more satisfactory. My going to jail completely answered my expectations. It enraged the people with the inactivity of the Party and threw upon them the burden of moving. P. tried hard to shirk doing anything himself, but when he found it would be done without him he made a virtue of necessity and now whatever strength the Party has is pledged to us.[41]

Parnell had been compelled to proceed with the money-raising conventions and parish collections, but his support was, at best, lukewarm. He persisted in his refusal to be directly involved in the plan, which now concentrated on the struggle on Smith-Barry's estate, where the tenants had abandoned Tipperary town to found New Tipperary. Three actions on Parnell's part give clear evidence of his attitude. He declined to meet the deputation from the Tipperary tenants while they were in London. He did not attend the grand opening of New Tipperary in April 1890; this could be interpreted by the public as a personal slight to O'Brien, after whom the Butter Mart, the main focus of the town, had been named. Finally, he had asked Sexton to stand in for him at the inaugural meeting of the Tenants Defence Association at the Thurles Convention the previous October, thus underlining his aloofness even from the new organization.

Friction between Parnell and O'Brien arose once again in the autumn of 1890 as O'Brien and Dillon made their plans for their American tour to raise the urgently needed funds for tenants evicted during the plan. Parnell could not appreciate O'Brien's single-mindedness of purpose, which asserted that the lion's share of their resources in Ireland and America should go to the plan in the coming year. Parnell, quite naturally, argued for other worthy causes: parliamentary and other political expenses, as well as the support of tenants evicted during the Land League, for whom he felt a particular responsibility.[42]

Parnell had, none the less, publicly announced his personal concern for the tenants involved in the plan. In July, he had delivered a key speech on the plan in the House of Commons. He admitted that he may have been wrong to insist on limiting its operation, and he recalled the argument O'Brien had put to him at the Greenwich Observatory: that if the movement could be widespread throughout the country, it would be too strong for the government and the landlords to resist; but if too small, then some tenants would be sacrificed – as, indeed, appeared to be happening. At the same time, Parnell declared, he had feared a 'general agrarian struggle' as the greater evil. He now offered himself as the tenants' protector: they should not suffer; but the clear inference in his words was that all should seek agrarian peace, that the plan could be quietened, if, in return, the chief secretary, Arthur Balfour, could allow the plan tenants to take advantage of the 1887 Land Act. Parnell was, above all, motivated by a desire to bring practical help to tenants against whom the odds were heavily stacked.[43] Conciliation – as O'Brien was later to recognize – was the best course of action. This gesture to Balfour underlined that Parnell was not the Land War combatant he had once been.

However, with this speech and his offer of peace to the Tories, Parnell was in danger of undermining the 'Liberal alliance' he had worked so hard to protect, and which had dictated his attitude to the plan. The agrarian agitation – or rather government coercion and evictions – had, in fact, provided the Liberals with a stick with which to beat Balfour and the Tories. Contrary to Parnell's fears, the plan had, in the end, helped to cement the 'Union of Hearts'. It could also be argued that the plan, by keeping alive an active movement throughout Ireland, had helped to strengthen Parnell's hand at Westminster. But there is little indication that Parnell acknowledged that the plan had had these political effects.

In his speech to the House on the plan, Parnell also stated firmly that the long-term solution he really favoured was land purchase to create a peasant proprietorship. This, for him, had long been his answer – as indeed it was for most of the agrarian radicals, O'Brien included (with the notable exception of Davitt). However, where he differed from O'Brien was in his view that the transfer of ownership should be voluntary; compulsory land purchase was something to which O'Brien clung for many years. Parnell believed that Irish landlords should be induced to stay in Ireland – like Thomas Davis, he argued that the Irish nation was made up of all classes and creeds. This was a doctrine which O'Brien himself in the twentieth century, inspired by the Land Conference of 1902 and the ensuing Land Purchase Act, was to preach with an obsession that alarmed his former colleagues in the Land War. But Parnell would very probably have approved of O'Brien's 'conversion', and he would have endorsed O'Brien's enthusiasm for the idea of a bonus to woo landlords into selling their lands to their tenants.[44] Even in the plan years there were signs that O'Brien was not totally committed to waging war on landlords, and could share his leader's views. On the eve of one of his prosecutions, in September 1887, he delivered a lecture in Dublin on 'the lost opportunities of the Irish gentry', in which he suggested that a permanent settle-

ment of Ireland's problems must come from a friendly agreement
with the landlord class:

> If in the morning the Irish gentry proposed frankly to draw a
> wet sponge over the past, there is not a politician in Ireland who
> would answer with a churlish or contumelious word. They would
> be welcomed. They would be honoured. . . . Irish forgiveness is
> to be had to this hour for the honest asking.[45]

An even clearer sign was his first novel, *When We Were Boys*,
which he wrote while he was in prison for his part in the plan. One
of the main messages in this book was that it was possible to
reconcile differences between England and Ireland and between
landlords and their tenants.[46]

In the midst of the crisis over the leadership of the Irish party,
O'Brien sent Parnell a letter on 7 December 1890 which confirmed
his feelings towards him:

> I appeal to you as a leader I have for ten years been proud to
> follow and as a friend for whom I still feel a warm affection.
> Can you not see some way by which, while safeguarding your
> own reputation, the country may be saved from the ruin that
> threatens it.[47]

When he wrote those words, O'Brien must have been aware of the
fatal consequences a division in the party would have on the Plan
of Campaign. The split was a major factor in the total collapse of
the second phase of the Land War; but O'Brien never reproached
Parnell for this, nor in his later reminiscences did he rebuke him
for his lack of help with the plan. In his book, *The Parnell of Real
Life*, published in 1926 (only two years before his own death), the
chapter on 'Parnell of the Plan of Campaign days' was devoted
entirely to the meeting at Greenwich and their subsequent dinner.
No other reference was made to Parnell and the plan, and O'Brien's
admiration and affection for Parnell, and his mourning for his
passing, are evident throughout this book. He even suggested that
the problems Ireland had faced after the 1922 treaty would never
have arisen if Parnell had been listened to in 1890, and the country
had obtained self-government under his leadership rather than as
a result of 'the rude diplomacy of insurrection'. However, it must
be stressed that in the 1920s O'Brien was consumed with his own
bitter feelings about Partition, and above all about Dillon and the
Irish parliamentary party, whom he blamed for the events that
overtook Ireland after 1912. He drew a parallel between himself

and Parnell. Both had been sacrificed by the party, and on both occasions unprecedented opportunities had, in his opinion, been lost. In 1890 this had been caused by the anti-Parnellites' 'tenderness for English liberalism, approaching to a vice', while in 1903 (when O'Brien himself broke with the parliamentary party as a result of his defence of the Wyndham Land Act and his espousal of conciliation of landlords), the party had shown 'a wholly vicious incapacity to collaborate with English Toryism'.[48]

In the twentieth century, O'Brien was also extremely reluctant to be critical of Parnell over the O'Shea divorce suit; he now stated that if only Parnell had been allowed to go into the witness box during the hearing of the case, he would have been fully exonerated, and he 'would have been shown to be rather the victim than the destroyer of a happy house and the divorce would never have taken place'. He declared that Parnell had implied this to him at Boulogne, and he also recalled the assurance Parnell had given to him in a letter written in January 1890, when the divorce issue was first talked of, that he would come out with his honour unscathed.[49] O'Brien must have forgotten his own reaction to the news of Parnell's subsequent marriage to Katharine O'Shea; a letter he sent to his wife, Sophie, from Galway jail in July 1891 showed that he now had no illusions about the true nature of the Irish leader's relations with Mrs O'Shea:

> I was not surprised to hear how the marriage affected Mrs Douglas. Curiously enough, in that as in all other things, she is a reflection of the simple Irish mind. I find his marriage (followed by his astounding folly in talking of bringing Mrs O'Shea to Ireland as a sort of Goddess) has done him more harm with the country people than all that went before. The explanation is simple. P. had been so often traduced that, when he said there was another side to the case, the simple-minded believed really that he was innocent and that the whole thing was a fabrication of the *Times*, and now that he is married they are shocked to find that it is all true, and the revulsion of feeling is all the greater.[50]

However, the passage of time had distorted O'Brien's memory, and, in hindsight, he could only think well of Parnell.

Arthur Griffith once said that O'Brien knew more of Parnell and was more trusted by him than any other man, and O'Brien himself claimed that, unlike others, he had not found Parnell's personality elusive.[51] Theirs was a close relationship; they had worked well together in the days of the Land League, and even after their paths diverged with the Plan of Campaign, the friendship they had established was capable of surviving these tensions. However, their differences had been fundamental ones: over priorities – the land question or home rule – and over methods – constitutional or militant agrarian action. During the Land League, and even up to 1885, the land and national questions had converged and helped one another. Thereafter, the two themes, according to Parnell, had come into conflict. However, O'Brien's hurt tone on a number of occasions, their attempts to resolve their differences, and their contacts during the plan years do indicate the importance they attached to their relationship. After all, it was Parnell who had singled out O'Brien, and brought him to the forefront of Irish politics. In many ways he owed his career to Parnell, who in turn recognized O'Brien's qualities. It is doubtful that Parnell would have achieved all that he did achieve, especially in the early to mid 1880s, without O'Brien's help and support. Proof of their enduring friendship – despite the strains of the recent years – was provided by Parnell's presence at O'Brien's wedding in June 1890. His insistence on attending meant that O'Brien and Sophie had to abandon their plans for a small private affair. O'Brien later recalled how Parnell had been in very good spirits at their marriage: 'His refined face, so brilliantly handsome for all its pallor, his shy gentleness and words of affection, are remembrances never to be dimmed.'[52] Parnell's praise for O'Brien on this occasion, which Wilfrid Scawen Blunt has described as the best speech everyone had ever heard him make, came from the heart and clearly reveals the high regard he had for his former colleague in the Land War:

> Whether we take him as a distinguished Irish journalist or as a man of letters, whether we look on him as a wise and prudent statesman, as a brilliant, courageous and determined Irishman, we search our ranks, we search our country, we search the nations of the world for a man with whom we would rather go into battle or conclude an honourable and lasting peace.[53]

NOTES

1 The topic of William O'Brien and the Land War is fully explored in Sally Warwick-Haller, *William O'Brien and the Irish Land War*, Dublin, 1990. This article draws upon and develops some of the ideas and material about the relationship between O'Brien and Parnell that have

74   *Sally Warwick-Haller*

been mentioned in that book, see particularly ch. 2, 'The editor of *United Ireland*', and ch. 3, 'The Plan of Campaign'.

2 F. H. O'Donnell, *A History of the Irish Parliamentary Party*, London, 1910, vol. I, p. 457.

3 J. M. Wall to W. O'Brien, 20 June 1924 (W. O'Brien papers, University College Cork, AT 213–16).

4 W. O'Brien to Sophie O'Brien, three letters, n.d. (1891) (W. O'Brien papers, UCC, BA 94, 117, 152).

5 W. O'Brien, *The Parnell of Real Life*, London, 1926, p. 130.

6 W. O'Brien's diary, 15–17 November 1878, as cited in W. O'Brien, *Recollections*, London, 1905, p. 198.

7 C. S. Parnell to W. O'Brien, 22 July 1886, in *Cork Free Press*, 6 September 1913.

8 C. S. Parnell to W. O'Brien, 11 February 1891, cited in W. O'Brien, 'Was Mr Parnell badly treated?' *Contemporary Review*, LXX, November 1896, pp. 691–2.

9 O'Brien, *Recollections*, p. 233.

10 C. S. Parnell to T. W. Croke, 16 May 1881 (Croke papers, Cashel Diocesan Archives, National Library of Ireland microfilm, P. 6011, 1881/7).

11 O'Brien, *Recollections*, p. 233.

12 C. S. Parnell to W. O'Brien, 1, 5 July 1881, in *Cork Free Press*, 27 September 1913.

13 O'Brien, *Recollections*, pp. 72–3, 298–9 (précis of correspondence, 1, 9, 24, 28 February 1868; extracts from his diary, 3, 4 July 1881); *Cork Free Press*, 27 September 1913; P. Egan to W. O'Brien, 3 July 1881; J. O'Kelly to W. O'Brien, 2 July 1881 (W. O'Brien papers, UCC, Box AA).

14 J. Dillon to W. O'Brien, 12 July 1881 (W. O'Brien papers, UCC, Box AA).

15 C. S. Parnell to W. O'Brien, 12 July 1881 (T. P. Gill papers, NLI, MS 13478/1); W. O'Brien to J. Dillon, 18 July 1881, in *Cork Free Press*, 27 September 1913.

16 O'Brien, *Recollections*, p. 307.

17 Journal entries for 22 September, 11 October 1881, in T. W. Moody and R. Hawkins (eds), *Florence Arnold-Forster's Irish Journal*, Oxford, 1988, pp. 248, 268; O'Brien, *Recollections*, p. 318.

18 O'Brien, *Recollections*, p. 308.

19 *United Ireland*, 13, 20 August, 3, 10, 17, 24 September, 12, 19, 26 November, 3 December 1881.

20 O'Brien, *Recollections*, pp. 353–5, 365–6; A. J. Kettle, *Material for Victory*, Dublin, 1958, p. 56.

21 Quoted in P. Bew, *Land and the National Question in Ireland, 1858–82*, Dublin, 1978, p. 63.

22 *United Ireland*, 14 October 1882.

23 Ibid., 10 June, 30 September 1882.

24 Ibid., 14 June 1884.

25 See Warwick-Haller, *William O'Brien and the Irish Land War*, pp. 150–9.

26 C. S. Parnell to W. O'Brien, 13, 15 June 1882, in *Cork Free Press*, 27 September 1913.

27 J. Morley, *The Life of William Gladstone*, London, 1903, vol. III, p. 370.

28 W. O'Brien to T. Harrington, 25 November 1887 (Harrington papers, NLI, MS 8576/34).

29 W. O'Brien, *Evening Memories*, London, 1920, pp. 156–7; M. Davitt, *The Fall of Feudalism in Ireland*, London and New York, 1904, p. 518; R. Barry O'Brien, *The Life of Charles Stewart Parnell*, London, 1898, vol. II, pp. 170–2; T. M. Healy, *Letters and Leaders of my Day*, London, 1928, vol. I, p. 266; *Weekly Freeman*, 26 November 1887.

30 O'Brien, *Evening Memories*, p. 177.

31 Morley, *Life of Gladstone*, vol. III, p. 370; K. O'Shea, *Charles Stewart Parnell: his Love Story and Political Life*, London, 1914, vol. II, pp. 113–14.

32 O'Brien, *Evening Memories*, pp. 176–90; O'Brien, *Parnell of Real Life*, pp. 139–44, 181.

33 Healy, *Letters and Leaders of my Day*, vol. I, p. 267.

34 W. O'Brien to T. Harrington, 27 November 1887 (Harrington papers, NLI, MS 8576/34).

35 *Freeman's Journal*, 9 May 1888.

36 Text of article and Dillon's comment dated 9 May 1888; W. O'Brien to J. Dillon, 10 May 1888 (Dillon papers, Trinity College, Dublin).

37 W. O'Brien to J. Dillon, 29 June, 14 July, 4 August 1888; Dillon's journal, 5 November 1888 (Dillon papers, TCD); O'Brien, *Evening Memories*, pp. 351–4.

38 W. O'Brien to J. Dillon, 24 July 1889 (Dillon papers, TCD); T. Harrington to W. O'Brien, 10 July 1889 (T. P. Gill papers, NLI, MS 13500/6).

39 *Weekly Freeman*, 13, 20 July 1889; W. O'Brien to J. Dillon, 24 July, 14 August, 11 November 1889 (Dillon papers, TCD).

40 W. O'Brien to J. Dillon, 14 August 1889 (Dillon papers, TCD).

41 W. O'Brien to J. Dillon, 21 October, 11 November 1889 (Dillon papers, TCD).

42 C. S. Parnell to W. O'Brien, 3 October 1890 (T. P. Gill papers, NLI, MS 13506/2).

43 *Hansard*, 3rd series (Commons), vol. CCCXLVI, cols 1516–23, 11 July 1890.

44 See Warwick-Haller, *William O'Brien and the Irish Land War*, p. 149, and chs 6 and 7.

45 Lecture delivered on 8 September 1887, in W. O'Brien, *Irish Ideas*, London, 1893, pp. 13–29.

46 See Warwick-Haller, *William O'Brien and the Irish Land War*, pp. 124–8.

47 W. O'Brien to C. S. Parnell, 7 December 1890 (Dillon papers, TCD).

48 W. O'Brien, *The Parnell of Real Life*, pp. 93, 181; this book is largely a reproduction of material in the first two volumes of O'Brien's memoirs.

49 *Cork Free Press*, 6 September 1913; the text of Parnell's letter to O'Brien of 14 January 1890 is given in this newspaper article.

50 W. O'Brien to Sophie O'Brien, n.d. (late July) 1891 (W. O'Brien papers, UCC, BA 146).

51 O'Brien, *The Parnell of Real Life*, pp. 52, 203.

52 *Cork Free Press*, 6 September 1913.

53 W. S. Blunt, *The Land War in Ireland*, London, 1912, p. 448; *United Ireland*, 14 June 1890.

4 Parnell in the spectrum of nationalisms

Michael Hurst

In the country of the deaf the one-eared man is king. Provided, of course, he is ready and willing to bid for the crown. Overall, Irish circumstances in the 1870s required anyone seriously intending to be both elected for and sitting for an Irish parliamentary constituency in the United Kingdom House of Commons to be well economically healed. But for throne-sitting, be it for unionism of any brand, or for the renewed home rule cause, they ruled he must be distinctly well-born. To the beat and *cri* of the heart of the 'Irish Irish' people almost all the monied and/or upper-crust community of Ireland, Protestant and Catholic alike, was either deaf or unheeding. Some, like those restarting an autonomy movement in 1870 and intensifying it in 1873,[1] were certainly (for a whole series of frequently mixed motives) easier of hearing. Half-comprehension, nevertheless, rapidly becomes intolerable to the totally hopeful distressed, actual or *soi-disant*. Their attention turns all too immediately to those who fit their practical needs and satisfy the cravings of their psychological wavelengths.

From 1877 to 1880, when chronic agricultural depression gave a truly gigantic fillip to Irish Irish discontents, Biggar, middle class, commercial and hideous, proved every bit as resourceful in method and as insolent in mode, when attempting to wreck the workings of the legislature, or to inflame the Irish Irish electorate, as his gentry, agrarian and handsome partner in 'crime'. Yet in this scramble for the laurels of *enfant terrible* it soon became crystal clear that Parnell was destined for 'William' status and Biggar for that of 'Ginger' in what had become the home rule ginger group. For the Irish Irish it was doubtless a source of great encouragement to recruit a Belfast businessman to the 'Whitefoot' mood; and one of exaltation when he came to embrace Catholicism. Landing one who, like St Patrick himself, was a born gentleman was, however, something altogether more exhilarating. Even Isaac Butt, rejoicing at the advent of Parnell on the political scene, banked heavily on the effect of the 'historic name' and had the wit to perceive him as an 'ugly customer' for the 'Saxon'. And, snobbery apart, he saw at once what millions later came to see – that here was a biter to get the biters bit and revenge the bitten. What eluded him was the truth that, however moderate or slowly delivered home rule demands might be, the Irish Irish people as a whole liked extreme and millenarian ways of having them put and explained. Here was an overwhelmingly agrarian community with a history of soul-searing suffering fouled by three major post–1800 famines at the least, living under a land law the 1870 Act [2] had only begun to rectify. How was it to appreciate that its educational jugular vein had been savagely slashed by the Catholic hierarchy when it stymied the Queen's College scheme of 1845,[3] and thus prevented the emergence in Ireland among the Irish Irish of the counterpart of Scottish and Ulster graduates? Without them the confidence between 'managers' and 'men' so lamentably lacking in Irish Irish areas could never easily be built. An uncomprehending people facing ruin and aware of past disaster naturally needed and turned to the liveliest lad. Butt heard but patchily, and dug his own political grave by inviting in Parnell. The times were made for the younger man.

That Parnell was an Irish nationalist would and could not be disputed. It is none the less all too easy to dispute what he was a nationalist for, and by no means easy to arrive at a clear-cut conclusion. Though highly significant and successful in the prime of his own lifetime, he was in so many ways an anachronism in Irish life – a man of the past and of the future. Being neither an intellectual expositor by word of mouth, nor one given to writing books or diaries, Parnell left us no coherent ideological messages to mull over. Not for us 'The Thoughts of Chairman Charles'. What was on his mind, or what he wished his audiences to think was on his mind, at particular points in his political career stands out in the overwhelming proportion of his speeches. Correspondence is too scant for building a complete interpretation, and conversations so much a matter of dispute as often to be well-nigh valueless. Except, that is, for use in a great game of probabilities. Even so, some pronouncements are so consistent as to form the basis of a number of confident claims. Serious contenders for consideration in the Parnell Irish nationalist categorization competition are three-fold: first, it can be argued he was a traditional polity nationalist; second, that his views assumed that the Irish were not of two, and possibly three, ethnicities, as so often claimed, but one indivisible group, for the comprehensive happiness of which he sought political change; and third, that he was arguing on behalf of all those, be they British Irish or Irish Irish, who wanted national legislative institutions, without regard to any of whichever ethnicity did not.

So much nationalism in modern Europe has had to drive forward on current fuels reinforced by artificially created ones purporting to be from the past, and a virtually unbroken past at that. Very often the latter draw heavily on the extremely dim and distant, not to say murky, periods, the historical accounts of which (like Cardinal Newman's 'Life of Ninian') consist not only of all, but more than all that is known about them. Parnell had no time for any of that. Like Daniel O'Connell before him, he was nothing if not the man of action, basing his arguments on the times of Grattan's Parliament operating in the more liberal constitutional, civil rights and economic climates immediately prior to the passing of the Act of Union in 1800.[4] The combination of law and menace, represented by the predominantly Protestant Volunteers raised to relieve pressures upon the British forces and to intensify those upon the British Parliament to extend the powers of the Irish one, appealed most powerfully to a man over-endowed with ego, who took it as self-evident that he was born to lead wherever he went, and who regarded any manifestation of favour to Irishmen of the kinds he valued as an unmixed blessing. In other words, it was the mood of 1782 that appealed to him most; the disloyalty of the 'loyal', who could rally behind them the Irish Irish masses, mollified by the prospects of bigger and better laws in their favour. As a peripheral and debt-ridden gentleman he felt, like George Washington before him, the potent call of the politics of envy so effective for forging the passionate union, so urgently required in his view, for the benefit of the high, low and all intervening conditions of mankind in his land. For him 1782 stood for the 'all against England' line. Operate that and Ireland's internal problems could be overcome.

The craving for a Grattanite world ignored its technicalities and its human factors. Parnell appears to have disregarded certain political realities: London's influence over the Irish Parliament after 1782 was not markedly reduced; the Irish political majority was less pro-emancipation than the Westminster government; Irish agrarian society was not bonded together, and this, together with the failure of Catholic emancipation in 1795, led to the 1798 rebellion; and the rebellion, and the dangerous international situation, convinced Britain of the need for the absorption of Ireland into a United

Kingdom polity. Ulster factors, though he himself was partly of Ulster stock and half-American, never impinged meaningfully upon his mind either. And their influence in Irish discontents compounded all of the preceding items of friction – the first above all. Like so many 'frontier' politicians he shared a passion for having in public life elements of the lawful and the violent running in tandem. Think only of the great Scottish notables in the days of the Scottish parliament, deploying their clansmen 'volunteers' up the road to encourage their national assembly to take the 'right' decisions. Did not Lord Charlemont and the Earl of Argyll have that feature of matters public in common? As with them, so with Parnell – the hope was a peaceful solution.

After one bout in Kilmainham, Parnell swore never to return. Violent politics are not limited liability companies. The playboy shies at their consequences. For Parnell, therefore, the game is 1782 not 1798. When in 1886–90 an actual home rule scheme had to be actively worked on, his knowledge of the Grattan period improved somewhat. Never to mastery of the subject, but to levels leading to meaningful discussion and sensible pronouncements. Had home rule actually passed the House of Commons in 1886, mastery could well have followed. When land legislation, however complicated, was definitely going through, no one excelled Parnell in knowledge or comprehension of it. It was then real enough to get him off his backside. As one who read virtually as little as he could get away with and wrote even less, he was moved by extreme urgency alone. Capable though he was of gargantuan effort, nature had made him in mind (and possibly in body) one of those very able and indolent men a *Wehrmacht* chief-of-staff pronounced as the only ones truly fit for supreme command – their nerves being of the strongest.

Here then was an Irish nationalism which blithely assumed a past polity status should be restored to what was the discrete kingdom of Ireland, although subsumed within the archipelago overall state. What had had a parliament should have it once again. So the unit was taken for granted. For Parnell the truth was so self-evident that it never occurred to him to suppose that problems associated with profoundly changed attitudes to a separate legislature, whatever its precise nature, might preclude any restoration in ways largely inoperative in 1800 and therefore not actively militating then for abolition. He ignored the significance of the fact that, whereas the Anglo-Irish had run Grattan's parliament and its predecessors, and dominated Irish representation at Westminster almost totally until O'Connell's celebrated capture of County Clare in 1828 and the changes wrought by the 1832 Reform Act, they had not had anything like their own way for nearly fifty years before Parnell's election to the leadership of the more zealous home rule party in 1880. Nor did he take much account of the huge shift to Conservative and Liberal unionism among the overwhelming proportion of those Anglo-Irish – nor their extra power afforded them by the legislative linkage to the British British nationalists. Added political clout at the disposal of the northern British Irish masses, developed alongside and to some degree in response to enormous rises in the influence (*de facto* and *de jure*) of their Irish Irish contemporaries, likewise left him largely unimpressed. Just why derived from his special notions of himself as a person, himself as a gentleman and himself as a leader of Ireland. So, though he most certainly was an old-fashioned polity nationalist, he did look to Irishmen as if they were of one indivisible group. And he regarded those not behind him as traitors, whatever labels they attached to themselves. Whether milder home rulers or unionists, all were thoroughly Irish to his mind. Apart from the complex composite class of which a suburbanite squireen like Captain O'Shea and his wife were highly interesting examples (one Catholic, the other Protestant), a goodly number of Anglo-Irish Whigs nurtured and treasured the view that truly the Irish were one and undivided. Be they all-out assimilating unionists (and after all, they, the Whigs, far, far more than Tories and Conservatives, played the role of arch-British Isles homogenizers), or uneasy unionists, or hankerers after pre–1800, all craved and quested reconciliation in their land. The wish for it was father to the thought that, because a series of tenuous connections linked one grouping to its neighbours in opinion on either side of it, the whole set might be regarded as desirous and capable of operating as a coherent whole. Home rule movements were, evidently, proofs to the contrary.

Yet even here, political alliances and the blurred edges between both Liberalism and moderate home rule, and moderate Home Rule and its extremer Parnellite manifestation, offered them loaves of comfort. Most of all, Parnell's Anglo-Irish and Protestant identities proved to him that, if he (with his impressive Irish patriotic pedigree of modernizing Whiggery behind him)[6] could command the Catholic masses in the role of virtual dictator, invested by a huge proportion of the peasantry with 'uncrowned king' features, then for all intents and purposes oneness was alive and kicking hard. Without doubt, duality in Irish identity has been overplayed, with the composite groups largely ignored as to both numbers and influence, and the willingness and ability in many to overlook the deep religious divide and the ethnic 'realities' it brought in its wake. Nevertheless, much of Parnell's assurance rested on and within himself.

As a person, he was boundlessly imperious and accepted all deference, even near-worship, as another portion of the self-evident truth surrounding himself and his causes. The greater the scope of his authority, the greater that of his would-be exploitation of it. The more the opposition that might gather against him, the more arrogant and unprincipled he became. The first was brilliantly illustrated by his ventures in political strife in Parliament and over in Ireland, as the agrarian crisis grew and the Land League spread like wildfire through the Irish Irish countryside. The period 1877 to 1882 saw him as boldly irresponsible as the full concatenation of circumstances allowed. The first and second could not have been more dramatically and devastatingly highlighted than by the successful imposition of Captain O'Shea (husband of his mistress and most assuredly never a true Parnellite Irish nationalist) upon the parliamentary borough of Galway City as the Parnellite candidate – and hence, in the circumstances of the day, its MP. Anything that could be got away with would do.

Gentry status did more than set him on his parliamentary way. In the Ireland of 1874 to 1891 the very rarity among the more extreme home rulers of gentry prepared to be 'pals' as well as 'friends of the people' was in itself of immense help in propelling him first to the position of chief agitator 'indoors' and 'out of doors', and then to the chairmanship of the more extreme nationalist faction which then absorbed the less moderate of the depleted moderates in very short order. Doubly a 'frontiersman' from his Anglo-Irish and American sides, he lived in the cul-de-sac of the self, draped for public purposes with the flags of Ireland. Though of the Whig tradition he was the reverse of Whiggish in individual philosophy or modes of conduct. Unless in some strait-jacket he was not unlikely to give friends, let alone enemies, hard metaphorical kicks. In so many respects he was a gentleman only in name. On the European continent, unlike the general practice in the British Isles, the word 'gentleman' was and is used very often in a purely pejorative sense. Paris, Boulogne and Madrid assuredly had less difficulty with the word than Dublin and London. Yet whatever the personal failings of Parnell on this front, he never spared himself once in battle, however deep the mire and however overwhelming the odds against him might be. This, though, involved matters of challenge; when thwarted he moved into his most reckless and dangerous moods.

Denied all but a smattering of upper-class support, Parnell had as his principal lieutenants men whose education was based on journalism, the practical world of the law courts and life in the round. Spliced with intelligent gentlemen like the Redmond brothers and a few medical graduates, they constituted a formidable 'front bench'. But all the fair-minded were obliged to admit that none of them was a Parnell – a 'Chief'. Gentlemen among nationalists had long contended for influence in Irish Irish politics – O'Connell among them. But he was from that rare commodity, the Celtic gentry, so probably never really should have counted. Parnell was older than his assistants (and as he ruefully made clear, had helped Timothy Healy to great purpose in his career); he was usually vastly bolder too. Though hating discipline, he employed it as a form of animal cunning in battling for mastery in all levels of struggle. He was a man of *kampf* particularly his own. Something remarked as royal rather than Führer-like. Not only did he act (once in leadership and on the move) as though invested with power foreign to the world of a political party questing after a fairer form of liberal constitutionalism in Ireland, but as a royal populist. Parnell's Protestantism was not imbued with the sense of proportion so strong in Anglicanism. His individualism was rife with American-style egalitarianism of the sort decreeing that, not only is nobody better than you, but you are manifestly (by destiny) better than they.

Davitt, alone of the prominent Irish Irish nationalists, had moral power coming within quality and quantity range of Parnell's demonic variety – where The Chief seemed so often to say: 'Good, be my evil.' What chance, though, does a full giant stand, when he lumbers himself up with a socialist ideology crowned by land nationalization in a land where the impact of English property notions have bitten so very deep. Landlords' property was an affront to the moral law of Irish Irish Ireland. For tenants to have it, and to do so in freehold, was the way of the saints. Socialist collectives stank of the latifundia when men (off as well as on the 'hillside') wanted a place of their own. In that way and that alone was the Irish Irish psyche to be brought to agrarian content. Real understanding of past clan life was virtually dead. Rent was only an abomination when paid to the landlord class. It was all, after all, a matter of scale. Everybody would then be a somebody and remain one for life. Heirs would then usually repeat the same somebodyship from generation to generation. Such was the vision. During the last dreadful phase of his life a cornered Parnell appeared to veer in a Davittian direction without Davitt. That, however, smacked of a Jacobinical variant of dirigisme led from on high, not the grass-roots rural and urban proletarian credo so dear to Davitt himself. The militancy, not the apparent socialism, was the key to the Parnell bid to combine extreme-tending trade unionists with the bitterness of the Irish west and the remnants of the 'hillside men'. Then, too, it was a losing and, subsequently, a lost cause. Davitt in addition never enjoyed the blessing of the Irish Irish Catholic hierarchy. It, too, would not condone grass-roots leadership as desired by the truly radical radicals. Parnell's similar lack once the divorce scandal broke in November 1890 was always seen as a potent source of his undoing.

Justin McCarthy and T. P. O'Connor, in contrast to their fellow 'front benchers', had a most marked duality about their political identity. There was a lot of the 'transplant' about both. The former, especially, presented a species of near diplomatic devotion to the ways of the Irish nationalist party – Liberal alliance; in so much, that is, as his inaccuracy of mind permitted. Dillon, O'Brien and Healy had real power of sorts in Ireland. But like the influence of Joseph Chamberlain in Britain *vis-à-vis* Gladstone, the position of each in relation to Parnell was at Ireland level never better than that of 'good littlun' dealing with a 'good bigun'. The outstanding gentleman, therefore, had his automatically strong position further buttressed by the Irish social scenes and their effects upon the character of the meritocratic and aspiring leaderlets of the Parnell Irish nationalist party in the 1880s. During the split this lesson was driven yet further forward. In the Parnellite coteries 'The Chief's' standing became more heightened still. Ironically, the presence there of almost all those of gentry origin of the formerly united party, and of potentially restless 'Fenian'-style groups, did not tend to intensify any of the to-be-expected trends of independent thought and action. The sustained crisis simply ruled out any such thing. Among the anti-Parnell factions unity proved a tender plant. No one was either able or allowed to be bigger than a battle cruiser. Fleet flag battleship was there none.[7]

For most of his political leadership Parnell was head and shoulders above any potential challengers – a fact making for yet more idiosyncrasy in the Irish nationalist party as a British Isles political formation. Pursuit of the ideal of an 'Irish independent party'[8] necessitated tight discipline in Parliament and at the grass or bog roots anyway, and any departure from it provoked a distinct intensification. Entry of the 'uncrowned king' effect from the numerous lower peasants accelerated and deepened this distortion, all the more when actually aided and abetted by the less critical of the better-off, of the party elites. Persuaded that he could run the party as his personal fief and get away with failing to develop the Irish National League of 1882 along the promised democratic lines, Parnell found himself able to shelter behind what was largely a lack of the very organizational activity so often thought by the less discerning to be the 'secret' of Parnell victories in influence, not only in Ireland, but in the Home Rule Confederation of Great Britain, of which he had become president as early as 1877.

Parnell extended his polity view to cover the very convenient opinion that everyone was Irish. This being so, as his party in 1885 won possession of 85 of the kingdom's total of 103 seats in a new and mainly single-member constituency system, Parnell found it easy enough to conclude and to insist that only the majority of Irish people mattered. That was liberal democracy for you and the total application to Ireland of the Third Reform Act was proof that the government of the United Kingdom considered it a place where notions of majority right should be gaily applied. It was also a species of populism veering well into the illiberal were it to be examined under the intellectual miscroscopes of those fully aware of the great gulf in Ireland between the Unionist and home rule parties. Polity tradition made for insistence upon the right as well as the need for Ireland's legislative autonomy. Facile use of majority notions made it less necessary actually to prove contentions about the oneness of Irishness 'in the final analysis', deeply felt though these were in Irish Irish nationalist circles at all social levels and in all four provinces.

During the periods of upset at the outset and end of his 'Chieftainship', the Irish home rule movement was a movement indeed. Behaviour on the ground was volatile in the extreme. Boycotting, injuries to man and beast and belief in some degree of political violence were endemic. Irish Irish nationalism could not be said to belong to what had long been the British norms in politics. Grassroots Unionism also had its 'dark' Orange side, albeit undeployed for most of each year. The Irish nationalist party in the 1880–2 stretch became the agrarian orientated 'Labour' party which Parnell recreated in the split phase. Between 1882 and the Parnell split it was adjusted to accommodate a short-lived and expedient alliance with Gladstone's second ministry, a promising, if in the end unsuccessful, rapprochement with the Conservatives in 1885, and an alliance with the Gladstonian opposition between 1886 and 1890. So though 'The Chief' was from a normal source in British Isles politics, his party was a precursor, one in which the control of an abnormally backward and unusually unaffluent Irish Irish majority rested with a handful of vital lay lives and with the hierarchy and clergy of a Catholic church out of kilter with the general majority Protestant trends in the whole archipelago. Radical politics and economics, coupled with reactionary social and philosophical ideas, were both very 'non-Westminster' and phenomena under active manufacture in numerous European continental lands. Charles James Fox and Parnell were bridge figures: men of a temporary phase which would not necessarily be succeeded by straightforward constitutionalism ameliorated by economic and social advance. Naturally enough, the Parnell-O'Shea divorce has usually been seen in its narrow context. Nevertheless, it should be thought of in the light of aborting 'Chieftain'-style leadership among the Irish Irish. While strongly rekindled by the paramilitary and military phases of Irish life in the period from 1912 on into the mid 1930s, such leadership had cut a pretty poor figure during the previous two and a bit decades and encountered a most efficacious enmity from one who could so easily have been tempted into its orbit – de Valera himself. 'Blue Shirt' phenomena among the main opposition party forced him to face up to what might happen were he not to curb harrassment by the IRA of the Irish Irish right in what was then the Irish free state.[9]

Maybe the very nature of the 'fall' of Parnell ensured the return of 'Chieftain' phenomena. The upholding of the home rule cause and prospects through adherence to the Liberal alliance made sense, but not romance. It left so much of the collective Irish Irish ego aching with frustration and injured pride. Revived Gaelic culture quickened its drive to fill intensified needs. The cul-de-sac mentality simply refused to die and its gradual recovery threw up those who wished Irish Irish nationalism to live feverishly and to bid for a British Isles 'dual monarchy'.[10] In the background, craving for 'autarchy' began to flourish. Simultaneously, a *de facto* alliance attitude taken up by so much of United Kingdom Unionism in the 1890s and early 1900s diffused the intensity of, or distinctly redirected the interests of, very many nationalist activists back into the quest for development. Home rule in the senses attached to the phrase as a term of art there certainly would not be. Of anything short of that there was a great deal. Plunkett in agricultural science and Wyndham in land purchase together placed a huge question mark over the Irish Irish future. The fact was that in 1905, whatever the status of the lions of Gaelic revival and the disappointment at Balfour's inability to produce a more modest than home rule autonomy out of the Unionist camp, fever-pitch levels of politics in Ireland were in pleasantly short supply.[11]

While the precise troika-like character of Parnell's brand of Irish Irish nationalism and the intricate interconnections between the three strands can then be explained, it is precisely this phrase 'fever pitch' and what is associated with it which takes us to what must necessarily be the next stage of the discussion – the question of just how much intensity went into his Irish nationalism and exactly how the temperature of events arose. So much in politics depends, after all, on more than a specified credo. Even given that no essential rubric of it suffers abandonment or sizeable modification, any change in the extent and heat of party feeling up or down the intensity of feeling and drive scales is well nigh certain to affect the speed at which a policy could be attempted and the chances of its success. In politics intensity is usually thought of as exclusively the handmaiden of extremism. The vehemence of moderation to be found in countless liberal causes (the Broad Church party of Anglicans not least among them) nevertheless proves the contrary. Determined pursuit of restraint can so often know little restraint. Hence at times the Parnell record during periods of the highest constitutional propriety recalls the Hungarian Politburo member who, in the onset of liberalization, solemnly told a British audience of how those dilly-dallying in the cause of enlightenment were being ordered 'forward', and those over-eager in it were being ordered 'back'. Freedom was subject to heavy 'Chieftain' planning – all full of intensity.

The position of Ireland in the United Kingdom was one all its own. And the degree of 'ownness' had increased mightily as the nineteenth century progressed. The essential oneness of the countries of Britain in matters political, religious, economic, social and cultural so far advanced by 1880 had been distinctly less marked when the Union with Ireland began. Widened voting rights, evangelical work-ethic inspired behaviour, industrial high development, individual social mobility, and the progressive mentality – all were then if not in their infancy then just past the stage of adolescence. But every category was very much on the move – if only because of an ever-growing wealth. So was the modernization of agriculture. Demographic increase likewise. Ireland in 1800 boasted some political reformism, an increasing strictness in Protestant religion, a few lately successful industries, heavy emigration, and sectors of the progressive mentality. Agricultural modernization, however, was a matter of certain areas only, but demographic burgeoning was an endemic outbreak. In contrast with the overwhelmingly 'onward and upward' surges in Britain, Ireland presented a picture of daunting melancholy and stark discouragement. While the facts were undoubtedly often harsh in themselves, they were steeply worsened by the geographical curse imposed upon Ireland by placing her cheek by jowl with Britain, compounded time and time again by the apparently malicious twists and turns of history. Politics were deeply flawed by tendencies towards localized violence, rampant in the hugely predominant agrarian sector of the centre, south and west, being taken willy-nilly into those urban industrial developments in and around them. Politics were deeply flawed by the vast religious gulf between the Protestant voters and their Catholic colleagues in these same areas – things severely aggravated by the gradual democratization moves in the voting system of the United Kingdom. Religion was similarly sullied in turn by politics and the aggravating factors deriving from the frictions inherent in the severe contrasts between Protestant-minority wealth and Catholic-majority poverty. It was, moreover, to become more troublesome because more efficient. By the 1840s evangelical supremacy in the Anglican church of Ireland and the other Protestant sects meant added theological and conversionist aggression. To this the Catholics responded and eagerly counterattacked, literally expressing their zeal in the physical form of a whole plethora of new and imposing ecclesiastical buildings.

Conditions such as these held good and more in 1880. No modern-style notions of work ethic spread among Catholics in the Irish Irish heartlands, however. Older notions of the equal value to God of all human beings and of the right they had to the things of the earth held sway. Industry meant little to the Irish Irish masses at home in 1800 or 1880. Its competitive needs remained beyond the mental horizons of Irish Irish workers convinced that each should have according to his demand, and that demand should equal the better kinds of British wages. Widespread mental and moral indolence on the part of the aristocracy and gentry, or cowardice in the face of ignorant peasant opposition, went far towards ensuring that scant meaningful improvement occurred in most heartland agriculture until the 1870 and 1881 Land Acts.[12] Individual social mobility for the Irish Irish had necessarily to be (if useful) emigration abroad, to the few promising centres in Irish Ireland, to Protestant-dominated industrial or more efficient agricultural districts, or to Britain itself. Any 'progressive' mentality they may have had was due to their social grievances. Modernization of Irish Irish agriculture never came in Parnell's lifetime. Nor was it helped on by the free trade system which step by step took over in the United Kingdom from the 1820s to the 1860s. Much of Irish Irish Ireland bought as well as sold food.

The buoyancy of 1800 in Ireland had eight decades later become more regionally constricted. Irish Irish Ireland had dropped back, whereas in east and north Ulster things had forged ahead. The 'advanced' part of England, so much associated with the Parliamentary party in the English Civil War, had followed up its mastery of British achievement by building on the positive industrial, commercial and agricultural trends visible in pre-1800 northern Ireland. Although the Belfast cotton industry had declined, the linen industry emerged successfully into the modern age. And while shipbuilding in Irish Irish Ireland slumped, that in British Ireland went on from strength to strength – reaching its zenith in the years following Parnell's death. In 1880, therefore, Belfast was already powerfully integrated into a tri-complex industrial giantry based on Clydeside, Merseyside and the Lagan Valley, with industrial Cumberland and, through it, the English north-east, plus Barrow-in-Furness and its various roots, thrown in for good measure.[13] The Irish Irish populations in east and north Ulster were fed by both immigration and better conditions. Yet, as in the full heartland, they were even more heavily affected by a British Irish community. This time, though, it was not a mere upper-crust needful of police and soldiery from time to time for the bolstering of its position, but an integrated mass which, while not free of severe internal tensions (as between Anglican landlords and many Presbyterian tenants, or between industrialists and workers), could be relied upon to raise a virtual wall of *völkisch* unanimity in the face of Irish Irish Ireland. Put in position by James I[14] for precisely that function, this community only appeared moderate because few enquirers went into its midst – and because circumstances were such as to call upon them for very little while the House of Lords could veto non-financial legislation indefinitely, and before the Liberal party adopted a home rule stance in 1886. Parnell's psychology worked on a west-east political axis. When what he termed 'the march of a nation' in a discrete territory, being part of a multi-ethnic polity, moved in directions called for by majority opinion sponsored and mobilized by him in an age increasingly liberal democratic in Britain and populist in Irish Irish Ireland, British northern Ireland could not count in his book. Neither Ulster nor any part of it had ever been more than partially differentiated from the rest of Ireland. Tradition and modern majority facts both challenged the idea that a literal province, still less a portion of one, could block, call in question, disperse or otherwise hamper the Irish Irish national 'march'. Holism in the creed of the Irish nationalist party had therefore a logic which many in Britain found respectable – especially in a conflict said to involve autonomy, not sovereignty issues.

In 1874 the Irish Irish were the sole ethnic group in the United Kingdom the majority of which – indeed, any substantial proportion of which – was interested in working for home rule in the generally understood sense of political autonomy. The same was true in 1891. Parnell, leading odd man out among the Protestant Irish, led the odd man out community *par excellence* of the United Kingdom for more than ten years of the intervening time. Singularity in the religious sphere underwent no attenuation either. Had the Catholic hierarchy backed the Queen's Colleges scheme and allowed the emergence of what by Parnell's entry into politics would have been a sizeable and highly significant tertiary educated Catholic public, professional and business lay leadership, the position could not but have been different. Without a main and unfaltering stream of well-educated Catholics, lay successfuls tended to public (as opposed to private) impotence – even to being regarded as renegades, virtually British Irish. Moreover, such an absence aborted the best consequences that have flowed from legislative reforms like the disestablishment of the Church of Ireland in 1869, the two Gladstone Land Acts and the Land Purchase Acts themselves.[15]

The very sense of the static or of going backward in the absence of striking moves forward undoubtedly constituted a vital part of the Irish Irish nationalist psychology – one deeply alarmed, too, by the apparently endless bouts of emigration and a gradual lowering of the Irish Irish population percentage in the total island figure. Political moderation the Catholic hierarchy almost unfailingly advocated and sincerely practised, yet its hysterical desire to keep its flock from lay influence, be it from the dread Anglo-Saxon hordes or independent-tending Catholic graduates, was in many ways the creator of discontent. After crucial reforms were through, free trade, lack of scientific agricultural skills, but, most of all, the Catholic hierarchy, were mainly responsible for failures denying the tenant farmers and new small owners the highest personal satisfactions. Not so much the landlords, however much old tensions resurfaced during major distress phases like those of 1879 to 1882 and 1887 to 1888. Not so much the viceregal administrations. Though the purposes they served on the grass-roots levels and the relations between them all and the paramilitary police naturally highlighted the 'system' as an affront. Yet much of the British Irish and immigrant British presence in Irish Irish counties was there *faute d'autre*. Fine Gaelic sports were doubtless healthy in themselves.[16] They did not, however, enable farmers' sons to rise to being anything else. Had an adequate form of tertiary education been available the farming community would have been able to enjoy the fact of some of their male young having joined the ranks of the graduate professionals, of having prevented the British Irish and other British from inevitably hogging key jobs in county administration, and of having taken the self-esteem of the Irish Irish people several stages forward. Every farming family could not but have benefited.

Strong differences, too, pervaded the structure of the Irish Irish economy. Only there did agriculture predominate. Not in England and Wales; not in a Scotland where by 1880 a mere fraction of the population lived beyond the 'Highland line', as compared with 50 per cent in 1800;[17] and not in east and north Ulster either. The sovereignty of the United Kingdom Parliament was total and the English predominance in it ensured that no 'agricultural party' of the sort so powerful in France and Germany, and now so stridently influential within the EEC, was ever able to rise, take grip of and slow down the development of large-scale industry and its control of political influence. Disraeli had fondly hoped this might be, and that he and O'Connell might do a deal. Ethnic differences and acute Tory/Conservative-Whig/Liberal/Repealer civil rights and constitutional quarrels ruled it out. But Ireland was the prime loser as the prime agrarian unit in the polity and the one with by far the fewest resources for coping with the downfall of Lord Liverpool's ministry's protection of United Kingdom agriculture and the *coups de grâce* of 1846 and on. All those in Ireland who were not connected with the Britanno-Ulster commercial and industrial nexus were losers: the Parnells fundamentally every bit as much as their tenants. Representation patterns aggravated the socio-economic realities on each side of the Irish Sea and made mutual comprehension that much more difficult. The Act of Union gave 100 seats to Ireland in the United Kingdom House of Commons. To achieve this each of the 32 Irish counties retained its 2 members, giving counties almost two-thirds of the kingdom's quota. Of the 236 borough members in the Dublin Parliament only 36 were taken over into that of London. The 1793 County Franchise Act (retained in 1800) meant the county seats acquired the most generous regulations for concocting electorates – electorates highly attracted to Repeal once O'Connell broke the County Clare 'barrier' in 1828. Nor did the restrictive concomitants to Catholic emancipation in 1829 and the still strict ones of 1832, aimed at undoing these effects, come near to bringing that off, but zest for Repeal dropped mightily before the Great Famine and was but partially resuscitated by it. Acts of 1850 and 1868 again increased the county electorates, yet not until 1884, when single member county constituencies rose to 85 in Ireland and borough seats sank to 16,[18] did the near democratic franchise reach the point where the agrarian impact reached its Union period peak.

In Britain pre-Reform conditions meant exactly half the Welsh and exactly one-third of the Scottish representation belonged to boroughs. How different, though, in England, where a mere 80 out of 469 seats had been allotted to counties. City and town were vastly overrepresented before the industrial revolution and remained so during its first and middle stages. Ironically, English domination of the United Kingdom House of Commons took the form of what turned out to be a distortion of the most felicitous variety. It gave an upper-, upper-middle- and middle-middle-class population an automatic institutional means of maximizing the advantages facilitating national economic change. It made the assault upon agricultural as well as industrial protection highly feasible in 1846 and made possible the virtual switch to free trade in the next two to three decades a piece of political cake. County seats rose to nearly two-thirds of Welsh representation by 1885, but lost ground in Scotland, amounting to no more than slightly over half its seats by then. When county seats were increased to 144 out of 471 in 1832 and to 172 out of 465 in 1867, in England industrialization had already taken a striking series of turns. In 1885 a county increase of 234 out of 465 arrived when the pattern of what was to remain industrialized England until the First World War had been fully made. Moreover, such were the huge net demographic increases in cities and towns throughout Britain that many county seats were essentially urban in terms of population percentages. Seat categorization shifts in favour of counties in England and Wales brought scant comfort to an agriculture badly beleaguered after 1877. The slippage in Scotland for the counties by 1885 appeared to bring no substantive disadvantages in its train. But in Ireland, outside north and east Ulster and the leading centres of the south and west, towns were something of a wasting asset – like whole tracts of countryside.

The island's startling overrepresentation was in itself a political advantage of top importance to the Irish Irish in their Parnellite phase. So, too, was the fact that the north and east of Ulster were underrepresented – above all, Belfast and its thriving surrounds. Odd-man-outship had obtruded yet again. Given the highly disciplined nature of the Irish nationalist party, the fact that it could win 85 seats in Ireland made it a particularly formidable bargaining force.[19] However threadbare many of the least prosperous county seats actually were, they had exactly the same value in the House of Commons as the ones from the best of all Britain's, and Ulster's, 'gardens'. And whatever Parnell's parliamentary strength – that of its greatest extent in 1886, the lesser following of the second Gladstone ministry, or the handful of pre–1880 – its power and influence were substantially helped by the categorization of United Kingdom legislation. Like England with Wales and Scotland, Ireland enjoyed its very own set of laws. Theoretically, all members of both Houses of Parliament determined the nature of all laws. But in practice, although governments took care to safeguard their majorities at all times, members from particular areas took the leading roles when their especial affairs were under consideration. Imagine, then, the impact of Parnell-style politics inside this procedure for Irish Bills. Add to the picture the strong desires of the Conservative and Liberal parties to attain or retain office and to acquire or consolidate support in the country, and the great potential for nuisance power in the hands of zealous home rulers stands out a mile.

Technical advantages over-used do none the less bring on misfortune. Former opponents can create cabals to down what has become hateful to them all; parties can split as the Liberals did in 1886 and a partial joining of one side with a whole party of erstwhile enemies springs forth. Intensification of feeling and action on the part of the Irish nationalist party in Ireland and in British areas of Irish Irish settlement will almost certainly be answered and more by the British Irish and deeply inflamed British millions. Parnell's career is a convincing illustration of just how constricted his general capacity for political manoeuvre actually was even at the best of times. The gigantic character of United Kingdom might lie all about him and about Ireland and about huge sectors of the world. Whatever comfort he might get from the Irish Irish Americans, material and otherwise, the influence of a mellowed American attitude towards things British, and the substantial pull of the Scots Irish, ruled out any possibility of the Irish nationalist party acquiring anything beyond the means for financing politics and in certain cases for pursuing limited revolutionary or semi-revolutionary ends. And to whatever extent the ire of the Irish Irish rose, the real possibility of Fenian sentiment being able to bring about mutiny and revolution in Irish United Kingdom army regiments simply did not exist, however much Fenian songs might be heard during duty marches on the North-West Frontier of India. Nor was the Royal Irish Constabulary to be suborned, let alone British forces of any kind, no matter what the proportion of radicals in their ranks.

So when in his first fine and often careless political raptures upon entering active politics in 1874, upon becoming an MP in 1875, during the run up to the 'New Departure' and the Land League in 1879, for his ambitious American tour and for the rest of his pre-prison period, Parnell could only go a certain way before heaving in sight of that great surrogate of the Himalayas – the law and order of British authority. The man who emerged from Kilmainham jail had learned a lot. The person who had sounded off in Cincinnati, Ohio, on 20 February 1880,[20] in a way many have taken to mean he wished Ireland to destroy all links with Britain, knew full well by May 1882 that though London had not put links round him it had certainly and easily put him behind bars – and a Liberal-Whig London at that. Real politics was not facing schoolmasters, the dons of Magdalene College, Cambridge and irate, outraged cricketers in County Wicklow. Brutal and primitive terrorism in Phoenix Park a seeming moment after his release matured him further at the speed of light. A youngish civilian had learned in a moderately hard way just what Gladstone and company wished to teach him: that Liberals were prepared to be reasonable and friendly, provided he, Parnell, played liberal constitutional ball. Home rule might ultimately be achieved. Lord Salisbury's willingness to drop coercion added distinct hopes of right-wing flexibility to thinking about matters Irish. Parnell smelled breakthrough. For the time being the Liberals could and would offer no more. Yet already Parnell was actually being handed good fortune on a plate because of Gladstone's decision to extend the Irish electorate on lines more or less identical to those planned for Britain. The Conservatives were merely playing 'futures' and outflanking Gladstone on the land issue from which so much motive power for home rule politics was generated.

Working in any way with the Conservative party put an enormous strain upon Parnell's authority. It came too, of course, after the undoubted 'U-turn' of Kilmainham and the essentially unsatisfactory result the alleged 'Treaty' had had. Turning to Salisbury was in itself proof of disappointment. Certainly the Right hoped for advantage. But that did not signify Parnell was in the clear. His 'wild' men were ill at ease and the Right might prove an empty vessel. If the Conservatives failed him, he had only Gladstone, revolution or inaction – or withdrawal from the fray – to hope for. Nationalism trapped in the parliamentary system without irresistible powers of blackmail was inevitably a troubled phenomenon. It depended so much upon sustaining discontent overall at white or near white heat temperatures. Leadership needed to deliver goods on the central policy front – and often. Before the 1885 general election, the Irish nationalist party had no bird in hand except the Land Purchase (Ashbourne) Act [21] and a cessation (possibly temporary) in coercion. Extremists, though, were zealots for Irish autonomy as a first step to republican sovereignty. This first step alone posed vast difficulty. Anything more belonged to the wildest worlds of Celtic dream.

It cannot be said that Parnellite machinations of top Machiavellian-level cunning presented the Irish nationalist party with the ability to hold the balance between the Conservatives and Liberals following the general election of 1885. Proof that Irish nationalist votes in British constituencies could be or actually were swung around at will is not anywhere near full or convincing. That any attempt was made is yet another major test of Parnell's authority and credibility. 'Orange'–'Green' conversations and parliamentary co-sculduggery were bad enough, but (even with Anglican-Catholic school board sympathy in mind) the order to vote 'Orange' for the ultimate greater glory of the 'Green' was a tall one. The more so as Parnell's stint as President of the Home Rule Confederation of Great Britain, begun in 1877, had not been one of caucus triumph. No Chamberlain he – not in design and still less in execution. Organization in Ireland was never as sometimes suggested.[22] There, key compensating factors none the less generally righted matters at the drop of a mitre and accompanying birettas. Britain was not that easy. All these stages of the Irish nationalist story called for imagination, energy and organization at all levels from 'The Chief'. Dalliance at Eltham or elsewhere left the party and its causes neglected – and opened Parnell to dangers never posed even by his relations (such as they were) with the revolutionaries, actual or would-be.

Very often during his ascent to the radical nationalist leadership in 1880 Parnell had let things ride – ride right into his capable hands. The experience continued frequently thereafter, but once power was his it never fell from his grasp except through the workings of arrogant and unperceptive neglect. No matter what stage of his game the Irish nationalist party needed tight discipline. Its Chief let his lieutenants argue yet exercised a species of osmotic control over them as the talk progressed. He took it for granted that he held his post and that decisions he had seemingly willed into being would be carried out unquestioningly. Tendencies to fissiparism were self-evidently anti-national. That truth provided his psyche with the great justification for autocracy and something more. The second great switch into an alliance with what soon turned out to be the third Gladstone ministry Parnell took most seriously and made a hard sell. Yet in psychological terms it was a markedly easier affair, while at the same time an infinitely more binding and near irreversible development. Conservatism and Liberal Unionism first defeated a home rule scheme sponsored by Gladstone (with backing ranging from Whigs to members of the American Clan na Gael), defeated a Gladstonian-Irish nationalist combination in the general election of 1886, and then joined to back a Conservative Unionist government. A remarkably high proportion of the Liberal vote in Britain was radical and Conservative-loathing rather than positively friendly in approach to Irish nationalist ends. Knowing that, the Irish party was only too aware of not being 'independent' in the pre-Kilmainham way, or even in the much attenuated one palely alive until Parnell committed himself and his to the Gladstone scheme for home rule. More remarkable was that on top of this change Parnell had feet of immense coldness towards moves climaxing in the Plan of Campaign in 1887, when bad agrarian conditions drove Dillon and O'Brien to the edge of the law and beyond.[23] Coupled with indifferent health, prolonged public absences and an undeniably supine line in nationalism in the face of renewed coercion and a controversial Land Bill, Parnell's leadership position became further eroded.

It was further eroded because near disastrous problems had threatened over the official Irish nationalist candidature for the parliamentary borough of Galway,[24] where a by-election arose because T. P. O'Connor had been elected in two seats at the 1885 general election – Liverpool (Scotland) and Galway – and had chosen to stay with the former. Despite a strong preference for the candidature of one, Michael Lynch, both locally and amongst Parnell's lieutenants, The Chief foisted a Captain O'Shea, blatantly unwilling to take the truly watertight party pledge of August 1884, upon the unhappy constituency with an arbitrariness of unprecedented force and egocentricity. True though it was that dalliance had in itself done irreparable damage to the Irish nationalist party by the time the stench of the divorce court sullied the political air of the United Kingdom, it did not constitute a political sin of commission. On the contrary, it was one of startling and sustained omission – in short, dereliction of duty. At Galway the aberration was a full-blown act of corruption and betrayal of principle taken in the mainstream of public life – and for reasons most despicable. Great though that divorce court stench undoubtedly was, the one issuing from the public convenience into which Parnell had devalued the borough of Galway more than rivalled it. In fact it rendered him vulnerable in relation to Liberal allies in ways not touched in *The Times*'s 'Parnellism and crime' onslaught of April 1887[25] and on. Total innocence over the Phoenix Park murders he found protection enough in itself. Danger of exposure in things where his guilt was strong and continuing could and did prove a different kettle of fish, something of which Parnell was obviously more than aware. By the point when the 1887 Coercion Act was about to become operative and create risks for him like those which soon erupted over the condemnation of the National League by the lord lieutenant that 19 July, he certainly found profound comfort in the prospect of a hero's welcome from the Liberals of the National Liberal Club the next day. Here indeed was a 'Cave of Adullam' and one (as for King David before him) of especial personal convenience. In so many ways from this time until the divorce crisis broke in November 1890 he was, if not a Liberal, then an Irish nationalist deviously striving to maintain synchronized beats in the Union of Hearts. Yet it was, all too tragically, the Liberal attitude to the divorce scandal that brought him down.

Stuck as we are in the facts of history, it is necessary to view Parnell as a nationalist confined willy-nilly by United Kingdom power at home and abroad ultimately to follow (albeit often unwillingly) the dictates of the English-invented King-in-Parliament system. As what might be termed in the final analysis a 'prisoner' nationalist he was denied openings taken by several in the Anglo-Saxon tradition with whom he had much in common. Not for him the great distance of the Atlantic and the widespread support which the Virginian gentry and Bostonian elites afforded George Washington. Nor the ready-made colonial assemblies (the incipient home rule); nor the stupidity or power of George III to help him mightily on his way. Before 1883, Parnell was not able to live so far away from economics as he was thereafter.[26] From economics Washington never escaped in the run up to war, during war, or the first period of Independence. A large party equivalent to the Irish Volunteers so attractive to Parnell and one of Scots Irish so elusive for him in Ulster were mainstays on the colonial battle-fields. The latter most of all at the worst of times. No Patrick Henry graced the Belfast scene, zealous for 'liberty or death'. Or take the case of Gough Whitlam, the man who in a brash breach of the constitution was declared 'out' – here is someone, eyes ablaze with the greenish glint of disloyal loyalty, all agog to found a republic in a long royal Australia. 'Cheeking' the Crown has long been the 'right' of the discontented throughout the white and not so white metropolitan and peripheral areas. The United States was in so many ways the place where the latterday Cromwellians secured lasting victory. Washington was where the Lord Edward Fitzgeralds and the Wolfe Tones of North America could rejoice; Boston where its 1798ers (Belfast-style) might fill mighty tabernacles and, like the Banbury Puritans 'Sing psalms through their noses'. Parnell, Washington and Whitlam can all be deemed frontiersmen. As the nearest in to the metropolitan country, Parnell was the worst placed for pranks. Whitlam, though furthest out, attempted his deeds in times of wiser loyalism among masses of loyalists, devoted to that bigger Union of Hearts called the Commonwealth. On the frontier, upper-crust figures feel disadvantaged by simply being there. Until after the Second World War most extra-metropolitan imperial territories were consistently less wealthy than the United Kingdom. Law may be easily challenged in thought as well as in word and deed. All too often the opposition and complaints of the Anglo-Irish have become obscured by the subsequent paramountcy of Irish Irish challenge and the switch to post–1800 loyalism of previously (and often rightly) red hot, even republican, British Irish.

In continental Europe, the search for comparisons must begin with constitutional nationalism. Switzerland, the first such entity to operate in any of its components beyond the boundaries of oligarchy, offers us little. Like the United States (but more loosely) it was built up from agreements among previously self-operating parts; all of them retained powers, albeit much reduced in 1848, 1874 and at several points in the twentieth century. Before 1800 Ireland, like the American colonies before Independence, boasted an assembly; a colonial one outside the metropolitan state. After

1800 it was simply part of a centralized and extended version of that imperial hub. Only in so far as 'Jura Libre' was able to secede from Canton Berne in recent times and to illustrate how equality could be achieved relatively peacefully in the current confederation, do Swiss affairs impinge on issues like home rule within home rule, possible variations on the theme of British and Irish shared heads of state and the Government of Ireland Act 1920 (with North and South home rule).

The Netherlands, too, is not a fecund field. Early partition between Protestant and Catholic provinces and population exchanges meant community problems in the Protestant provinces became easily containable within the 'rule of law'. Governance of Catholic Dutch-inhabited areas south of the Waal, which were retained for reasons of military security, did raise issues like equality of civil rights in ways more serious than those of Catholic minorities inside the Dutch Protestant heartland. Dutch Protestants, like those Anglo-Irish in the 1826 general election who acted as precursors of O'Connell, did work hard to establish a juster society. But within those Dutch frontiers ethnicity was not at issue. At no time in France's revolutionary or post-revolutionary history was the like of Parnell on the stage. None of the sub-nationalisms has ever taken meaningful grip on the ethnic phenomenon they coveted. When the 'Big Holland' of 1815 burst asunder in 1830, the latest version (Belgium) of what had been the Spanish or Austrian Netherlands, or a chunk of an extended Napoleonic France, saw a Walloon-directed culture and politics supreme over it.[27] The 60 per cent Flemish majority, roughly comparable to the Irish Irish Catholic majority in Ireland, found itself remaining in what had long been its inferior role. Not until the German occupation during the First World War, and then the creation of a discrete Flemish government area, did a serious sea change occur. But the subjugation, such as it had been, was one of Catholics by Catholics. Those most like Parnell in politics had espoused the modernist liberal cause glorying in the partial suppression of Flemish peasant Catholicism. Boulanger, not Parnell, graced the streets of Brussels.

Scandinavia has at least one important area of comparison with Ireland and Irish nationalism Parnell style. Not in the Norway-Sweden state, also founded in 1815 and undone in 1905 – a divorce of mutual relief with none of the Irish-type ethnic complications in either unit.[28] Norway's two languages counted for next to nothing in the rows. The overall picture was what counted. But in Finland things were different.[29] When surrendered by Sweden to Russia in

1809 its constitution was allowed to stand. While not in constant active use, it and the concomitant distinct Finland-serving armed services allowed under its provisions, made a most extraordinary contrast when compared with the autocratic wasteland of all the vast rest of the tsarist empire. The Diet met rarely until 1863 but, as in Sweden itself, Poland and Hungary, it provided the means for the development of modern national aspirations, in what were already or would become nation states, or the means for achieving greater autonomy, be it moderate or extensive. Initially, and indeed for much of the nineteenth century, the Swedish-Finnish aristocracy dominated public life in this grand duchy. The situation was distinctly Grattan-like – except that, whereas the British Irish always had the disadvantage of having ethnic unity with the British and religious divides from the Irish Irish, the Swedish Finns were not Russian or Russian Orthodox and shared their Lutheran religion with the overwhelming proportion of Finns. They were able in fact to raise the Finnish Finns from cultural and economic backwardness as part of a general process of overall modernization aimed at the benefit of all Finns. The great symbolic triumph of the composite nationality ideal was that a former aide-de-camp to Tsar Nicholas II, of Swedish Finnish background (derived in part from the immigration of Dutch and German ancestors) and commander of the Finnish army, should have been a much loved president of Finland. Parnell was never able to aspire in realistic moments to anything like that.

Not even the most extreme Irish Irish republican could seriously entertain the view that the partition of Ireland matched the horrors inflicted upon Poland[30] by Russia, Prussia and Austria. Polish nationalists for most of the nineteenth century and some of the twentieth were 'noble' led. Inside Russian territories after 1815 until the rising of 1830 a large, mainly Polish-inhabited chunk of what had been Polish state territory was given a species of 1782-type constitution. It was operated by men with much in common with the Anglo-Irish of the late eighteenth century. Other former Polish lands were not so privileged, yet were essentially run until rebellion ruled it out by their Polish upper classes – rather like Irish counties by the Anglo-Irish justices after the Union had abolished the Irish Parliament. Polish-run tsarist areas were notably agrarian, with many Germans and Jews in the cities and towns. However, the Polish landed interest had fellow Poles, or majority-Uniate White Russians or Ukrainians upon their estates. All shared the basics of religion. As with the Swedish Finns, so with the Poles, the locals could so often be gathered behind them against Russia and Russian Orthodoxy. Much of the abandon and self-indulgence of the European east conjures up the self-indulgence of Parnell. So too, though, do the junketings of spoiled rich young men who compounded the fact of having American mothers with the enormity of having fathers of the same breed. The second Polish revolt (1863) was often better supported by Uniate White Russian peasants than by actual Polish lower orders. Here not the slightest element of an American analogy will hold. Nor can any with the subsequent decimation of the lower gentry and the end to effective Polish-run local rule. Constitutionalism ended until the Revolution of 1905. In the Russian Duma at last some mini-Parnells surged up; only to sink at the end of its short life. Only the re-emergence of Poland in 1918 allowed them to resurface – in roles never lived through by the essentially aborted Parnell.

In Prussian Poland the Poles approached the odd-man-outship of the Parnellite party. Association in politics with the German centre (Catholic) party never proved anything near an adequate defence. For leaders of the Polish ethnic group the position in the late nineteenth and early twentieth centuries frequently involved desperation of the kinds seen in Parnell's 'last stand'. Their language and their property were under constant, officially favoured hostile pressures, in what was anyway a deeply anti-Catholic atmosphere; it could be argued that conditions in Ireland infrequently seen after 1800 were matters of everyday life in Prussian Poland. Here was an essentially pre-O'Connell scenario. Austrian Poland (Galicia) presented what for the Poles was a felicitous contrast. After 1871 the Polish leadership ran what amounted to a home rule scheme within what had in 1867 become the Austrian (Cis-Leithanian) portion of the Dual Monarchy. Parnells and Parnells plus abounded in the union parliament (the Reichsraat) in Vienna. Some occupied ministries and some even penetrated to the three joint ministries (Foreign Affairs, Defence and War) at one or another level. But Ukrainians plus Jews outnumbered them. They had 'rightly' struggled to be largely free, but still dominated others:[31] a condition becoming dire in 1907 with the democratization of the Cis-Leithanian voting franchises.[32]

That same democratization destabilized much of the rest of Cis-Leithania – the lands of the Austrian and Sudeten Germans, the Czechs and the Slovenes. In the kingdom of Bohemia and the Margravate of Moravia Czechs were the majority. Sudetens, though, amounted to approximately one-third of the population.

Before 1848 many of the nobility installed by the Habsburgs after 1620, to replace recalcitrant and often Protestant Czechs, had treasured the notion that a united Bohemian or Moravian identity embracing the entire population and led by them was just the political ticket – for use against the emperor and ethnic nationalists as required. This was the cue for the local Parnells and Parnells plus. The chances to answer it were none the less cut short. Old and new Czech and Sudeten nationalisms put paid to it before Parnell had as much as made a single political speech.[33] Austrian Germans by definition and Slovenes in fact cannot be usefully brought into comparison with the Parnell or Parnellite phenomena. Austrian Germans were never supplicants, peaceful or otherwise. Slovenes had no Austrian German leaders and were at an altogether more modest level of aspiration than the Irish Irish while the Habsburg empire lasted.[34] Of Hungary much too much has been made in connection with Ireland.[35] Certainly the 'Ausgleich' of 1867 created an institutional structure for the new Austria-Hungary dear to the hearts of many leading Irish nationalists. Its status of Grattan-quadruple-plus was undoubtedly something to which O'Connell would have lent support, for which Parnell would have pressed, and which Arthur Griffith of Sinn Fein actively advocated – despite the fact that Magyar supremacy was maintained through the medium of a limited suffrage law and that at least five sizeable ethnic groups were under pressure to Magyarize in a way most strongly at variance with the dearest basic principles of the Irish Irish movements from the outset. While the Magyars in earlier times were struggling to secure effective autonomy or even independence from Vienna, there are grounds for comparison with what Parnell would have liked Irish conditions to be. The Magyar leaders had allowed nationalism to triumph over religious differences. The quest for modernization was notable, with Count Istvan Szechényi in the role of a proto-Horace Plunkett.[36] Though no Magyar party championed anything approaching Land Purchase, Magyars urgently called upon their citizens of non-Magyar ethnicity (largely without success) to join them. Religious tolerance, however, both strengthened and weakened the Magyar hand against Vienna. Solidarity among the Magyars was invaluable. But religious bigotry among many Catholic non-Magyar groups, above all the Croats, and the necessary exclusion of the Orthodox Rumanians and Serbs from what the Magyar leadership and, indeed, the general Magyar community represented, worked against them. In so far as several ethnicities aimed at no more than home rule within Hungary or a redrawn Habsburg state, some comparative possibilities with the Irish Irish exist. Polity nationalism has, nevertheless, been the hallmark of Irish nationalism at most times – a factor working for talk of the Hungarian state rather than of these others; except for the Croats, whose relationship with Budapest bore some similarity to what the second Gladstone Home Rule Bill planned for Ireland *vis-à-vis* Westminster.[37]

The Italian Risorgimento is inappropriate for comparisons with Ireland. The idea was to make a centralized united kingdom, not to subject one to a partial dismantling. It could not be pursued without a military component and power politics involving the greatest states of western and central Europe. And in any case, on the personal level with which we are here principally concerned, Parnell lacked the steady cunning, and control of a sovereign bailiwick (i.e. Piedmont) afforded to Cavour, lacked and was unwilling to use guns *à la manière* Garibaldi, had no great corpus of exciting rhetorical works like Mazzini – and, unlike Victor Emmanuel of Piedmont, was an 'uncrowned king'.[38] In the Spanish scene, too, though dismantling trends have been powerfully at work in the twentieth century among Basques and Catalans alike, the sheer difficulty entailed in the putting of the Spains together in the aftermath of the Moorish invasions had far exceeded anything awaiting those eager to reconstruct Humpty Dumpty.[39] Autonomists and separatists were and are, therefore, seldom assisted by the Spanish proper within their nests. Swifts, Molyneauxs, Grattans, Parnells and Childerses have scarcely shown their faces, let alone risen to the dazzling heights of leadership.

Many in Italy talked bombastically of their country liberating itself. Events proved them badly wrong. Ireland, on the other hand, seldom spoke thus, yet achieved much in the Parnell period through the factors in her favour being used to some advantage. It was, then, poignantly tragic that Charles Stewart Parnell should have thrown away the Liberal alliance for a mess of Kitty. Parnell's determination to hold on to the leadership could only have disastrous consequences, as the Irish nationalist 'fold' came down in 1891 upon their 'Assyrian' leader.

NOTES

1 For a thorough survey of these processes see Lawrence J. McCaffrey, 'Irish federalism in the 1870s: a study in conservative nationalism', *Transactions of the American Philosophical Society*, 52, Part 6, 1962, *passim*.

2 An excellent account of these circumstances is fully set out in E. D. Steele, *Irish Land and British Politics: Tenant-Right and Nationality, 1865–1870*, Cambridge, 1974, *passim*.

3 Much of the data on this are to be found in D. A. Kerr, *Peel, Priests and Politics: Sir Robert Peel's Administration and the Roman Catholic Church in Ireland, 1841–1846*, Oxford, 1982, ch. 7.

4 Considerable light is thrown upon this period by T. H. D. Mahoney in his *Edmund Burke and Ireland: the Lifelong Efforts of the Great Statesman to Help his Native Land*, Cambridge, Mass., 1960, esp. in chs 5–10.

5 Quite the best account of this achievement is splendidly presented in O. MacDonagh, *Daniel O'Connell, 1775–1829: the Hereditary Bondsman*, London, 1988, ch. 12.

6 A clear and succinct account of this is included in F. S. L. Lyons, *Charles Stewart Parnell*, London, 1977, ch. 1.

7 Key material upon all the leading figures in Parnell's Irish nationalist party is available in C. C. O'Brien, *Parnell and his Party, 1880–1890*, Oxford, 1957, *passim*.

8 For this see O. MacDonagh, *Daniel O'Connell, 1830–1847: the Emancipist*, London, 1989; J. H. Whyte, *The Independent Irish Party, 1850–1859*, Oxford, 1958; McCaffrey, 'Irish federalism'; and O'Brien, *Parnell and his Party* – all *passim*.

9 Fascinating comment on this theme abounds in M. Manning, *The Blueshirts*, Dublin, 1970.

10 See Arthur Griffith, *The Resurrection of Hungary*, 3rd edn, Dublin, 1918.

11 Extremely interesting aspects of this phase of Irish history are most intelligently dealt with in T. West, *Horace Plunkett, Cooperation and Politics: an Irish Biography*, Gerrards Cross, 1986.

12 See Steele, *Irish Land*; B. L. Solow, *The Land Question and the Irish Economy, 1870–1903*, Cambridge, Mass., 1971; S. Clark, *Social Origins of the Irish Land War*, Princeton, NJ, 1979, Part C; and P. Bew, *Conflict and Conciliation in Ireland, 1890–1910*, Oxford, 1987 – all *passim*. Likewise (to explain the 'Northern Question'): D. W. Miller, *Queen's Rebels: Ulster Loyalism in Historical Perspective*, Dublin, 1978; and J. Loughlin, *Gladstone, Home Rule and the Ulster Question, 1881–1893*, Dublin, 1986.

13 See L. Kennedy and P. Ollerenshaw, *An Economic History of Ulster, 1820–1939*, Manchester, 1985; and I. Budge and C. O'Leary, *Belfast: Approach to Crisis: a Study of Belfast Politics, 1613–1970*, London, 1973.

14 See Miller, *Queen's Rebels*; and P. Robinson, *The Plantation of Ulster*, Dublin, 1984, both *passim*.

15 As a stimulant to informed comparative thinking, T. E. Cliffe Leslie, *Land Systems of Ireland, England and the Continent* (albeit published

as early as 1870) is most helpful on the Irish land question and the issues arising from it.

16 The 'healthy' side of Celtic 'retooling' is well explained in M. Tierney, *Croke of Cashel: the Life of Archbishop Thomas William Croke, 1823–1902*, Dublin, 1976, ch. 10.

17 See R. H. Campbell, *Scotland since 1707: the Rise of an Industrial Society*, Oxford, 1971; and A. Slaven, *The Development of the West of Scotland, 1750–1960*, London, 1975 – both *passim*.

18 See *McCalmont's Parliamentary Poll Book of All Elections, 1832–1918*, Introduction, 1971 reprint.

19 Ibid.

20 A discussion of what was said by Parnell in Cincinnati appears in Lyons, *Charles Stewart Parnell*, pp. 111–12.

21 Of 1885 – the first extensive measure of this kind for Ireland.

22 See O'Brien, *Parnell and his Party, passim*. Chapters 4, 5 and 8 err strongly in this regard.

23 Ibid., ch. 7.

24 Ibid., ch. 6, section 2.

25 Ibid., ch. 7, *passim*.

26 Lyons, *Charles Stewart Parnell*, pp. 245–6.

27 For a vivid and informative picture of pre–1914 Belgium, see D. C. Boulger, *Belgian Life in Town and Country*, London, 1904.

28 See T. K. Derry, *A History of Modern Norway, 1814–1972*, Oxford, 1973, ch. 5; and Section 1 – 'Norway' (two articles: 'The economic basis of Norwegian nationalism in the nineteenth century' by Alf Kaartvedt, and 'An outline of Norwegian cultural nationalism in the second half of the nineteenth century' by Kjell Haughland), in R. Mitchison (ed.), *The Roots of Nationalism: Studies in Northern Europe*, Edinburgh, 1980.

29 The whole Finnish case history is beautifully laid out in A. Upton, 'Finnish nationalism' – part of 'Section Two – Nationalism entire' in M. Hurst (ed.), *States, Countries, Provinces*, Oxford, 1986.

30 The issues here are well explained in F. Wandycz, *The Lands of Partitioned Poland*, Washington, 1975.

31 In A. S. Markovits and F. E. Sysyn (eds), *Nation Building and the Politics of Nationalism: Essays on Austrian Galicia*, Cambridge, Mass., 1982, all eleven essays provide significant insights into this subject.

32 The best full treatment of this democratization is W. A. Jenks, *The Austrian Electoral Reform of 1907*, New York, 1950.

33 Both C. A. Macartney, *The Habsburg Empire, 1790–1918*, London, 1968, and A. J. May, *The Habsburg Monarchy, 1867–1914*, Cambridge, Mass., 1965, deal most lucidly with this Czech topic.

34 Macartney, *Habsburg Empire, passim*.

35 Griffith, *Resurrection of Hungary, passim*.

36 See G. Barany, *Stephen Szechenyi and the Awakening of Hungarian Nationalism, 1791–1841*, Princeton, NJ, 1968.

37 For an extensive analysis and discussion of many polity and ethnic nationalist issues, see M. Hurst, 'States, countries, provinces', in M. Hurst (ed.), *States, Countries, Provinces*.

38 In his *Life and Times of Cavour*, 2 vols, Boston and New York, 1911,

W. R. Thayer delineates the essentials of the Italian unification movement with telling skill. No later writer has improved upon his gifts of context-setting and causational analysis.

39 For sheer brilliance of perception and explanation, G. Brenan, *The Spanish Labyrinth*, Cambridge, 1943, remains unequalled in this field.

5 Parnell and Bagehot

D. George Boyce

When in 1866 Walter Bagehot published his *English Constitution* he identified what he regarded as the central reason for the success of the British way of government: the fact that party was integral to the British House of Commons, 'bone of its bone, and breath of its breath', yet without in any way impeding the working of the House. This was because 'The body is eager, but the atoms are cool'.[1] British parties were based upon a deferential society, where natural leadership was given its due; they were composed of fundamentally like-minded men; they were devoid of any significant ideological divisions. And because they were loose and shifting entities they provided a check on the power of the executive; for the cabinet was but a 'committee' of the House, working in a kind of fruitful tension with the House. Cabinet could dissolve Parliament; Commons could dismiss cabinet. This understanding enabled the cabinet to govern; and yet only allowed it to govern as long as it held the confidence of the House. Bagehot, in calling his book the *English Constitution*, chose his words carefully: for the essential style and character of the constitution was English; and Bagehot nowhere in his work acknowledged, or even mentioned, the role of Irish parties, Irish MPs, in the working of the system. When Bagehot published the second edition of his book in 1867, he was concerned lest the franchise reform of that year undermine the essentials of the system; but he took comfort in the reflection that, after all, the existing political parties would enlist the new voter, and secure his deference, as they had secured that of his predecessors.[2]

This constitutional theory prevailed when Isaac Butt's home rule party first entered Parliament as a recognizable force following the general election of 1874. Before then the home rulers had won some by-elections and it owed its sudden breakthrough to its fifty-nine seat achievement in 1874 to its ability to absorb other issues

besides home rule: to its concern for land reform and denominational education. As soon as the election was over the successful
candidates met in Dublin and adopted resolutions constituting themselves 'a separate and distinct party in the house of commons', fully
prepared for a parliamentary career.[3] But the problem lay in defining how the party could operate effectively in the British parliamentary system. For if the atoms were hot, yet the body cold, then the
home rulers were confronted with a real dilemma. They could press
their case in discussion and debate, and Isaac Butt was a practised
and eloquent advocate of the cause. Ireland, he argued, did not
enjoy the full benefits of the constitution of England; she did not
benefit economically from the Union; her people were not protected
by the ordinary law of the land. He declared that the Lord Lieutenant of Ireland could make it a crime for a man to be out of doors
after dark.[4] But all this was absorbed by the British members
of the House with equanimity; this was standard Irish political
rhetoric.

Butt's early experience revealed the dilemmas of home rule on
a British political platform. It is not unlikely that, had the Liberals
been in power in 1874, Butt's party might have found the best and
only route to political influence lying in some alliance with them;
for after all, a number of Butt's followers were Irish Liberals who
had changed their tune (much to the disgust of more advanced
nationalists, who labelled them derisively as 'Whigs'). It is possible
that in this event the home rule party would have been absorbed
into the British parliamentary body almost before it could find a
distinct independent tradition. But because the Conservatives were
in office, then at least the home rulers had time to find their
bearings in the House. But herein lay the other side of the dilemma:
independent existence might simply lapse into impotent existence,
as Butt discovered when his eloquent pleas for justice for Ireland
fell on, if not deaf, then indifferent ears. And this raised another
dimension of home rule in the English constitution: home rulers
were elected in a society, parts at least of which were far from
deferential. Even in Butt's day the rhetoric of home rulers, when
they stood on their own ground in Ireland, was far from 'cool'.
Attacks were launched on Irish landlordism, on past British rule in
Ireland, on present iniquities.[5] And while the influence of this
aspect of home rule must not be exaggerated, none the less it was
clear that a more aggressive style at home had to be reconciled
with a parliamentary language in Westminster. This would become
more acute when the home rulers were obliged to face the question:

where was 'home' anyway? Was it in Cork or Galway, or was it located in the corridors, committee rooms and floor of the British Parliament?

Walter Bagehot's description of the House of Commons was based on the assumption that, while members appeared not to be playing the game according to the rules, in reality they were: their conflicts did not make government or the business of the House impossible. When Parnell entered the Commons as member for Meath in April 1875 he found himself in a party whose leader did not favour 'a policy of exasperation'.[6] But his arrival coincided with the policy which has been so closely associated with his own rise to power, and with the arrival of the home rulers as a serious political force: the policy of obstructionism, of using the rules of the House to delay its business, and thus declaring a kind of 'war' on the 'Saxon' Parliament.

Obstruction was initiated by J. G. Biggar, one of the members for Cavan, whose purpose it was to 'rub them up, sir, that's the thing to do; rub them up. Make them uncomfortable'.[7] But obstruction was not the sudden plunge into revolutionary activity that it later appeared. It was a consequence of the nature of Parliament itself as it had developed even in Bagehot's day, and of the home rule party's desire to play a full and active role in the proceedings of the House. Butt's intention was to make his party an integral part of the political process; and for it to assume this role, he was determined to seek to initiate legislation on a whole range of Irish subjects, and not merely debate the merits of Irish federalism. The only way Butt could do this, since he would never be in a position to form a government, was to use the time allocated to private members. Parliament sat for only six months; and business was often taken late at night, and after midnight. Yet Butt was determined to make his party one dedicated to the offering of Bills relating to Ireland, even if, as was so often the case, they would meet with defeat; and he was determined also to oppose legislation which his party believed was inimical to the interests of Ireland. In July 1874 he fought against a Bill for, amongst other matters, the retention of certain special powers for peace preservation in Ireland; and the party's opposition lasted for seventeen hours, with the House being divided three times. This was not new: in July 1860 a radical Liberal member, Sir John Trelawney, noted that

The labour of attendance at the House has become almost beyond the endurance of giants. Certainly, Palmerston is of Heroic mould. Between 3 & 4 on a summer's morning, he was still at his post baffling the Irish Brigade, who hoped by factious motions for adjournmt. to get rid of the Peace Preservation Bill. Maguire suggested that the House shd. go to bed, Palmerston proposed that the minority only shd. go – & when that body dwindled to 7, he observed, on giving way, that the Public would, at least, see there were still seven wise men.

Butt was not, as Parnell's admirers liked to claim, a feeble lackey of the British parliamentary system; on the contrary, it was because he was anxious to make his party work that system that he first gained the disapproval of the House for what turned out to be – given the shortage of time for debates – 'obstructionist' policy.[8]

This policy was one of firmness combined with a respect for the rules of the House; it was not meant to 'rub them up the wrong way', even though that was its effect. Biggar took the opportunity to press Butt's firm policy beyond its proper sphere, and deliberately seek to waste the time of the House. This was most easily done when the House was in Committee, for then each member had the right to make repeated motions for reporting progress. Despite Biggar's first excursion into wasting the time of the House, it was not as effective as its advocates claimed: as R. Barry O'Brien acknowledged, 'the year 1875 passed quietly away in Parliament and in Ireland'. As for Parnell, he 'remained chiefly a calm spectator of the proceedings of the House of Commons'; promising himself, however, that he 'must try and ask a question myself some day'.[9] And when in June 1876 he made his most celebrated interjection in the House, declaring that the 'Manchester Martyrs' were not, as Sir Michael Hicks Beach called them, 'murderers', his intervention was handled calmly and professionally by Beach, who contented himself with pointing out that the prisoners had been convicted by an English jury for a crime committed on English soil, and that the restoration of an Irish parliament would make no difference to their fate; and then turning, as he put it, 'to a more material question'.[10]

The British Parliament, then, seemed capable of absorbing the Irish home rule party; and even the apparently original tactic of obstruction was by no means new in the House, and so far not particularly successful. Obstruction could only work if it were mounted as a systematic campaign against the government and the business of the House; and it first began to take serious effect in the session of 1877, when Parnell and his group turned the half-past twelve rule against the government. This rule, first introduced in 1871 and then reinstated in 1875, had the purpose of turning obstruction against its practitioners. No order of the day or motion was to be taken after half-past twelve at night if a notice of opposition to it had been printed on the notice paper, or if such notice of motion had been given on the immediately preceding day (with the exception of money Bills). This provided an appropriate parliamentary revenge on the Irish party, which saw its Bills disappear without discussion.[11] But in 1877 Parnell and Biggar entered notice of opposition against every important English or Scottish Bill in the ministry's programme. None of this legislation could be proceeded with after 12.30 a.m. on the day following which it was down for debate, and an Irish member could talk it out until the hour arrived. This policy was described by Parnell's biographer as 'war';[12] but the commotion it engendered must not obscure the fact that when Parnell came to defend himself against the charge of deliberately wasting the House's time, he did so on parliamentary grounds, and in constitutional language. When the Chancellor of the Exchequer moved a resolution that the rules of debate be altered to overcome obstruction, Parnell replied that the changes were drawn up to 'muzzle' him and prevent him taking part in debates. In past sessions members had used the rules to obstruct measures brought forward by Irish MPs; his intention was to put to a 'practical test' the bona fides of the assertion constantly made in the House that 'Irish Members were free to take that part in the debates on English measures which English members frequently took, with disastrous effects, in the debates on Irish measures'. He went on:

> as long as the House insisted on doing the work of England, Ireland and Scotland – or rather trying to do it; as long as it insisted, also, in legislating for the Colonies and for the Indian Empire, there would be obstruction of a practical character which would prevent them from doing work which they could not possibly do, however necessary.[13]

Parnell was here shifting his ground, from the Irish intruder, bent on upsetting the 'alien' Parliament and the too 'comfortable' English,[14] to the Member of Parliament pointing out that obstructionism was a way of exposing the unworkable nature of the present English constitution. When he stood on his own ground, in Dublin, Parnell claimed that the home rulers had a right to obstruct because they were punishing the English for the misgovernment of Ireland;[15] but even in Ireland – in Belfast – he was capable of arguing his case on the grounds of constitutionalism:

> If some curb is not immediately put on the arbitrary tendencies of the Minister there will soon be an end of Constitutional Government. Parliamentary representation will be a farce, and the boasted 'Mother of free Parliaments' will become a mere registering machine for endorsing the acts of the British Minister. Alas! How changed are Englishmen, even in regard to their own liberties. The spirit of Liberty seems to be departing from Protestant England. They have submitted tamely to an encroachment on their liberties during the present Parliament totally unworthy of the descendants of those Catholic Englishmen who wrung from King John, on the battlefield, the fundamental principles of the British Constitution (cheers).[16]

Parliament was vulnerable because Parliament tried to do too much: a proposition that was increasingly heard in the 1870s and 1880s, not least from the leader of the British Liberal party, W. E. Gladstone.

Isaac Butt, for his part, regarded these tactics with disgust; for him 'no man can damage the authority of the House of Commons without damaging the cause of representative government and of freedom all over the world'. In May 1877 Parnell pointed out to Butt, after Butt had publicly rebuked him, that

> my clause on the Prisons Bill regarding the treatment of political prisoners was supported by all sections of the English Liberal party, and the Government were compelled to accept it lest they should be defeated on a division. Here, then, no adverse effect as regards the support of Englishmen was produced by my course of action. Subsequently, on the Marine and Army Mutiny Bills, amendments that I moved were supported by the full strength of all sections of the Liberal party present, as many as 146 and 150 voting for some of the amendments.[17]

Parnell was here demonstrating his developing sense of parliamentary procedure and timing, not to mention his efficacy in parliamentary intervention and debate. But his tactics had the virtue of enabling him and his followers to create popular interest in the home rule party, and depict themselves as more aggressive than they really were. For the home rulers were unable, even had they desired, to avoid engagement in the ordinary legislative processes of the most experienced legislature in modern politics: they participated in debates on foreign and imperial policy; they were keen observers of, and contributors to, the proceedings of the House.[18] Yet they managed to convey the impression that their behaviour in the Commons was a species of warfare. This enabled the home rulers, and Parnell in particular, to place themselves at the head of two significant wings of the (far from 'deferential', in the Bagehot sense of the word) Irish nation: the Fenians and the Land League, both of which helped Parnell to his mastery of the home rule party by 1880.

The Fenians, several of whom had already met Parnell secretly in June 1878, were impressed by his lively parliamentary tactics; and some of them believed that, in the absence of a revolutionary movement, they could, without compromising their principles, adapt their movement to the rising star of nationalist Ireland. This Fenian link had other important implications for Parnell, for it was Fenian leadership that was instrumental in the channelling of Irish agrarian discontent into the organized form of the Land League in the summer of 1879. Parnell hesitated, before finally placing himself at the head of the league in October 1879; but even while acting as the leader of agrarian discontent, he remained a Member of Parliament, and pursued his ambition of ousting Butt's rather colourless replacement, William Shaw, from the head of the Irish parliamentary party. Ironically, while Parnell and his parliamentary following sat with the opposition Conservatives in the House of Commons, Shaw and his supporters sat with the Liberals, on the grounds that the Liberals were the friends of Ireland. But already there were prefigurations of the day when the Parnellites would sit with the Liberals as the friends of Ireland. When Lord Hartington threw his weight behind the government's Compensation for Disturbance Bill, the Irish nationalists to a man supported the government: and the Bill was read a second time, despite the fact that twenty Liberals opposed it and twenty walked out.[19] It was the first time, but not the last, that Irish home rulers were to provide a source of support for the Liberal party when it divided on a controversial Irish issue.

Despite Parnell's leadership of what might be called the popular movement, his parliamentary position in 1880 was weak. In the general election of March 1880, out of some sixty MPs reckoned to be home rulers, Parnell's following numbered only twenty-four definite adherents, though as the life of the Parliament wore on he gained more supporters; and he was helped by the fact that the rest of the home rule representatives did not form a separate party, thus leaving him the undoubted leader of the home rule cause.

Parnell enjoyed the same kind of advantages and disadvantages as another rising star of the House, the radical Joseph Chamberlain. Chamberlain was able to mobilize popular opinion in the form of provincial urban Liberalism to gain rapid advancement to the cabinet; but once there he was no more powerful than any other minister, or, rather, he enjoyed no particular advantage over any other minister who lacked his popular base.[20] Parnell, of course, had no ambition to join the British cabinet; but the use of provincial popular following to draw attention to his public power was similar, if more dramatic and more risky.

The power of Parnell in Parliament lay in his ability to challenge the Liberal government which took office under Gladstone in April 1880 and to challenge it both in Ireland and in Westminster. Parnell's leadership of the Land League was a subtle combination of restraint and force; and once again he was able to reconcile his position as popular leader with a distinct parliamentary role – one, however, that was not to last much longer. Parnell's advantage was summed up by Gladstone on 23 October 1880. The question of obstruction in the proceedings of the House became acute as the Irish members fought a rearguard action against the government's coercive measures giving it the power to suspend the ordinary law in parts of Ireland whenever necessary. The sitting on 25 January lasted for 22 hours; that on 31 January for 41 hours without a break, the second longest sitting recorded for the Commons. But Gladstone was aware of the difficulty of curbing the excesses of the home rulers. The labours of Parliament had become 'unduly and almost intolerably severe'; and the extreme pressure of business was the secret of the 'obstructor proper' and 'makes it pay him so well to pursue his vocation at all costs'. Parliament, then, was the author of its own difficulties, since its legislative programme was ever increasing. But to amend its rules to curb Parnell was to provide the Irish obstructor 'with a new national grievance: and as his extremist resistance would probably be popular with his constituents, the House might find that it had more than a merely personal conflict to handle'. Moreover, the Bagehot concept of the British Parliament once again came to the aid of Parnell: for any great changes in the role of the House of Commons 'if repressive of the liberty of debate, would be grave public evils'. This latter reflection provoked Gladstone to draft some notes on what he called 'devolution': the need to devolve 'upon other bodies' a portion of the Commons' 'overwhelming tasks' and thus enable the House at once to 'economise its time, reduce its arrears and bring down to a minimum the inducement to obstruct; for obstruction will then be only the infliction of suffering, whereas now it is the frustration of purpose, the defeat of duty'. Devolution would still leave the power of repression at the command of the House; and 'of this Devolution, part may be to subordinate or separate authorities. But part may also be to subformations out of the body of the House itself.'[21] Gladstone thus saw Parnell as only part of a longer term malaise affecting the British constitution: that of the 'long term corruption' of the legislature.[22] This 'corruption' had concerned Gladstone long before the home rulers exploited it; the answer to it, he noted, might supply the 'means of partially meeting and satisfying, at least so far as it is legitimate, another call. I refer to the call for what is called (*in bonam partem*) Local Government and (*in malam*) Home Rule'.[23]

Gladstone's 'devolution' idea was discussed without much enthusiasm in cabinet, where only Joseph Chamberlain and John Bright showed much interest.[24] But the necessity of changing the rules of the House to draw the sting of obstructionism gained general support.

Gladstone was moving towards the idea that the Irish problem was in essentials a constitutional one, and could only be resolved if, as Gladstone hoped, 'a more intelligent and less impassioned body has gradually come to exist in Ireland'; otherwise, 'if we are at war with a nation we cannot win'.[25] But he acknowledged that he must curb Parnell's activities, and especially his opposition to Gladstone's Land Act of 1881 setting up land courts to fix 'judicial rents' between landlord and tenant; and his conviction that Parnell was intent upon wrecking the Bill persuaded him to imprison the Irish leader in Kilmainham jail in October 1881.[26] Gladstone had no illusions about the impact of his actions in Parliament where he anticipated 'rough work when the Session opens both as to the suspects whom we are obliged to keep in prison, and as to the proposals we shall probably have to make for enabling Parliament to get through its work'.[27] But, once again, this was not due solely to the Irish members. The House was legislating more frequently, and transacting an increased amount of business; and the wider representation of social classes throughout the kingdom, Lord Hartington's biographer asserted, imported into parliament 'a much larger number than formerly of ambitious and energetic men, whose position depends, not on social status, but on their power to make themselves heard and noticed'. When Hartington defended the proposal to introduce the 'cloture' he did so on the grounds that the 'time of the House belongs not to every individual member of the House, but to the House itself'.[28]

The final defeat for the possibility of renewing obstructionism was not long in coming. In May 1882 Gladstone and his cabinet agreed to release Parnell and his two fellow prisoners, 'with a view to the interests of law and order in Ireland'.[29] The murder of the newly appointed Chief Secretary for Ireland, Lord Frederick Cavendish, in Phoenix Park on 6 May was condemned by Parnell, but caused the government to introduce fresh coercive measures in the Commons, in the course of which the home rulers, having resisted to the last, withdrew from the House altogether:[30] only to return to oppose the attempts by the government to put an end to such influence as 'obstruction' allowed. Gladstone moved towards a series of changes to the standing orders of the House to streamline its procedures, congratulating himself on 'a great day, as I think, for the House of Commons itself',[31] when these were finally accepted after thirty-four nights of debate. And once again, as in 1877, the Parnellites fought against the procedural changes on the grounds of parliamentary liberties. The 'cloture', Parnell alleged, would not facilitate the business of the House. He used the language of Bagehot when he declared that the new measures would 'increase the friction of Parties in the House of Commons to a very remarkable extent'. He also warned the House that the result would be to 'increase the drive and the tendency in "another place" to throw out Bills which have been passed apparently by the agency of the cloture' – a prophetic utterance. So far from facilitating legislation, Parnell declared, the 'cloture' would 'do nothing except crush and check the liberties of the House of Commons'. The restriction of the rights of the Irish members must be followed, one day, by similar restrictions on the people represented by others as well.[32]

It was significant that Parnell, the so-called 'alien force' in the British Parliament, should end up defending the freedom of that institution against Gladstone, one of its greatest ornaments. Parnell went so far that he was obliged to account for his actions in December 1883, when he told an audience in Cork that he had not 'leaned unduly towards the Government in the discussions on the rules of procedure which have just passed through Parliament'; there were sixty-seven divisions on the rules of procedure during the autumn session, in which the Irish party voted fifty-eight times against the government. If anything, the party had leaned towards the Tories. Then he moved on hastily to distract his listeners from the parliamentary scene and towards 'the question of national self-government' which, he assured them, 'is a question which is rapidly coming to the front'.[33]

In steering through his procedural changes Gladstone thought he had struck a balance between the power of the Commons and that of the executive; and while making allowance for the expedient nature of Parnell's reaction to these changes, the language he used reflected his development as a parliamentary performer, ever more deeply embedded in the parliamentary process, and using these as best he could to further the 'national cause'. The potential of these tactics was limited. Parnell's admirers spoke of his manipulation of the party and parliamentary system, and claimed that he demonstrated his mastery of both;[34] and their claims seem justified in the light of the political events as they unfolded between 1884, when Parnell's party accepted the 'pledge', by which a candidate committed himself, if elected, to 'sit, act and vote' with the party, and to resign his seat if he failed to do so; and Gladstone's 'conversion' to home rule for Ireland which was publicly disclosed in December 1885. But the reality was different; for the British parliamentary system was not so easily bent to the wishes even of the uncrowned king of Ireland.

Parnell – conveniently ignoring his predecessor Butt – claimed that he had got his idea of an independent Irish party from Charles Gavan Duffy and the Tenant Right League of the 1850s; and

> whenever I thought about politics I always thought that that would be an ideal movement for the benefit of Ireland. The idea was an independent party reflecting the opinions of the masses of the people; acting independently in the English House of Commons, free from the influence of either English political party; pledged not to take office or form any combination with any English political party until the wants of Ireland had been attended to.[35]

So Parnell told the Special Commission in 1889; but the most significant phrase was his qualifying one, 'until the wants of Ireland had been attended to'.

So far it seemed hardly likely that attending to these wants would involve any move by the two British political parties towards home rule; and between Parnell's release from Kilmainham jail in May 1882, and 1884, no such possibility was seriously entertained. Yet some sort of Irish policy, necessarily involving a modification of the way in which Ireland was administered and governed, followed from the desire to keep the Irish question firmly in the context of

Westminster, firmly within the confines of a parliamentary resolution: and neither Gladstone nor the Conservatives envisaged any other mode of action. In October 1883 the Marquis of Salisbury, in an article published in the *Quarterly Review*, warned that the British parliamentary system was changing. We still lived under 'Parliamentary Government', but now the 'control of the machine' was in the hands of the democracy. Salisbury singled what he called the 'Whigs' out for special condemnation; for it was they who, through their assistance to the Irish (past and present), were undermining the fortress of Parliament from within. Salisbury's polemic was not without insight, however; for he noted the vital element in the British parliamentary state that rendered the Parnellites a significant force in British politics, even though their numbers were at this time but few: the fact that 'as far as after half a century of experience we may judge it, has been to add another illustration of the difficulty of keeping people as subjects against their will by the instrumentality of highly popular institutions; and the more real the popular institutions are, the more arduous does the undertaking become'. The Irish minority could never form a government, therefore they were 'free to practise on the weaknesses of those who are'. Their votes in a division could be made the price of legislative concessions. Salisbury alleged that the Irish party, through its obstructionist tactics, was hoping to gain its end: to oblige us to prefer that 'Ireland shall be ruled by the Irish, rather than that England should not be ruled at all'.[36]

It may be said that the first of Salisbury's propositions was true, the second was not. Obstruction could not have wrung from Gladstone nor anyone else what he did not want to give; and obstruction was in any event an exhausted policy by 1882, for the change in the rules of the House rendered it of marginal effect. As Gladstone put it – rather unkindly – 'He did not think the Parnellites strong enough ever to cause real danger or do serious mischief: they would be . . . like vermin about a man's person, troublesome and disagreeable, able to give annoyance, but not to interfere with his action.'[37] But Salisbury's point about the difficulty of a parliamentary institution 'keeping people as subjects against their will' was a substantial one; for it was the key both to the Conservative flirtation with Parnell in 1885, and to the Gladstonian identification of Parnell as the prime minister of a home rule Ireland in 1885–6. Gladstone himself contributed to this identification when his cabinet decided, whatever the consequences for Ireland, to proceed with a franchise reform measure for the whole United Kingdom which, Gladstone acknowledged, would cost the Liberals about twenty-five seats in Ireland.[38] After the government resigned on a defeat on the budget in June 1885, to be replaced by Salisbury's 'caretaker' government, a general election the following November-December revealed that Parnell was the master of nationalist Ireland. This may have been due to reasons other than the Franchise Act of 1884; but it put beyond doubt the claim that Parnell was indeed the spokesman of the majority of his nation: his eighty-six strong party was the measure of his power.

Even before this election, it was clear that, if the Irish question were to be 'domesticized', then it was important to discover what Parnell wanted, and what he would accept – within the limits laid down by British politicians. From January to June 1885 Joseph Chamberlain made contact with Parnell through the offices of Captain O'Shea to discover what Parnell's attitude would be to the 'central board' scheme of local government reform drawn up by Chamberlain. Chamberlain's proposals did not find favour in the cabinet;[39] but the discussions which took place at one remove between Chamberlain and Parnell revealed Parnell's strengths and weaknesses as a British parliamentary figure. The fact that his views were elicited – as within a few months Gladstone was to elicit them on the possibility of a home rule bill – revealed that the Irish question was of central concern to the British political elite. By 1 August 1885 the Conservative Earl of Carnarvon was in secret session with Parnell, and listening to assurances from the Irish leader that Parnell had 'always kept on the side of moderation, that he had quieted violence, that he had kept the National League within the bounds of law and that he should do so still'.[40]

But Parnell the parliamentarian must play the parliamentary game; his only leverage lay in the perception held by others of his indispensibility in a constitutional settlement of whatever sort would ensue. The Parliament which assembled after the 1885 general election gave Parnell a strength equal to the Liberal majority over the Conservatives; but this revealed, not the certainties, but the vagaries of the role of 'independent opposition'; for while Parnell could keep either party out of office, he could put in only the Liberals. Parnell was in desperate need of a hand of friendship from either of the British parties. His position was now no different from that which he himself indicated in 1882–4: 'we struggle today for that which may seem possible for us with our combination'.[41]

This explains Parnell's anxiety to discover Gladstone's intentions during the general election; and his placing (after months of delay) in Gladstone's hands of his 'Proposed Constitution for Ireland' in early November, which revealed Parnell as a moderate constitutionalist with a flexible approach to the finer details of a home rule settlement.[42] He had already discussed, amongst other matters, the position of Irish representation at Westminster with Lord Carnarvon.[43] But once Parnell revealed his hand, then he was vulnerable to the imposition of a solution upon him by a British party. Barry O'Brien was wont to refer to Parnell's skill in 'playing one English party against the other, and out-manoeuvring both';[44] but the opposite was more nearly true: for each of the English parties played him off against the other. Salisbury flirted with Parnell; but when the moment for electoral advantage had passed he was by January 'feverishly eager to be out'.[45] Meanwhile Gladstone had got through the election without committing himself publicly beyond his rather vague pre-election address on Ireland. 'An immense loss of dignity,' he told Lord Spencer, 'in a great crisis of the Empire, would attend the forcing of our hands by the Irish or otherwise.'[46]

In the course of December 1885 Gladstone began to canvass the possibility in his own mind of some kind of association between the Liberals and the Irish, as a means of settling Ireland.[47] This was a stage beyond his previously held belief that he could and should stand upon a clear Liberal majority in Parliament alone. When, finally, Gladstone's commitment to home rule was publicly acknowledged, the resting place of parliamentary Parnellism was reached: even before Gladstone announced any detailed scheme of Irish home rule; even before any Bill was placed before the House; even before Parnell was able to explain to his electorate in Ireland what was envisaged, what was on offer, the home rule party had become the partners of the Gladstonian Liberals. Parnell had no other choice – at least, no other choice within the context of parliamentary politics. To do other than support the Liberals would be for Parnell to cast himself adrift on the sea of Westminster politics. As Labouchere predicted, in a conversation he had with T. P. O'Connor on the way to the railway station:

> I said that I supposed it would end in some sort of alliance with the Liberals as the Conservatives would give nothing. He agreed, and said that he himself was a Radical, and that he would do anything in reason.[48]

The way in which Parnell and his party were now part of the Liberal party front, 'bone of its bone, breath of its breath', to use Bagehot's phrase, was illustrated by Gladstone in his speech during the second reading of the Home Rule Bill in May 1886. Gladstone – who had earlier sought for a Conservative initiative on Irish self-government, and hoped for a bi-partisan approach to the problem – now berated the members on the opposition bench who had said that 'if we cast away the Party spirit' in dealing with Ireland we should do well. 'What', asked Gladstone,

> is meant by this? Is it meant that the Party spirit is to be expelled generally from the circuit of English politics? Is that so? Is there a dreamer who, in the weakness of his dreams, has imagined that you can really work the free institutions of this country upon any other principles than those in the main which your fathers have handed down to you and which have made this country what it is?[49]

And in the debate on the Queen's Speech on 24 August 1886, shortly after the defeat of Gladstone's Home Rule Bill, and the return of a Conservative government to power, Parnell reciprocated. 'As regards our own position,' he declared, 'we have every reason to feel, I must not say satisfied with the result of the General election, but certainly satisfied with our present position.' For the first time

> in the history of the Irish national movement a large section, the great majority, of the Liberal party have declared at the polls that Ireland is entitled to autonomy. That declaration has been endorsed in the country by the great majority of the Liberal electors – the vast majority.

Parnell believed that the Liberal electors would cease to hesitate on Liberal policy; for after the Tories had tried to govern Ireland for a year or two

> I am convinced that there will be no such hesitation, so we have every reason to be patient . . . we have every reason to be moderate, and to urge our people at home to be moderate, and to keep them within the limits of loyalty, as far as any advice of ours can possibly so keep them, because ours is a winning cause. It can only be damaged by excesses of any kind.[50]

W. S. Blunt was sceptical about the power of endurance of what he termed the 'alliance between the Catholic Irish and the atheistic English radicals' which was 'not a natural one and may be broken at any moment'; but, as Professor Lubenow demonstrates (with an awesome statistical power), the voting lists 'show it to have been pervasive and durable'.[51] The Parnellites, for most purposes, were a manifestation of the radical wing of the Liberal party; an accession of strength after the departure of the arch-radical Joseph Chamberlain and some Liberals over the Home Rule Bill. Parnell's difficulty as a parliamentary politician lay not in Westminster, but in that aspect of Irish nationalism that he had singled out in his speech of August 1886: 'our people at home'.

For the Gladstonian policy of making the Irish question a 'creature of parliamentary politics' and thus 'containing it for thirty years'[52] presupposed that Parnellite nationalism was indeed constitutional and non-separatist: a proposition denied by its Conservative and Irish Unionist supporters. Was Parnell, as he now claimed, standing outside the United Kingdom and the empire trying to get in; or standing inside the United Kingdom and empire trying to get out? The nature of Irish nationalism can never be put to the test, since Parnell did not get home rule (nor, for that matter, did John Redmond). But it must be said that Irish nationalism spoke with two voices. When Parnell stood upon Irish ground, he was as liable as any fellow home ruler to denounce the evils of the Saxon, and then declare that the story of Anglo-Irish relations was (as Thomas Moore had it) on our side Erin and virtue; on their side the Saxon and guilt. Yet there was always implicit in his nationalism, and that of many of his party, the notion that a settlement of the constitutional problem would bring about a 'union of hearts'. Ireland was, in this view, outside the United Kingdom and the empire; yet not unwilling to come in, if all past wrongs were redressed. This latter stance was perfectly compatible with the parliamentary way, with the English constitution; indeed, it was axiomatic, unless – as Parnell sometimes mused – the home rulers were to withdraw from Westminster altogether.[53] And it was this policy that Parnell now stressed, as he established himself under the wing of the Liberal party: a policy severely strained within months of the failure of the first Home Rule Bill when Ireland was again disturbed by agrarianism in the 'Plan of Campaign'.

The Plan of Campaign has been dealt with elsewhere in this volume, and need not here be discussed in detail; its importance for this essay lies in the response that Parnell made to it. Parnell did not set his face against the new agitation right away, claiming later that he was unable to do so because of illness.[54] But in December 1886, in a secret encounter with William O'Brien in the fog at Greenwich Observatory, he urged O'Brien to moderate the campaign.[55] This encounter took place at a time when Parnell had lapsed into one of his withdrawal periods, neglecting his political duties and remaining what his biographers liked to call 'inactive'. His intervention (which had little effect) was the direct consequence of Liberal advice. Following a characteristically exaggerated diatribe against the landlords by John Dillon on 5 December 1886, John Morley informed Parnell that the Plan of Campaign was having a very adverse effect on English public opinion; Parnell disavowed any part in the plan, and was 'anxious to have it fully understood that the fixed point in his tactics is to maintain the alliance with the English Liberals'.[56]

Charles Stewart Parnell had begun his noticeable parliamentary career by associating himself with the policy of obstructionism; this was how he first brought his name to the attention of the 'advanced nationalists'. But, unless he were prepared to lead a genuine revolutionary movement in Ireland, he must play the parliamentary game. His decision to place himself at the head of the Land League agitation propelled him to the leadership of nationalist Ireland; but his intention was, as he himself later admitted to R. Barry O'Brien, to keep to the constitutional path: 'I have never gone for separation. I never said I would. The physical force men understand my position very well. I made it clear to them that I would be satisfied with a Parliament, and that I believed in our constitution movement.'[57] Parnell's political leadership, however, placed an Irish crisis into an English parliamentary context; but that context was one which British parliamentarians believed firmly was able to resolve political crises, and to bring them to a political conclusion. For all his obstructionist activity, for all his claims to have founded an independent Irish party, Parnell's room for manoeuvre in the British parliamentary system was limited. It was limited not only because of his relatively small party which, even when it seemed to hold the balance of power in 1885, was still obliged to seek rather desperately for an Irish Government Bill from one or other of the English parties. But it was also constrained by the confidence of British parliamentarians that their institution was old enough and strong enough to contain even the unprecedented Irish nationalism of the 1880s. The parliamentary culture would prevail. It would prevail even if it were somewhat altered in style. It was ironic that Parnell, who had built his early parliamentary reputation on the policy of obstructionism, should have found himself, in 1887, combining with the Liberals to oppose the Conservative government's Criminal Law Amendment (Ireland) Bill, and provoking, through their joint action, the use of the Closure on 18 March after a marathon debate; and, thereby, occasioning the introduction of even more sweeping changes to the rules of parliamentary procedure.[58]

Parnell was a master of what Conor Cruise O'Brien called the 'intelligently applied techniques of power', techniques applied, not merely against a 'panorama of fenianism and the land movement', but in his 'immediate political surroundings'.[59] The exigencies of these surroundings explain what seemed to be his extraordinary volte-face between 1887 and 1890. In the aftermath of the Liberal alliance Parnell went out of his way to praise the Liberal party which had 'always striven to do justice to Ireland', and had 'acted upon principle and from deep conviction from the first to last in this Irish question'.[60] In 1888, in a speech at the Eighty Club in London, he urged his people and especially the tenant farmers to 'remember that a great and historic party are committed to their cause, and that they are not standing alone'. This was when Ireland seemed to be fulfilling what Gladstone told Queen Victoria in 1884 was 'something like a political axiom when we say that the adoption of a legislative project into the creed of the Liberal party at large is the sure prelude to its accomplishment'.[61] But when Parnell's personal life made it essential for Gladstone to demand Parnell's leadership of the Irish party as the price of that 'axiom', then Parnell in December 1890 warned Gladstone that he and his followers 'declined to surrender to you that independence of our party which has produced in you the mind in which you are today'.[62]

But a closer reading and de-coding of Parnell's last speeches reveal him as a parliamentarian still: and, moreover, one anxious to treat with his old ally, Gladstone. In his December 1890 speech he declared that there was a distinction between 'a man and his colleagues sometimes'. But the distinction in Gladstone's case was a little out of order:

> It is a distinction between the tail wagging the head and the head wagging the tail, and the message that Ireland sends back to the Grand Old Man is this: 'Resume your place as leader of your party. Back up your legitimate authority, and when you put yourself in the position of an independent leader such as ours, then, and not till then, will we allow our leader to treat with you upon those equal terms which alone can assure a lasting, possible, and permanent settlement.'

Parnell went on to offer his assistance in helping the 'English Radical party to strengthen the back of the grand old man. We can break down unwillingness which exists on his part to face this question [the needs of the Irish artisans and labourers] in common with many other questions'. A pan-British radical alliance could be constructed. 'Independent Opposition', even in the extremity of Parnell's last desperate effort to retain power over his party, was a highly qualified concept.

It is tempting to see Parnell as a kind of scourge of Walter Bagehot and his complacent assumptions about the 'common sort of moderation essential to the possibility of parliamentary government';[63] and then to regard Parnell's resting place in the Liberal alliance as a kind of Bagehoterian revenge. There is much truth in this, but it is not the whole truth. The British Parliament itself was poised between the world of Bagehot and an age which witnessed the 'losing of the initiative by the house of commons'.[64] It was also a Parliament whose membership was changing. New men were coming into Westminster; and the Irish party itself was representative of the transition from the predominance of landed men in the Commons to 'individuals from the various strata of the middle classes'.[65]

New men brought new styles. In 1886 Gladstone singled out what he regarded as the greatest change in the House of Commons, which was

the want of reverence. I notice with alarm the growing irreverence and not in the House alone, but throughout society. I say with *alarm*, because the decline of reverence means the decline of liberty. Reverence is a barrier, a check upon licence, but once Reverence is gone, then that licence runs riot and liberty is necessarily curtailed.[66]

Gladstone was not here referring specifically to the Irish nationalists, but to the changing character and style of the House as a whole; and, while making allowances for the natural distaste of an old man for new ways, there was substance to what he said: in 1885 the House of Commons, for the first time, was one in which the landed gentry did not predominate.[67]

The Parnell experience seemed to contribute to the decline of the Bagehot model, with the home rulers shifting Parliament away from the forum for discussion, as obstruction, heated debate and partisanship became the order of the day. But the arrival, and then postponement, of home rule in 1885–6 helped retain the place of Parliament in the constitution as a body concerned with essentially political, not social and economic, issues. As Gladstone's distinguished editor observes,[68] the continuance of home rule as the defining policy of both Liberals and Conservatives checked any advance towards the collectivist state, and the transformation of Parliament's purpose and function which, after 1918, rendered it unrecognizable to a survivor of the Victorian high age of parliamentary government. Had Parnell succeeded in his last design to construct a pan-British radical alliance with 'equal justice and equal measures . . . meted out to Ireland as well as England',[69] then the Parliament of Bagehot would have succumbed more quickly to the onslaught of collectivism.

Parnell's unexpected death halted any such possibility. But it did not affect the determination of the bulk of his party to pursue the constitutional goal of the Liberal alliance. This had the effect of lengthening the experience of the home rulers as parliamentary politicians, who never doubted, until the last (and perhaps not even then) that the British House of Commons could resolve the Irish question. It was not the least of the many paradoxes of Parnell's career that, through his placing of Irish home rule firmly on the parliamentary agenda, he should have ended up by delaying the transformation of Parliament from the assembly celebrated by Walter Bagehot to the legislative factory that it was, after 1918, to become. In a real sense, then, Parnell was one of the last great figures of the Victorian constitution, with its unshaken belief in the resolution of political conflict through parliamentary means: a belief whose limitations were finally and starkly revealed in the Ulster Crisis of 1912–14 which threatened, not only the Liberal party, but the whole British constitution. If it did nothing else, the rise and fall of Parnell preserved the *raison d'être* of the British Parliament: Bagehot made possible Parnell; and Parnell gave a significant, if in the end illusory, extension to the life of Bagehot.

NOTES

1 Walter Bagehot, *The English Constitution*, London, 1909 edn, pp. 142–3.
2 Ibid., pp. xix-xxiv.
3 J. C. Beckett, *The Making of Modern Ireland*, London, 1966, p. 381.
4 Karen B. Stroup, 'Ending the quarrel of centuries: a rhetorical analysis of the persuasion of Isaac Butt and Charles Stewart Parnell, leaders of the Irish', Ph.D., Indiana University, 1984, pp. 92–5.
5 D. G. Boyce, *Nationalism in Ireland*, London, 1982, ch. 7.
6 R. Barry O'Brien, *Life of Charles Stewart Parnell*, London, 1910 edn, p. 68.
7 Ibid., pp. 68–9.

8 David Thornley, 'The Irish home rule party and parliamentary obstruction, 1874–87', in *Irish Historical Studies*, 12, 1960–1, pp. 38–57. T. A. Jenkins (ed.), *The Parliamentary Diaries of Sir John Trelawney, 1858–1865*, London, 1990, p. 136.

9 R. B. O'Brien, *Life of Parnell*, pp. 68–72.

10 *Hansard*, 3rd series, vol. ccxxx, cols 808–10, 30 June 1876.

11 F. S. L. Lyons, *Charles Stewart Parnell*, London, 1978 edn, pp. 58–9.

12 E.g. by R. B. O'Brien, *Life of Parnell*, ch. VII.

13 *Hansard*, 3rd series, vol. ccxxxvi, cols 54–7, 27 July 1877.

14 R. B. O'Brien, *Life of Parnell*, p. 83.

15 *Nation*, 25 August 1877.

16 *Ulster Examiner*, 16 October 1879.

17 R. B. O'Brien, *Life of Parnell*, pp. 97, 145.

18 Alan O'Day, *The English Face of Irish Nationalism*, Dublin, 1977, *passim*.

19 R. B. O'Brien, *Life of Parnell*, pp. 181–2. For examples of nationalist-radical co-operation see T. W. Heyck, *The Dimensions of British Radicalism: the Case of Ireland, 1874–95*, Illinois, 1974, pp. 47, 189–90, 197. Privately, Hartington urged the Cabinet to drop the bill.

20 J. P. D. Dunbabin, 'Electoral reforms and their outcome in the United Kingdom, 1865–1900', in T. R. Gourvish and Alan O'Day (eds), *Later Victorian Britain, 1867–1900*, London, 1988, p. 124.

21 H. G. C. Matthew (ed.), *The Gladstone Diaries*, vol. IX, *January 1875-December 1880*, Oxford, 1986, pp. 598–9.

22 Ibid., p. lxxvii; J. L. Hammond, *Gladstone and the Irish Nation*, London, 1964 edn, pp. 206–8.

23 Matthew, *Gladstone Diaries*, vol IX, p. lxxviii.

24 Ibid., p. lxxviii.

25 H. G. C. Matthew (ed.), *Gladstone Diaries*, vol. X, *January 1881-June 1883*, Oxford, 1990, p. 145.

26 Hammond, *Gladstone*, pp. 246–50.

27 Matthew, *Gladstone Diaries*, vol. X, pp. 169–70.

28 Bernard Holland, *The Life of Spencer Compton, Eighth Duke of Devonshire*, 2 vols, London, 1911, vol. I, pp. 370–1.

29 Matthew, *Gladstone Diaries*, vol. X, p. 248.

30 R. B. O'Brien, *Life of Parnell*, p. 277.

31 Matthew, *Gladstone Diaries*, vol. X, pp. ci-cii; Holland, *Spencer Compton*, pp. 371–8.

32 *Hansard*, 3rd series, vol. cclxxiv, cols 721–2, 2 November 1882.

33 *Freeman's Journal*, 18 December 1883.

34 R. B. O'Brien, *Life of Parnell*, p. 314.

35 Ibid., p. 180; C. C. O'Brien, *Parnell and his Party*, Oxford, 1974, pp. 140–3.

36 Paul Smith (ed.), *Lord Salisbury on Politics*, London, 1972, pp. 346, 361, 366–7, 372.

37 H. G. C. Matthew (ed.), *Gladstone Diaries*, vol. XI, *June 1883-December 1886*, Oxford, 1990, p. 658.

38 Matthew, *Gladstone Diaries*, vol. X, p. cxxiii, and vol. XI, pp. 87, 192.

39 Matthew, *Gladstone Diaries*, vol. X, pp. cxxiv-cxxv; vol. XI, p. 337; C.

H. D. Howard, *Joseph Chamberlain: a Political Memoir, 1880–92*, London, 1953, pp. 148, 150–6; Hammond, *Gladstone*, pp. 366–71.
40 Sir Arthur Hardinge, *The Fourth Earl of Carnarvon, 1831–90*, London, 1925, pp. 78–81.
41 Alan O'Day, *Parnell and the First Home Rule Episode*, Dublin, 1986, p. 13.
42 Matthew, *Gladstone Diaries*, vol. x, p. cxxxix; vol. xi, p. 382; O'Day, *Parnell and the First Home Rule Episode* p. 114.
43 Hardinge, *Fourth Earl*, p. 181.
44 R. B. O'Brien, *Life of Parnell*, p. 314.
45 Hardinge, *Fourth Earl*, p. 210.
46 Matthew, *Gladstone Diaries*, vol. x, pp. cxxxvii-cxxxviii, cxliv-cxlv; vol. xi, p. 467; Hammond, *Gladstone*, pp. 400–2.
47 Matthew, *Gladstone Diaries*, vol. xi, p. cxliii.
48 W. C. Lubenow, *Parliamentary Politics and the Home Rule Crisis: the British House of Commons in 1886*, Oxford, 1988, p. 157.
49 *Hansard*, 3rd series, vol. cccv, col. 580, 10 May 1886; for Gladstone's earlier initiative to the Conservatives, see Robin Harcourt Williams (ed.), *The Salisbury-Balfour Correspondence, 1869–1892*, Hertfordshire, 1988, pp. 126–9.
50 *Hansard*, 3rd series, vol. cccviii, cols 383–5, 24 August 1886.
51 Lubenow, *Parliamentary Politics*, p. 158.
52 Ibid., p. 285.
53 R. B. O'Brien, *Life of Parnell*, p. 199; Lyons, *Parnell*, p. 444.
54 L. M. Geary, *The Plan of Campaign*, Cork, 1986, p. 88; R. B. O'Brien, *Life of Parnell*, p. 431.
55 Geary, *Plan of Campaign*, pp. 90–1.
56 Ibid., p. 90.
57 R. B. O'Brien, *Life of Parnell*, p. 539.
58 Thornley, 'Irish home rule party', p. 55.
59 C. C. O'Brien, *Parnell and his Party*, p. 38.
60 *The Times*, 21 July 1887: Parnell at the National Liberal Club. In April 1887 Michael Davitt described Parnell as 'practically part of the Liberal party'; C. C. O'Brien, *Parnell and his Party*, p. 227.
61 *Nation*, 12 May 1888; Matthew, *Gladstone Diaries*, vol. xi, p. 194.
62 *The Times*, 11 December 1890; speech in Dublin.
63 Bagehot, *English Constitution*, p. 163.
64 Valerie Cromwell, 'The losing of the initiative by the House of Commons, 1780–1914', *Transactions of the Royal Historical Society*, 5th series, 18, 1968, pp. 1–23.
65 C. C. O'Brien, *Parnell and his Party*, ch. 1, esp. p. 34.
66 Lubenow, *Parliamentary Politics*, p. 330.
67 Ibid., p. 333.
68 Matthew, *Gladstone Diaries*, vol. xi, p. clxi.
69 *The Times*, 11 December 1890.

6 The fall of Parnell
The political context of his intransigence

Philip Bull

I

The story of the fall of Parnell has been told and retold countless times, and its significance discussed and assessed in many contexts. In particular, F. S. L. Lyons and Conor Cruise O'Brien have, one at length[1] and one more briefly but succinctly,[2] analysed the crisis in depth. Both of them, and others who have written on these events, were in turn indebted to the earlier and very thorough investigative and analytical work done by Henry Harrison.[3] As these events recede further into the past, two conclusions emerge from this body of literature. The first of these is that Parnell's behaviour, from the moment that the majority of the Irish parliamentary party sought to reverse its decision to re-elect him as its chairman, had more to do with passions, personal pride and desperation than with the processes of rational political choice. The second conclusion is that, no matter how much Parnell's actions had been determined by these factors, his fall from power, and in particular the manner of that fall, was of immense significance in influencing the subsequent course of Irish nationalism, and especially the concepts and the strategies of the next generation of nationalists.

The main purpose of this essay is to look again at Parnell's behaviour at that time, applying to it a hypothesis which might help us to make more political sense of that behaviour and to relate it in a more coherent way to an analysis of Irish politics capable of accommodating both Parnell's own perspective at the time and the longer-term political developments which appear to give some degree of retrospective legitimization to that behaviour. The crucial period for this purpose is from his re-election as chairman on 25 November 1890 to 11 February 1891, when Dillon and O'Brien crossed from France to England and gave themselves up to the imprisonment which they had been remaining abroad to elude, thus marking the end of negotiations with Parnell. Prior to the party's action in re-electing Parnell there was little in his behaviour that defies ready explanation. It is true that in retrospect some of his close associates could not understand his imperturbability in the months preceding the divorce court verdict; they were mystified as to how he could have apparently believed that the personal revelations of the divorce court would not impinge upon his political life. His assurances to colleagues – like that given to Michael Davitt in about February 1890 that he would emerge from the divorce case 'without a stain on his name or reputation'[4] – need to be seen, however, in the light of what we now know to have been his expectation that Captain O'Shea could be bought off. To this must be added what appears to have been his naïve belief that the crucial question in the event of the case entering the public arena would be that of his 'honour' in the rather narrow sense in which he defined it, namely that Captain O'Shea had not been deceived. In other words, Parnell – caught in a web from which there could anyway be no absolute escape – could see a path forward on which he might elude too serious a consequence for his public position, and accordingly he was unlikely to sound an alarm by appearing other than confident of his capacity to ride this new storm.

The decision of his colleagues, fully cognizant as they were of the evidence and the verdict from the divorce court, to re-elect Parnell to the chairmanship must have confirmed him in that view. Their subsequent change of mind, within so short a time, had very different consequences from those which would have followed a decision not to re-elect him in the first place. For one thing, the attempt to dislodge him involved an affront to his dignity which was bound to maximize the personal resentment and passion in his reaction in a way which might not have been so strong had he simply not been re-elected. More to the point, however, the belated action of his colleagues actually changed the issue at stake. The timing of their change of heart enabled Parnell, with some considerable foundation, to see their action not as a response to his illicit relationship with Mrs O'Shea, nor even as an acknowledgement of the views of the Irish Catholic hierarchy, but as a direct consequence of the intervention of Gladstone in the question of the leadership of the Irish parliamentary party. It was on this basis that Parnell chose the ground on which he was to fight, publicly condemning both those of his followers who had turned against him at the behest of the British Liberal party and the very alliance with that party which had been one of the two most signal achievements of his own career. On both counts he appeared to his contemporaries to have lost all sense of proportion as to the political realities by which he, like his followers, was constrained.

It was this question of the Liberal alliance which now lay at the heart of Parnell's disputation with his colleagues. His manifesto against Gladstone inflamed feelings within the party, his condemnation of his colleagues was couched in terms of their preference for the Liberal alliance over their commitment to Ireland, and he embarked on a series of negotiations in France with Dillon and O'Brien which seemed largely to turn upon the exigencies of that alliance.

II

Parnell, like his colleagues, embraced the Liberal alliance with an enthusiasm never before associated with a British initiative in relation to Ireland. He did not participate as fully as some of his colleagues in the public occasions through which the 'Union of Hearts' was consummated, but for this there are explanations. His health had not been good, and more particularly the increasing complexity of his private life had caused a degree of withdrawal from the public arena, although – as Roy Foster has pointed out – his attendance in the House of Commons was much more regular than has often been claimed.[5] The strength of his public commitment to the Liberal alliance is, however, beyond question. It was his concern for possible adverse effects on the alliance which caused him to adopt a hostile attitude towards the Plan of Campaign, despite its importance to his most prominent colleagues.[6] By 1888 and 1889, as F. S. L. Lyons has demonstrated, Parnell had become increasingly fulsome in praise of the Liberals and optimistic of the achievement of home rule; speaking of Gladstone, he claimed that 'Under the genius and guidance of that great devoted Englishman, a new hope has come into our hearts and our breasts today'.[7] This strong defence by Parnell of the alliance must, however, be seen in a proper context.

It is not surprising that Irish nationalists were powerfully affected – even perhaps swept off their feet in some cases – by Gladstone's bold initiative on home rule. There has not, however, been adequate recognition of the extent to which that support masked important differences of attitude to the alliance. Some nationalists,

no doubt deeply affected by what seemed such a dramatic change
from their normal stereotype of the politics of the English, were
more absorbed than others in this new relationship, to the point
even of seeing the new alliance as an immutable characteristic of
the political world in which they were now to operate. Others, more
cautious, were drawn more subtly into the relationship through their
own political proclivities. For those like Dillon and O'Brien, deeply
immersed in the struggle against landlordism in Ireland, there was
a natural affinity of outlook with many Liberals who saw the rural
elites of England as major obstacles in the path of their own pursuit
of reform. Even more for Davitt, with his socialist commitment
and his English labour connections, a Liberal party which looked
increasingly like a potential midwife for the birth of labour politically was a not entirely unattractive parliamentary context within
which to work. For others less sophisticated politically, and necessarily resident in London because of their parliamentary duties, the
alliance provided an opening for social and political associations
which was both welcome and seductive. Yet others, as Alan O'Day
has pointed out,[8] were already resident in England prior to their
election, and so the Liberal alliance helped to consolidate their
normal social and political habitat. Together these factors added
up to a situation in which the independence and autonomy of the
nationalist party was potentially at risk. As a recent writer has
suggested, one should see the home rule issue in 1886 not as
revolutionizing the British party system, but as being revolutionized
by it; this the party system did to home rule 'by domesticating it,
by making it a creature of parliamentary politics, and by so containing it for thirty years'.[9] That was partly an unavoidable consequence
of the alliance; it was also partly an aspect of the wider purposes
of the British Liberals, who were not immune to a belief in the
civilizing mission of the Englishman and for whom the alliance
represented a special opportunity to tame the beast of Irish politics.

In the case of Parnell these factors had minimal effect. While he
was committed absolutely to the Liberal alliance, he saw it as a
major advance in the achievement of home rule – and entirely
conditional on it. Moreover, few of the enticements which drew
many of his colleagues closer to the Liberals were relevant in his
case. In social terms he had no need of the Liberal context, nor
was he drawn, as many of his colleagues were, to the particular
political culture of his allies. Most importantly, his relative detachment from the individual elements of the Irish political coalition on
which his power was based enabled him to stand above the current

situation and take a longer view than his colleagues appear to have been taking. Indeed, one of the attributes of his particular form of leadership was that he provided little opportunity for even the most able of his party members to share his mind on strategic questions, either immediate or longer term. Even less did he expose his views on the future to public sight. It is therefore difficult to delineate the lines of his thinking. Fortunately there is one very significant public insight he allows which indicates that his commitment to the Liberal alliance was accompanied by a realistic view of its limits.

In February 1888 Parnell had maintained that Ireland 'was ripe for self-government' because, whereas for every person favouring parliamentary action when he entered public life there were nine or ten who looked to violence, by 1888 these proportions had been completely reversed'.[10] While allowing for some arithmetical exaggeration, it is clear that this represented welcome news to the Liberal audience which, as Lyons shows, Parnell was at this time seeking to placate;[11] for them it was evidence that the wild beast had indeed been tamed. But it is also perfectly compatible with a view that such proportions were capable of reversal, something for which Parnell had always to be prepared. The remark – made when speaking of his amendment to the address in the House of Commons – was a caution as well as a tribute. It was to another audience, and in a context where anger rather than gratification was intended, that he makes much more explicit his continuing recognition of the ambiance within which that parliamentary action must be set. On 23 May 1889 Parnell received from the representatives of the nationalist municipal bodies of Ireland an address of congratulation on his vindication before the Special Commission over the Pigott forgeries. On that occasion, he gave a speech which deserves careful consideration for what it tells us about Parnell's continuing perception of the role of Irish MPs at Westminster. It is a speech which attracted the attention of Conor Cruise O'Brien in his *Parnell and his Party*, and it is to his treatment of it that I wish first to turn.

Dr O'Brien refers to this speech, together with one made later in Edinburgh, as an illustration of Parnell's new confidence in home rule, the achievement of which would end all justification for rebellion (for the ears of his Edinburgh listeners); the denial of which would justify withdrawal from parliamentary action (for his Irish audience). Dr O'Brien then quotes from the speech the essence of Parnell's point about withdrawal from Westminster:[12]

If our constitutional movement were to fail, if it became evident
that we could not, by parliamentary action and continued representation at Westminster restore to Ireland the high privilege
of self-government . . . I for one would not continue to remain
for 24 hours longer in the House of Commons at
Westminster. . . . The most advanced section of Irishmen as well
as the least advanced have always [thoroughly][13] understood that
the parliamentary policy was to be a trial and that we did not
ourselves believe in the possibility of maintaining for all time,
[or for any lengthened period,][14] an incorruptible [incorrupt][15]
and independent Irish representation at Westminster.

Dr O'Brien makes his substantive analysis of this passage in a
footnote, in which he correctly asserts that it is 'remarkably unlike
any other of Parnell's utterances of this period' and then – whether
or not partly by answer to this earlier point is not clear – that 'it
was also the only important political speech he addressed to an
Irish audience' in this period. The analysis of the speech is thereafter based on what Dr O'Brien calls a 'tempting conjecture',
namely that Parnell was being influenced by an expectation that
divorce proceedings would go ahead, and he concludes

that the parts of this speech which concerned the Irish representation at Westminster reflected not so much anxiety about the
'corruption' of the Irish representatives by the liberals, as anxiety
about the effect of the divorce on Parnell's own leadership. He
was preparing a possible line of counter-attack in advance.[16]

This is weak as conjecture, and indeed it is far-fetched to suppose
that the prospect of divorce proceedings could, as early as this,
have had such a major impact on Parnell's thinking and in a form
which so closely fitted the details of the actual unfolding of the
divorce crisis. In seeing in Parnell's actions so early an intimation
of a later event, Dr O'Brien has allowed himself to be over-influ-
enced by his own retrospective view. It also stretches the credulity
of the reader to suppose that Parnell shaped one of his most important speeches of these years around the prospect of a divorce case
about which he managed to display so little concern when it was
actually upon him. More importantly, this treatment of so major a
speech deflects attention away from an analysis based on its actual
context and from an attempt to discern what it can tell us about
Parnell's views.

First of all, we must recognize what it was that Parnell intended by this speech, and to do so we must see it as a reflection of a milieu of nationalist thought dating back at least to Young Ireland in the 1840s. Nowhere is Dr O'Brien's retrospective bias more evident than in his supposition that Parnell intended to imply no more than that the Liberals were to be the agents of the 'corruption' he predicted. Parnell's party had been constructed on a premise that it was to go to Westminster in order to get out of Westminster, and this was a purpose clearly at variance with the ethos of that institution and of the other parties inhabiting it. It was an object which would not over a long period of time be sustainable, for Irish representatives were bound to be drawn increasingly into the culture and purposes of the host institution. In a section of the speech which Dr O'Brien has omitted from the middle of the passage he quotes, Parnell makes clear that it would be no mere personal preference to discontinue attendance at Westminster, but that 'the Irish constituencies would not consent to allow us to remain, and that has been the view which our countrymen at home and abroad have always taken of our action'. Parnell then continued:

> They don't believe that we came here as mere parliamentarians to humbug and cheat the just expectations of our people at home. They know we came here to obtain this definite and one object, and if by the way we tried to obtain other concessions it was because we were anxious to do good to the humbler classes of our countrymen as we went along.[17]

This is indeed an accurate interpretation of the publicly declared basis of Parnell's movement, but it also indicates a perception of the dangers inherent in parliamentary action which is much broader than a fear of 'corruption' by the Liberals. Parnell was aware – and his whole career points to this awareness – of the dimension pointed out by W. C. Lubenow, namely that the British political system had the capacity to 'domesticate' the Irish issue,[18] and the Liberal alliance was an important, although not the only, facilitator of that process. Important as that alliance was to the pursuit of home rule, no nationalist movement could survive in Ireland in the longer term if it were to become dependent upon it.

It was natural enough that Parnell should make such a point at this time to an Irish audience; it would have been neither appropriate nor particularly intelligible to an English one. It did not qualify, nor contradict, Parnell's commitment to the alliance. It helped, for those for whom it mattered, to set the limits within which that

alliance could operate effectively. The speech was delivered, moreover, at a time and to an audience appropriate for the expression
of anger, and it was this aspect – entirely ignored by Dr O'Brien
– which drew the major editorial comment at the time in the
Freeman's Journal. Parnell was being congratulated on his vindication over the forged letters, but he wished to make a point about
the way Ireland had been treated by the process of the Special
Commission. Expressing his anger that three English judges, knowing nothing of Ireland, should have presumed in effect to have put
a whole people on trial, Parnell confessed:

> I should have preferred to have gone to my grave with the stigma
> of the letters upon me – cowardly, mean, and contemptible as
> these letters were – rather than submit my country and my
> countrymen to the humiliating ordeal that was forced upon us as
> the accompaniment of the inquiry into the authenticity of these
> letters.[19]

It was, to a large extent, the Liberal alliance which had made
Ireland vulnerable to this humiliation; the politically motivated
Special Commission had been as much a Tory exercise in discredit-
ing their Liberal opponents as an exercise in besmirching Irish
nationalism with criminal associations. It was an appropriate
moment to remind the Irish people that Parnellite participation at
Westminster could not be taken for granted if the premise on which
it had been founded no longer applied. In the sentence which
directly links his comments on the Special Commission to his speculation about the effect of the constitutional movement failing, Parnell said, 'We are told that it was our intention in this agitation of
ours to subvert the authority of the Crown, and to organize an
armed rebellion.'[20] So monumental a misconception is this that it
is hardly surprising that Parnell should restate the central principles
of his movement.[21]

This speech is a major indicator of the underlying continuities in
Parnell's perception of his movement. Its theme is not one that he
could have been expected to assert very commonly during a period
in which commitment to the alliance, rather than definition of its
limitations, was the immediate need. The very significance which
he himself gave to these remarks, by the occasion he chose and by
the connection he drew with the Special Commission, shows that
they were intended as a serious comment on the continuing nature
of the Irish nationalist situation. It is equally important with all
those speeches in praise of British Liberalism and of the alliance

in setting a proper context for his reactions to the major crisis which was about to destroy his political career.

III

Many bridges had been burnt in the party debates in Committee Room 15 between 1 and 6 December 1890, and in the events which followed. Notwithstanding this, a genuine attempt was to be made to negotiate a compromise, commencing with William O'Brien's arrival in France by ship from America on Christmas Day 1890, and continuing with the arrival of John Dillon from America for the second phase of negotiations on 18 January. These negotiations were to prove futile, but they are important for an understanding of the influences shaping Parnell's actions in these critical months.[22]

O'Brien and Dillon were crucially placed to conduct these negotiations, and indeed it is hard to imagine any other member of the party with the status and outlook to do so. They, particularly O'Brien, were amongst those members whom Parnell held in most respect. They had been part of a group of six nationalist MPs on a fundraising tour in America when the crisis arose, and had therefore been able to remain aloof from the partisanship of Committee Room 15 and subsequent events. Moreover, they were unable to return to the British Isles, where warrants existed for their arrest to serve prison sentences, and so they had the best of all reasons for remaining detached from the internecine strife occurring in Ireland. Another reason they were well placed to conduct negotiations with Parnell was that they had a distinct political purpose in doing so over and above the need to reconcile Parnell to his withdrawal from the leadership. The opposition to Parnell had unleashed elements in Irish politics extremely distasteful to them. Whereas they had both taken the view that Parnell's continued leadership was impossible, particularly after his manifesto against Gladstone, they were fiercely opposed to the way in which the moral question of his relationship with Mrs O'Shea, as distinct from the political issue, was being used to revive clericalist and sectarian elements in Irish politics. In seeking to rescue Parnell, not as leader but in terms of his continuing role in Irish politics, they were quite deliberately seeking to undermine those elements, and to create between the currently polarized forces of Parnellism and anti-Parnellism a middle ground as a basis for the continuation of the secular political structures characteristic of their movement hitherto.

In this they were eventually successful, although not in their immediate aim of inducing Parnell to accept a compromise which would avert the disintegration of their party.

It was this wider political purpose which made it possible for them to offer Parnell terms as generous as they did.[23] The question, then, is why Parnell refused to accept them. F. S. L. Lyons has addressed the problems involved in answering that question, and he arrives at a number of views, the most significant of which is that any answer must be a highly speculative one. He refers to the widely held suspicion at the time that Parnell had no intention of withdrawing from the leadership, and that he kept negotiating only as part of a 'grand strategy' to divide his Irish opponents and 'to drive a wedge between them and the liberal party'. Apparently dissatisfied himself with these more devious motives as explanations of Parnell's behaviour, Lyons draws attention to the conviction of many of those close to Parnell that he genuinely wanted a settlement and to what must have been the innate attraction of terms so generous.[24] Inconclusive in this analysis, Lyons in another place turns back to mood and mischief as his principal explanations.[25] Nowhere, however, does Lyons – nor for that matter any other analyst – turn to the possibility that Parnell's political judgement, rather than the general and emotional attitudes to which his action is usually attributed, might better explain his intransigence. It is the purpose of this chapter to posit such an explanation.

Even though Parnell was fighting for his political survival, even though he may have felt considerable contempt for the followers who presumed to dislodge him, and even though his judgement might well have been impaired by emotional distress, the fact remains that he had a choice to make, and essentially a simple choice: whether to secure certain and substantial political advantages, including an assured role for himself politically, by shifting to the wings of the stage, perhaps only temporarily, or whether to make the dramatic gesture of fighting for his status and leadership at the risk of losing everything. In choosing the latter course, he was giving his own answer to the argument most pressed upon him by his colleagues in support of compromise, that by so doing he would save the Liberal alliance and home rule. In rejecting that argument, he might well have come to two views about it: first, that there was little chance anyway that the Liberal alliance would secure home rule; and second, that by the time that failure had become evident, the divorce case would have receded into the past, and the need of the hour would be met more by a Parnell who had taken the fighting course than by one who had compromised. The development that invalidated such a calculation he could not foresee, his own death within a year.

A framework for such a supposition is clearly present in the terms of Parnell's speech of May 1889. He can hardly have thought that the achievement of home rule was a foregone conclusion. The most that Gladstone had the power to promise was the passage of a Home Rule Bill through the House of Commons. It needed no special wisdom to see that such a Bill had no chance of passing the House of Lords, no matter what the electoral support. Nor would a wise observer have placed any great odds on the problem being resolved by a second election, specifically on home rule, and a consequent constitutional crisis, with or without the involvement of the Crown, even supposing the Liberals were to take their commitment as far as that, which in the event they did not. Moreover, these speculations on what Parnell might have foreseen as the prospect for home rule through the Liberal alliance are in no way inconsistent with what actually happened after his death. In the end the failure to translate a successful House of Commons Bill into legislation must be attributed to an ultimate unwillingness of the Liberal party to commit its whole political future to that single issue, as well as to a fundamental structural obstacle, in the form principally of the House of Lords, to the achievement by purely parliamentary means of Irish self-government. All of that was foreseeable, and if the likelihood of Liberal failure was high in Parnell's consciousness, he would have viewed arguments based on the need to save the Liberal alliance and home rule in a context very different from the one in which they were constructed. The constant reiteration of these arguments by his colleagues might well have weakened, rather than strengthened, their appeal for his withdrawal.

If such a supposition is correct, then it has significant implications for how Parnell would have seen his own longer term political interests. While the pattern of his career indicates that he felt threatened by extra-parliamentary activity which was directed towards social rather than political objectives, there is no doubt of his constant awareness of the significance of what he called the 'more advanced nationalists'. This is not to suggest that he ever entertained any notion of revolution or violence. His commitment to constitutionalism was absolute, but that did not necessarily entail an equally absolute commitment to attendance at Westminster.

The concept of withdrawal from Westminster was not new to Irish nationalist thinking, nor even to Parnell's own calculations, and a later organization of nationalists, essentially non-violent and constitutionalist in its methods, was to make a dogma of it. Given the clear message of his May 1889 speech, it is more credible that Parnell saw that possibility than that he did not. Faced with the choice offered him in the negotiations in France it might well have seemed a better political choice that, compromised as he now clearly was in guiding the process of testing the Liberal will and capacity to deliver home rule, he should make the most of the situation by holding himself aloof so as to be more acceptable to those who might help build a different kind of constitutional movement in the event of Liberal failure. Parnell might then be in a position to draw on new concepts of political action, just as he had done in the late 1870s with parliamentary obstruction and the New Departure.

A further major factor which could well have influenced Parnell's choice was a perception that the intervention of Gladstone in the affairs of the Irish party, and the subsequent dispute over the relationship of the two parties, had irreparably destroyed the Irish party's capacity to remain adequately autonomous, and that in these circumstances the party as it was presently constituted would not survive as a politically effective force beyond a Liberal failure to effect home rule. In this event, to have turned himself into a discredited 'back-room boy' would have contributed little to the advance of nationalism. On the other hand, provided that he could in the short term hold his ground in Ireland, limited as that ground was, he might help to give space for his colleagues to take home rule as far as it was capable of being taken on the present assumptions while keeping himself freer than they to re-establish a new basis of autonomy for a new phase of nationalism, taking up the reins which then fell from their hands. His moral lapse by then would be more remote in the public consciousness and his criticisms of the Liberals, at least in so far as they related to that party's inability to deliver home rule, vindicated by events. Again, the course that his colleagues followed – and in this his Parnellite colleagues proved little different from his anti-Parnellite ones – found them by 1895 at the end of a road with no apparent direction forward. It was to be left to others to attempt to find new directions, but they had not the benefit of Parnell's involvement, nor had they any basis of continuity with the structures and experience which were the principal legacy of Parnell's leadership in the 1880s.

The divorce crisis created for Parnell a major dilemma. Having failed to ride the storm, the choices he faced were uncomfortable ones, and he did not find them easy to make. But in the last analysis, his instinctive shift to the apparently more intransigent position was based on political judgements, not only as to his own personal future, but as to what he saw, in the now fundamentally changed circumstances which he himself had done so much to create, as the path most likely to allow for political advance of the nationalist movement. The wisdom of his choice is beyond test, for the grave closed off all possibility that his judgement in this might be weighed.

IV

By the time of the negotiations in France, at which Parnell's apparent intransigence frustrated any rapprochement between the warring factions, the coalition of broad nationalist elements built up in the 1870s had already been effectively dissolved. Precipitate actions – by the parliamentary party, by Gladstone and by Parnell himself – had all contributed to a situation which was now irreversible, even had Parnell been willing to withdraw his claim to the leadership. As Conor Cruise O'Brien – whose view is that Parnell's decision to cling to the leadership was indefensible – acknowledges, the party had by its action in acceding to Gladstone's bidding 'forfeited the substance of its power and independence'.[26] Already Parnell's own sights were set beyond the immediate crisis and upon the conditions in which such a coalition, essential to nationalist success, might again be constructed.

Parnell had been prepared for a contingency such as had now occurred, albeit not one so centred on his own personal position. Recognizing the possibility – perhaps the probability – that even though Gladstone might honour his commitment to seeing a home rule Bill through the House of Commons the Liberal alliance would not succeed in achieving home rule, he had already foreseen the eventual need for a significant change of direction as a response to such a failure. The pressure generated by the Special Commission had led him to reflect publicly on that need in May 1889. In the event of such a failure the Irish parliamentary party would need to recover its independence of action to enable it once again to exploit all means of applying pressure within the British political system. A concept long inherent in Irish nationalist thinking, and one which had been again debated during Parnell's time,[27] was that of withdrawal of Irish MPs from Westminster as a tactical manoeuvre and their convening in some form or other as an alternative assembly in Ireland. Deriving its origins in part from O'Connell's abandoned concept of a Council of Three Hundred and given more circulation by Gavan Duffy and the Young Irelanders, the idea emerged naturally enough from the strong sense in nineteenth-century Ireland that the Act of Union lacked legitimacy, both legal and moral, and that this necessarily qualified Irish involvement at Westminster. The idea had been strengthened by a pattern of experience in which Irish representatives at Westminster had invariably become more and more absorbed in the momentum and ethos of that institution to the detriment of the pursuit of policies directed to the recovery of greater Irish autonomy. This was a history of which Parnell was well aware; it was reinforced by his own political instincts as to how an Irish nationalist movement needed to relate to British politics and British institutions. Once the crisis of his own leadership had arisen, it was this context which became most relevant for understanding his reactions.

The crisis over his leadership was not one in which withdrawal from Westminster was possible or appropriate, and he did not argue for it. But it was one in which the question of over-absorption of the Irish party into the British political framework was highly relevant. Parnell's articulation of that dimension might seem – and almost unavoidably so – to be disingenuous and self-serving, but given his underlying view of the nature of the relationship of the two countries, appeals from his colleagues to abase himself to save the Liberal alliance and enable home rule to go through could have nothing other than a passing attraction. Tempted though he might have been by terms offered to him, in the final analysis the premise on which they were based was one he could not share. The crisis over his leadership had caught him, in terms of his political strategy, on the wrong foot. Instead of being seen to be reactions to the failure of the Liberal party, his behaviour looked more like actions defensive of his own personal position. However, given an assumption that he had already serious doubts as to the likelihood of success through the existing arrangement with the Liberal party, it is perfectly explicable that he should not have acceded to the pressure for compromise.

In fact, there was a significant political reason for him not to compromise. Given that so much had already been destroyed, there was in his own *persona* something worth preserving as a basis of continuity between the past and the future. If he allowed himself to remain outside the framework of the majority party, while not actively hindering its pursuit of whatever might be wrung from the Liberals when they returned to office, he would retain a potential to develop another 'new departure' when the need arose; he could become a focus of 'oppositional' politics in an environment in which 'official' politics was caught in a cul-de-sac. He carried into this task a significant strength. In making the claim in Committee Room 15 – preposterous as that claim was by the normal standards of democratic conduct – that he stood above the party, that he owed his leadership not to the members who elected him but to the Irish people, he had some weight on his side. His success, and that of his party, had to some extent depended upon the willingness of elements of Irish nationalism to accept his leadership over and above any question of commitment to a parliamentary party as such. In this sense he personally – and no one else – had the capacity to provide a crucial link between the successes of the 1870s and the 1880s and any future new expression of nationalist purpose. This hope was necessarily null and void once he was dead, and his followers in the small Parnellite party then subordinated themselves as much as did the majority party to the exigencies of Westminster politics. Had he lived, the potential for him to focus the imagination and energies of those with a renewed commitment to a broad and innovative nationalist strategy would have been very considerable, and it was on this potential that he was prepared to gamble everything.

Judgements about Parnell's actions in the last year of his life have generally been clouded by two misconceptions, one that his decisions were made with very little reference to rational political considerations, the other that he was preoccupied with the immediate preservation of his own personal dominance. It is possible to see in Parnell's somewhat reluctant recourse to the non-compromising position in the negotiations in France a recognition, confused as it was by the highly charged emotional circumstances, of what was politically sensible for him in these tumultuous events and also of the longer term context within which the decisions being made would have to be accommodated. Although evidence is sparse in terms of any record of Parnell's thinking, better sense can be made of his behaviour by allowing for the possibility that his actions were informed by the shrewd judgement of Irish politics which had characterized his earlier achievements. Bombastic the circumstances may have made his response, but correctness of judgement was not thereby necessarily absent.

Parnell the man did not survive to play a part in working out the next phase of Irish nationalism; Parnell the symbol did. It is generally assumed that the impact of the memory of Parnell related not to the soundness of his political judgement in his final months, but to the romantic and heroic image cast by his bitter struggle and tragic death; that he had, as Conor Cruise O'Brien contends, 'deviated from politics into literature'.[28] The two pictures, the political and the romantic, can be integrated, however. His actions were constructed out of a particular perception of the political context, which is what gave the memory of those actions such potency in the reshaping of the next phase of nationalist politics. Appalling as the implications of his final decisions were to him personally, in the mortification of his severe electoral defeats and in his death, he was not so much a victim as a moulder of destinies.

There is a postscript to this analysis of Parnell in the way in which the interpretation of the political situation here attributed to him can be seen working itself out in the attempt of one of his closest colleagues to relocate himself politically in the changed environment created by Parnell's fall and the split in the nationalist movement. As has been seen, William O'Brien and John Dillon did not have to take an immediate stand on these issues, as did their colleagues, first because of their role in conducting negotiations with Parnell, and then by their incarceration in Galway jail. It was not until July 1891, with their release from prison, that they had publicly to place themselves politically. Their time in prison had enabled them to discuss, by notes secretly passed between them, the situation they would face on their release. This correspondence has survived, and the discussion between them has been recounted and analysed elsewhere.[29] Initially, and on the basis of a suggestion from Dillon, they discussed holding aloof from either party, thus – as O'Brien later put it – preserving themselves as a 'dispassionate tribunal' 'to whose good offices the best men on both sides, weary of the savage conflict, might some day have recourse'.[30] However, as the rout of Parnell at by-elections became sufficiently clear, Dillon shifted to a conviction that they should join the anti-Parnellite majority, given that Parnell obviously enjoyed the support of only a small proportion of the voters. O'Brien, on the other hand, continued to argue against that proposition, taking the longer view that

> these results in no way changed the fact that enormous masses of the electors' sons, as well as of the staunchest militant

Nationalists of the old wars, stood as firmly as ever behind Parnell – indeed, all the more firmly and bitterly for these defeats.[31]

In the end, both Dillon and O'Brien joined the anti-Parnellite party, but it is important to note that O'Brien had not done so as a result of any change of judgement on his part; he had, he claimed, 'with many misgivings', subordinated his judgement to Dillon's to avoid a split between them. He did not, however, remain very long as a parliamentary member of the majority party. Having thrown himself into the negotiations with Gladstone and his colleagues after their return to office, he chose an early opportunity – using the excuse of a politically motivated bankruptcy suit against him – to resign from Parliament. He then began, from his new home in the west of Ireland, to lay the basis for the United Irish League organization which he was to launch in January 1898. Through the experience of that organization he found that the parliamentary party was no longer capable of responding to political innovation in Ireland, let alone leading it, and the basis was laid for the delayed – but probably inevitable – alienation of O'Brien from Dillon and from the existing parliamentary party.

In this tale we can see the working out of what is suggested here to have been Parnell's own strategy, but in circumstances much less opportune than if he himself had been its guiding influence. Effective as in many ways he was, O'Brien failed to take the parliamentary party on the more radical path which he believed was required in the aftermath of the Liberal retreat from home rule, nor did he succeed in attracting to his new league and to its strategy the emerging nationalist group soon to become Sinn Fein. It was that group which was to develop new policies and strategies for a constitutional nationalist movement, but it did so in isolation from any structural continuity with the foundations which had been laid by Parnell. O'Brien, imbued as he was in the land dimension of the national question, was not well placed to nurture such links. Parnell would have been. These younger nationalists were, in any case, devotees of his memory.

In a summary of why Parnell rejected the compromise terms offered him in France, Professor Lyons has focused on mood as a major determinant of his decisions and on an instinctive tactical joy 'at the opportunity to sow discord among his enemies'.[32] It is argued here that the instinctive element in his actions was much more politically sophisticated than that. He saw a means of preserving an element of continuity through the course of the disaster in which he was now embroiled, and it was that which ultimately determined the choices he made. His actions may not have been palatable or defensible in terms of the normal codes of political behaviour, but neither were they lacking in the political judgement, nor in the understanding of the dynamic of Irish nationalism, which had made him so effective a leader of a movement which had always needed a dimension which went beyond such codes. To have taken the supposedly more rational course of compromise might have saved his life, but it would also have very likely destroyed any potential for future effectiveness in the only terms in which Parnell measured success.

NOTES

1 F. S. L. Lyons, *The Fall of Parnell, 1890–91*, London, 1960; also *Charles Stewart Parnell*, London, 1977, chs. 15–20.
2 Conor Cruise O'Brien, *Parnell and his Party, 1880–90*, Oxford, 1957, ch. IX.
3 Henry Harrison, *Parnell Vindicated: the Lifting of the Veil*, London, 1931.
4 Lyons, *Charles Stewart Parnell*, p. 463.
5 R. F. Foster, *Charles Stewart Parnell: the Man and his Family*, Hassocks, Sussex, 1976, p. 150.
6 O'Brien, *Parnell and his Party*, p. 205.
7 Lyons, *Charles Stewart Parnell*, p. 426.
8 Alan O'Day, *The English Face of Irish Nationalism: Parnellite Involvement in British Politics, 1880–86*, Dublin, 1977, pp. 23–5.
9 W. C. Lubenow, *Parliamentary Politics and the Home Rule Crisis: the British House of Commons in 1886*, Oxford, 1988, p. 285.
10 Lyons, *Charles Stewart Parnell*, p. 382.
11 Ibid.
12 O'Brien, *Parnell and his Party*, pp. 233–4.
13 Word inadvertently omitted by Dr O'Brien.
14 Words inadvertently omitted by Dr O'Brien.
15 The word in the original which Dr O'Brien has misquoted here.
16 O'Brien, *Parnell and his Party*, p. 234, fn. 1.
17 *Freeman's Journal*, 24 May 1889.
18 Lubenow, *Parliamentary Politics*, p. 285.
19 *Freeman's Journal*, 24 May 1889.
20 Ibid.
21 F. S. L. Lyons also deals with this speech in some detail, and rejects O'Brien's 'tempting conjecture' on grounds similar to those above. Lyons attributes the sentiments expressed in the speech to two factors. One is essentially the reason given by *The Times*, that 'A great deal of what Mr. Parnell says seems to be intended to satisfy persons who are likely to be discontented at certain recent statements of his in a different strain' (quoted in *Freeman's Journal*, 24 May 1889), but put more kindly

by Lyons as his tactic of 'balancing'. The second reason is that 'he said what he did because he believed it', which is essentially the view given above, but with Lyons building less upon it (Lyons, *Charles Stewart Parnell*, pp. 444–5).

22 This discussion follows closely, and relies heavily upon, Lyons, *Fall of Parnell*, pp. 193–250.
23 Lyons, *Fall of Parnell*, pp. 246–50.
24 Ibid., pp. 245–6.
25 Lyons, *Charles Stewart Parnell*, p. 575.
26 O'Brien, *Parnell and his Party*, p. 348.
27 See especially Lyons, *Charles Stewart Parnell*, pp. 146–9.
28 O'Brien, *Parnell and his Party*, p. 356.
29 Lyons, *Fall of Parnell*, pp. 281–9; Lyons, *John Dillon: a Biography*, London, 1968, pp. 136–40; William O'Brien, *An Olive Branch in Ireland and its History*, London, 1910, pp. 54–7; P. J. Bull, 'The reconstruction of the Irish parliamentary movement, 1895–1903: an analysis with special reference to William O'Brien', unpublished Ph.D. thesis, Cambridge, 1972, pp. 52–9.
30 William O'Brien, *Olive Branch*, p. 54.
31 Ibid., pp. 55–6.
32 Lyons, *Charles Stewart Parnell*, p. 575.

Part II
Ideas and images

7 The political thought of Charles Stewart Parnell

Tony Claydon

I

Trying to discover the true political ideals of Parnell can resemble a parlour game. When faced with a man who espoused so many varied solutions to the Irish question, and who appealed at different times to Gladstone, Fenians, tenant-farmers, the Roman Catholic hierarchy and the English working class, historians might feel tempted to ask the 'real' Charles Stewart Parnell to stand up. The politician left few clues to resolve his biographers' dilemmas. He was not given to introspection. He wrote no books, kept no diary, engaged in little enlightening correspondence. All that survives are his speeches, altering considerably in tone and content, according to their audience and the course of events. So slippery was Parnell that some commentators have doubted whether he had any under-lying political principles. F. S. L. Lyons has argued that Parnell's great achievement was not in ideas, but in methodology. His central idea was simply to balance moral and physical force.[1] Oliver Mac-Donagh has presented the home rule agitation as devoid of precise political theory. Parnell had no propositions or specific requests, but was merely attempting to mobilize the Irish into a pressure group 'under cover of a seeming political demand'.[2] This chapter attempts to cut through this confusion by a close study of Parnell's speeches. It asserts that his rhetoric, despite its ambiguities, was always generated from certain traditions of political theory. These traditions could account for all the variety of his oratory and provide a consistency beneath his tactical shifts. There was a 'real' Parnell beneath the contradictions.

II

It seems probable that we can learn something about Parnell's fundamental beliefs from his earliest political behaviour. In 1874 and 1875 Parnell began his public career with a series of election campaigns, first speaking for his brother, John, who stood unsuccessfully for the parliamentary seat of County Wicklow, and then supporting his own candidatures for Dublin and Meath. In all these campaigns the greatest emphasis was laid on the patriotic record of the Parnell family.[3] The young orator's ancestors had been active in public affairs for over a century before 1875, and had left a testimony of opposition to English rule in Ireland. Sir John Parnell, Charles's great-grandfather, and a leader of the pre–1800 Irish administration, had spoken against the Union in the old Irish House of Commons, whilst his son, William, had attacked the new Imperial Parliament in a series of pamphlets and novels. What is crucial for understanding Charles Stewart's position is the exact nature of the nationalism his family bequeathed.

It was based firmly on parliamentary liberalism. The ancestral Parnells held that no government could be legitimate if denied the basic ideal of liberal representative theory – a legislative assembly, dependent on and responsive to the people, which embodied the principle of government by consent. William once stated that there was no substitute for a 'pure representation chosen by the people'[4] whilst Sir John, in the debates over Union in 1800, appealed for a dissolution of Parliament so the people 'could speak their sentiments by the representatives they would choose'.[5] The Parnells' nationalism grew out of this parliamentarianism. They demanded to be ruled from Dublin because they believed the liberal ideal could only be realized if parliaments were close enough to the governed to be swayed by public opinion. Government by consent could only be delivered by local assemblies. The family contended there was a special genius in small legislative units, since in these 'The distance between the governors and governed is lessened, public opinion has more force . . . [and] dependence of the government on the people is evident and acknowledged'.[6] Thus William argued his 'pure representation' had to be 'resident in Ireland', because if it was not, the MPs, 'at a distance from their friends and acquaintances', would 'receive no check from public opinion'.[7] On these, clan, principles Westminster could not govern Ireland legitimately. It sat in a distant country and tried to govern too large an area ever to give proper consideration to Irish affairs and aspirations. The Irish MPs in London, removed from their constituents, and swamped by the English, were not effective representatives. Westminster would never listen to its remote province, and could lay no claim to govern her by consent. 'The English ministry have no sort of knowledge of affairs in Ireland,' William lamented. 'It is a dispiriting task to endeavour to interest English ministers, and English parliament in the welfare of Ireland.'[8] According to Sir John, the Irish, denied their own local assembly, were 'entirely at the mercy of the United Parliament'.[9]

There were other problems besides the theoretical illegitimacy of the Imperial Parliament. The Parnells also objected to the effects of English rule on the Irish character and on an Irishman's independence. Here the family were borrowing from an English tradition of 'Country' principles. These were a set of arguments which had been adopted by eighteenth-century oppositions at Westminster, and had centred on government corruption and oppression. J. G. A. Pocock has made an impressive attempt to analyze 'Country' principles with reference to Florentine political thought, and it is sometimes useful to use his term 'civic humanism' when discussing the ideology. Basically, however, the 'Country' position rested on the perverting effects of centralized power.[10] 'Country' politicians insisted that liberty and virtue were only possible whilst citizens and their representatives remained independent of central government. An overbearing government impinged upon the autonomy of the individual, and without this autonomy the moral qualities which fostered freedom declined. Civic humanists argued that a powerful state forced its citizenry into submission. It used military force and, more invidiously, the corrupting potential of office, to undermine men's independence. Citizens lost their self-reliance, and with that went self-respect and public spirit. Men sank into slothful dependence on their rulers and the nation declined into slavery and political degradation. The Parnells adapted these ideas to the Irish situation. They suggested that since the English could not govern Ireland with justice at such a distance, they were tempted to use force and corruption to hold the country. A powerful state was the substitute for legitimate rule. Sir John Parnell had hinted at the process when claiming the Union had only proceeded when an Irishman's right to assemble had been 'bourn down by cannon' and after a borough-buying campaign 'most calculated to degrade parliament'.[11] William, after 1800, saw his country garrisoned by a landlord class 'who held it lawful to shoot a mere Irishman',[12] and described Irish MPs bribed by the court party in Westminster.

William's novel, *Maurice and Berghetta*,[13] illustrated the doleful effects of 'English influence and government'.[14] Over the years the Irish population had lost its virtue with its independence. It had been bribed and brutalized, and the degraded Irish character, recalcitrant and incapable of exercising liberty, had been formed by bad English laws. The 'Country' picture of moral decay, stemming from force and corruption, had joined the image of a local parliament in the Parnell family gallery.

The Parnells' position can be neatly characterized by comparing it to the rhetoric of those who had tried to restructure the English Atlantic empire in the 1770s and 1780s. The Founding Fathers of America and the Irish Patriots of 1782 had both used a mixture of parliamentary liberalism and 'Country' ideals to press for a devolution of power from London. When men like Washington and Jefferson had agitated for an end to English interference in American affairs, they had argued, first, that Westminster did not represent them, and second, that the English stationed large forces on their continent and attempted to bribe Americans with office.[15] Grattan and Flood, the Irish leaders, borrowed many of these points in pressing for legislative independence.[16] Both groups suggested models of devolution in which local assemblies, close to and responsive to the people, exercised most power. What might be called 'Atlantic principles' underlay both Irish and American movements. These late eighteenth-century traditions influenced the Parnells. Where the family library contains works dealing with history or politics, it is remarkable how many of them (such as the works of Edmund Burke and Thomas Jefferson, or the life of Washington) deal with the 1770s crisis in the English empire.[17] Sir John and William were inspired to ask for the restoration of Grattan's parliament – the great achievement of 1782 – and their rhetoric echoed that of the American Patriots. Their nationalism, based on liberalism and civic humanism, was an extension of 'Atlantic principles' into the nineteenth century.

Charles Stewart Parnell was a child of his ancestors. Parliamentary liberalism and 'Country' ideals ran as parallel tracks through his oratory. He was determined to break up the distant mass of Westminster to provide a parliament in Dublin. He was determined because he believed only a Dublin parliament would be close enough, and responsive enough, to the people, to govern by consent, and because he believed only a Dublin parliament could dispense with degrading force and corruption. An analysis of his rhetoric through his career reveals that, although he allied with people from many different traditions of Irish nationalism, he never said anything inconsistent with his family's ideals. At the end of our parlour game, it will be C. S. Parnell, the exponent of 'Atlantic principles', who will arise.

III

The family ideals can make sense of the first period of Charles's career. From his election to Westminster in 1875 to the start of the Land War around 1879, Parnell became the chief exponent of an aggressive parliamentary policy for Irish MPs. In contrast to the existing home rule members, led by Isaac Butt, who pursued gentlemanly lobbying of ministers, Parnell opened a campaign of 'obstruction'. This involved vigorous demands for justice for Ireland in Commons speeches, attempts to block coercive legislation by making endless amendments and filibustering, and slowing the whole legislative programme of the government by taking an interest in the minute details of measures relating to the mainland of Britain.[18] This policy was more aggressive than anything tried by Parnell's ancestors (Sir John and William had both been Westminster MPs) but it should not be taken as evidence that Charles had rejected their traditions. The rhetoric which accompanied 'obstruction' served several purposes, all of them supportive of ancestral philosophy.

At one level Parnell used obstruction to demonstrate the 'Country' point that government power could corrupt. He contrasted his vigour in Parliament with the indolence of Butt's supporters, and attributed the ineffectiveness of the Irish in the Commons to their being seduced by the English. When the Irish came over to London, the lifestyle of a Westminster MP, coupled with the lure of working with the powerful, made them forget their national virtue and their constituents. As Parnell, graphically, put it, 'one hundred and three Irish representatives were affectionately invited over to London to help the English govern themselves. . . When they got over they were bribed not to interfere'.[19] Obstruction, by highlighting the difference between an uncorrupted Parnell and the seduced placidity of his colleagues, drove home the principle that only those who stayed away from big government could retain their independence. 'It is', Parnell claimed, 'only Irishmen in the House of Commons who can never be Irishmen.'[20]

The defence of obstruction also allowed a rehearsal of liberal parliamentarianism. Parnell justified his actions in this period by placing them in the context of a Westminster assembly which was too distant from Irish opinion to allow its representation by normal parliamentary means. He told those who questioned his tactics that the Imperial Parliament could not govern Ireland by consent. It sat in a foreign city, contained too few Irish MPs and remained profoundly uninterested in Irish affairs. So distant and unconcerned was it that 'anti-Irish prejudice' reigned amongst the majority English MPs, the 'House was generally conspicuous by its absence'[21] when Irish matters were considered, and the forms of the House were deliberately used to kill Irish measures, 'not by means of argument, but by brute force'.[22] Parnell concluded that the experience of the present legislative Union had shown that successive governments had been unwilling and unable to attend to the legislative requirements of Ireland.[23] This supported the family belief that distance crippled Westminster's legitimacy. Charles justified obstruction in prose haunted by his grandfather William. 'It was', he complained, 'a physical impossibility that that House [the Imperial Commons] could be able to make laws for us. Even if they desired to . . . they had not got the capacity to understand our needs and necessities'.[24] A distant parliament was so unrepresentative that it could never be made to take notice of some of its charges. In these circumstances, obstruction could be offered as the only remaining option for those who believed in representation.

Obstruction, finally, was a practical demonstration of the contention that the British Isles were too large and varied to be governed from a single point. Parnell brought both strands of the family philosophy together by arguing that the Imperial Parliament could only function by denying representation to Ireland, and corrupting her representatives. In the post–1800 settlement, he claimed, Irish MPs were treated as second-class legislators. They were expected to stay quiet until the English ministry introduced Irish legislation. They were bribed, or forced, to comply. They had no right, as British MPs had, to introduce Bills demanded by their constituents or to contribute to debates on non-Irish issues. Parnell contended that the Irish had to be forced to be silent because, if they began to contribute to discussion on general issues or raised the grievances of their countrymen without invitation, Westminster's system would fail. The legislative programme of the Commons would grow beyond the capacity of the House to consider, and politicians could not even pretend to the English people that they were attending to all the needs of their constituents.

Obstruction was a campaign to demonstrate all this. If Parnell, and other Irish members, refused to be second-class legislators, and claimed the right to raise their constituents' demands or comment on non-Irish debates, Westminster would fail. Parnell claimed that much of his 'obstruction' was not cynical wrecking, but merely him taking the sort of detailed interest in English measures not yet shown by Irish MPs. To some extent his record on measures like the Prisons Bill, where he introduced several useful amendments, bore out this claim.[25] Parnell wanted to show what proper Irish participation in legislative business meant for the Commons time-table. He said he was accused of obstruction when he had 'asserted as a matter of right, that an Irish member might take an equal part in the deliberations of the House with any English member'.[26] Parliamentary chaos had ensued merely because

> he ventured to do a thing which he thought no Irish member had done before – he ventured to put to the test the bona fides of the assumption constantly made in the House; that the Irish members were free to take that part in the debate . . . which English members took.[27]

Obstruction, therefore, was designed to expose the fraud of 1800. It was a vigorous campaign opposed to the ancestral Parnells' style, but not their philosophy. It tried to expose the lie that the British Isles could be administered from London without corruption, and without denying the benefits of parliamentary government to Ireland.

IV

The first problem with this 'Atlantic' interpretation of Parnell is his close contact with those republican exponents of armed struggle – the Fenians. By 1880 he had had close discussions with men of the stamp of James O'Kelly and John Devoy (who had both been involved in organizing Fenian violence in the 1860s), and had established contact with the Clan na Gael, the American-Irish secret society.[28] His campaign to wrest the leadership of the home rule movement from Butt also involved an appeal to Fenian support.[29] Speaking at Manchester in 1877 he glorified the republicans' violent actions. Gladstone had only disestablished the Irish church, he claimed, because 'there was an explosion at Clerkenwell and because a lock was shot off a police van at Manchester'[30] (two notorious incidents from the Fenians' 1867 campaign). The problem was that the Fenians were not of the 'Atlantic' tradition. Rather than concentrating on the people's right to representation, or the danger of power, their rhetoric centred on the romance of force, the sanctification of the struggle of earlier heroes, and national virility.[31] How could Parnell associate with such men and yet remain true to his ancestors?

One answer to this is that Parnell did not come as close to the Fenians as all that. He usually appealed to Irishmen to cool their agitation and avoid violence. He pointed out that there was no faster way to destroy Irish nationalism than leading it into a war with the English in which the latter's superior resources would certainly triumph. Much of Parnell's most aggressive oratory did not contain explicit support for force, and this politician was an expert in the equivocal speech, which signalled any support for the Fenians only tacitly. Yet Parnell did make the Liverpool address, and others like it. His defence of violence was real.

In fact, Parnell could meet the Fenians half way, without straying outside the family traditions. It was the genius of the clan creed that, whilst it set up a dream of peaceful representation in a Dublin parliament, it allowed an espousal of violence. The civic humanist in a Parnell could point out that an armed citizenry was a traditional counterbalance to the power of government. It provided a safeguard for an individual's independence.[32] The liberal parliamentarian, meanwhile, could view a government without consent of its people as a tyranny. A tyranny (as the Founding Fathers of America had argued) permitted resistance. Violence could be embraced, so long as it was always placed carefully in the context of tyrannical, corrupting and unrepresentative government. William Parnell had understood this when stating that the Irish were not rebels by nature, but that laws denying 'liberty, security and respectability'[33] had formed the national character. His grandson took the short step from explaining the violence of his countrymen to justifying it.

English tyranny was at the centre of Parnell's approach to violence. On his first trip to America in 1876 Parnell spoke of 'the arbitrary force of England'[34] and of Britain as 'the tyrannous power'[35] which had tried to strangle American liberty at birth. It was now doing the same in Ireland. On returning home he developed the argument, stating that his campaign of obstruction 'shall show the world that England governs her Irish provinces just as the Turk governs her Christian provinces'.[36] There was a plot to 'disenfranchise the Irish nation from using ordinary privileges', and the hundred Irish MPs at Westminster were camouflage for an illegitimate form of government. The style of English rule was (in Parnell's frequently employed imagery) a 'mask' which, when torn off, would reveal the despotism beneath. Once this view of England's rule as a tyranny was in place, it was easy for Parnell to hang his account of violence on it. His speeches, where they sympathize with the use of force, suggest that force was provoked and justified by the tyrannical actions of government. In Dublin in 1877 he laid down his philosophy.

If they care for retaliation upon those who have never hesitated to exercise every means of coercion and cruelty in their power, I can say this – that the Irish members can help the Irish people to punish the Englishmen who have shown themselves utterly unable to govern this country. Do you conciliate the housebreaker who has broken into your house in the depth of night to rob you of your possessions and cut your throat into the bargain? Do you conciliate the highwayman who stops you on the high road and puts a pistol to your head saying 'Your money or your life'?[37]

This is one of those equivocal speeches which might just refer to vigorous parliamentary action, but there is a deliberate, latent, justification of violence there, and it is a justification based on the despotism of government. This remained the basis of Parnell's thought. In 1880 Parnell told the Americans about an incident at Carraroe where an angry crowd had beaten off legal officers trying to serve an eviction order.

You will agree with me that they exhibited a remarkable degree of courage, judgement and respect for the law, until the police commenced the attack by bayoneting the women. [Then] they behaved with the courage of their race because they threw themselves at the constabulary in their unarmed conditions and gained a splendid and gallant victory.[38]

The only time Parnell talked of force without prior provocation by England was when he suggested Ireland should have a militia. This fell outside liberal justifications for force, but it was squarely inside the civic humanist glorification of an armed citizenry as protection against government power. Parnell could defend a militia as a check to the humanist's nightmare of moral degeneration. 'When Grattan threw away the sword . . . by consenting to the disbanding of the Irish volunteers,' he claimed, 'it was the death-knell of Irish independence. Force, fraud and corruption won over the majority of the Irish Parliament, and the Irish Parliament of the past became a thing of the past'.[39]

The full subtleties of Parnell's attitude to violence are brought out in his consideration of past struggles. Fenians tended to glorify *any* attempt to overthrow British rule by force. They could present Emmet's 1803 Dublin street brawl or Young Ireland's 1848 battle in the Widow McCormack's cabbage patch as major blows in a heroic heritage.[40] Parnell, by contrast, concentrated on a narrower range of events. True to his 'Atlantic' heritage, he was inspired only by the American War of Independence and the Irish Patriots of 1782. Parnell frequently cited the great names of these struggles, and drew political lessons from them, whilst skating quickly over the events of 1803, 1848 or 1867. For Parnell these later risings were understandable, but are not exalted as worthy of emulation. For instance, in 1877 Parnell, addressing a vigorous crowd of Irishmen in Sheffield, presented the efforts of Young Ireland and the Fenians as little but a natural reaction to huge provocation.

> If in '48, when the country was devastated by a famine such as the Indian famine did not equal, they had again tried physical force, the Irish people would have been more or less than men if they had done anything else. And when in 1867, seeing their country rapidly depopulated to make room for English bullocks, they again rebelled, let it be remembered there were only those occasions in 77 years.[41]

This passage illustrated English oppression rather than Irish heroism. Violence in 1848 and 1867 was a human, but not particularly glorious, reaction.

By contrast, Parnell chose to highlight the great Atlantic struggles. Parnell's speeches make it clear he saw his struggle as exactly analogous with those of Washington, Jefferson, Grattan and Flood. He drew comfort from their example and held them up as models to his followers. In 1876 Parnell wrote to the American secretary of state that 'Ireland sympathizes in an especial manner with the great principles of civil government that constitute the strength and glory of the American Republic',[42] whilst in a speech in Liverpool he claimed Ireland's demands were an application of the 'same principles'[43] which had led to American independence. By the time of his 1880 American tour he was equating stages in the War of Independence with the unfolding struggle in Ireland.[44] The identification with the American colonists remained a comfort to Parnell throughout his career. In his very last year, when he felt most isolated, it was their use of force which he used to defend his past actions. Should he have bowed to Gladstone's request that he step down as leader of his party after being implicated in the O'Shea divorce? 'Why you might as well have told Washington at Lexington or at Bunker Hill, that unless he surrendered his trenches to the British Army, he would lose all the fruits of his exertions.'[45] Similarly, the 1780s Irish Volunteers could be said to have been fighting Parnell's type of battle, and their use of force was condoned. Grattan enjoyed a starring role in Parnell's rhetoric. An early appearance was in 1876.

> They [the English] know Ireland is determined to be an armed nation, and they fear to see her so, for they remember how a section of the Irish people in 1782, with arms in their hands, wrung from England legislative independence.[46]

Thus Parnell could make speeches which would excite Fenians, without going over to their principles. The Fenians saw violence as a sign that Ireland was developing the moral strength to be a nation, that it proved itself a virile country which was creating itself through struggle. They glorified confrontation for its own sake. Parnell disagreed, seeing the Irish nation as an existing corpus of people with the right to proper representation in a parliament. It did not have to be born in arms. Parnell could, however, still accept violence as the permitted response of a people to despotism. It was part of a struggle for consent in government, and independence from centralized power.

V

Parnell's acceptance of violence was to prove particularly useful in the early 1880s. In this stage of his career, Parnell was involved with the Land League, the movement founded by Michael Davitt to prevent mass evictions of tenants in time of agricultural depression.[47] As president of the league, Parnell would have to explain, or at least to excuse, the intimidation by its supporters of new tenants who had taken others' holdings, legal officers and landlords. However, Parnell's support of agrarian agitation, raised more problems than his attitude to physical force. The Land League's ultimate demand was for the abolition of landlordism in Ireland through the compulsory purchase of estates by their tenants. If Parnell agreed with this, and his speeches show he did, he could have been far more radical than the liberal, humanist gentleman portrayed so far. He was proposing an alternative property and social structure for Ireland – far beyond the family demand for a Dublin parliament.

Yet in fact, Parnell's views on land were of a piece with his views on politics. He pressed social change, because his vision of an ideal settlement had social preconditions not met by existing Irish landlordism. As a liberal parliamentarian, Parnell believed that, although a local assembly was the only sort of government with the potential to reflect public opinion, this potential could not be realized without a certain social group. A truly representative system needed a class of men prepared to act as a channel of communication between government and people. It needed individuals who would be willing to transmit public opinion upwards by acting as representatives in the assembly, whilst also being ready to implement the legislature's decisions by taking positions of local authority. Such men would be able to report back the actual effects of measures to national leaders. Government by consent would be secured because the legislators would be in touch with and active amongst their population.

Parnell believed that a public spirited, local and landed gentry were ideal candidates for such a class of men. They were the natural leaders of their communities and had the education and leisure the role demanded. This is why he idolized his family in his earliest speeches. They had understood the duties of landed gentry in a liberal society. They had been MPs, JPs, and lord lieutenants of their counties, high sheriffs and benevolent landlords prepared to listen to the needs of their tenants.[48] Similarly Parnell approved of the gentry of England. In his Land War tirades against landlords he excepted the landowners in England because of their traditions of public service and because they had 'been more or less reasonable to their tenants'.[49] Unfortunately in Ireland such a public spirited gentry was virtually nonexistent. Parnell saw the Irish landlords as alienated figures, often absentee, who had totally lost touch with public opinion. Their lack of concern with anything but the collection of rent had rendered them incapable of fulfilling any representative role. Characteristic were Lord Leitrim, 'a scourge to the human race',[50] and Lord Kenmore who 'would not leave a roof over the heads of his tenants'.[51] The lack of anything like the gentry of England left a gaping hole in Parnell's vision of a liberal Ireland.

Parnell became a social radical to suggest a remedy for this deficiency. He said bad landlords had to go because they had failed in the duties required of the gentry in liberal society. They had not listened to their tenants and neighbours, had not tried to help them or represent them in centres of power, had not understood their economic problems.[52] Even the English state felt they had betrayed the trust implied by the original grant of their land. As Parnell put it,

> [The landlords] were given those lands originally free of charge on condition that they perform certain duties. They were given them under English rule in order that they might make the Irish people content – but it was not intended that they should oppress these tenants, that they should rack rent them or that they should starve them. . . . When the land of Ireland was given to these men for nothing it was given with corresponding duties, and they have failed in those duties.[53]

From the style of this attack it is clear that Parnell was not objecting to a landlord class as such. His liberalism meant he did not wish to see his enemies eliminated, but transformed into men who would not fail in their representative role. Paul Bew has recognized this and has argued that Parnell supported land purchase to end the competition over rents.[54] This would allow landlords to join their tenants in a united demand for home rule. Bew's interpretation can be supplemented by numerous speeches in which Parnell suggested that when the tenants had purchased their land, those whose only interest in Ireland was rent would be removed. Then a class of propertied men would be left, who would be able to assume a leading role in public affairs.[55] This determination to produce a responsible gentry class explains why Parnell always protected land-lord interests against the true social radicals of his movement. He opposed Davitt's ideal of land nationalization, and insisted that the landlords receive a fair price for the land they were forced to sell.[56] The hope was to produce that class of men so vital for his political vision, not for a fight to the death with the propertied. Parnell's support for agrarian agitation for these reasons explains why he cooled to the movement after 1882. With the No-Rent Manifesto, and extremist rhetoric, the league seemed about to attempt a show-down on the land issue. This would detract from Parnell's main aim of a parliament in Dublin.

The civic humanist in Parnell could also support land purchase. A man's landed property had always been seen as a guarantee of his independence from government. The English 'Country' party in the eighteenth century had seen freehold as a badge of virtue, and a qualification for citizenship.[57] Parnell's rhetoric took up these arguments in the Land War. He insisted that self-respect and industry would flow from the peasantry's emancipation, and that landownership could break their degrading reliance on landlords and state.[58] He tied the land agitation emphatically to 'Atlantic principles' when insisting that gaining freehold would not diminish Irish enthusiasm for nationalism, but would rather provide the independence, virtue and courage needed to demand proper representation. As he pointed out, 'the men who won American independence . . . were the owners of their land, and I am not going to believe that improvements in the conditions of the Irish people will make them less worthy Irishmen'.[59]

VI

The next stage of the career, 1882–5, provides few difficulties for Parnell, the exponent of 'Atlantic principles'. In these years he concentrated on the National League, the political organization of the home rule party. By having a branch in each Irish constituency, and working for the return of home rule MPs, the league kept Irish issues publicized and hoped to prove once and for all that the Irish population did not consent to rule from Westminster.[60] The period also saw a rapprochement with the Catholic church.[61] Parnell, however, never made religion an important plank of his nationalism. The English treatment of Catholics was used simply as one example among many of corrupt tyranny, and Parnell never really got to grips with questions of faith. His rhetoric swept away the tensions between Ulster Protestants and southern Catholics by naïvely insisting that a local, Dublin parliament would be representative enough to dissolve the problem.[62]

Early in 1886, by contrast, came an event which troubles any consistent interpretation of Parnell's politics. William Ewart Gladstone offered the Irish a degree of legislative independence. Parnell's reaction to the Liberal's First Home Rule Bill has always posed the central dilemma for his historians. It is difficult to know how seriously to take his assertion that he accepted it as a 'final solution' to the Irish question. Parnell's welcome for the measure, which reserved important areas like trade, foreign policy and defence to Westminster, seems at odds with some of his more fiery rhetoric before it was proposed. At Cincinnati in 1880 Parnell may have gone as far as asking for the 'last link'[63] between Ireland and England to be broken, whilst in Cork in 1885 he had memorably reminded his audience that no man had the right to fix the boundary of the march of a nation.[64] Was it likely that such a man would really be happy with the glorified county council offered in 1886?

Parnell's thoughts on the final political structure of the Irish nation are most unclear. He said he would accept Gladstone's home rule, but he never ruled out further development towards full independence once it had been granted. He told the Irish parliamentary party in 1890 that the Bill would 'enable us to take the first steps, the first necessary steps, for the creation and consolidation of Irish nationalism'.[65] Before 1886 Parnell had supported a variety of possible frameworks, from the restoration of Grattan's parliament to out and out republicanism.[66]

The idea that Parnell was an exponent of 'Atlantic principles', if not entirely clearing this confusion, at least sets bounds to the man's wandering rhetoric. The crucial point to grasp is that 'Atlantic principles' were, in many ways, vague. They did not insist on a precise constitutional structure as the ideal framework for the English empire. Parnell's guides in political thought, the American and Irish Patriots of the 1770s and 1780s, although steady in their ideals, had not been doctrinaire about the shape of a settlement. The Founding Fathers of the United States had never strayed from parliamentary liberalism or civic humanism – but they had used these principles to argue for everything from simple protection of colonial assemblies' control over local affairs to full independence. The Irish Patriots had become thoroughly confused about how much autonomy from England was required to satisfy their demands.[67] 'Atlantic principles', as handed down from the eighteenth century, gave no clear decision about which responsibilities could be left to an imperial parliament, and how much power should be allowed to local assemblies.

This vagueness allowed Parnell to be flexible. Parliamentary liberalism and civic humanism determined the direction in which an acceptable solution to the Irish question would be found, but they did not tie him down to a particular constitutional structure. 'Atlantic principles' insisted that a settlement create a local legislature more responsive to public opinion, and dispensed with force and corruption. This was the bedrock of Parnell's position, and could not be compromised. Yet, if a proposal satisfied these conditions, the precise organization of the English empire which it envisaged was not of crucial importance to him.

This theory allows Parnell's acceptance of Gladstone's proposals to have been sincere. The 1886 Home Rule Bill conceded the important demands. It met the Atlantic conditions for a solution outlined by Parnell the previous autumn.

> It is necessary that we should exchange the dark, terrible suffering history of the past for a future of freedom and prosperity, when it may be possible for the freely elected representatives of the nation to shape the future of our country. I do not know of any conditions under which it is possible for a nation to shape her course with justice to herself save under the fostering guidance and care of a freely elected parliament.[68]

If there were any reservations, as over the retention of Westminster control over trade, they were overshadowed by the abolition of the distance between people and government, and the end to coercion and English influence, implied by the restoration of the Dublin parliament. Yet the theory of indifference to precise structure also allows Parnell's support for rival frameworks at other points in his career. The primacy of those vague 'Atlantic principles' rather than precise political structure in Parnell's thought left him free. He could speak republicanism to Fenians, and moderate home rule to constitutional monarchists, without contradicting his principles. The question of exactly how far Ireland should separate from Britain was relatively unimportant. Any proposal which provided a proper representative assembly, and favoured small government over large, would be welcomed.

Once Gladstone put his Home Rule Bill on the table, Parnell was almost impeccably loyal to it. Although other frameworks were possible, Gladstone's had the inestimable advantages of being concrete and on offer. Parnell argued for the Bill in its Commons debates, and did not desert after parliamentary defeat for the measure questioned Gladstone's ability to deliver. In the general election which followed the measure's rejection, he toured the country urging the Irish resident in England to vote Liberal and praising Gladstone.[69] He entered into an alliance with the Liberal party and addressed their conferences.[70] The theme of his oratory was that home rule was central to the establishment of the Irish nation.

> It will enable us to take part in the government of our own country – and none of us wish for any higher or better future – will enable us to direct the energies of our people into proper and safe channels, will enable us to develop the long neglected resources of our country.[71]

This style of oratory was not abandoned even in 1890–1 when the

O'Shea divorce split Parnell's party and ended his alliance with Gladstone. He still viewed the 1886 Bill as the culmination of his career. All Parnell's defences of that measure reaffirmed his commitment to 'Atlantic principles'. The assembly offered would be able to represent the Irish people and to protect, rather than enslave, them. In the 1886 proposals, the English had accepted that they could not govern Ireland by consent, or without force and corruption. William and Sir John had been vindicated.

VII

'Atlantic principles' help to solve the riddle of Parnell. They provide a set of underlying political ideas which give coherence to a confusing mass of rhetoric. Yet parliamentary liberalism and 'Country' principles allow historians to do more than tidy their conceptual desks. They allow an assessment of Parnell's contribution to the Irish question.

There is no doubt that Parnell's great achievement was the focusing of Irish discontent into a mass agitation for home rule. 'Atlantic principles' played a vital role. They suggested the panacea of a local parliament, clarified the effects of English government in the Irish mind, and stressed the importance of political action independent of the corrupting influence of Westminster. Parnell's principles created a movement with more coherent demands and more recognized leaders than previous campaigns. A solution to the Irish problem was, perhaps, brought nearer as English ministers came to know with whom, and about what, to negotiate. Against this, however, Parnell's 'Atlantic' mind did a great disservice to Ireland. It failed to recognize the 'Irishness' of the Irish question. Parliamentary liberalism and the 'Country's' civic humanism were 'universal' principles. They were, supposedly, applicable to people everywhere. They refused to acknowledge that there might have been emotions, desires and tensions peculiar to Ireland. Most damagingly, they failed to account for the growing pride in Gaelic language and culture as a basis for nationalism, and for the almost unbreakable connection between nationalism and Catholicism. 'Atlantic principles' might look appropriate to men like the Parnells. They were the philosophy of independent gentry, willing to take starring roles in representative government. Yet the Parnells – landed, English educated, Protestant – were untypical Irishmen. 'Atlantic principles', by presenting nationalism as a political rather than a cultural force, and by playing down Catholic identity, misunderstood and misrepresented the passions which were creating modern Ireland.

NOTES

1 F. S. L. Lyons, 'The political ideas of Parnell', *Historical Journal*, 16, 1973, pp. 749–75.
2 Oliver MacDonagh, *States of Mind: a Study of Anglo-Irish Conflict 1780–1980*, London, 1983.
3 F. S. L. Lyons, *Charles Stewart Parnell*, London, 1977, pp. 44–5. For the family influence on a wide range of Parnell's social and political beliefs, see R. F. Foster, *Charles Stewart Parnell: the Man and his Family*, Hassocks, Sussex, 1976.
4 [William Parnell], *An Enquiry into the Causes of Popular Discontents in Ireland*, 2nd edn, London, 1805, p. 41.
5 *A Report on the Debates in the House of Commons of Ireland on Wednesday and Thursday the 5th and 6th February on the King's Message Recommending Legislative Union*, Dublin, 1800, p. 46.
6 [Parnell], *Enquiry . . . Causes . . . Popular Discontents*, p. 45.
7 Ibid., p. 52. Sir John also doubted English MPs' ability to represent Ireland. See his contributions in *A Report of the Debate in the House of Commons of Ireland, on Tuesday and Wednesday 22nd and 23rd January, 1799*, Dublin, 1799.
8 [Parnell], *Enquiry . . . Causes . . . Popular Discontents*, p. 39.
9 *Report on the Debates . . . 1800*, p. 46.
10 For 'Country' ideology and its roots in civic humanism, see J. G. A. Pocock, *The Machiavellian Moment: Florentine Political Thought and the Atlantic Republican Tradition*, Princeton, NJ, 1975, part III; also Isaac Kramnick, *Bolingbroke and his Circle: the Politics of Nostalgia in the Age of Walpole*, Oxford, 1968. Civic humanism is nicely summarized by John Robertson in 'The Scottish Enlightenment at the limits of the civic tradition', in Istvan Hont and Michael Ignatieff (eds), *Wealth and Virtue: the Shaping of Political Economy in the Scottish Enlightenment*, Cambridge, 1983, pp. 141–51.
11 *Report on the Debates . . . 1800*, pp. 11, 46.
12 [Parnell], *Enquiry . . . Causes . . . Popular Discontents*, p. 5.
13 [William Parnell], *Maurice and Berghetta; or the Priest of Rahery. A Tale*, Dublin, 1819.
14 William Parnell, *Letter to the Editor of the Quarterly Review*, Dublin, 1820.
15 For the transfer of English 'Country' and parliamentary ideas to America, see Pocock, *Machiavellian Moment*, last chapter; and Bernard Bailyn, *The Ideological Origins of the American Revolution*, Cambridge, Mass., 1967.
16 For Irish borrowing from America, see D. N. Doyle, *Ireland, Irishmen and Revolutionary America*, Dublin, 1981; and R. B. MacDowell, *Irish Public Opinion 1750–1800*, London, 1944, pp. 39–50.
17 'Avondale, County Wicklow, Residence of the late C. S. Parnell M.P. catalogue of the library . . . to be sold at auction', Dublin, 1901.

18 Lyons, *Parnell*, pp. 57–66.
19 *Nation*, 22 September 1877, speech in Killmallock.
20 Ibid.
21 *Hansard*, 3rd series, vol. ccxxxvi, col. 306, 1 August 1877; see also *Hansard*, 3rd series, vol. ccxxxviii, col. 938, 7 March 1878.
22 *Nation*, 29 September 1877, speech in Navan.
23 *Nation*, 21 July 1877, speech in Manchester.
24 *Ulster Examiner*, 2 October 1877, speech in [London]Derry.
25 Lyons, *Parnell*, p. 59.
26 *Hansard*, 3rd series, vol. ccxxxvi, col. 55, 27 July 1877.
27 Ibid.
28 Lyons, *Parnell*, pp. 72–82.
29 Ibid., p. 70.
30 *Nation*, 21 July 1877.
31 MacDonagh, *States of Mind*, pp. 76–77.
32 Pocock, *Machiavellian Moment*. The glorification of a citizens' militia is a major theme of this book.
33 [Parnell], *Enquiry . . . Causes . . . Popular Discontents*, p. 3.
34 *Nation*, 11 November 1876. Joint statement issued by Parnell and O'Connor Power on President Grant's rejection of the Centennial Address by the Irish people.
35 Ibid.
36 *Bradford Observer*, 27 August 1877, speech in Bradford.
37 *Nation*, 25 August 1877.
38 *Indianapolis Daily Sentinel*, 22 January 1880, speech in Indianapolis.
39 *Nation*, 29 September 1877, speech in Navan.
40 They were included in the six risings, commemorated in the manifesto read from the Dublin post office steps during the 1916 Rising.
41 *Sheffield Daily Telegraph*, 14 September 1877.
42 See note 34.
43 *Nation*, 25 November 1876, speech at Liverpool.
44 See, for example, the speeches published in the *Brooklyn Daily Eagle*, 9 January 1880; *Boston Globe*, 13 January 1880.
45 *The Times*, 11 December 1890, speech in Dublin.
46 *Nation*, 29 September 1877, speech in Navan.
47 For Parnell's involvement in the Land War, see Paul Bew, *The Land Question and the National Question in Ireland 1858–82*, Dublin, 1978; Lyons, *Parnell*, pp. 116–207.
48 Foster, *Parnell . . . Family*, pp. 3–54; Lyons, *Parnell*, pp. 15–40. For William Parnell's views on benevolent landlordism, see [Parnell], *Enquiry . . . Causes . . . Popular Discontents*, p. 61.
49 *Nation*, 27 September 1879, speech in Tipperary.
50 *Freeman's Journal*, 13 October 1879, speech in Navan.
51 *The Times*, 26 August 1886.
52 See, for example, *The Times*, 20 May 1881, speech on second reading of a Land Bill. Also *The Times*, 7 March 1885; *Milwaukee Daily Sentinel*, 24 February 1880.
53 *The Times*, 20 December 1889.
54 Paul Bew, *C. S. Parnell*, Dublin, 1980, pp. 26–30.
55 *Nation*, 27 September 1879; *Freeman's Journal*, 20 April 1890.

56 For the breach with Davitt, see speech given in Drogheda in *Freeman's Journal*, 16 April 1884. Parnell described land nationalization as a 'will of the wisp which may lead to serious disunion'.

57 See Pocock, *Machiavellian Moment*, Part III. Glorification of the landed interest in 'Country' thought can be seen in Henry Neville, *Plato Redivivus*, London, 1681 – often seen as a seminal text for English civic humanism.

58 This was the central contention of Parnell's 1880 speeches in America. See also the series of speeches in the west of Ireland in the autumn of 1879, just as Parnell was becoming closely associated with the Land War. *Freeman's Journal*, 13 October 1879 and 29 November 1879; *Nation*, 14 June 1879.

59 *The Times*, 20 April 1891, speech in Irishtown.

60 See C. C. O'Brien, *Parnell and his Party, 1880–90*, Oxford, 1957, pp. 119–50.

61 Early mistrust and reconciliation is traced in Emmet Larkin, *The Roman Catholic Church and the Creation of the Modern Irish State 1878–1886*, Dublin, 1975. By 1885 Catholic priests were integral to the National League organization. See O'Brien, *Parnell and his Party*, pp. 128–30. Parnell was speaking frequently on denominational issues. See Alan O'Day, *The English Face of Irish Nationalism*, Dublin, 1977, p. 139.

62 *The Times*, 8 June 1886; *Hansard*, 3rd series, vol. ccxxxxiv, col. 207, 4 March 1879.

63 *Cincinnati Commercial*, 20 February 1880. Other Cincinnati papers did not report the exact words 'last link', but they agreed on Parnell's impassioned plea for much greater Irish independence.

64 *Nation*, 24 January 1885.

65 *The Times*, 30 June 1890, speech to the Irish parliamentary party at Westminster.

66 See *The Times*, 2 March 1891, for Parnell's hope that he could one day address the citizens of 'Royal Meath' as men of 'Republican Meath'. The *Iowa State Register*, 2 March 1880, and *Cincinnati Commercial*, 20 February 1880, report radical language on Parnell's American tour. By contrast in Chester in 1886 – *The Times*, 30 June – Parnell suggested he would be happy with less than Grattan, or even the Canadians, had won.

67 For constitutional squabbles between Grattan and Flood see R. B. MacDowell, *Ireland in the Age of Imperialism and Revolution*, Oxford, 1979, pp. 287–8.

68 *Nation*, 5 September 1885, speech in Dublin.

69 See *The Times*, 26 and 28 June, 1 and 5 July 1886.

70 See, for example, *The Times*, 21 November 1887, speech to the National Liberal Club – Parnell claimed Gladstone's offer had turned the Irish towards peaceful politics.

71 *The Times*, 30 June 1890.

8 The economic thought of the nation's lost leader: Charles Stewart Parnell

Liam Kennedy

'I would throw what is called "political economy" to the wind', exclaimed Charles Stewart Parnell, addressing a labour conference in Dublin.[1] This was after the 'Fall', during the brief, bitter interval before his death. Still, it hardly augurs well for any sustained treatment of his economic ideology. Worse still, Parnell left few written documents of any kind. Of necessity, therefore, any reconstruction of his economic ideas must be based on oral testimonies: his reported speeches at meetings, demonstrations and in the House of Commons. Fortunately, these exist in great number: Parnell was a prolific speech-maker, while the melodramatic aspects of his career ensured extensive coverage in contemporary publications.

An exploration of his economic ideas is worthwhile for a number of reasons. Parnell was the commanding figure in Irish public life during the turbulent final quarter of the nineteenth century; indeed, looking across the century as a whole, only the Liberator himself, Daniel O'Connell, bears comparison with Ireland's uncrowned king. Moreover, as the potential leader of an independent Irish parliament, his views on national economy command particular attention. These cannot of course be isolated from his political views, the twin streams of thought being essential to an understanding of his parliamentary and agitational activities. To an extent also, his politico-economic ideas influenced his relations with the two major parties at Westminster, the Liberals and the Tories. In terms of an intellectual legacy, one may note that the discourses thrown up in the course of his political career, especially those fashioned during the first phase of the Land War (1879–82), both reflected and helped shape the canon of nationalist economic historiography.[2]

Irish economic problems, according to Parnell, manifested themselves in a variety of ways. Agriculture was unproductive, at least relative to its potential, and in the late 1870s was in the grip of deep recession. Industrialization had largely passed the country by. Ireland had experienced massive famine at mid century, and ever since had been losing tens of thousands of its people annually through emigration. How was the Irish problem, in its economic dimension, to be explained? For Parnell, as for other Irish nationalists, the answer was seductively simple. The colonial nature of the relationships binding the two countries, and given merely a new form with the Act of Union, was the fundamental cause of Irish underdevelopment. In particular, he asserted, there was the 'notorious and continued unwillingness or incompetency of the imperial parliament to legislate for Ireland in accordance with its wishes and its wants'. An exotic comparison served to highlight the point. 'Christian England governs her Irish province no better, perhaps not half as well as Mahommedan Turkey governs her Christian serfs.'[3] How, and to what extent, these colonial ties might have inhibited economic development is not spelled out. There are some scattered clues, however. Stung by a question in the House of Commons in 1881 as to why there were no industries in Ireland, Parnell did not point to industrial Ulster.[4] Instead, he observed that without a spirit of enterprise there could be no industry. But enterprise presupposed the likelihood of gain from expenditures of labour and capital. In Ireland, the Irishman, and his forefathers, had grown up in the knowledge that the fruits of their effort would be appropriated by others. Quite rationally, therefore, Irish people had not responded to apparent economic opportunities.[5] One can only comment that it is debatable if this argument held much force in relation to agriculture; in the realm of manufacturing industry it held none.

Some years later, at a St Patrick's day dinner in Westminster Town Hall, Parnell delivered a more detailed statement in which he specified some of the British institutions which were adversely affecting economic development in Ireland.[6]

We are encircled by a system of Government of the most extraordinary kind (hear). Apart altogether from the criminal administration . . . the jury-packings, the secret inquisitions, the Crown prosecutors on the bench, the herd of informers, and the whole system from top to bottom of the criminal administration under which Ireland labours at present, we have a civil administration of the most extraordinary character.

Parnell then singled out a number of government boards for special criticism. There was the Board of Public Works, staffed by incompetent engineers, which had studded the country with monuments to its incompetency. There was the Board of National Education, which would not allow Irish children to learn the history of their own country. There was the ineffective Fisheries Board. The Local Government Board was engaged in encouraging Irish people to emigrate. Ireland might be a much 'beboarded country' but each and every one of these English-imposed boards had been a signal failure.[7] What is striking about this inventory of ills, irrespective of what validity particular criticisms might have had, is how peripheral most of them were to issues of economic change.

It is tempting to dismiss these sentiments as little more than rhetoric but this would be a mistake. On specific economic themes, from land redistribution to industrial protection, Parnell's ideas can only be appreciated when set against this backcloth of colonial images and assumptions.

THE LAND QUESTION

The land question was second only to home rule among the array of issues pursued actively by Parnell. The two were closely connected, not only at the level of agitation but also in his scheme of thought. In April 1875, at the very outset of his parliamentary career, Parnell pronounced himself unhappy with Gladstone's Land Reform Act of 1870.[8] The Act offered no protection to the majority of tenants who were not leaseholders. He held that the tenant, as well as the landlord, held property rights in the land, and that these should be protected by legislation.[9] 'Without fixity of tenure and fair rents the tenants would never be happy, nor would the country be prosperous.'[10] In essence this was a traditional tenant right platform, with the emphasis on regulating landlord-tenant relations through the medium of the 3 Fs – fair rent, fixity of tenure and free sale of tenant right. Two years later, in the House of Commons, Parnell made clear that he had come to more radical conclusions: 'he firmly and strongly believed . . . the question would never be settled on any other . . . than that of giving to the Irish people the right and liberty of living on their own farms as owners'.[11] Curiously, a year later he was less sweeping in his judgement. While the sale of lands to tenants was 'not an unimportant branch of the settlement', there was a variety of ways in which the land question could be solved.[12] This may have been only a brief tactical deviation, in pursuit of more immediate legislative gains in the House. Later that year, when addressing a very different kind of audience, composed of farmers and townsmen in Galway, he predicted that owner occupancy should, and one day would, prevail in Ireland.[13] At a home rule and tenant right meeting in Cavan in the spring of 1879 Parnell was again speaking in unequivocal terms on how the land question might be settled.[14] In the coming parliamentary session, he urged, Irish members should

> devote their energies, not to obtain a final settlement of the land question – because the final settlement of that question under present circumstances was impossible – but he thought this much was possible, that they might obtain a measure from the present Government which would go a long way towards preventing evictions and unjust raising of rents (cheers). What he believed ought to be the final settlement of the land question was the settlement which obtained in France and Belgium, where the man who cultivated the soil is the owner of the soil, and he looked forward to the times, sooner or later, when by purchasing the interests of the landlords it might be possible for every tenant to be the owner of the farm which he at present occupies as tenant-at-will or otherwise (cheers). He thought this was a matter which might not come perhaps for many years, but still things were marching very fast in that direction. When this became a burning question in England they would be near a settlement of it in Ireland.

The speech is interesting for a number of reasons. It shows a firm commitment to the idea of peasant proprietorship, a position to which Parnell adhered for the remainder of his political career. It was made before the outbreak of land agitation in the west later that year. He held out no immediate prospect of success. It seems also that the line of causation, in terms of achieving the final settlement, ran from England to Ireland, in the first instance at any rate.

Peasant proprietorship logically entailed abolishing the landlord class in Ireland. Parnell, though himself a landlord, had early on criticized the overbearing manner of many landlords towards their tenants. Echoing Drummond's dictum, he warned about the duties as well as the rights of property.[15] This critique developed more fully over time. At the famous Westport meeting, on 8 June 1879, Parnell argued that landlordism was an unnatural institution.[16] Significantly, the system had been abolished elsewhere in Europe[17] – in France, Belgium, Prussia and Russia. No matter that he was here conflating quite different historical experiences or that the landlord and tenant system was still firmly entrenched in parts of Europe, the argument had striking economic and political resonances in the hungry conditions of 1879–80. In later discussions of landlordism, Parnell made clear that his target was not landlords as such, but rather the system itself (a distinction very probably lost on his fellow landlords).[18] This iniquitous system, implanted by force in the seventeenth century, had inhibited investment and enterprise on the part of tenants, had led to rack-renting and periodic famines, and ultimately pitted the 10,000 landlords of Ireland against the 600,000 tenant-farmers of the country. The result was that the gentry had been necessarily estranged from the national movement and national life. But divested of their estates, they would be released from their impossible role and enabled to play a constructive part in a post-landlord Ireland.[19] This is a strand in Parnell's thought on which Paul Bew, for instance, places special emphasis, seeing this as a pointer to Parnell's innate social conservatism.

There is no doubt that Parnell envisaged a role for the Anglo-Irish in his home rule Ireland. The key question is the extent of this role, particularly after the confrontations of 1879–81. Given the consistency as well as the ferocity of his attacks on landlordism and, on occasion, on individual landlords, one suspects that Parnell, the political realist, can hardly have entertained serious notions of a leading role for the remnants of the *ancien regime* in a self-governing Ireland.[21] Even if he did, the strategies he pursued during the 1880s suggest that he accorded the prospect a low priority.

The uprooting of landlordism and its replacement by a peasant proprietorship served important political functions in Parnell's scheme of things. But he also envisaged more purely economic consequences arising from a social revolution in land ownership. Pointing to the case of the 5,000 or so tenant-farmers who had bought their holdings under the Church Temporalities Commissioners, Parnell argued that the security conferred by ownership had resulted in farm improvements on a scale which would never have been possible under the old system.[22] 'It was the magic of property which turns sand into gold, that has produced this extraordinary state of affairs.'[23] The more general argument, which is familiar to economic historians and development economists, is that a rearrangement of property rights can result in improved incentives, and hence greater productivity, on the part of the working farmers.[24] The subsequent history of owner occupancy in Ireland, however, failed to bear out these sanguine expectations. There was no 'agricultural revolution'.[25] The reason this was the case was that Parnell's economic, as distinct from his social or political, critique of landlordism was basically flawed. Post-famine Irish agriculture was not plagued by insecurity of tenure, evictions were relatively unusual, and rents were not raised capriciously or exorbitantly by most landlords.[26] Effectively the tenant had achieved co-ownership rights in the soil long before the major land purchase Act, that of Wyndham, in 1903.

Discussions of the relative merits of different kinds of land tenure might well have retained their abstract and speculative character but for a specific conjuncture of circumstances. The crisis – part economic, part political – which gripped rural Ireland between 1879 and 1882 helped to push the issue of peasant proprietorship onto the political agenda at Westminster. But it was rent levels and fear of eviction, not visionary schemes, which provided the real impetus behind the agrarian agitation. The fall of agricultural prices in the late 1870s, poor potato harvests and a drying up of opportunities for migratory labour in Britain, plunged the rural economy into depression. After some initial hesitation, Parnell committed himself wholeheartedly to the task of channelling these currents of discontent. His pivotal role in the Land War made it essential that he should formulate a working definition of that most elusive of terms, a 'fair rent'.[27]

Parnell's notion of a fair rent, and its relationship to the actual rent, derived ultimately from his belief that the tenant was entitled to co-ownership rights in the land he worked. We need not take too seriously Parnell's contention that, before the Anglo-Norman conquest of Ireland, the tenant enjoyed joint ownership of the land with his Gaelic chieftain and that this was the ancient origin of these modern claims.[28] More to the point, at an open-air meeting in Hilltown, high among the Mourne mountains and under the watchful eye of his Orange chairman, Parnell posed a challenge to conventional theories of rent: 'Look at these plains and hillsides – cultivated hillsides – that lie stretched before us . . . how much were these lands capable of producing rent before the tenant farmers came on them, and made them worth what they are now?'[29] Neither the Lord nor the landlord had 'made' this farm land.[30] Indeed a fair rent for landlords in the north of Ireland would leave very little for the landlord as his just right. During the course of 1881 Parnell returned to this theme a number of times.

Well, my definition of a fair rent is this (cries of 'no rent' and 'order'), that the landlord might have whatever the land was worth originally, before it was improved by the tenant or his predecessors in title. . . . Now, gentlemen, I would measure the original value of the rental of Ireland before it was improved by the tenant at about two or three millions of pounds sterling a year – not more.[31]

As his estimation of the current rental of the country was about £17 millions, this meant that rents in Ireland were grossly exploitative, even if one allowed for changes in the price level. (This was on the assumption – a reasonably accurate one, as we know for the nineteenth century – that most farm improvements had been undertaken by the tenants.)[32] However, in the course of the same polemic, Parnell modified his estimate of over-renting, suggesting that a fair rent should be in or about the poor-law valuation of the land. If this was taken as the guideline, then, at a guess only about one-quarter of the rents in the country were at this fair level. About a half were rack-rents, that is 20 to 30 per cent above the poor-law valuation. The remainder he described, rather inelegantly, as 'very exorbitant rents'.

These images of economic and tenurial relations have embedded in them an interesting model, albeit an implicit one, of how rent is determined. This had been a major preoccupation of the classical economists of the early nineteenth century, and had been resolved intellectually along the lines proposed by David Ricardo. Briefly stated, orthodox economic theory held that the supply of land, for all practical purposes, was fixed, hence changes in the price of land (rent) were due solely to changes in the demand for land. The demand for land, in turn, was determined by agricultural prices.[33]

Parnell's explanation for changes in rent levels was quite different. To use one of his examples, the value of the nation's rental income had increased enormously since the time of Sir William Petty, two hundred years earlier. (Petty had estimated Irish rents as totalling about £0.9 millions in the 1670s.)[34] Taking Petty's estimate as an approximation to the original value of the land, then the rise in rents since then had been due to improvements effected by landlords and tenants. However, as the landlords had invested little in the farms of their tenants, most of the increases in rental values were due to the exertions of the tenants.[35] What we have, then, is an investment-driven account of rent increases.[36] This was, of course, most convenient because it meant that the bulk of the rental income from land should properly accrue to the improving tenant and not to the landlord. The problem with this is that it neglected the role of demand factors. Had food markets not expanded over time, the demand for land, and hence rents, would have changed little.

Parnell's theory of rent was not only partial, it was also internally contradictory. He perceived, more sharply than some contemporaries and indeed some later historians, that there was an inverse relationship between the rent paid for a holding and the value of its tenant right.[37] Parnell claimed that most rents were excessively high, and presumably therefore had been set at a competitive or market rate. But if rents were competitive, then the value of what has been termed 'pure tenant right' (that is, the net payment after making allowance for any unexhausted improvements undertaken by the outgoing tenant) should have been zero. Though difficult to quantify, this was patently not the case in the later nineteenth century, when payments by incoming tenants were ten, even twenty times the annual rent.[38] Only a small part of the (gross) tenant right payment could have arisen from compensation for unexhausted improvements. Parnell did not see, or affected not to see, a contradiction between alleged rack-rents and large payments for tenant right. But then a firmer grasp of the economics of rent would have been nothing but a political embarrassment in his quest for the higher truths of 'a nation once again'.

One can still concede that the conclusions (if not always the arguments) deployed by Parnell held some persuasive power, and not just in the realm of politics. Why should landlords, who were monopolistic suppliers of a factor of production whose supply they could do little to influence, be the beneficiaries (through rising rent rolls) of secular gains in agricultural prices? As Parnell himself pointed out, it was hardly through the operation of 'natural' economic forces that the ancestors of his fellow landlords had come to own the land resources of Ireland. In the final analysis, discussion of the most appropriate beneficiaries of the monopoly rent from land ownership partakes of an ethical debate. In this sense, Parnell's conclusions might be viewed as a tenable 'moral economic' argument which transcended the categories of thought of conventional political economy.

This edges us in the direction of debates about land nationalization, which formed one of the sideshows on the land question in this period. Partly under the influence of the American economist, Henry George, and drawing sustenance also from the writings of James Fintan Lalor, various schemes for the ownership of the land by the whole people of Ireland were in circulation.[39] The most eminent Irish agrarian radical to espouse these ideas was the founder of the Land League, Michael Davitt.[40] It should be stated immediately that Parnell had no sympathy with schemes of nationalization whereby the state appropriated the rental surplus from land for the use of society as a whole. In an oblique attack on Davitt in April 1884, he warned against the notion that 'ownership of land by anybody . . . was theft, whether that anybody be landlord or tenant'.[41] Such ideas would set town against countryside, tenant-farmers against artisans and working men, and were altogether preposterous. It is true when Parnell was approaching his political nemesis in 1891 he claimed that he had 'always believed in the principle of the nationalization of the land'.[42] This was before a labour conference in Dublin, and the setting is obviously significant. Moreover, he defined the concept in deliberately narrow terms, that of a tax on land. Lest this might prove unpalatable to his constituents in rural Ireland, he could reassure them with the thought that the tax could be levied in such a way that the burden was transferred to that ready source of largesse in nationalist schemes, the Irish landlord class.

CONGESTION AND RURAL POVERTY

The drive towards a solution to the land question, along the lines of peasant proprietorship, carried a number of ancillary agrarian concerns in its wake. Chief among these was the plight of smallholders in the west, crowded onto small uneconomic holdings, and frequently dependent on earnings from migratory labour in Scotland and England. Parnell recognized the problem of congestion and, to his credit, gave it considerably more thought than many of his strong-farmer supporters in the east of Ireland. Addressing the House of Representatives during the course of an American tour in early 1880, he argued for 'a more natural distribution' of Irish farming land.

I should like to see the rich plains of Meath, Kildare, Limerick and Tipperary, instead of being the desert wastes that they are today, supporting the teeming and prosperous population that they are so capable of maintaining. . . . Let the next emigration be from the West to the East, instead of from the East to the West – from the hills of Connemara back to the fertile lands of Meath. When the resources of my country have been fully taken advantage of and developed, when the agricultural prosperity of Ireland has been secured, then if we have any surplus population we shall cheerfully give it to this great country. Then our emigrants will go willingly and as free men – not shovelled out by a forced emigration, a disgrace to the Government whence they came and to humanity in general.[43]

The inverse relationship between population density and land quality was one of the peculiar features of nineteenth-century rural Ireland (see Figure 8.1)[44] and very much at variance with Colin Clark's observation of a direct association between the two in a number of other countries.[45] Some redistribution of the farming population was therefore possible. Parnell fairly quickly shifted his policy recommendation from a west-to-east axis – a rhetorical flight of fancy, as he later described it[46] – in favour of local, less disruptive population movements.

I have nowhere seen so much land suitable for settlement as you can see in any of the Irish counties (loud applause). I don't care what county you go to – whether you go to the county Waterford, or the county Cork, or the county Kerry, or the county Westmeath, or the county Meath, or Mayo or Galway – everywhere you go to you see all the rich lands without any inhabitants, and on the poorer lands and on the bogs you see people crowded together in small holdings (hear, hear). Well, then, before we talk of emigration to some other country wouldn't it be better for us to develop the fields of migration which exist in our own country (cheers).[47]

Parnell singled out for special obloquy the unoccupied tracts of land let out each spring on a short-term basis by landlords to graziers.[48] Under this 'vicious system of farming' the lands were under-capitalized, under-cultivated, and employed virtually no labour.[49] For economic, social and ecological reasons these large reserves of land should be taken away from the landlords and divided up among smallholders. This theme of land redistribution, which at times coexisted uneasily with the less controversial demand for owner occupancy, was to prove an enduring feature of debates on the rural economy. It found expression in the political discourses of the United Irish League, in the anti-grazier agitation of the ranch war (1906–8), and in justifications of spontaneous land seizures in the west during and after the Great War.[50] It significantly influenced also the agrarian programme of Fianna Fail in the interwar period.[51] This ideological legacy of the Land League and Land War is, in part also, the legacy of Parnell.

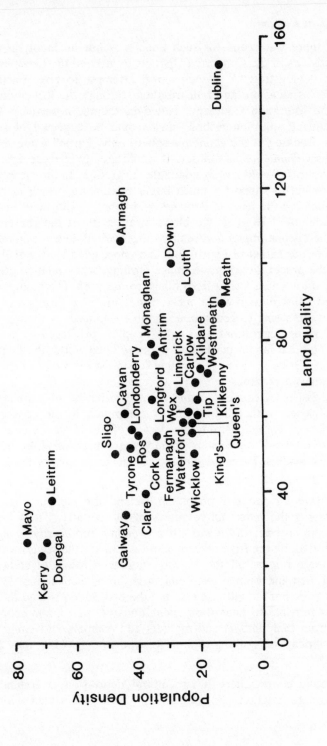

Figure 8.1 The relationship between land quality and population density in Ireland, 1881
Calculated from *The Agricultural Statistics of Ireland for the Year 1881*, BPP, LXXIV, 1882

That there was scope for such policies is not in doubt, as the later activities of the Congested Districts Board and the Land Commission demonstrated.[52] Parnell's own attempts to give practical effect to his ideas on land redistribution, through the formation of a private Migration Company, ended in failure, however.[53] The more difficult question is how much could be expected of such policies. Looking at the economic sphere only, Parnell made some astonishing claims for its efficacy. It would greatly increase agricultural output. It would largely eliminate emigration. In time it would allow Ireland to support a much larger population, which in turn would increase the level of demand, and hence employment in the Irish economy.[54] Even if one blows away much of the rhetorical froth, the distinct impression remains that Parnell held exaggerated notions of the extent of improvable and unoccupied land available, and of the practicality of more tillage farming (when relative prices continued to dictate a shift from tillage to pasture). The reality was that land redistribution was a once-off measure, that farm sizes had to go on increasing to generate acceptable standards of living, and that the rising generations of country people – privileged by access to the two great labour markets of the developed world, the United States and Britain – were not willing to subsist on a diet of piety, patriotism and potatoes.[55]

These issues of congestion and a maldistribution of population connect closely with the problem of emigration in the economic world view of Parnell. During the decade of the 1880s the country lost close on a million persons, mainly young people.[56] Like other nationalist leaders, Parnell deplored this haemorrhaging of the Irish population:

> they have far too few people in Ireland for the purposes of developing the industrial resources of the country. They could not spare anyone; and it was a heart-rending and horrifying sight to travel along the Irish railway lines, and to see the scenes which were occurring at all the railway stations. Crowds of stalwart young men and women were emigrating from their homes, leaving nobody but the old, useless, and the bed-ridden behind them. It was horrible to hear the lamentations of these poor people, torn from their fathers and mothers and compelled to emigrate to America with nothing to look forward to even when they got there.[57]

The specific context here is agricultural depression in Ireland – giving rise to eviction and emigration – which coincided with a cyclical downturn and rising unemployment in the American economy. Government support for emigration schemes, such as those of the Quaker philanthropist, Mr Tuke, were denounced 'as an indecent attempt to assist the Government in getting rid of the Irish difficulty by getting rid of the Irish people'.[58] If emigration was the means towards a solution to rural poverty, then given Ireland's long experience in this regard, the problem should have resolved itself years ago. The alternative to state-encouraged emigration in tackling congestion, according to Parnell, was to break up the three million acres rented by large graziers and people them with smallholders.

As emigration was crucial to the economic strategies pursued by Irish families – influencing decisions as diverse as marital fertility, the timing of family dispersion and inheritance practices – these views merit assessment. Land redistribution, as we have seen, could alleviate the problem of rural overcrowding. But it could not provide a long-term solution. Moreover, while it could make a contribution to the issue of densely packed households – in the west, for example – it could not really address the problem of surplus sons and daughters *within* households right across rural Ireland. Parnell's observations on the social costs as well as the endemic nature of emigration are also fair points, though the implications are far from clear. Whether, in the circumstances, less rather than more emigration would have been to the benefit of the country in the later nineteenth century, as Parnell implied, is hard to say. The costs and benefits of emigration remain among the unresolved problems of Irish historiography.[59] My own impression is that the outflow raised material living standards on average among those who remained at home and most certainly among those who emigrated to North America.[60] It is noteworthy that income per capita rose markedly, albeit with interruptions, between the Great Famine and the Great War.[61] It is difficult to see how a piling up of population, especially on the land, could have done other than reduce average living standards.

Only widespread industrialization could have generated jobs on the scale necessary to match the reproductive powers of the Irish family. It should be said immediately that Parnell was deeply committed to the development of modern industry, seeing this both as an end in itself and a means of taking 'the strain off the land'.[62] There is no hint here of the agrarianism or narodnik world view, with its anti-urban and anti-industrial bias, which infected sections of the nationalist revival movement in the decades before 1914.

Towards the end of his career Parnell went so far as to state that
'Ireland without trade, without industry, but merely as an agricultural country, never can be a nation'.[63]

There is more than a little ambiguity, not to say disingenuousness
in Parnell's view of emigration (a failure of will as much as of
intelligence, and one shared by later generations of Irish politicians). Was it primarily forced, or was it voluntary? In a new
Ireland, would there still be room for some emigration? If so,
might this be desirable? These problems were never fully explored.
Presumably there is an optimal level of ambiguity in any working
politician's treatment of contentious issues. But one thing was clear.
Loosening the connection with England was a prerequisite to solving the interrelated problems of employment and emigration.

> The first necessity for the obtaining of prosperity to Ireland is
> the banishment of English misrule from Ireland (cheers). We
> may endeavour to foster native industry, we may encourage
> amongst you the desirability of using articles of Irish manufacture,
> and may succeed to a certain extent in that, but we can never
> hope really to obtain the prosperity of our country until we have
> fulfilled the first condition of national life and prosperity – that
> our people should rule themselves.[64]

In Parnell's mind the economics of nationalism and the nationalism
of his economics were inseparable.

INDUSTRIALIZATION

Parnell took it as self-evident that Ireland had failed to industrialize
during the nineteenth century; the industrial success of the north
of Ireland occupied him but little. But Ireland had the potential to
industrialize. According to Parnell in 1881, there was no shortage
of capital in the country, its industrial resources were numerous
(this assessment was later reduced to more modest proportions),
and the people were enterprising (as was demonstrated by the
success of emigrants in the USA).[65] All that was needed to release
this economic potential was fair play for Irish industry and the
restorative powers of a self-governing Ireland.[66] It is not quite clear
what Parnell meant by 'fair play'. Sometimes it seems to carry
allusions to restrictive legislation affecting Irish industry in the past
– what was a very distant past by the 1880s. But it may also have
been an attack on the complacent assumption, current in British
political economy but not shared by many European economists,

that free trade between national trading partners was necessarily the best way of promoting economic development. Certainly Parnell was an early advocate of tariff protection for Irish industry. In Cork in 1881, at a monster meeting attended by large contingents of skilled workers – masons, cabinetmakers, cordwainers, tailors, builders – he regretted the fact that 'we cannot yet have our own Parliament to protect Irish manufactures'.[67] On the occasion of a visit by members of Dublin Corporation to his quarrying works at Arklow in 1885 he delivered himself in stronger, more dogmatic terms: 'without a freely-elected National Assembly with power to control all the affairs of Ireland, and with power to protect her struggling industries . . . it is impossible for us to revive our native industries'.[68] These views were elaborated in more detail, and with some suggestive insights, later that year.

> I am of the opinion . . . that it would be wise to protect certain Irish industries at all events for a time (hear, hear); that it is impossible for us to make up for the loss of the start in the manufacturing race which we have experienced owing to adverse legislation in time past against Irish industries by England, unless we do protect these industries, not many in number, which are capable of thriving in Ireland (applause). I am not of the opinion that it would be necessary for us to protect these industries very long, possibly protection continued for two or three years would give us that start which we have lost, owing to the nefarious legislative action of England in times past (hear, hear). I think also that Ireland could never be a manufacturing nation of such importance as to compete to any extent with England. I believe there are several industries which would thrive, and could be made to thrive, in Ireland. But I think that, as regards many other branches of manufacture, of which we have now to seek our supply from the English markets, we should still have to go to their markets for supply on account of natural reasons.[69]

The emphasis on the competitive disadvantages facing late industrializers would find sympathetic echoes among some contemporary economists, particularly those influenced by the dependency school of writing.[70] It is noteworthy also that Parnell envisaged a specialized industrial structure, and did not entertain fatuous notions of self-sufficiency in the manner espoused by later ideologues of an independent Ireland. Most surprising perhaps is the brief interlude of protectionism anticipated, though this may have been dictated by the passions aroused in British politics at the mention of tariffs operating between the two countries. Certainly, if the infant-industry argument, which is the one being invoked here, has validity, then one could not expect most new or struggling Irish firms to make the transition to international competitiveness in such a short space of time.

Within a year of this major pronouncement Parnell felt obliged to sacrifice his aspiration for control of tariff policy in the interests of securing Liberal support for home rule. He never expected concessions on protectionism from a Liberal, as distinct from a Tory, government, he declared. But he was prepared to accept Gladstone's home rule proposals 'as final without Protection'.[71]

This did not, however, rule out a state role in promoting industrialization. In an address to a mainly Liberal assembly at Nottingham in 1889 he defined the home rule movement as being primarily concerned with the national regeneration of the country, aiming especially at the revival of its industrial fortunes.[72] The best way, in fact, of promoting Irish nationality was by constructing harbours, clearing the rivers, reclaiming waste land, developing existing mineral resources and, so far as possible, restoring manufacturing industries which had proven successful in the past. Teaching the agricultural classes how to farm their land in a better fashion was mentioned in passing. But, with an almost Gladstonian concern for sound national housekeeping, he made clear that he was no advocate of profligate state expenditure.

> Do not suppose that I believe in any lavish system of State-aided industries or works of reclamation or of communication, either at the expense of Government – the future Government of Ireland – or at the expense of the English Government. I think you must in all these things look to the individual effort and to the local effort as your main impulse and the chief factor upon which you have to rely for success. . . . We do require from the state . . . some little assistance in the direction of the making of lines of communication, and so forth, to enable capital in Ireland to have, in the improvement of land and of navigation, a chance, when judiciously expended, of getting its head above water.[73]

What is disappointing about this strategy, when every allowance is made for likely *laissez-faire* prejudices among sections of the audience, is its modesty. Some of these proposals were already being acted upon by the Tory government of the day, to the scorn and derision of members of the home rule party. More far-reaching initiatives would follow in the next decade or so under the impetus of what has been labelled constructive unionism.

INDUSTRY AND AGRICULTURE

Although we have discussed Parnell's ideas on industry and agriculture separately, there is some evidence to suggest that he saw the two major sectors of the Irish economy as interlinked. Speaking to an audience in Belfast, at the end of the 1870s, he warned: 'The land may not be a very interesting question to an audience such as this, but depend upon it the question is one that must lie at the root of Ireland's prosperity, in the town as well as the country.'[74] (Interestingly, this prefigures the set of assumptions which guided agricultural and to a lesser extent industrial policy in the Irish Free State during the first decade of political independence.)[75] Referring to the depression in trade in the city, it was his opinion that this would not have been so severe but for the fact that the country laboured under a defective system of landholding. Furthermore, the large food import bill for the United Kingdom – of the order of £100 millions annually – could be saved through substituting home produce. These funds, rather than leaking away on imports, would circulate within the UK economy to the benefit of, among others, manufacturers in Glasgow, Manchester, Newry and Belfast. Then there was the fact that British and Irish industry was handicapped by virtue of the heavy rent burden on land. 'It is impossible for a country like England when there was such a tax as that of rent upon it, to compete in the manufacturing line with a country like America, where the lands are free to the people to cultivate it.'[76] The longer term result, therefore, would appear to be deindustrialization (and a failure to industrialize in the case of Ireland).

Parnell might appear to be close to espousing agricultural protectionism here, and perhaps implicitly he was. Otherwise, how could British and Irish farmers compete with their counterparts in America? Parnell saw clearly that new sources of supply, particularly the burgeoning food exports from the USA, were forcing down prices on the British market and threatening the livelihoods of farmers.[77] There is no doubt that American grain producers in particular enjoyed an absolute advantage over UK producers.[78] A tariff barrier against cheap food imports was the obvious remedy in terms of overcoming this cost disadvantage and safeguarding the incomes of domestic producers. This course of action was in fact advocated by a number of Tory landowners and was widely adopted in continental

European countries. The interesting point, though, is that Parnell's argument does not rely on such conventional lines of thought.

With a good land system, he claimed, agriculture in the UK could be much more productive. In the case of Ireland, the natural fertility of the soil (not to mention the imagination) was such that food output could be trebled in relation to existing levels. The positive incentive effects of owner occupancy presumably would bring about this surge in output. The reduction of rents would lower production costs, increase competitiveness, and reduce food prices for the non-agricultural population. The last would be beneficial to industry in terms of the raw material and, more importantly, the labour costs it faced.[79]

In forming an assessment of these ideas, it is convenient to begin with the burden-of-rent conundrum. Is this the long-lost explanation for British industrial decline in the late nineteenth and twentieth centuries? Was the level of rents a major barrier also to Irish economic and industrial advance? The answer to both questions is a simple no. Despite the common-sense ring to Parnell's comment, it is in fact based on fallacious reasoning. Food prices determine the level of rents, and not the other way round. At the margin of cultivation the cost of production equals the price of the agricultural commodity. But at the margin there is no rent payment. Hence, a general reduction of rents – even their total abolition by, for example, political fiat – would not affect prices. Hence, also, there can be no favourable knock-on effects for the competitiveness of industry.

A radical reduction of rents could, however, have had some unintended and adverse consequences from the point of view of farm output and productivity. Let us assume, for the sake of argument, that an overnight transition to a rent-free land economy would have been possible. An immediate problem is that the benefits might be consumed, in whole or in part, on the farm itself, in the form of increased leisure and auto-consumption.[80] There is the likelihood, in the longer term, of an increasingly inefficient distribution of land and labour resources. This is because rent, whatever its distributional implications, serves the useful economic function of acting as a spur to efficiency. By putting a price on the use of land, rents tend to squeeze out incompetent farmers and release land to their more efficient fellows. That this is no remote hypothesis is illustrated by the serious misallocation of land resources apparent in mid and late twentieth-century rural Ireland under conditions of very low land taxation.[81] One can only conclude that the prospect of a highly productive and competitive agriculture, once the pressure of rent had been relaxed, was more than doubtful, while the anticipated knock-on effects for industry were likely to have proved equally illusory.

The other strand of the argument, in terms of the agriculture-industry nexus, is that of the rural economy's demand for the industrial and other goods of the north-east. No doubt a more prosperous rural Ireland would have resulted in some expansion of demand for goods and services produced in the Belfast region. One is not being wholly facetious, I hope, in remarking that there was little demand for ocean-going ships on the part of west of Ireland fishermen, that textile machinery was not part of the furniture of the typical Irish workshop and that high-quality linens had little place in the homes of Irish peasants. The general point is that the export-oriented industry of the north-east had weak linkages to the rest of the island's economy. Economically speaking, the industrial north and the agrarian south were only faintly complementary.[82]

SOCIAL ECONOMY: THE QUESTION OF LABOUR

One might not expect a product of the Anglo-Irish 'caste' to show much interest in labourers and the labour question.[83] Yet it can be argued that it was precisely because he was a landlord, and not for instance a strong farmer, that Parnell evinced such sympathies. A paternalistic concern with the plight of labour, particularly that of rural labour, animated sections of the British and Irish landed classes in the later nineteenth century. There were of course other reasons for such interest, ranging from the economically self-interested to the more purely political. In Parnell's case it is clear that he saw it as most important to involve labourers in the land and home rule movements.[84] At the end of his life, as his manifold enemies closed in, he made desperate attempts to carve out a distinctive constituency among Irish and British workers. But his concern with issues of labour cannot be dismissed as simply opportunistic.

Before either the land or the national questions became pressing issues at Westminster, Parnell was contributing to discussions on social legislation. During debates on the Factories and Workshops Bill he supported state intervention relating to the hours of employment of married women and children (though not adult single women).[85] He also argued for regular meal-times in workshops and factories and, where possible, the extension of factory holidays to all employees. Later on he supported an extension of the Bill which would exempt women from working in flax scutch mills, on the grounds of the unhealthiness of the work.[86]

As concern with agricultural depression mounted, it is hardly surprising that Parnell sought to link the land and labour questions in Ireland. In the winter of 1878 he urged vigorous parliamentary action to alleviate 'the sufferings of the poor labourer who famished, perhaps, on eight or nine shillings a week', simply because the farmer, 'owing to high rents and grasping landlords', was unable to pay more.[87] The point was made in more stark form at an election meeting in Dungannon. 'We have often heard that the labourers have been badly treated by the farmers, but why is this?' There was a ready, indeed congenial, answer: 'It is because the farmer is compelled by rack-rents to starve both himself and his labourers.'[88]

Within a month of the passing of Gladstone's Land Act of 1881, and the establishment of a Land Commission to fix 'fair rents', Parnell proposed an ingenious solution to the problem of low wages. They should bear in mind, he advised a meeting of the Irish National Land League in Maryborough, that if they commenced to pay good wages to their labourers before the Land Commission reviewed their rents, then the commission would be obliged to take these labour costs into account when fixing a fair rent.[89] So, he continued, 'I wish to impress upon you that liberality to your labourers will come, not out of your pockets, but out of the pockets of the landlords.' It is doubtful if many, or indeed any, of the listening farmers took this advice seriously, given its speculative and uncertain character.

Was there a link between high rents and low rural wages, as Parnell suggested? The demand for agricultural labour, it may be worth reminding ourselves, depends on the physical productivity of that labour and the value of the farm output it produces. Rent simply does not enter into the farmer's calculation of how much to pay labour. The effect of a reduction in rent, or even its abolition, would be to transfer income from the pockets of landlords to those of farmers, without any direct implications for wages.

It is of course possible that farmers might share some of this increased income with their labourers, thereby allowing them to benefit indirectly from rent reductions. In other words, they might have reacted in an altruistic rather than in a purely business fashion, as assumed here. But Parnell himself would not have subscribed to such a sentimental view of employment practices. At Enniscorthy in 1881 he felt obliged to point out to farmers that 'there are other interests in Ireland besides their own; that there are the interests of the labourers (cheers), of the artisans, of the traders, the shopkeepers, the manufacturers, and the merchants'.[90] A few years later he warned farmers that they must treat their labourers well. 'Recollect this', he said, 'in a very short time these [labourers], who some of you show you think so little of, will have equal rights with yourselves – their votes will reckon just as much as yours in the ballot-box.'[91] He appealed to Tipperary farmers for justice for their employees, stating categorically that he had 'always been most desirous for the settlement of the labourers' question'.[92] Nor was this simply platitude. He continued: any class who resisted the labourer's just demands would have to be 'coerced into doing him justice'.

A clear appreciation of the reality of rural class relations is also evident in Parnell's treatment of issues such as housing and allotments for labourers. In 1881 he argued for special housing for labourers and plots of land on which to grow vegetables and other food. In a passage, which is revealing also of his conception of proper social relations, he concludes that this would leave labourers *independent* of farmers and landlords.[93] Neither could be trusted to look after the labourers' interests.

> Before he left home in Ireland to come to that House he had a visit from a labourer, who said to him – 'The farmers are the worst men in the world as regards the labourers. They will grind them down and do nothing for them, and make them exist on starvation wages.'[94]

Reforms in the area of land and housing could be introduced, however, without interfering with farmers. Labourers could be given a small stake in the soil from the large reserves of untenanted land held by landlords.[95] If he did not know it then, Parnell must have realized fairly soon that the spatial distribution of landlord properties was such as to be incapable of solving the intensely localized housing problems of labouring households. To Parnell's obvious disappointment, farmers were quick to resist any encroachment of cottages and gardens onto their farms.[96] On a number of occasions he urged farmers to respect the needs of labourers, and in particular to refrain from obstructing the provisions of the Labourers' Housing Act, passed in 1883. Knowing that merely appealing to sentiment was unlikely to prove successful, these pleas tended to be couched in political and electoral terms as well. 'I think it would not be to your interest or to the cause of Ireland that this important though long-suffering and badly-treated class should be further neglected.'[97]

These sympathies extended also to the urban working class; Parnell had powerful political bases in Dublin and Cork but not, significantly, in Belfast. The strongest statement of the case for labour was, however, reserved for the last months of his life. The scope as well as the stridency of his proposals are surely related to his beleaguered political position at the time. On his return to Dublin, immediately after the split in the Irish party in December 1890, he assured an audience at the Rotunda that he would fight to ensure 'for labour, and the dignity of the labourer, a rightful and proper and overwhelming position in the council of the nation'. The social composition of the audience is interesting, *The Times* correspondent pointedly noting that 'the respectable classes were but slightly represented'.[98] It was in an address at Clerkenwell that Parnell's labour manifesto assumed its most advanced form.[99] Observing the strained relationships between labour and capital, he indicated his support for shorter working hours for civil servants, miners, workers engaged in dangerous occupations and also those workers whose bargaining position in relation to employers was weak. He also urged state intervention in the case of monopolistic concerns such as the great railway companies. In industrial relations, he felt that certain institutional innovations developed in the course of dealing with the Irish land question might be used more widely. Just as the Land Commission intervened between landlords and tenants, so boards of conciliation could be created to mediate between employers and workers. Thus he was opposed to the 'rude agencies of strikes and combinations' to achieve what could be done easily by means of legislation.[100] Irish MPs could not take the lead in promoting labour reforms at Westminster – this would leave them open to the charge that they were seeking to damage English prosperity – but they would certainly co-operate with the leaders of the British working class in pursuing social reform.

A few days after the speech in Clerkenwell he told a meeting in Newry of the importance of solidarity between the English and Irish working classes in pursuing labour objectives. None the less, they must never forget that 'above all things and beyond all things, they are Irish Nationalists, and that their first . . . duty is due to their motherland'.[101] In effect Parnell was saying that the labour question was a subordinate one, and that their patriotic duty lay with supporting Parnell and his faction of the Irish party. The grand labour strategy need not be taken too seriously. It was a desperate resort to radicalism so as to shore up a deteriorating political position. But viewing Parnell's career as a whole, there is no doubting a sincere, sometimes courageously expressed, sympathy with the position of labour in the two countries.

CONCLUSION

Parnell was neither an original nor a profound thinker on economic matters, Irish or otherwise. This was despite a lineage which included Sir John Parnell, Chancellor of the Irish Exchequer at the time of the Union. His reading of treatises on economic matters seems to have been limited;[102] in important respects he was a graduate of the university of the hustings and smoke-filled rooms. The manner in which economic and party political arguments neatly fused suggests that the former were subordinated to the latter.[103] An outstanding case in point is Parnell's political and economic analysis of landlordism.

The politicized nature of economic debates in the context of the rise of the home rule movement left little room for detachment. It was an article of faith among home rulers that the essential source of Irish underdevelopment was the constitutional link with Britain; by implication, self-government, in some ill-defined manner, would regenerate the economy. As Parnell put it: 'The reason the Irish do not succeed in Ireland is because a nation governed by another nation never does succeed . . . The curse of your rule – of foreign rule in Ireland – overshadows everything.'[104] The great likelihood is that a blanket assumption of this kind inhibited serious economic enquiry. Indeed one might hazard the generalization that a preoccupation – both intellectual and emotional – with the political, to the neglect of the economic, determinants of development is a characteristic failing of nationalist leaders in many countries in most time periods.

Parnell and his party never achieved state power in Ireland. Thus it cannot be assumed that his ideas would not have evolved further, in response to the pressures and opportunities of office. Still, a strongly interventionist Irish parliament does not seem especially likely under Parnell's leadership. There is a repeated acceptance of market forces or 'natural causes'.[105] On land reform, for instance, the corollary of his drive for peasant proprietorship was the desire to make it as easy 'to sell and buy land as to sell a hay-stack or a bale of cotton'.[106] There is also at times an almost Smilesian emphasis on allowing Irish people to help themselves.[107] Moreover, Parnell's necessity, as the leader of a mass nationalist movement, of stressing solidarity between different social classes would also tend to militate against policies of income and wealth redistribution. Even setting aside political imperatives, Parnell's personal disposition was to favour social harmony across the major socio-economic divides, in an Irish version of 'one-nation' toryism.[108] At a guess, one suspects he would have pursued economic policies akin to those followed by Cumann na nGaedheal in the 1920s.

Parnell's own self-image was that of a practical man.[109] An almost pure political animal might be a more apt description. In either case, it may be too much to expect a rigorous analysis on his part of the implications of some of his economic pronouncements. Moreover, the message had often to be attuned to the predilections of his listeners, or shaped to serve some larger strategic purpose. Despite these constraints, there are consistently recurring themes throughout most of his public life. These include a critique of landlordism, a preference for peasant proprietorship, an emphasis on industrialization, and a concern with improving the conditions of labour. The poverty of analysis notwithstanding, this was a worthwhile *agenda* for economic policy-making.

Parnell frequently claimed more for his policy ambitions than they could possibly yield. This is a species of inflation characteristic of the political sphere. It was endemic in nationalist politics. But he was no evangelist of utopian schemes. Notions of self-sufficiency or economic autarchy, for instance, found no place in his thought.[110] While it is true he failed to acknowledge adequately the nature and extent of Ulster industrialization, it can also be said that he entertained no illusions of a swift transition to an industrial society in a self-governing Ireland. Despite the rural and Catholic clerical backing that sustained him politically during most of his career, he did not subscribe to primitivist notions regarding the superiority of rural over urban industrial life. In this level-headedness he compared favourably with later leaders of nationalist Ireland, from Arthur Griffith to Eamon de Valera.

NOTES

1 *Freeman's Journal*, 16 March 1891. In preparing this paper I have benefited enormously from the help of Alan O'Day who not only suggested the theme, but also made available to me his extensive

collection of speeches by C. S. Parnell. I am deeply grateful for his help and encouragement. I am also grateful for the valuable comments of my colleagues D. S. Johnson and Mark Graham.

2 It is instructive in this regard to compare the economic assumptions made and the conclusions drawn by Parnell and his lieutenants with those of George O'Brien, the father figure of Irish economic history. In important respects O'Brien's trilogy of works on the Irish economy is a sophisticated version of arguments current within the home rule movement. For a critical assessment, see L. Kennedy and D. S. Johnson, 'Nationalist historiography and the decline of the Irish economy', in Sean Hutton and Paul Stewart (eds), *Ireland's Histories: Essays on Ideology, Politics and Economics*, London, 1990.

3 *Nation*, 1 September 1877.

4 *Hansard*, 3rd series, vol. cclxi, cols 895–6, 19 May 1881.

5 Ibid.

6 *Freeman's Journal*, 18 March 1885.

7 Ibid. For further criticisms, on economic grounds, of the imperial Parliament, see his speeches on Castlebar (*Nation*, 15 December 1877), at Westminster (*Hansard*, 3rd series, vol. ccxxxix, cols 597–8, 4 April 1878), and in Belfast (*Ulster Examiner*, 11 February 1879).

8 *Drogheda Argus*, 17 April 1875.

9 Ironically, it was the attempt in the 1870 Act to define legally the rights of tenants under the system of Ulster custom which had the perverse effect of increasing rather than reducing uncertainty on the part of tenants. See B. M. Walker, 'The land question and elections in Ulster', in S. Clark and J. S. Donnelly (eds), *Irish Peasants: Violence and Political Unrest, 1780–1914*, Madison, Wis., 1983, p. 237.

10 *Drogheda Argus*, 17 April 1875.

11 *Hansard*, 3rd series, vol. ccxxxiv, col. 178, 1 May 1877.

12 *Hansard*, 3rd series, vol. ccxxxix, col. 1604, 9 May 1878.

13 *Nation*, 9 November 1878.

14 *Freeman's Journal*, 15 April 1879.

15 *Hansard*, 3rd series, vol. ccxxiii, col. 1644, 26 April 1875, speech opposing a coercion Bill for Ireland.

16 *Nation*, 14 June 1879.

17 Share-cropping flourished in parts of France and central Italy. In southern Spain and Italy large estates dominated, while in east Prussia the Junker landowning class monopolized economic and political power. For a concise treatment of landholding systems in Europe, see A. Milward and S. B. Saul, *The Development of the Economies of Continental Europe, 1850–1914*, London, 1977.

18 *Freeman's Journal*, 13 October 1879, speech at Navan.

19 *Hansard*, 3rd series, vol. cclv, cols 2017–18, 24 August 1880; vol. cclxi, col. 897, 19 May 1881.

20 P. Bew, *C. S. Parnell*, Dublin, 1980, pp. 137–8.

21 There are interesting parallels here with the views of another rural reformer, also from a Protestant and landed background but a unionist in politics – those of Sir Horace Plunkett. See his *Noblesse Oblige*, Dublin, 1908. More surprisingly, perhaps, James Fintan Lalor had argued in the 1840s for leadership from the gentry within the context

of an Ireland of peasant proprietors (L. Fogarty (ed.), *James Fintan Lalor: Patriot and Political Essayist, 1807–1849*, Dublin, 1919).

22 *Globe*, 8 March 1880, speech in Toronto.

23 Ibid.

24 See, for example, A. A. Alchian and H. Demsetz, 'The property rights paradigm', *Journal of Economic History*, 33, 1973, pp. 16–27; and D. C. North and R. P. Thomas, *The Rise of the Western World: a New Economic History*, London, 1983.

25 R. Crotty, *Irish Agricultural Production*, Cork, 1966, pp. 102–7; J. J. Lee, 'Irish agriculture', *Agricultural History Review*, 17, 1969, pp. 64–76.

26 See J. S. Donnelly, jr, *The Land and the People of Nineteenth-Century Cork*, London, 1975; and W. E. Vaughan, *Landlords and Tenants in Ireland, 1848–1904*, Dublin, 1984.

27 For an incisive discussion of the distinction between 'fair rent', competitive rent and rack-rent, see B. Solow, *The Land Question and the Irish Economy, 1870–1903*, Cambridge, Mass., 1971.

28 *Glasgow Herald*, 19 April 1881.

29 *Freeman's Journal*, 25 April 1881.

30 While this was not an original line of argument – variations on it had been propagated in radical Presbyterian farming circles since at least mid century – it was well attuned to a religiously mixed Ulster audience. On this doctrine of rent and tenants' rights, see J. McKnight, *The Ulster Tenants' Claim of Right, or Landownership a State Trust*, Dublin, 1848.

31 *Freeman's Journal*, 3 October 1881, speech in Cork.

32 C. Ó. Gráda, 'The investment behaviour of Irish landlords 1850–75: some preliminary findings', *Agricultural History Review*, 23, 1975, pp. 139–55.

33 For a modern discussion see C. Ritson, *Agricultural Economics: Principles and Policy*, London, 1977. Early theories of rent are usefully traced in R. Prendergast, 'James Anderson's political economy – his influence on Smith and Malthus', *Scottish Journal of Political Economy*, 34, November 1987, pp. 388–401.

34 C. H. Hull (ed.), *Economic Writings of Sir William Petty*, Cambridge, 1899, vol. i, pp. 214–16.

35 *Glasgow Herald*, 19 April 1881, speech at Glasgow City Hall. In a similar vein, see the speeches reported in the *Freeman's Journal*, 2 September 1881, 3 October 1881 and 24 March 1891.

36 This line of thought also led Parnell into blackly humorous discussions of the numbers and proportions of 'good' and 'bad' landlords in Ireland.

37 For valuable early discussions of this interdependence, see the *Report from the Select Committee on Tenure and Improvement of Land (Ireland) Act*, BPP, xi, 1865.

38 For example, on the Abercorn estates these averaged twenty-one times the annual rent in the period 1881–6, while on the Earl of Ranfurly's estate the corresponding figure was fourteen. See *Reports from Commissioners, Inspectors and Others: Land Acts (Ireland)*, BPP, xxvi, 1887.

39 H. George, *Progress and Poverty*, New York, 1956. Two chapter titles convey the flavour of his views on land ownership: 'Injustice of private property in land' and 'Enslavement of labourers the ultimate result of private property in land'.

40 On Davitt the best, if incomplete, biography is T. W. Moody's *Davitt and Irish Revolution 1846–82*, Oxford, 1982. Davitt's unorthodox views on the land question are contained in his very fine work, *The Fall of Feudalism in Ireland*, London, 1904.

41 *United Ireland*, 19 April 1884.

42 *Freeman's Journal*, 16 March 1891.

43 Address to the House of Representatives in Washington, *Congressional Record*, 2 February 1880, X, Pt 1, pp. 664–5.

44 It is strikingly revealed in Figure 8.1 how some of the poorest counties (Mayo, Kerry, Donegal, Leitrim) also experienced acute population pressure. The opposite is true of the rich eastern counties of Meath, Westmeath and Dublin. Land quality is measured here in terms of the valuation (£) per 100 acres. Population density is defined as the rural population in a county in 1881 divided by the value of farmland in that county. The correlation coefficient for the two variables is -0.62 (Ros is Roscommon; Tip is Tipperary; Wex is Wexford).

45 C. Clark, *The Value of Agricultural Land*, Oxford, 1973.

46 *Hansard*, 3rd series, vol. cclxi, col. 893, 19 May 1881.

47 *Freeman's Journal*, 6 December 1880.

48 The major accounts of the grazier system are to be found in D. S. Jones, 'Agrarian capitalism and rural social development in Ireland', unpublished Ph.D. thesis (1977). Queen's University, Belfast, and in P. Bew, *Conflict and Conciliation in Ireland, 1890–1910*, Oxford, 1987.

49 *Freeman's Journal*, 6 December 1880.

50 P. Bew, 'The Land League ideal: achievements and contradictions', in P. J. Drudy (ed.), *Ireland: Land, Politics and People*, Cambridge, 1982, pp. 77–92.

51 M. A. G. Ó. Tuathaigh, 'The land question, politics and Irish society, 1922–60', in Drudy, *Ireland*, pp. 167–89.

52 W. L. Micks, *History of the Congested Districts Board*, Dublin, 1925.

53 For Parnell's explanation – essentially that landlords discreetly boycotted the company – see *The Times*, 20 December 1889.

54 See, for example, *Freeman's Journal*, 1 April 1880, 6 December 1880; *The Times*, 18 December 1882.

55 On the minimum viable size of farms, and how it increased during the twentieth century, see P. Commins, 'Land policies and agricultural development', in Drudy, *Ireland*, pp. 219–20.

56 W. E. Vaughan and A. J. Fitzpatrick (eds), *Irish Historical Statistics: Population 1821–1921*, Dublin, 1978, p. 262.

57 *Hansard*, 3rd series, vol. ccliv, cols 416–17, 14 July 1880.

58 *The Times*, 12 December 1883.

59 For pre-famine Ireland, see J. Mokyr, *Why Ireland Starved*, London, 1985, pp. 255–9, and, for the later nineteenth century onwards, K. A. Kennedy, T. Giblin and D. McHugh, *The Economic Development of Ireland in the Twentieth Century*, London, 1988.

60 The economic costs of emigration to Irish society were potential rather

than real if the emigrants could *not* have been absorbed into productive employment at home.

61 K. A. Kennedy, *et al.*, *Economic Development*, pp. 12–15.
62 *The Times*, 18 December 1889, speech in Nottingham.
63 *Freeman's Journal*, 18 March 1891.
64 *United Ireland*, 15 October 1881.
65 *Hansard*, 3rd series, vol. cclxi, col. 896, 19 May 1881.
66 Ibid. See also *Freeman's Journal*, 11 October 1881 and 21 August 1885.
67 *Freeman's Journal*, 3 October 1881: the point was later repeated at Drogheda (*United Ireland*, 19 April 1884).
68 *Freeman's Journal*, 21 August 1885.
69 *United Ireland*, 10 October 1885.
70 On dependency theory in relation to Ireland, see E. O'Malley, *Unequal Competition: the Problem of Late Development and Irish Industry*, London, 1989, and L. Kennedy, *The Modern Industrialisation of Ireland, 1940–88*, Dublin, 1989.
71 *Hansard*, 3rd series, vol. cccvi, col. 1181, 7 June 1886.
72 *The Times*, 18 December 1889.
73 Ibid.
74 *Ulster Examiner*, 16 October 1879.
75 G. O'Brien, 'Patrick Hogan Minister for Agriculture 1922–1932', *Studies*, vol. 25, 1936, pp. 353–68.
76 *Ulster Examiner*, 16 October 1879.
77 'American competition would continue, and will forever check the resumption of prices that we have been having during the last four or five years' (*Ulster Examiner*, 18 October 1879). Note also his analysis of the crisis in a speech to the House of Commons (*Hansard*, 3rd series, vol. ccxlvi, col. 1397, 27 May 1879), and at meetings in Tullow, County Carlow (*Freeman's Journal*, 29 September 1879) and in Roscommon (*Freeman's Journal*, 18 November 1879). On his American tour in the following year, Parnell placed the emphasis on the 'unequal and artificial tenure of land which prevails' (*New York Times*, 5 January 1880).
78 J. Foreman-Peck, *A History of the World Economy: International Economic Relations since 1850*, Brighton, 1983, pp. 39–45.
79 *Ulster Examiner*, 18 October 1879.
80 As happened, for example, in Russian peasant agriculture immediately after the Bolshevik revolution in 1917 and the expropriation of the nobles. For an overview see M. Lewin, *Russian Peasants and Soviet Power*, London, 1968.
81 P. Commins and C. Kelleher, *Farm Inheritance and Succession*, Dublin, 1973.
82 L. Kennedy and P. Ollerenshaw (eds), *An Economic History of Ulster, 1820–1939*, Manchester, 1985, Preface.
83 Though an exaggeration, the term 'caste' has some validity and was used in this loose sense by Sir Horace Plunkett to describe fellow landowning families (*Ireland in the New Century*, London, 1903, p. 63).
84 *Freeman's Journal*, 29 December 1880.

85 *Hansard*, 3rd series, vol. ccxxxviii, col. 94, 21 February 1878.
86 *Hansard*, 3rd series, vol. ccxxxviii, col. 590, 1 March 1878.
87 *Nation*, 23 November 1878.
88 *Freeman's Journal*, 2 September 1881.
89 *Freeman's Journal, 27 September 1881.*
90 *Freeman's Journal*, 10 October 1881. There are some ways in which
    a reduction in the rent burden might have benefited labourers (but
    these do not form part of Parnell's thought). One is through economic
    ignorance. Farmers experiencing an increase in net income, and unable
    to distinguish between returns from land and other factors of pro-
    duction, might be misled into believing that additional inputs of labour
    would increase their incomes still further. Another is that a rise in
    income could lead to an increase in farmers' demand for leisure. This,
    in turn, could take the form of substituting hired labour for their own
    labour.
91 *United Ireland*, 19 April 1884.
92 *Freeman's Journal*, 9 January 1885.
93 *Hansard*, 3rd series, vol. cclxi, col. 895, 19 May 1881.
94 *Hansard*, 3rd series, vol. cclxi, col. 1987, 6 May 1881.
95 Ibid.
96 *Hansard*, 3rd series, vol. cclxxix, cols 1247–8, 30 May 1883.
97 *United Ireland*, 19 April 1884. See also *Hansard*, 3rd series, vol.
    cclxxxviii, cols 967–8, 21 May 1884.
98 *The Times*, 11 December 1890.
99 *The Times*, 5 March 1891.
100 Ibid.
101 *Freeman's Journal*, 9 March 1891.
102 F. S. L. Lyons, 'The economic ideas of Parnell', in Michael Roberts
    (ed.), *Historical Studies*, vol. ii, London, 1959, pp. 60–78. This is a
    valuable essay, concerned more with an exposition than an evaluation
    of Parnell's ideas.
103 The priority of the political was reflected also in Parnell's ordering of
    issues. In a famous passage from a speech in Athenry (*Freeman's
    Journal*, 25 October 1880) he proclaimed, in relation to the land
    agitation: 'I would not have taken off my coat and gone to this work
    if I had not known that we were laying the foundation in this move-
    ment for the regeneration of our legislative independence.' Parnell's
    cool response to the Plan of Campaign is also indicative of the priority
    attached to political and constitutional change.
104 *Hansard*, 3rd series, vol. cclxi, col. 896, 19 May 1881.
105 *Freeman's Journal*, 12 October 1879; *New York Times*, 5 January 1880.
106 *New York Times*, 5 January 1880. See also *Ulster Examiner*, 16 Octo-
    ber 1879.
107 See, for example, his speeches in Arklow (*Freeman's Journal*, 21
    August 1885) and in Nottingham (*The Times*, 18 December 1889).
108 See, for example, the speeches reported in the *Ulster Examiner*, 29
    September 1877; *Nation*, 14 June 1879; *Freeman's Journal*, 27 Septem-
    ber 1881 and again on 9 March 1891.
109 *Freeman's Journal*, 21 August 1885.

110 One can cite occasional loose statements to the contrary, but these should be indulged as simply excesses of rhetoric.

9   Parnell: Orator and speaker[1]

Alan O'Day

Oratory is the usual avenue to leadership in a democratic movement, and Mr Parnell is one of the few who have arrived at
power neither by that road nor by military success. So far from
having by nature any of the gifts or graces of a popular speaker,
he was at first conspicuously deficient in them, and became at
last effective only by constant practice, and by an intellectual
force which asserted itself through commonplaces of language
and a monotonous delivery. Fluency was wanting, and even moderate ease was acquired only after four or five years practice. His
voice was neither powerful nor delicate in its modulations, but it
was clear, and the enunciation deliberate and distinct, quiet when
the matter was ordinary, slow and emphatic when an important
point arrived. With very little action of the body, there was
often an interesting and obviously unstudied display of facial
expression. So far from glittering with the florid rhetoric supposed
to characterise Irish eloquence, his speeches were singularly plain,
bare, and dry. Neither had they any humour.[2]

That Parnell possessed exceptional qualities placing him above the
ranks of talented or even gifted politicians scarcely is a matter of
dispute. Alone among the champions of Ireland Parnell was
acclaimed the leader not simply of the nation but of the Irish race
everywhere. That notion of an Irish people, of course, was restricted to those of national inclinations but Parnell's achievement is
hardly diminished by this caveat. Daniel O'Connell and Eamon de
Valera, too, were charismatic figures receiving an adoration at least
as intense as Parnell's, and it certainly is possible to argue that
both men gained more for Ireland, but neither they nor other Irish
politicians could lay claim to so complete an allegiance of the 'race'.
By comparison with Parnell other leaders were parochial figures.

Yet, despite Parnell's status, the sources of his compelling ascendancy, along with his continued grip on the imaginations of subsequent generations, have evaded easy definition. Usually, inspirational leaders, as James Bryce observed, were moving orators purveying uplifting sentiments. Parnell has never been seen as an orator or man of ideas but as a shrewd leader with a remarkable political antenna who constructed an effective organizational machine and won certain material boons for Ireland.[3] Valuable as such attributes may be, they are not the qualities to ignite mass enthusiasm nor the stuff to excite poets. Perhaps no one captured Parnell's attraction on paper so persuasively as R. Barry O'Brien, though his portrait, too, tantalizes without quite penetrating the mystique of the man.[4] Later writers have sought to grapple with the forces that transformed Parnell from a stumbling speaker into a revered leader without significantly improving on O'Brien's picture. Indeed, if anything, a modern scholarship dissecting both Parnell and his movement has obscured rather than illuminated his magnetism.

Parnell's speeches have never been ignored – they are the stable source for assessing his views and the progress of the nationalist movement. However, it has been usual to examine his speeches piecemeal rather than as an approach to Parnell's manipulation of social and political communication, a theme to be investigated here. It is suggested that his speeches had more importance in establishing a personal charisma than has been acknowledged, though primarily by how they were transmitted to the wider audience. Additionally, evaluation of Parnell's speeches allows an assessment of how he viewed politics, his own function in political life, and most pertinently, the extent of his commitment to the Westminster House of Commons as an Irish forum.

It seems unlikely that any revisionism can transform Parnell into a moving orator. Bryce, as quoted, treated Parnell's speaking skills sympathetically but he was mainly concerned with his performances in the House of Commons. Parnell's Irish contemporaries were not bashful about recalling his initial fumbling platform efforts.[5] Nor had he improved dramatically by 1880. During Parnell's American tour in early 1880 several newspapers commented on his oratorical shortcomings. Following an address in the city of brotherly love, a Philadelphia newspaper pointed to his 'manifest sincerity' rather than qualities as a speaker as the source of support engendered there.[6] In Boston his appearance was greeted less generously. It was noted, 'he has some hesitancy in his speech, often corrects a word or phrase which he has uttered, and during the latter part of his address he was visibly affected'.[7] On moving inland where folk allegedly were more receptive to plain speaking, Parnell's skills continued to be depreciated. In St Paul, Minnesota it was reported,

> his manner is quiet, and his gestures few and it is evidently his subject more than his style that appeals to the audience. He makes no oratorical displays, and attempts no rhetorical flourishes, but states his views and facts so calmly that he seldom rouses the enthusiasm for which his countrymen are so noted.[8]

Of his address at Peoria, Illinois, it was remarked drily that 'his manner is not calculated to produce very much enthusiasm'.[9] Even in 1890 the *Nation* noted that he was not an orator and would never seek to claim distinction as a public speaker.[10]

Though Parnell had a distinctly limited speaking style, he also showed a penchant for the apt phrase, the *bon môt*. Many of his statements were the political currency of the day and remain frequently cited now. Phrases like 'keep a firm grip on your homesteads', his characterization of Gladstone as a 'masquerading knight' and the ringing affirmation that 'no man has the right to fix the boundary to the march of a nation', the last forming part of the inscription on the Parnell Monument in Dublin, are but a few of the well-known illustrations of this gift.[11] Great orators, including O'Connell, Isaac Butt and John Redmond, were less quotable.

It is a cruel irony that virtually the only substantial first-hand source for Parnell should be his speeches. He wrote little in his own right. His letter-writing generally was confined to brief issuances of instructions, acknowledgements, apologies and occasional requests for information. Few of these terse efforts have been preserved. Parnell's main indulgence in correspondence was open letters, usually to the *Freeman's Journal*. Where these documents survive and are accessible, they generally are of modest importance. Parnell did not keep a journal or diary; he did not attempt a memoir. There is an abundance of later reminiscences by contemporaries but the accuracy of these is suspect. Parnell, in any event, was not given to introspection, at least for the benefit of colleagues, and even Mrs O'Shea's volumes published in 1914 do no more than lift a corner of the shroud which has concealed his private emotions.[12] Only the speeches exist in something like complete form.

Nearly the whole of The Chief's vast corpus of parliamentary and public addresses is available. Curiously, until lately, no systematic attempt to compile these valuable documents was undertaken. Evidently supporters intended to gather together the speeches following Parnell's death but, if the project was begun at all, it rapidly languished.[13] As he was primarily a man of words, the neglect has deprived posterity of an indispensable resource. To date, historians have tended to rely on small or random selections of Parnell's speeches, frequently taking from them only the emotive or colourful phrases and ignoring the context in which each was given. Several attempts to discuss Parnell's American tour of 1880, for example, have relied upon an examination of a few speeches only but have none the less suffered no bashfulness in rendering verdicts on the episode. However deficient Parnell was as an orator, he remained a traditional politician in his resort to public and parliamentary platforms in attempts to state positions, influence opinion on policy and rally support. In the months following December 1890, after abstinence from speaking in Ireland, he unhesitatingly stumped the country in a campaign to retrieve his ascendancy over national opinion.

Parnell's speeches can be classified by time, place, purpose and audience though many cross the neat boundaries imposed by this type of categorization. Usually, his addresses have been treated in the context of a radical to moderate axis but, as will be seen, other perspectives on them can be inserted which are important as well. Most, though, showed evidence of meticulous preparation and were succinct. Bryce noted that the parliamentary speeches 'were carefully prepared, and usually made from pretty full notes, but the preparation had been given rather to the matter of arrangement than to diction, which had rarely any ornament or literary finish'.[14] He emphasized of Parnell,

> when he interposed without preparation in a debate which had arisen unexpectedly, he was short, pithy, and direct; indeed, nothing was more characteristic of Parnell than his talent for hitting the nail on the head, a talent which always commands attention in deliberative assemblies.

Impromptu remarks at public or party meetings showed that Parnell was a man seldom caught off-guard.

The content and tone of his speeches differed over time, by place, audience and political exigencies. This is no less than might be expected; nor does it distinguish Parnell from other Irish or British politicians. Most of his speeches, totalling several thousand, were delivered within the precinct of the Palace of Westminster. Most of these outpourings consisted of interjections in debates.

Parnell's most intense periods of parliamentary activity were between 1877 and 1881; during 1882; from 1885 to 1887 and then in 1891. Prior to 1877 he was a minor player in debates. Though certainly less vigorous in the sessions of 1883 and 1884, he by no means can be said to have drifted into the shadows. Also, from 1888 to 1890 he was less involved but continued to be present and to speak in major debates.[15] Parnell's pattern of participation did not strictly reflect his own importance or influence either inside or beyond Parliament. Simple statistical analysis of his parliamentary activity would conceal qualitative dimensions of Parnell's speeches.

Before gaining the party chairmanship in 1880 Parnell had been regular in parliamentary attendance and vigorous in debate though his addresses by common consent lacked artistry. His rise to the formal leadership did not result from an abundant display of skill in the House of Commons. Bryce appropriately labelled this period educative.[16] During this time Parnell took up a substantial range of Irish and other wide-reaching topics. His impact on national consciousness came from dramatic insistences that Ireland was not merely a 'geographical fragment' of England but 'a Nation' and by stating 'that I do not believe and never shall believe that any murder was committed at Manchester'.[17] But the volume of such utterances was limited. While Parnell upheld orthodox national positions, for instance, on home rule and the land, he had almost nothing original to say on these matters. In other ways he marked himself out as a diligent constituency member, taking up local questions, pressing the government over the small numbers and salaries of Catholic military chaplains, alleging that Catholic soldiers in Meath, his constituency, were prohibited from attendance at Sunday Mass, and similar problems.[18] Parnell deviated most from the bulk of home rule MPs in his assiduous attendance and attention to detail in a party notoriously lax on both counts.

After 1876, though, Parnell did strike a different note from the majority of Butt's party when he practised parliamentary obstruction by advocating an aggressive or active policy for home rulers in the House of Commons, and for his vigorous pursuit of issues like the South Africa Bill and anti-flogging campaign. Parnell's standing in Ireland resulted from these differences, especially as a consequence of his spirited resistance. The admiration which he received from a section of the Fenian movement and his appeal to advanced nationalists generally was the dividend of Parnell's militancy in the House of Commons. By 1877 and 1878 he was seen as the main alternative to Butt; his policy as the one more likely to advance Ireland's case. During the latter part of 1877 the bitter dispute over the 'active' approach broke into the open again in the demand for a National Conference to consider future courses of parliamentary action.[19] Controversy surrounding the conference served further to exalt Parnell as the personification of Irish intransigence.

Parnell's attitude had a negative quality. Emphasis on that side alone masks his abiding commitment to parliamentarianism. Even the extent of his 'obstructionism' is a moot point.[20] Parnell never resorted to it on more than an occasional basis, and then at certain moments of the session. It was not an all-purpose weapon. Most instances of 'obstruction' took place late at night when few MPs were present in the House and the actual inconvenience to the Conservative government was minimal. By 1877 that regime had lost its earlier legislative impetus[21] – in fact, Parnell's tactics offered a tempting scapegoat for Tory remissness. But the chief characteristic of 'obstruction' was that it, and Irish discussion concerning application of the tactic, recognized the centrality of Parliament. Activism was a parliamentary weapon. Though Parnell cautioned the Irish people that they could not depend on MPs or Parliament to carry their cause unaided, his own role in the movement was to wage the fight at Westminster. His first real incursion into the land agitation was at Westport in June 1879 though he maintained a distance from the movement until well into the autumn.[22] In the meantime he devoted himself to other political business including the Ennis by-election, the anti-flogging campaign and general parliamentary affairs.

Parnell's parliamentarianism was reinforced by an enlarged contingent of followers returned at the general election of 1880 and his selection as party chairman. During 1880 and 1881 a major part of the land battle was fought within the walls of Westminster. He did not, to be sure, rely on parliamentarianism alone, but the emphasis of Parnell's strategy was to pressure the Gladstone ministry to legislate on the land question. His advice to people at home was to help themselves but also to do nothing which would discredit their claim in England or weaken the resolve of the regime to pass a Land Bill. After 1882 Parnell was certainly more of a parliamentarian than an agitator. His coliseum was the House of Commons. The general election of 1885 from an Irish point of view was meant to strengthen Parnell's arm at Westminster. He specifically called upon the Irish people to give him the gladiators necessary for the combat ahead in Parliament. In February 1886, at the Galway by-election where he forced Captain O'Shea upon the party and constituency, Parnell claimed he held 'a parliament for Ireland in the hollow of my hand' and pleaded that this grip not be loosened by rejecting his nominee.[23]

Gladstone's advocacy of home rule in 1886 underlined the primacy of parliamentary action, but it was only an increment in the policy of the party and of Parnell. His main theatre had been the House of Commons from the moment of entry into that assembly. Between 1887 and 1890 Parnell was a parliamentary figure almost exclusively. Even in 1891 he did not counsel rejection of parliamentarianism but urged the Irish people to repudiate those who overthrew him for they could not be relied upon to meet governments on an equal footing or press the cause effectively in the House of Commons. Not surprisingly, Parnell made more speeches in Parliament during 1891 than in Ireland, though this was a period of intense public speaking as well.

Several observations about Parnell's parliamentary speaking can be offered. Clearly, it was regarded by him as an important, usually the main, venue for political activity. It was in the House of Commons that he appeared most frequently, spoke often and had fewer periods of comparative inaction. Parnell never renounced the primacy of parliamentarianism – indeed he used his public appearances to promote or enhance his title to leadership in the House of Commons. And, as Bryce noted, his speeches at Westminster were constructed with care. He showed a thorough grasp of issues and of detail. Many of the speeches, including his early interjections into debates, were the product of a sharp, well-informed mind. Yet it has to be borne in mind that the parliamentary addresses were not stirring inspirational pieces but the product of an efficient politician. Bryce observed that many of the pre–1885 speeches were marked by a 'hard attorneyism' which was less obtrusive in the later years. Nevertheless, he noted that even then,

> there was nothing genial or generous or elevated about them. They never soared into an atmosphere of lofty feeling, worthy of the man who was by this time deemed to be leading his nation to victory, and who had begun to be admired and honoured by one of the two great historic English parties.[24]

Extra-parliamentary addresses were less voluminous but still totalled in excess of five hundred. These had four forms – the set-piece public speech delivered at demonstrations or important meetings; impromptu remarks to crowds; responses to Irish deputations; and statements made at party or other organizational sessions. The major public address normally was prepared carefully, though Parnell displayed a capacity to respond in a ready fashion to moods and remarks from his audience. Public speeches had varying degrees of importance ranging from such famous occasions as at Ennis in 1880 and Cork in 1885 to several venues in 1891, but most were simply repetitious. Serial addresses where Parnell faced different audiences in quick succession, but spoke on the same subject, were the norm. His tour of northern and Scottish towns in 1877, the speeches in America in 1880, Land League demonstrations and many of the appearances during 1891 are instances when he essentially repeated himself for the benefit of separate audiences. Significant addresses were comparatively few. Moreover, impromptu speeches and reported comments at party meetings far exceeded the total of public occasions anyway. His addresses for whatever audience were nearly always topical – those in 1877 concerned the active parliamentary policy; speeches given between 1879 and 1881 treated the land issue; in 1885 he spoke on home rule and the need for an enlarged party; between 1886 and 1890 Parnell praised the benefits of the Liberal alliance; while in 1891 the subject of the hour was the split. Whereas in parliamentary debates, especially prior to 1880, Parnell's speeches showed breadth, those given outside were restricted to a narrow band of topics, virtually limited to Irish matters.

The speeches in the House of Commons have been accessible, if scattered through the volumes of *Hansard*. For practical purposes, they comprise a full and accurate rendering of The Chief's words. Sources for the extra-parliamentary efforts are more diffuse. Because of Parnell's almost instant prominence, his speeches from the beginning received attention in Ireland and were reported fully in the press. A number of omissions, though, can be identified. Some speeches in 1875 and probably also in 1876 were not reproduced in Irish newspapers. Parnell's appearances in England and Scotland were liable to receive reduced coverage or be omitted altogether. In August and September 1877 he and John O'Connor Power undertook an extensive speaking tour of northern and Scottish towns to argue for the active policy. Few of these addresses were published in Ireland or in the London press, but can be found in the local newspapers of the towns visited. There is no complete text for three of his speeches in Scotland. However, the largest number of omissions occurred during the American tour in 1880. At the time Parnell was engaged in a dispute with the proprietor of the *Freeman's Journal*, Edmund Dwyer Gray, and his newspaper restricted its reporting of the tour. Only the eastern seaboard portion of the visit received more than cursory attention. As a consequence, Parnell's alleged declaration at Cincinnati that he would not be content until the 'last link' binding Ireland and England had been broken went unnoticed then though it later became a bone of contention.[25] The record of public speeches, therefore, is less complete than for Parliament but, overall, the voids are few. Texts of most extra-parliamentary addresses were published though not all appeared in any single newspaper. Thus, there exists a fairly full, reliable account of The Chief's utterances.

Parnell's uneven pattern of parliamentary speaking has been noted. Distortion in the extra-parliamentary efforts was more marked. His speeches were concentrated disproportionately into three sequences – 1879–81 (land war), 1885 (general election) and 1891 (party split). Beyond these clusters he spoke outside Parliament as many as twenty times in a single year only in 1877. His total for that spell was inflated by the serial addresses delivered in England and Scotland under the auspices of the Home Rule Confederation immediately after his election as its president. Before 1877 he gave very few speeches in Ireland. In 1883 Parnell's platform appearances rose narrowly into double figures though half of that number were delivered over a two-week period in the Monaghan by-election. During the next year his total dipped to seven with his visit to Tuam being the only speaking engagement outside the ambit of London and the east coast of Ireland. Between February 1886 and December 1890 Parnell did not mount a platform anywhere in Ireland. Even in those spans of comparatively dense speaking, Parnell gave most of the addresses over a brief period, usually when the House of Commons was not sitting. The 'demonstration season' of early autumn was much favoured. The bunching effect tended to over-state Parnell's accessibility. So far as public speech-making was concerned, it clearly existed as an exercise undertaken with varying intensity.

Analysis of Parnell's speaking by venue also reveals a circumscribed pattern. A large number of the total were given in Dublin and Cork. Many of the addresses in Dublin took the form of remarks at meetings. When Parnell attended the land demonstration at Westport in early June 1879, it was merely the fourth speech he had made in Connaught. It can hardly be said that he traversed widely in Ireland before autumn 1880. Even then and during 1881 Parnell addressed few audiences in the western half of the country.

His initial appearance in King's County was in February 1881.[26] In 1882 Parnell's speaking in Ireland was restricted to Dublin and Cork; in 1883 to those two cities plus Monaghan; in 1884 to Drogheda, Tuam; and even in 1885 his circuit was remarkably narrow. During January he spoke in several small centres in western Cork, Limerick and Clare but his pilgrimages to the west were confined to the Galway and Castlebar conventions in the autumn. Most of Parnell's speeches were delivered in Munster and Leinster though in these provinces, also, only a few places were visited. Not until 1891 did he truly barnstorm the country. Generally, Parnell confined his travels to the market towns served by the rail network. Many areas never had the honour of a visit, or saw him only once or twice in a political career which stretched over sixteen years. Apparently, for example, he never spoke in, and possibly did not visit, Donegal, the native county of Isaac Butt. In contrast, particularly in 1891, the folk of Limerick Junction, Tipperary, an important railway stop, had quite exceptional opportunities to see and hear The Chief.

Parnell's extraordinary charisma was exerted at a distance. No more than a tiny fraction of the Irish people ever heard Parnell speak or even caught a glimpse of him in the flesh. His absence of oratorical gifts proved no more than a modest embarrassment in a society which did not hear him. Of those fortunate few who attended his addresses, many would not have heard his words with any clarity. Often the crowds, especially outside, were restless and noisy and Parnell's voice did not carry a great distance. Some demonstrations were held in inclement conditions, further adding to the burden of listening. That the occasions were memorable pieces of theatre, though, has been attested to repeatedly. Being present for one of Parnell's addresses was a major and exciting moment.[27] Although the proposition cannot be tested fully at present, there appears to be a correspondence between places where Parnell spoke with some regularity before December 1890 and support for him during the split. Even during 1891 his trips to previously neglected areas were an important influence in mustering the people in his favour. Yet the overwhelming reality remains that Parnell was neither seen nor heard by the country as a whole.

To suggest that Parnell was largely unknown in the flesh does not negate the impact he made on those who did hear him. A case can be made for his effectiveness as a communicator. His public speeches generally were of modest length, were well constructed, and used an appropriate but not over-elaborate vocabulary.[28] Parnell did not talk down to his audience and the speeches had the merit of avoiding a strain on patience. Many of his important addresses were delivered in halls in Dublin and Cork but others, especially those outdoor demonstrations, demanded that people stand for long periods and the length of the whole occasion was likely to be considerable.[29] A short pithy speech was effective on such platforms. But the real influence Parnell exerted was contained in what he said, as Bryce observed of the complementary efforts in the House of Commons.

In his Irish addresses a comparatively small number of essentially nationalist themes received repeated emphasis. The need for self-government was always a key demand. Parnell, perhaps more than any other leading Irish politician, appreciated that the coalition which sheltered under the national umbrella could only hold together if one universally endorsed demand was given pride of place on the agenda. In 1876 and 1877 he deplored the failure to give primacy to the home rule issue and believed that its neglect led to splits and a decline in popular backing of the Irish party.[30] In 1885, when confronted with internal squabbles, he reverted to an emphasis on the self-government claim.[31] Predictably, in 1891 Parnell attempted to seize the home rule initiative for himself. From February that year he gradually realized that opponents had successfully appropriated home rule for themselves, particularly its likely achievement under a Liberal regime. At that juncture Parnell began to abandon his traditional stress on a single unifying issue and then widened the programme to include labour and social questions. Land, also, was a key weapon in Parnell's speaking arsenal. He spoke on it especially between 1879 and 1881, but additionally in autumn 1885 and during 1891. Administration of justice in Ireland, coercion, the development of home manufacturers and Irish self-reliance were themes which he treated as well. Parnell's expanded platform in spring and summer 1891 has been cited as evidence of the desperation of a cornered man.[32] Then, he gave attention and support to labour and social questions. No doubt his broadened outlook reflected opportunism but it harked back to Parnell's interests in the 1870s which necessarily had been relegated to the back burner during the post–1880 era.

Excepting for the brief spell after he entered the House of Commons, Parnell's speeches were notable for an absence of reference to the grievances or injustices experienced by specific individuals or locales. His preference was for the high ground, to argue from principle. In this respect his public performances were an accompaniment to the parliamentary speeches. Even when Parnell visited his Cork constituents after 1880 – a city with strong localized concerns – he rarely gave these much heed. His indifference to such parochial issues could be seen in most situations. For much of his career Parnell appeared regularly in mainland British cities with substantial Irish populations. Prior to autumn 1879, in fact, Parnell was a frequenter of these centres to a greater degree than he was of many districts in Ireland. The combined total of his speeches in Ulster and Connaught had not equalled his addresses to the Irish in Britain. Between 1880 and 1885 he continued to speak on the mainland; from early 1886 to late 1890 it was the only place where he spoke. Even in the thick of the leadership battle in 1891 he did not abandon British platforms. Parnell had many intimate links with the Irish in Britain. They had been the earliest group to support his policy, had chosen him President of the Home Rule Confederation of Great Britain in 1877, and at several points (1883, 1885, 1890) he gave special emphasis to their political influence.[33] In May 1890, following an attempt to improve the exiles' electoral organization, the *Nation* expanded on Parnell's remarks, noting that 'while at home the vote can only be used to demonstrate Ireland's unalterable attachment to the principle of self-government, in Great Britain it can be used in large measure to decide the issue'.[34] Parnell was at pains to stress the 'obligations' of the Irish to aid the movement. But, for him the 'duty' was one-sided. He devoted minuscule attention to the peculiar problems of the immigrant community.

A similar, if less surprising, case was the Irish in America. During the tour of 1880 he said very little about the difficulties they faced, regarding them as financial and moral props for his organization. The Chief's main reference to the situation of the Irish was to note their poverty. His promise to Americans was that a prosperous Ireland would cease to export Irish paupers. Parnell preferred the plateau of generalization and principle to the trenches of particularized or local problems. The parish pump was not Parnell's domain. He regarded his speeches as a weapon for educating public opinion on large questions.

Despite Parnell's limitations as an orator, he elucidated nationalist themes in ways which endeared him to the people. Certain of these have been cited already. No other speech had so resounding an impact as his address at Cork on 21 January 1885. There Parnell stated what has been seen as his testament of nationalist faith, telling his listeners,

But I go back from the consideration of these questions to the consideration of the great question of national self-government for Ireland. I do not know how this great question will be eventually settled. I do not know whether England will be wise in time and concede to constitutional arguments and methods the restitution of that which was stolen from us towards the close of the last century. It is given to none of us to forecast the future, and just as it is impossible for us to say in what way or by what means the national question may be settled, in what way full justice may be done to Ireland, so it is impossible for us to say to what extent that justice shall be done. We cannot ask for less than the restitution of Grattan's Parliament, with its important privileges and wide and far-reaching constitution. We can not, under the British Constitution, ask for more than the restitution of Grattan's Parliament. But no man has the right to fix the boundary to the march of a nation; no man has a right to say to his country: 'Thus far shalt thou go and no further', and we have never attempted to fix the *ne plus ultra* to the progress of Ireland's nationhood, and we never shall. But, while we leave these things to time, circumstances, and the future, we must each one of us resolve in our own hearts that we shall at all times do everything which within us lies to obtain for Ireland the fullest measure of her rights. In this way we shall not give up anything which the future may put in favour of our country; and while we struggle today for that which may seem possible for us with our combination that we shall not do anything to hinder or prevent better men who may come after us from gaining better things than those for which we now contend.[35]

The speech conveyed many central themes and had an electrifying effect similar to President Kennedy's declamation that Americans should 'ask not what your country can do for you – ask what you can do for your country'.[36]

Parnell's address at Cork was the anthem of Irish national consciousness. It contained elements congenial to constitutional and revolutionary traditions along with a pledge that nothing must be done to forestall the aspirations of those who would succeed the present generation of political leaders. Parnell's studied ambiguity has been a commonplace of historical interpretation of his career. This view also suited Unionist opponents nicely for it facilitated using his utterances as evidence of a revolutionary wolf in constitutional sheep's clothing. Barry O'Brien's portrait was equivocal on the matter. He cited contemporary Fenians to the effect that Parnell at heart approved of their methods. Yet O'Brien noted that Parnell was laid to rest under the shadow of the tower marking where O'Connell sleeps.[37] In the closing paragraph of the biography the ambiguity of Parnell's legacy received emphasis. Thus, a legend gained currency that Parnell was never averse to an armed struggle but only relied on non-violent methods as a matter of practical necessity. His alleged extremism was conditioned by time and place – he took a more moderate line after 1882, especially from 1885 until 1891, and spoke in a more extreme way the further he was from Westminster.

Most of Parnell's public speeches contained a nationalist declaration, usually near the conclusion. Yet, the vast bulk of addresses were neither as blatant as that at Cork nor as imbued with equivocation on the means for achieving national aims. Still, a number of speeches, especially in 1876, 1880, 1885, 1889 and 1891, complemented Parnell's stance at Cork. Nevertheless, Parnell ordinarily could be found upholding constitutional methods and advocating support for what was essentially a parliamentary approach to Irish grievances.

The American speeches in 1880 illustrate Parnell's speaking technique. That tour was exceptionally important for during it he raised an impressive booty to aid the Irish tenants and to carry on the political agitation.[38] It also had an enormous impact on Parnell's reputation at home and abroad. The trip was under the guidance of the Clan na Gael, noted for its extremism, and Parnell scarcely could be blamed for setting a tone which obliged his hosts. In nearly every address Parnell stated that the goal of his movement in the longer term was to re-establish Ireland's nationhood. However, references to more purely national themes occupied little time and always were placed towards the conclusion. The main points covered in each speech were the state of the Irish peasantry, the neglect of British government, the evil of landlordism, and quite early in the tour he engaged in criticisms of the three other relief funds then in existence. The burden of Parnell's comments was to emphasize the value and role of moral pressure on the British regime in order to secure legislation for tenant-farmers. On arrival in New York Parnell explained,

we want to relieve the people, but we also want to sweep away the bad system which has led to the distress. America has always come forward with unexampled liberality to relieve distress in

Ireland, but all the charity of America cannot permanently relieve us. We must shame the British Government into doing us justice. We don't want to come to you in the guise of mendicants every year. The American people must not forget that our great point is to reach the British Government by means of an open discussion of the Irish land question before the nations of the earth.[39]

In the most important venue of the American expedition, the House of Representatives, he stressed the same points.[40]

Throughout the visit Parnell dwelled on the responsibility of the landlord system for the plight of Ireland and his commitment to its overthrow. Eastern speeches received greater circulation than the later efforts but obscurity did not lead to an increase in the militant tone. At Peoria, Illinois, for instance, a minor stop which was scarcely noticed, Parnell reaffirmed constitutional principles in a speech anticipating, in part, his famous remarks at Ennis later that year. He asserted, 'the League will proceed with their work until the last vestige of landlordism shall be destroyed never to appear again. How is the League going to do it, you may ask'.[41] At that juncture a man in the audience interjected, 'Shoot them.' Parnell retorted, 'We haven't anything to do it with.' He then outlined what he called a more effective means, stating,

it is one of the principles of the English constitution that when anyone has any grievances against the Crown, he is not bound to contribute to its support. We will apply the same principle to the landlords and cut off their supplies. By so doing we will make the landlords think it is to their interest as much as the tenants to have the question settled.

At Peoria, as elsewhere, he affirmed the national demand as well. Near the close of his speech he declaimed,

the people will never submit to the degradation. Many must die of starvation. Many must be permanently enfeebled by want and disease, and many more must become degraded, but nevertheless they are going to stand by their country, and regain for Ireland her proper place among the countries of the world. If you help us now, you will have the proud satisfaction of knowing that you took a prominent part in restoring Ireland to her former glory and prosperity.

Certainly the precise words and tone of Parnell's remarks differed between stops though the content of the speeches remained little altered. The national claim received recognition though he gave it greater emphasis in some venues. It is improbable that Parnell actually used the phrase 'last link' at Cincinnati, but there and in several addresses around the same time he was explicit about the ultimate objective of Irish autonomy. Extremist declarations would not have met with favour from the American authorities or been treated kindly by numerous publishers. Parnell's appearances attracted considerable adverse comment in the press though most often for his condemnation of the British government, and excessive hostility to the landlords, but the largest volume of unfavourable publicity arose from the attack on the other relief funds. Controversy over the various funds posed a major threat to the success of the mission. Reaction to the dispute in Peoria was typical:

> his speech was well received, excepting only his personal explanations, and his attacks on the other relief funds, which were faintly applauded, the feeling seeming to be that all efforts to relieve the distress of the people are worthy of kinder consideration.[42]

The electrifying address at Cork, too, takes on interesting hues when placed in its context.[43] Parnell devoted the lion's share of attention to the position of the tenant-farmers, the need to support manufacturers even if the cost of goods rose, and the question of the agricultural labourers. Much of what he said was not particularly congenial to important interests. Parnell's remarks on the national demand, then, were, in part, a means of sugaring a rather unpalatable pill. He always had been adept at using national feeling as a means of papering over difficult situations. At the time there was a second incentive to emphasize the national issue. Parnell was faced with disquiet within his own ranks occasioned by a prolonged spell of relative inactivity and leaks about his adoption of local government schemes. Thus, he spoke out at Cork in a way designed to quell dissent. From both the perspective of his immediate situation and the policy on contentious matters, his resort to an affirmation of nationalist belief was calculated to ease him through an awkward moment.

Examination of the speeches suggests that Parnell was not a distinguished orator but had under-appreciated qualities as a speaker. His talent for the neat turn of phrase was matched by astute timing. Parnell had a strong sense for masking the mundane or the contentious with a judicious injection of national sentiment. In brief, he was an effective communicator. Examination of the speeches reveals a good deal about Parnell, his ideas, his use of techniques, and affords some insight into his grip on the political affections of the Irish people, but it does not wholly supply a satisfying explanation of how a humdrum orator was lifted into a charismatic figure.

As James Loughlin observes, the marketing of Parnell was a critical facet of his mystique. The speeches played a major part in that exercise. His addresses made an indifferent impression on the immediate audience but they did read rather better than the platform oratory of many superior speakers. Parnell had the good fortune to fall into a gap in the evolving process of political communication. Earlier, the spoken word enjoyed a pre-eminence, and in the twentieth century, with radio and then television, it reassumed its primacy. However, during the final decades of the Victorian era, the speeches made an immense impact on the newly literate Irish people. Illiteracy in Ireland fell dramatically (33 per cent in 1871, 25 per cent in 1881 and 18 per cent in 1891) and the people were hungry for literature of all sorts.[44] The large number of Dublin and provincial newspapers and journals catered for the emerging mass readership. Nearly all of these periodicals had small circulations and depended on cheap copy. The practice of reproducing parliamentary and public addresses served several purposes, not least in allowing many journals to operate with tiny staffs and meagre budgets. Reliance upon political speeches was encouraged by concessionary telegraph rates for transmission of this material, and the comprehensive railway network allowed some newspapers, mainly those published in Dublin, to be read across the country.[45]

Parnell's speeches placed in context make him an even more arresting figure, an extraordinary innovator in the uses of communication techniques. He seems to have been one of the first major leaders, certainly the earliest Irish politician, who comprehended that he was speaking for a reading rather than a listening audience. Many accounts relate his exceptional concern that journalists had advantageous seating on platforms and that he exhibited personal consideration to them when travelling.[46] In effect, he realized how important this group of men, often a despised class in political circles, were to his ambitions. Appealing to the larger group of readers suited Parnell's abilities and he made the most of the opportunity. In contrast, nearly all of his contemporaries in Irish politics remained wedded to traditional forms of oratory and had correspondingly less impact than The Chief.[47] There were, of course, numerous other ingredients in Parnell's charisma but it is surely an important strand to it that he saw most effectively the means by which a politician could project an image to a nation and 'race' without having to see his people or be physically accessible to them. His formula worked well through nearly the whole of his career.[48] Experience suggested that he could alternate periods of intense speaking activity to 'real' audiences with communication at a distance without a loss of influence. When required he could resort to public appearances to aid his position. That apparently being true, Parnell gave insufficient attention to day-to-day organizational matters. These he left in the hands of willing lieutenants. His forte was communication. In 1891 his situation was transformed – communication alone was insufficient when opponents dominated the local and national organizational apparatus. Politics at a distance really only worked when there were no or only weak counter-forces. Yet, there is no telling what the ultimate result might have been but for his early death in October 1891. His speeches during that final fateful year showed that the lion, even when severely wounded, knew how to reach out for and cast a spell over a section of the Irish people. If Parnell discovered after November 1890 that being a great communicator was not enough to carry the day, his successors learned subsequently to their cost that organization alone was inadequate. In the end Parnell the communicator captured the hearts of his people while the wire-pullers of Irish politics passed into oblivion.

NOTES

1 Earlier versions of the chapter were presented at the University of Durham and the Institute for Advanced Studies in the Humanities, Edinburgh. Paul Bew, George Boyce, Michael Bromley and Roland Quinault read and commented on the chapter. The speeches were collected partly under a grant from the British Academy. I am indebted to all of the above for vital assistance.
2 James Bryce, *Studies in Contemporary Biography*, London, 1903, pp. 241–2.
3 He may be underestimated as a political thinker, however. See Chapter 7 in this volume, Tony Claydon.
4 R. Barry O'Brien, *The Life of Charles Stewart Parnell 1846–1891*, 2 vols, London, 1898.
5 For example, see the comments of M. J. F. McCarthy, *The Irish Revolution*, vol. I, Edinburgh, 1912, p. 40.
6 *Philadelphia Enquirer*, 12 January 1880.
7 *Boston Evening Transcript*, 13 January 1880.
8 *Daily Pioneer*, 28 February 1880.
9 *Peoria National Democrat* and *Peoria Register*, 3 March 1880 for ident-

ical reports. I wish to thank Walter L. Arnstein for supplying copies of these newspapers.

10 *Nation*, 14 June 1890.

11 *Freeman's Journal*, 20 September 1880, 11 October 1881, 22 January 1885.

12 Katharine O'Shea, *Charles Stewart Parnell, his Love Story and Political Life*, 2 vols, London, 1914.

13 See, Jennie Wyse-Power (comp.), *Words of the Dead Chief; Being Extracts from the Public Speeches and Other Pronouncements of Charles Stewart Parnell, from the Beginning to the Close of his Memorable Life*, Dublin, 1892, where a full edition is promised. A facsimile edition of speeches, letters and interviews published in the *Freeman's Journal* between 1879 and 1888 was assembled for use at the Special Commission though the only extant copy which seems to have survived is deposited at Trinity College, Dublin. See *Mr Parnell's Speeches, Letters and Public Addresses (Out of Parliament) in the United Kingdom 1879–88*, Dublin, 1889, plus the many additional addresses not included in the published edition. A modern edition is Michael Hurst and Alan O'Day (eds), *The Speeches of Charles Stewart Parnell*, London, 1991.

14 Bryce, *Studies in Contemporary Biography*, p. 242.

15 Comments on the speeches are based on the edition of Hurst and O'Day (*Speeches of Parnell*) plus the vast collection of addresses not included in the published volume.

16 Bryce, *Studies in Contemporary Biography*, p. 244.

17 *Parliamentary Debates*, 233 (1875), 1644–5; 330 (1876), 808.

18 Ibid., 224 (1875), 1625, 1923–4; 225 (1875), 158; 227 (1876), 561, 988–9; 228 (1876), 687–8.

19 *Nation*, 20 October 1877. Also, report of National Conference, *Nation*, 19 January 1878.

20 D. A. Thornley, 'The Irish home rule party and parliamentary obstruction, 1874–87', *Irish Historical Studies*, XII, March 1959, pp. 38–57. The interpretation, though, is based on my own analysis of his activities in the House of Commons.

21 Paul Smith, *Disraelian Conservatism and Social Reform*, London, 1967, p. 266.

22 Paul Bew, *C. S. Parnell*, Dublin, 1980, p. 32.

23 See F. S. L. Lyons, *Charles Stewart Parnell*, London, 1977, p. 331, where he considers the episode and the slightly differing reports of Parnell's exact words.

24 Bryce, *Studies in Contemporary Biography*, p. 243.

25 The 'last link' phrase is cited without qualification in O'Brien, *Life of Charles Stewart Parnell*, vol. I, pp. 203–4. For the controversy and authenticity of the speech see Lyons, *Charles Stewart Parnell*, pp. 111–13. Reports from *Cincinnati Commercial, Cincinnati Gazette, Cincinnati Enquirer*, 21 February 1880.

26 *Freeman's Journal*, 21 February 1881.

27 Andrew Dunlop, *Fifty Years of Irish Journalism*, Dublin and London, 1911, p. 35. See also Chapter 10 by James Loughlin, in this volume.

28 Karen Bruner Stroup, ' "Ending the quarrel of centuries": a rhetorical analysis of the persuasion of Isaac Butt and Charles Stewart Parnell,

leaders of the Irish home rule movement, 1870–1891', Indiana University Ph.D., 1984, pp. 87, 119–20.

29 See Dunlop, *Fifty Years of Irish Journalism*, p. 35, for a discussion of Parnell's differing technique by type of venue.

30 *Nation*, 22 January 1876.

31 This theme is considered at length in Alan O'Day, *Parnell and the First Home Rule Episode*, Dublin, 1986.

32 Lyons, *Charles Stewart Parnell*, pp. 579–81.

33 Alan O'Day, *The English Face of Irish Nationalism*, Dublin, 1977, pp. 108–25; 'The political organization of the Irish in Britain, 1867–1890' in Roger Swift and Sheridan Gilley (eds), *The Irish in Britain 1815–1939*, London, 1989, pp. 234–79; *Freeman's Journal*, 21 May 1890.

34 *Nation*, 24 May 1890.

35 *United Ireland*, 24 January 1885.

36 *Washington Post*, 21 January 1961.

37 O'Brien, *Life of Charles Stewart Parnell*, vol. ii, pp. 352, 367.

38 M. V. Hazel, 'First link: Parnell's American tour, 1880', *Eire-Ireland*, xv, Spring 1980, pp. 6–24.

39 *New York Times*, 3 January 1880.

40 *Congressional Record*, 2 February 1880, x, Pt 1, pp. 664–5.

41 *Peoria Register*, 3 March 1880.

42 Ibid.

43 O'Day, *Parnell and the First Home Rule Episode*, pp. 1–14.

44 Ruth Dudley Edwards, *An Atlas of Irish History*, London, 1973, p. 228.

45 K. Theodore Hoppen, *Elections, Politics, and Society in Ireland 1832–1885*, Oxford, 1984, 461–2.

46 Dunlop, *Fifty Years of Irish Journalism*, pp. 30, 32–3, 74; J. B. Hall, *Random Records of a Reporter*, London and Dublin, 1928, pp. 207–8.

47 See Dunlop, *Fifty Years of Irish Journalism*, p. 35.

48 James Loughlin, *Gladstone, Home Rule and the Ulster Question 1882–93*, Dublin, 1986, ch. 1, makes some pertinent observations on the use of rhetoric.

10 Constructing the political spectacle[1]

Parnell, the press and national leadership, 1879–86

James Loughlin

It has rightly been said of the Land War that it was initiated from below; that when the masses became involved in agrarian struggle the leaders were swept along; and that in Parnell's case the Land War 'turned him from a coming young man into the "uncrowned king of Ireland" '.[2] What the masses could not do effectively, however, was give coherent 'national' meaning to the events they were engaged in. That required a focus of identity that transcended faction, and was acutely attuned to the opportunities and pitfalls inherent in a complex and rapidly developing political environment. This was the role Parnell performed as the Land War developed. The Land War made him because he made the most of the opportunities it presented; so much so, that his progress towards the unchallenged leadership of the nationalist movement in the period 1879–86 has all the appearance of an effortless development. The effectiveness of the presentation, however, obscures the extent to which the contexts within which Parnell's formidable skills were displayed – indeed, the public entity of 'Parnell' itself – were the creations of the leader, his lieutenants and the nationalist press. This chapter will attempt to enhance our understanding of Parnell's leadership through an examination of the strategies employed to market 'Parnellism'.

PARNELL: ASPECTS OF A NATIONAL ICON

The success of Parnellism as a national phenomenon was dependent in the first instance on developments that pre-dated Parnell's rise to prominence; particularly a remarkable rise in literacy levels and advances in mass communications. By the mid 1870s an extensive railway system had been established throughout Ireland along with the electric telegraph. The enormous political significance of the electric telegraph was quickly appreciated by Karl Marx, who observed in 1871 that it was creating and disseminating myth on an unprecedented scale.[3] The telegraph, which enabled the publication of speeches within a day of their being delivered, greatly stimulated the growth of both public oratory and the provincial press, while the autumn political campaign – during which Parnell was to make some of his most important speeches – was a practice established by Gladstone in his Bulgarian orations of 1876–7.[4] While these developments worked to promote the political integration of the community in Britain generally, in Ireland during the Land War they had a similar, though more special, role of assisting the mobilization and integration of the agrarian agitation, and especially in facilitating 'Parnellism' as *the* medium through which the political world was made comprehensible to the largely peasant population that had thrust itself onto the political stage in 1879, motivated in varying degrees by fear of famine and the protection of living standards.

But while Parnellism was effectively a product of the Land War it was developed within the context of an already well-established range of national symbols, which included the 'national anthem' 'God save Ireland', the green flag, the national festivals of St Patrick's day and 'memorial day', held on 23 November in honour of the 'Manchester martyrs', together with an iconography of nationalist heroes ranging from Brian Boru to Thomas Davis and O'Connell, whose exploits were extolled in a thriving cheap literature.[5] Parnell was soon to enter the pantheon of nationalist heroes and already had the advantage of a family lineage suited to the purpose – an ancestor, Sir John Parnell, who, as speaker of the Irish House of Commons, had opposed the Act of Union, and his maternal American grandfather who had a distinguished record against the English in the war of 1812. Parnell was not slow to exploit these associations on entering politics.[6]

He was also of course personally well equipped for the role of national deliverer, being endowed with imposing stature and physical attractiveness; traits which went together with an acute and complex psychological make-up, shy and introverted yet with distinctly aggressive tendencies.[7] These traits were to influence strongly Parnell's personal and public life. More exactly, the public Parnell, the national icon, was a construction of the private man, a dramatic construction intended to inspire awe and devotion through the possession of characteristics deemed to be out of the ordinary run of humanity. Of these the most perceptible were impassiveness: an absence of normal emotional feeling; natural force: the impression of unselfconscious political direction and destiny; and what many contemporaries described as a 'hypnotic' gaze. By any standard, Parnell's ability to project these qualities, given his acutely sensitive and highly strung nature, is impressive. Moreover he seems to have believed that his political role was predetermined by fate. We get glimpses of this belief in Katharine O'Shea's biography; for instance, when Parnell says, 'what the ultimate government of Ireland will be is settled, and it will be so, and what my share of the work has been and is to be, also'.[8]

Parnell's public persona was also conditioned by his oratorical limitations; never a fluent speaker, he perfected a tense, 'chilling' monotone and dramatic timing. Containing little or no incidental or superfluous material, Parnell's speeches were, like the lines in a play, usually intended to have direct consequences. Also noteworthy is how his public persona was designed to contrast with popular perceptions of Irish Celtic characteristics, especially verbosity, emotionalism and gesticulation. 'Contrast' has been identified as an important factor in the development of charismatic political leadership in the twentieth century,[9] but it is most unlikely that Parnell was not fully aware of its importance to public perceptions of his own political stature. Certainly the difference between his style and that of other leading nationalists impressed political commentators during the period when the leadership of the nationalist movement was still in contention. Comparing Parnell's reaction to the stresses of obstructing the House of Commons with those of F. H. O'Donnell and J. O'Connor Power in 1879, the *Pall Mall Gazette* declared:

> He is a standing wonder to his friends. Calm, cool, bloodless, he is a man whom nothing can move. O'Connor Power grows savage under the exasperating treatment of the house, and O'Donnell hisses wind through teeth with ill-disguised resentment. But Parnell remains invariably imperturbable.[10]

Compared with Parnell's monumental and apparently superhuman self-restraint, O'Donnell and O'Connor Power merely demonstrated their human fallibility. It would be difficult to overestimate the degree of contrivance in Parnell's public self and the importance he attached to endowing it with exceptional characteristics – excusing failure to attend public meetings without apology as part of the 'ethics of Kingship'[11] and acknowledging his brother in public only with a wink[12] so that the integrity of the national icon would not be compromised by any perceptible display of ordinary human affection. Even the limited insight into Parnell's private life that the press offered to the public, worked to enhance his political image, highlighting Avondale's links with the 1798 rebellion and the Parnell family's associations with the Volunteers of 1782.[13] Parnell's preoccupation with his public image is evident at the earliest stages of his career. During his campaign for Dublin County in 1874 he had the respected Protestant home ruler, the Revd J. A. Galbraith, inform a poorly attended meeting that he was detained in a far part of the country and could not be present, when he was in fact observing the proceedings from a nearby field.[14]

Maintaining the inviolability of his public persona, however, was not always within Parnell's control. During the 1880 general election, for example, he was subjected to abuse and struck in the face with a rotten egg during a stormy meeting in Enniscorthy where he opposed the local candidate. Parnell was so concerned about the effects of this incident on his public image that he followed the reporter who had witnessed the incident most closely to the telegraph office, asked to read his report and suggested that the missile was an orange rather than an egg. And despite the fact that the incident was fully reported in the Dublin press the following day Parnell, during a speech that night at Navan, astounded pressmen by 'roundly' denying that he had been struck at Enniscorthy and claimed that 'there was no place in Ireland where such an insult would be offered to him'.[15]

PARNELL, THE PRESS AND MASS AGITATION

The elements that came together to give Parnell his position of supreme power among Irish nationalists would be familiar to students of mass politics and charismatic leadership: a national crisis combined with widespread popular anxiety about living standards; a potential leader/saviour of outstanding ability committed to a Herculean task and assimilated to, or acting within, the traditions of prevailing national-political myths.[16] In Parnell's case these elements came together specifically in terms of a union of constitutional and revolutionary nationalists with mass land agitation, the unity of which was enhanced by largely unspecified demands for land reform and 'home rule', but especially by the ideological dimensions of Parnell's public persona, with its ability to be perceived simultaneously in both constitutional and revolutionary terms.

Essential, however, to the effectiveness of Parnellism as the medium through which the Irish masses comprehended the political world was an efficient means of mass communication, a role performed by the popular press. The relationship between the press and politics was symbiotic and mutually beneficient. The growth of the provincial press in Britain had stimulated political activity in the more settled political conditions prevailing there,[17] and this occurred, too, in Ireland, which was in the throes of a national crisis, and to a greater degree. Explaining the relationship between the press and politics, M. J. F. McCarthy, a *Freeman's Journal* reporter during the Land War, wrote:

> Print had become for the first time an actuality for the catholic peasants and part of their everyday life, speaking to them in a thrilling, palpitating language, intelligible – and there lay the marvel – yet different from anything previously known, for it enabled them to hear their friends at a distance talking to them in accents of power about the wondrous doings of the Land League.[18]

What in fact McCarthy is describing is the central role played by the press in establishing the ideological context of the agrarian struggle and in creating a sense of participation for the Irish peasantry in great national events. The importance of the press in this respect was illustrated by an incident in Limerick when, shortly before Parnell was to speak at a major banquet, the press corps walked out in protest at inadequate facilities. The organizers pleaded for their return, arguing that their proceedings had no point if they were not reported.[19] The press, however, not only gave a sense of participation in national activities but also created a link between the humblest member of the league and the supreme leader, Parnell. McCarthy observed that for the impressionable younger generation educated in the national schools 'the newspapers were their evangel, Mr Parnell their saviour, and his lieutenants their apostles'. Parnell's activities, he estimated, caused the newspapers 'to be read by ten people for the one who had read them before'.[20] For his part Parnell was always keen to facilitate the press.[21] Under this stimulus it is hardly surprising that the number of nationalist papers rose remarkably. Between 1880 and 1886, in fact, they increased by 25 per cent, from 41 to 55.[22]

It was not, however, only nationalist papers that served Parnell's interests. The Liberal Unionist *Irish Times* admitted unwillingly that all papers reporting his activities were thereby enlisted in giving effectiveness to Parnellism. It pointed up the centrality of the press to nationalist politics in the 1880s by comparing this period with O'Connell's, when

> it would have been a very extravagant proceeding to send a corps of accomplished reporters after not only the principal but the subordinates into every small country town. This has now been done, and the government's own telegraph service [is] profusely employed for months in the work of explaining to the whole nation the arguments and adjurations of the League platform in whatsoever field set up in all broad Connaught or Munster.[23]

The *Irish Times* also acutely pinpointed an important aspect of Parnell's political act as a mass obsession when it described it as a 'drama' in several acts, the suspense of which was maintained by his refusal to articulate a specific set of agrarian demands, and with a new act about to open now in November 1880 with the news that he was going to be prosecuted.[24] The scenario presented by the *Irish Times* was one in which Parnell, possessed of enormous 'force', was pitted against 'society' which would refuse to be defeated.[25]

By any standards, the demonstrations at which Parnell's most important extra-parliamentary speeches were usually made were impressive, newsworthy events. Extensive railway communications made possible the assembling of massive gatherings throughout the country on a weekly basis. Within a short period of the beginning of the land agitation they had assumed a highly formalized ritual, having, in this respect, much in common with similar gatherings in Europe. In keeping with an agitation articulated in terms of a struggle for freedom from English oppression these demonstrations were, in the main, great pseudo-militaristic gatherings, with the population arrayed in green banners and rosettes, often carrying imitation pikes and swords, and an abundance of green 'national' flags. The crowds would usually be divided into 'foot' and 'cavalry' – the latter representing better-off farmers – while streets would be bedecked in bunting and with triumphal arches displaying a range of nationalist slogans. The usual mode of procedure would be a procession of 'foot' and 'cavalry', preceded by a number of bands, which would make its way to the local railway station where Parnell and his entourage would be met and taken – frequently in carriages pulled by men instead of horses – to the site of the demonstrations.[26] These rituals, impressive enough in daylight, would take on an added dramatic, even mystical, dimension when, as often happened, they were conducted at night by the light of thousands of firebrands. At the same time, though, while these events had a serious political purpose, they were also, as one press observer noted, mini-holidays, occasions for celebration, drinking and 'sky-larking'.[27]

As with his political activities generally, Parnell's approach to public demonstrations was carefully planned. When addressing open-air gatherings, for example, his speech was slow and deliberate, designed to be audible to those on the outer fringes of the meeting; when speaking indoors, though, where it was not necessary to strain his voice, it became surprisingly rapid.[28] The content of Parnell's speeches has been noteworthy chiefly for specific policy statements and memorable phrases such as 'keep a firm grip on your homesteads' and his 'ne plus ultra' statement of 1885. The speeches are equally important, however, for understanding how Parnell defined for his mass public both his own role in the struggle and the context within which it was taking place. Conscious of the tendency in England to define it as a conflict between Irish lawlessness and civilized order, Parnell countered this argument by defining its parameters well beyond Anglo-Irish relations to include the whole 'civilized world'. In his speech at Westport in June 1879, to take one instance, he emphasized the reasonableness and progressive nature of the nationalist demands by citing France, Russia, Belgium and Prussia as cases where landlordism had failed and the land was either sold or given to the occupiers.[29] This was an enduring theme throughout the agitation: Ireland was not asking for anything that other European nations had not achieved,[30] and all Europe, the USA and Australia were with the Irish in their fight: 'The eyes of the world are fixed upon you. Do not let it be said that this, the best and greatest struggle that Ireland has ever made, will fall short.'[31] All the civilized nations of the earth were spectators of their struggle and all were convinced that victory was near at hand.[32] To give colour to this claim Parnell sought to enlist the support of influential Europeans, such as Victor Hugo, though with less than successful results. Hugo failed to endorse the nationalist struggle while Parnell would have strenuously to reject the claim of clerical opponents in Ireland that he was enlisting Red revolutionists in the agrarian campaign.[33] On the whole, though, despite occasional misjudgements, Parnell's presentation of the agrarian struggle was highly successful. Unlike the leader and his lieutenants, for whom the Irish demonstrations were merely one context among several that engaged their political activities, for the majority of their peasant followers, knowing little of the intricacies of Westminster politics or of nationalist politics at the higher levels, nationalism existed entirely in the state of consciousness that party rhetoric was designed to inculcate. For them the images of intense international preoccupation with Irish problems conjured up by Parnell would have had a credibility it is hard to believe the leader shared.

Another dimension of the international context that Parnell employed to enhance Irish commitment to the agrarian struggle in its early stages was to argue that Disraeli's government regarded them as on a par with Zulus and Afghan 'savages',[34] and to explain Disraeli's failure to respond adequately to the distress of 1879 by reference to his Semitic origins: 'the Jew prime minister'.[35] Undoubtedly the most important element of Parnell's propaganda, however, was how he presented himself as leader and defined his relationship to the people. In his study of German nationalism, G. L. Mosse argues that, while the leader has a special importance in that his charisma is necessary to draw in the masses and inspire them, he has yet to appear as but one part of the total scene: symbolism and universal participation are equally important.[36] There is evidence that Parnell also recognized the importance of collective identity. At the beginning of the land struggle he was at pains to deprecate the importance of his own role and to emphasize collective achievement,[37] and it became an enduring theme. When he was greeted by a massive demonstration in Cork city in December 1882, for example, he told the crowd that he knew

> it is not on account of your estimate of my personal worth or ability that you assemble to greet me, but rather because you believe that I have held firm to the principle which I first pledged myself to in the royal plains of Meath.

In this speech Parnell was also at pains to emphasize that his policies were not radically innovative but merely following through at Westminster policies on Irish land and independence first initiated by Lucas, Charles Gavan Duffy and John Blake Dillon in the 1850s.[38] In the same context, it is worth noting that Parnell, at the outset of the struggle, asserted that the agitation generally was intended to complete the great work begun by O'Connell,[39] while his assumption of the chairmanship of the Irish parliamentary party in 1880 was presented to the public as an onerous task reluctantly undertaken: 'events went against my intentions in this respect and I was compelled to accept the position'.[40]

The literature on charismatic leadership asserts that it is most effectively exercised within pre-existing political myth and traditions.[41] Parnell's is an excellent case in point. For the celebrations of collective achievement, the emphasis on following the initiative of nationalist predecessors and his modest assessment of his own contribution merely served to highlight by contrast both his uniqueness and his central importance to the agrarian struggle. Certainly by late 1880 Parnell was the focus of a national personality cult of enormous proportions. Any change in his appearance – as when he shaved off his beard and arrived wholly unrecognized at a demonstration at Ennis[42] – became the subject of intense public discussion as to its meaning.[43] M. J. F. McCarthy, in being coached to give a speech for the Land League at this time, was told he could give the crowd any sort of nonsense he liked 'and if you only say "Charles Stewart Parnell" half a dozen times . . . everything else will be drowned out by the cheering'.[44] The poorer, superstitious peasantry indeed appear to have invested Parnell with quite awesome abilities.

Irish folk culture abounded with beliefs about the protective, and destructive, powers of people and objects, e.g. men who could raise and calm storms, cause women to follow them and, by their 'evil eye, tongue or wish', could bring misfortune on others. Objects invested with protective powers included iron, nails, rings, pins, knives, stones, rope, cloth and religious medals, to name only a few.[45] On his speaking tours in rural Ireland Parnell appears to have acted as a magnet for such objects and he established a routine whereby he did not disturb these items, slipped unobtrusively into the pockets of his overcoat, leaving them instead for Mrs O'Shea to discover.[46] The peasant perception of Parnell as a leader endowed with superhuman qualities was 'validated' by a peculiar coincidence attending his arrest and imprisonment in October 1881. Just six hours after the arrest Ireland and England were blasted by the worst storm in fifty years, causing at least one death and the sinking of over one hundred ships at sea.[47] This event Parnell's peasant followers interpreted as the elements protesting against his arrest.[48]

But of course Parnell's appeal extended beyond the poorer peasantry to the population at large. The simple fact was that the readers of Parnell's exploits at Westminster in Irish newspapers during the Land War were following a serial which touched their own lives and which was presented in prose that might have been lifted from a political thriller. Thus the unsympathetic *Irish Times* on Parnell rising to speak on the Queen's Speech in 1881:

Mr Parnell assumed his usual freezing tone when he got up, speaking very low and very slow, but with the iciness of attitude, deliberation and distinctiveness which betokens a provoking self-possession under the gravest circumstances, and at once chills and startles the hearers.[49]

But while all newspapers contributed to Parnell's mythic status in some degree, certain newspapers played a central role, and foremost among these in the early years was T. D. Sullivan's *Nation*. Sullivan was the author of the Irish anthem 'God save Ireland', was an expert at putting nationalist propaganda into popular verse[50] and was credited by nationalist leaders with great influence with the peasantry.[51] His was the first nationalist paper to wholeheartedly support Parnell and to authenticate the effectiveness of his obstruction tactics for the Irish masses. Authentification could not have been convincingly done by reports from nationalist papers alone. It was important to have them corroborated by objective or hostile sources and this became a speciality of the *Nation* during the crucial period of Parnell's emergence as the leader of the nationalist movement. Extensive quotations from the gamut of leading British papers were employed to demonstrate Parnell's superior political abilities, the following from the *Standard* being a representative example: 'Mr Parnell is the real leader of the Commons. . . . The government has failed to assert its authority and the last thing it can do is admit defeat.'[52] The *Nation* contributed in other ways also. Thomas Sherlock's popular biography of Parnell,[53] largely composed from a manuscript written by Parnell's mother,[54] was first serialized in the *Nation*. The paper remained loyal to Parnell even after *United Ireland* was started as a party organ in August 1881, while Sullivan was to push Parnell's 'Kingly' claims to the extent of asserting that he was twentieth in lineal descent from King Edward I.[55]

However, while Parnell's success in engendering mass devotion was impressive it might be asked just how deep that devotion went. This question is pertinent in the light of K. T. Hoppen's argument that Parnellism was only a temporary phenomenon which overlaid the real local concerns of the Irish people.[56] Hoppen's argument is, in the main, persuasive, though the opposition or contradiction he posits between nationalism and localism rather stereotypes the relationship between the two. That relationship was symbiotic and multi-faceted rather than starkly antagonistic;[57] leading nationalists tended to be good local constituency MPs as well as national leaders.[58] In fact what contributed substantially to the effectiveness of Parnellism as a mass phenomenon when it was at its most effective during the Land War was how the national movement became the channel through which the local and material grievances of its supporters were addressed. Accordingly, in this period Parnellism as a mass phenomenon had an intense psychological reality, exhibited most obviously in the public adoration of Parnell. Yet, while the devotion to Parnell was real, it was nevertheless contained within certain boundaries by the nature of his political act. Parnell was adored less as a man than as a national icon. A *Freeman's Journal* reporter observed acutely: 'he was a man who could only be popular at a distance, his refined features and splendid appearance acting as a charm on the large crowds of people who were never to meet him at close quarters'.[59] On the rare occasions when this occurred the contrast between the fallibility of the private man and his idealized image could cause lasting disillusionment.[60] Also, the special conditions of the Land War ended with the 'Kilmainham Treaty' in 1882. This was a major landmark in the history of Parnellite nationalism; indicated by the suppression of the Land League and its replacement by the National League, with its emphasis on the parliamentary struggle for home rule, and also by a changed relationship between the mass of the people and the nationalist movement.

PARNELL, *UNITED IRELAND* AND HOME RULE POLITICS, 1882–6

An important factor identifying Parnell with the people during the Land War was widespread participation in the agrarian struggle. The campaign for home rule, being conducted in Parliament, had no place for continuous mass agitation and that connection was lost. It might also be argued that while the land legislation effected through agrarian agitation established the Parnellites as the undisputed political representatives of the Irish people it also removed the reasons for the mass anxiety and associated dependency that contributed so much to the deification of Parnell. Certainly the failure of the No-Rent Manifesto of October 1881 was a striking indication of the limits of leadership. It also appears that the Irish political context following the end of the Land War had significantly changed, with national concerns giving way to local interests.[61] At any rate, several leading nationalists, though not apparently Parnell, were worried whether there would be mass support for a home rule campaign divorced from the agrarian issue and whether the undoubted development of mass nationalist consciousness that had occurred during the Land War would be accompanied by an equal degree of commitment.[62] These fears were well founded. The years 1882–5 proved to be years of slow growth in building the National League, despite the fact that more meetings were held in this period than during the Land War, with the situation only improving significantly following the franchise reforms of 1884–5 and in the run-up to the general election of 1885.[63]

Perhaps the most graphic illustration of the new political environment was demonstrated by the events surrounding the 'Parnell Tribute' of 1883, a reaction to the news that Parnell's property, Avondale, would have to be sold to discharge debt. The accepted view of the tribute is that it represented a 'remarkable index of Parnell's personal popularity'.[64] Accounts by contemporaries, however, paint a rather different picture of the early stages of the campaign. T. P. O'Connor wrote: 'a few subscriptions came dropping in daily to the *Freeman*, but there was nothing like a spontaneous expression of public feeling'.[65] William O'Brien described its beginnings as 'hesitating and feeble'.[66] In fact it was not until the appearance of the papal rescript on 11 May, almost two months after the tribute was initiated on St Patrick's day, that a significant response appeared. With its rather crude attempt to dictate politics to the Irish people and with evidence of its origins in English intrigue, it was bound to have an effect opposite to that intended. As the *Nation* put it, English interference caused a massive reaction in the tribute's favour.[67] But another way of looking at it suggests that a mass response was only likely when a political context focused on a national issue linking the leader and the masses was created; that mass devotion was dependent to a significant degree on mass involvement and subscription to the tribute was as much an expression of political independence as gratitude to their national deliverer. Also, bearing in mind M. J. F. McCarthy's observation on the nature of Parnell's appeal, it is possible that the object of the tribute, presenting Parnell in terms of fallibility rather than of strength – even if the cause of that fallibility was put down to his sacrifices in the national cause – was presenting him in terms which were alien to those in which he had been popularly understood during the Land War.

It was fortunate that in the less favourable political climate that followed the Land War Parnell had a party organ, *United Ireland*, on which he could rely totally. Unlike the *Freeman's Journal*, whose commitment to Parnellism was reluctant and effected under duress,[68] and the *Nation* which, while wholeheartedly supporting Parnell in general, disagreed with his attitude to the 1881 Land

Act,[69] *United Ireland*, edited by William O'Brien, one of the party's leading propagandists, was fanatically loyal to Parnell. Unlike Parnell, who could compartmentalize his life into sharply defined public and private spheres, O'Brien was a true believer who lived for the movement. T. P. O'Connor's estimate of him as having divided the world into 'his slaves and his enemies'[70] may have been exaggerated but it contained a substantial element of truth. Certainly it aptly describes the paper's policy, which was to keep other nationalist papers in line, to confront enemies within and without the movement, and especially to develop the cult of Parnell's personality. This was essential now as Parnell, anxious not to risk another spell in prison, had effectively given up campaigning in Ireland. In *United Ireland*'s pages all of Parnell's actions, wise and unwise, were hailed as inspired. Thus the disastrous foray into Ulster at the Tyrone by-election of 1881 was presented as a triumph which established Parnell's right to campaign in a county he could not appear in before;[71] his failure to respond to W. E. Forster's impassioned condemnation of him in the Commons as the perfect tactic to 'baffle and baulk' Ireland's enemies;[72] while his failure to thank the organizers of the Parnell tribute for a cheque of nearly £40,000 – something which caused considerable offence – was glossed over with the observation that the money itself was unimportant and the Irish people thought so.[73] More generally, Parnell's defence of Ireland's interests in Parliament was described as 'seven years abjuration of pleasures . . . seven years of sleepless warfare against all the might and splendour of one of the greatest empires upon earth, in the very citadel of its power'.[74]

What is instructive to note in the context of *United Ireland*'s propaganda is the attitude of O'Brien to the paper's readership. O'Brien had a very low opinion of its political sophistication and was to justify the paper's rhetorical extremism of these years as 'fighting journalism . . . the picture writing which is best understanded [*sic*] by the multitude'.[75] In effect, although Parnell rarely visited Ireland in these years, O'Brien and *United Ireland* were at the forefront of a campaign to maintain the psychological reality of his mythic status with the Irish people, aided and abetted by his leading lieutenants writing press articles extolling his political genius[76] and also by a rather inept and counterproductive government policy of attempting to associate Parnell with crime. The campaign produced some interesting spin-offs. Waltzes were composed in honour of national leaders, especially Parnell. Also jewellery, both cheap and expensive, bearing Parnell motifs was manufactured, and a 'home rule medal' with a bust of Parnell on one side and the 'Brian Boru harp' and 'God save Ireland' on the other. Produced by the firm of J. J. Lalor of Dublin, a retailer of Catholic religious merchandise, it was priced at sixpence and was clearly aimed at a mass market.[77]

United Ireland's role in promoting Parnell was not without its down side. Those in the nationalist movement who disputed the leader's policies were subjected to vilification that would have been unbecoming in Parnell's role as national icon. Thus while Parnell's disagreement with Sir Charles Gavan Duffy over the 1881 Land Act and other issues was respectfully conducted, an unrestrained personal attack on Duffy appeared in *United Ireland*.[78] Similarly, while Parnell's rejection of Davitt's land nationalization scheme was firm but devoid of personal animus, *United Ireland* condemned both Davitt and Henry George[79] personally for wanting to engage in 'a chaotic socialist experiment';[80] and when the Belfast executive of the National League sought to have land nationalization debated at its conference in 1884 *United Ireland* was quick to blame 'the whole mischief in Belfast' on 'a few troublemakers'.[81] Among the paper's most virulent attacks, however, were those directed at nationalists who wished to democratize the existing leadership structure centred on Parnell and his talented lieutenants. In October 1884 the Revd Harold Rylett, the Parnellite candidate in Tyrone in 1881 and a leader of the land struggle in Ulster,[82] called with others for a division of power within the movement between the parliamentary party at Westminster and a 'National Council' in Dublin. Rylett incurred the wrath of O'Brien both for pushing this idea and for supporting it with the claim that the movement was being controlled by a 'ring' centred on Parnell and that he had personally heard O'Brien say that 'if there were five men to speak it would be enough for the others to follow' – a charge O'Brien rejected as 'misrepresentation' by 'one of the most wicked of the secret agents of Henry George', along with ridicule of the National Council idea.[83] There was, though, much in Rylett's charges.

As early as 1880 T. D. and A. M. Sullivan had waged a campaign to prevent Sir Charles Gavan Duffy from being selected as parliamentary candidate for Louth, fearing that his political stature would have the effect of diminishing Parnell's leadership.[84] In this respect it is worth noting that when Parnell was briefly panicked into considering resignation from the leadership of the Irish party in the wake of the Phoenix Park murders in 1882 it was Duffy he suggested to succeed him, but was told that since Duffy had no parliamentary seat he would not be acceptable to nationalist MPs.[85] The issue of control within the movement did not easily dissipate. When Andrew Kettle, a leading agrarian reformer and associate of Parnell, lent his support to the National Council idea in 1885, *United Ireland* attempted a smear by linking his name with Unionist newspapers that supported this proposal in order to damage the nationalist movement.[86] More generally, O'Brien and *United Ireland* sought to effect a crude news management by having reporters from Unionist papers expelled from the movement's demonstrations.[87]

Nationalist fortunes began to improve significantly in 1885. The franchise reforms of 1884–5 trebled the numbers entitled to vote in Ireland and gave political power to many thousands who previously had none. The run-up to the general election of 1885 saw the effective re-creation of a political context of national dimensions entailing mass participation as local branches of the National League sprang up all over Ireland geared to ensuring nationalist representation of the new Irish county seats. Meanwhile the primacy of national issues over local interests was confirmed in the winter of 1885–6 with the Parnellite triumph at the general election, and when it became clear that Gladstone intended to enact a home rule Bill for Ireland.[88]

The period of the first home rule crisis was to see Parnell at the pinnacle of his power, illustrated by his success in achieving what would undoubtedly have been impossible six months before – the foisting of the despised Captain O'Shea on Galway. At the same time, though, it was not an easy task, and among its several interesting features is how Parnell presented his case to the people. Gone now were the declarations of collective achievement and self-effacement; on this occasion Parnell found it necessary to pitch his argument explicitly in terms of the 'great things' his own outstanding leadership qualities had achieved in the past – 'I have never led Ireland wrong' – and the apparently necessary connection between their accepting his decision on O'Shea and obtaining the 'parliament for Ireland' that he now held in the palm of his hand.[89]

CONCLUSION

The major achievements of Parnell's career have been located in both the Irish and the parliamentary contexts. In Ireland, this entailed his role in rallying a demoralized peasantry to a belief that they could, by organized and disciplined protest, win a better life for themselves. In the parliamentary arena his major innovation is to have organized and led the first modern disciplined political party.[90] However, a wider and longer perspective than that offered by the Anglo-Irish relationship in the 1880s is needed to assess his significance more fully.

What is most striking about 'Parnellism' – that understanding of the political world articulated through the leader's epic struggle with the historic foe – as a nationalist phenomenon is its uniqueness. No Irish leader before and none since acquired the peculiar hold over the Irish people that Parnell did. The elements that came together to make it possible were several: an increasingly literate population, mass communications, a national economic crisis with widespread popular anxiety about living standards and physical well-being, a political movement with a virtual monopoly of power within the community, stereotyped terms of political debate structured around the dichotomy between the interests and rights of the nation as against the aggression of the occupying English power, and a national leader of outstanding political acumen, endowed with physical characteristics ideally suited for the purpose of engendering mass adoration.

The factors outlined in this chapter which were important to the success of Parnellism correspond closely to those identified as instrumental in the success of mass political leaders in this century. Studies of Gandhi, Hitler, Franklin Roosevelt, Mussolini and Sukarno reveal a similar set of factors, circumstantial and personal. For example, extraordinary personal qualities included perceived invulnerability; the ability to project supreme self-confidence, energy and determination; 'self control or composure under conditions of stress, challenge, or danger, where most men would be expected to be thrown off balance'; perceived genius and/or madness; and finally, and by no means least, extraordinary 'hypnotic' eye power.[91] As for Parnell, the social conditions that provided the environment for the emergence of leaders such as Hitler, Roosevelt and Mussolini were severe social crisis and psychic distress,[92] while the factors that ensured that these particular leaders would emerge supreme and not any of their rivals bear a striking similarity to those that applied in Parnell's case, i.e. the assimilation of the leader to dominant cultural myths, the performance of heroic feats, the projection of the possession of qualities with an uncanny or powerful aura, and outstanding – or in Parnell's case, unique and 'chilling' – rhetorical ability.[93] Seen in this context, then, it could be added to existing accounts of Parnell's significance that 'Parnellism' as a mass phenomenon was in several important respects the precursor of the mass politics of the twentieth century. There were, of course, enormous differences, certainly in the content of politics and especially with reference to the European dictators of the 1930s. Perhaps the most significant difference between Parnell and the most important of these – Hitler – lay in their attitudes to the relationship between public and private life. It has been argued of Hitler that he translated the private sphere of sentiment into the public sphere of political action.[94] To some extent this was also true of Parnell, in so far as his early experience of personal rejection in England[95] contributed to his decision to support home rule. But in the main Parnell kept the public and private dimensions of his life rigidly separate. Indeed it can be argued that Parnell only regarded the private sphere – his life with Mrs O'Shea – as truly authentic, and that the public sphere of politics was there to be exploited in any expedient way. Timothy Healy, for instance, was surprised at Parnell's lack of scruple in inventing interviews with pressmen when he felt that such procedures served his political purposes.[96] But more revealing evidence of the distinction he made between the public and private appears in his correspondence with Mrs O'Shea during the last bitter election campaigns of 1890–1. Parnell wrote to O'Shea that the insults hurled at her name during the Kilkenny election campaign did not distress him greatly as they invariably referred to her as 'Kitty O'Shea', a public term of abuse, and not by the private names by which she was known to him or her family.[97]

Nevertheless, while Parnell kept the public and private dimensions to his life separate there was a relationship between the two that had fateful political consequences. Parnell's failings as a political leader have been dated to the early 1880s when he started to neglect his duties as party leader and spend more time with Mrs O'Shea.[98] This coincided with the establishment of *United Ireland* as a party organ giving primacy to the glorification of Parnell's public persona. It may well have been the case that with *United Ireland* constantly keeping the mythic entity of Parnell before the Irish public, and ensuring that other nationalist papers towed the party line, he felt he was free to pursue his private interests more fully without political cost. And it could be argued that there was no necessary reason why this should not have been so. In the end, it was not Parnell's failure in managing his public persona that proved his undoing but his inability to prevent his private life from erupting into the political arena.

NOTES

1 Chapter title taken from Murray Edelman, *Constructing the Political Spectacle*, Chicago and London, 1988.
2 Paul Bew, *C. S. Parnell*, Dublin, 1980, p. 143.
3 See R. V. Comerford, 'Political myths in modern Ireland', in *Irishness in a Changing Society*, Gerrard's Cross, 1988, pp. 2–3.
4 H. C. G. Matthew, 'Rhetoric and politics in Great Britain, 1850–1950', in P. J. Waller (ed.), *Politics and Social Change in Modern Britain: Essays Presented to A. F. Thompson*, Brighton, 1987, pp. 35–42.
5 See Peter Alter, 'Symbols of Irish nationalism', in Alan O'Day (ed.), *Reactions to Irish Nationalism*, London, 1987, pp. 1–23; James Loughlin, *Gladstone, Home Rule and the Ulster Question 1882–93*, Dublin, 1986, pp. 12–14.
6 See his early election addresses in Roy Foster, *Parnell*, 2nd edn, Hassocks, 1979, app. 2, pp. 316–17.
7 For an interesting discussion of his characterists see ibid., pp. 125–7.
8 Katharine O'Shea, *Charles Stewart Parnell: his Love Story and Political Life*, London, 1914, vol. II, 160.
9 Ann Ruth Willner, *The Spellbinders: Charismatic Political Leadership*, New Haven, Conn., and London, 1984, pp. 93–4.
10 Quoted in *Nation*, 8 November 1879.
11 O'Shea, *Parnell*, vol. II, p. 160.
12 J. H. Parnell, *Charles Stewart Parnell : a Memoir*, London, 1916, p. 277.
13 See, for example, 'Mr Parnell at home', extracted from the *World* in *Derry Journal*, 26 November 1880.
14 Andrew Dunlop, *Fifty Years of Irish Journalism*, Dublin and London, 1911, pp. 27–9.
15 Ibid., pp. 149–55.
16 See Willner, *Spellbinders, passim*.
17 Matthew, 'Rhetoric and politics', p. 37.
18 McCarthy, *Irish Revolution*, London, 1912, vol. I, p. 129.
19 J. B. Hall, *Random Records of a Reporter*, Dublin, 1921, p. 215.
20 M. J. F. McCarthy, *The Irish Revolution*, vol. I, p. 129.
21 Dunlop, *Fifty Years of Irish Journalism*, pp. 32, 34; Hall, *Random Records*, pp. 215–17.
22 Loughlin, *Gladstone*, p. 29.
23 *Irish Times*, 2 November 1880.
24 Ibid.; see also issue of 18 October 1880.
25 Ibid., 1 November 1880.
26 See, for example, the demonstrations held between 26 October and 6 December 1879 at Enniscorthy, Galway, Balla, Roscommon, Swinford and Castlerea in *Freeman's Journal*, 27 October, 8, 18, 24 November, 6 December 1879.
27 McCarthy, *Irish Revolution*, p. 162.
28 Dunlop, *Fifty Years of Irish Journalism*, p. 35.
29 *Freeman's Journal*, 9 June 1879.
30 Ibid., 6 December 1880.
31 Ibid., 21 February 1881.

32 Ibid., 11 April 1881. See also *Freeman's Journal*, 17 August 1882.

33 See *Freeman's Journal*, 25 February, 7 April 1881; F. S. L. Lyons, *Charles Stewart Parnell*, 2nd edn, London, 1979, pp. 153–4.

34 *Freeman's Journal*, 23 November 1879.

35 Ibid., 18 November 1879.

36 G. L. Mosse, 'Mass politics and the political liturgy of nationalism', in Eugene Kamenka, *Nationalism: the Nature and Origin of an Idea*, London, 1976, pp. 49–50.

37 See Parnell at Galway, *Freeman's Journal*, 8 November 1879.

38 *Freeman's Journal*, 18 December 1882.

39 See Parnell at Navan, *Freeman's Journal*, 18 October 1879; also relatedly *Freeman's Journal*, 27 October 1879, 18 October 1880, 18 December 1882.

40 Parnell, interview with *Freeman's Journal*, 3 November 1880.

41 See Edelman, *Constructing the Political Spectacle*, pp. 31–8; Willner, *Spellbinders*, pp. 62–3. For an intensive study of the political influence of the Parnell myth, see William M. Murphy, *The Parnell Myth and Irish Politics 1891–1956*, New York, 1986.

42 See *Freeman's Journal*, 18 October 1880.

43 T. M. Healy, *Letters and Leaders of my Day*, London, 1928, vol. I, p. 101; McCarthy, *Irish Revolution*, p. 137.

44 McCarthy, *Irish Revolution*, p. 322.

45 See Séan O'Súilleabháin, *Irish Folk Custom and Belief*, Cork, 1967, 2nd edn, 1977, ch. 8.

46 O'Shea, *Parnell*, vol. I, pp. 185–7.

47 The most extensive coverage of the storm is to be found in *Irish Times*, 14, 15 October 1881.

48 Healy, *Letters and Leaders*, vol. I, p. 138.

49 Excerpt from *Irish Times* in *Nation*, 22 January 1881.

50 See, for example, T. D. Sullivan, *Green Leaves: a Volume of Irish Verse*, 12th edn, Dublin, 1888, *passim*.

51 See Michael Davitt, *The Fall of Feudalism in Ireland*, New York, 1905, p. 715; T. P. O'Connor, *The Parnell Movement*, London, 1886, pp. 347–51.

52 *Nation*, 21 June 1879.

53 Thomas Sherlock, *Charles Stewart Parnell: his Youth and Development*, Dublin, 1881.

54 Mrs Parnell's handwritten memoir of the Parnell family (N. L. I. T. D. Sullivan papers, MS 8237 (6)).

55 *Nation*, 2 January 1886.

56 K. T. Hoppen, *Elections, Politics and Society in Ireland 1832–85*, Oxford, 1984, p. 485.

57 See James Loughlin, review of Hoppen in *Fortnight*, February 1985, p. 23.

58 Alan O'Day, *The English Face of Irish Nationalism*, Dublin, 1977, pp. 17–19, 27, 133–6.

59 McCarthy, *Irish Revolution*, p. 369.

60 For a relevant example see James Mullin, *The Story of a Toiler's Life*, Dublin, 1921, pp. 187–8. Mullin was an Irish doctor working in Cardiff

and a devoted supporter of Parnell until he came to stay while on a speaking tour.

61 See, for example, A. C. Murray, 'Nationality and local politics in nineteenth century Ireland: the case of County Westmeath', *Irish Historical Studies*, xxv (98), November 1986, pp. 144–5.
62 Loughlin, *Gladstone*, pp. 26–8.
63 Ibid., pp. 30–1.
64 Bew, *Parnell*, p. 62.
65 T. P. O'Connor, *Memoirs of an Old Parliamentarian*, London, 1928, vol. i, p. 374.
66 William O'Brien, *Evening Memories*, London, 1920, pp. 12–13.
67 *Nation*, 19 May 1883.
68 See F. H. O'Donnell, *The History of the Irish Parliamentary Party*, London, 1910, vol. ii, p. 194.
69 Loughlin, *Gladstone*, pp. 31–2.
70 O'Connor, *Memoirs*, vol. i, p. 143.
71 *United Ireland*, 17 October 1881.
72 Ibid., 3 March 1883.
73 Ibid., 15 December 1883.
74 Ibid., 23 December 1882.
75 William O'Brien, *Recollections*, London, 1905, p. 360.
76 See, for example, T. M. Healy, 'The secret of Parnell's power', *Pall Mall Gazette*, republished in *Nation*, 5 January 1884.
77 See *Nation*, 8 April 1882; 26 June 1886.
78 *United Ireland*, 28 August 1881.
79 Henry George, a radical land reformer, whose book *Progress and Poverty* urged the public ownership of land. For Davitt's disagreement with Parnell on this issue see Lyons, *Parnell*, pp. 230–4.
80 *United Ireland*, 19 April 1884.
81 Ibid., 2 August 1884.
82 B. M. Walker, *Ulster Politics: the Formative Years 1868–86*, Belfast, 1989, p. 161.
83 *United Ireland*, 1 November 1884.
84 See Duffy to T. D. Sullivan, 28 November 1884 (NLI, T. D. Sullivan papers, MS 8237 (2)).
85 See Healy, *Letters and Leaders*, vol. i, p. 162. See also Duffy's chapter in R. B. O'Brien, *The Life of Charles Stewart Parnell*, 1898, 2nd edn, London, n.d. [1910].
86 *United Ireland*, 31 March 1886; Dunlop, *Fifty Years of Irish Journalism*, pp. 237–5.
87 Dunlop, *Fifty Years of Irish Journalism*, ch. 8.
88 Loughlin, *Gladstone*, pp. 30–4.
89 *Freeman's Journal*, 9, 11 February 1886.
90 See Lyons, *Parnell*, pp. 614–17, for an informed assessment.
91 Willner, *Spellbinders*, ch. 6.
92 Ibid., pp. 48–51.
93 Ibid., pp. 60–1.
94 J. P. Stern, *Hitler: the Führer and the People*, 3rd impression, London, 1976, p. 27.

95 See Ged Martin, 'Parnell at Cambridge: the education of an Irish nationalist', *Irish Historical Studies*, XIX (73), March 1974, pp. 72–82.
96 Healy, *Letters and Leaders*, vol. I, p. 97.
97 See O'Shea, *Parnell*, vol. II, p. 183.
98 Bew, *Parnell*, p. 145.

11 Parnell in Irish literature

John Kelly

I

Not the least of Irish history's many ironies is that Charles Stewart Parnell – perhaps the least literary of any Irish leader before or since – should have generated myths which engaged not merely two of the major writers of the twentieth century, but a host of other Irish playwrights, novelists and poets. He not only preferred a carpenter's bench and tools to 'all the poets, novelists and sages' but was also fond of pointing out that 'literature has no chance against the Freeman'.[1] His ignorance of Irish history astonished Gladstone and embarrassed his friends, he preferred watching walking contests to visiting the theatre, and Youalt's *The Horse* is the only book he is known to have read all through. Had he lived, would such a man ever have bothered to read the poems, novels and plays in which he appeared? This is a hypothetical question in more senses than one: not only did he not live, but if he had lived the myth would have been very different.

For, as far as his future literary reputation went, his death was a shrewd move: it abstracted him from the increasingly acrimonious recriminations among his former colleagues, so giving his frequently invoked shade purity and integrity, and it slotted him immediately into a messianic typology that was already potent in Celtic, Jewish and Christian tradition, and which was shortly to achieve an even wider resonance through the work of comparative mythologists and psychologists. In 1890, a few months before Parnell's death, Sir James Frazer published the first edition of *The Golden Bough*, a book enormously influential in modern literature, which identified the sacrificial leader as the universal human myth. According to Frazer's copious researches, a tribe's wellbeing was thought to depend upon the mysterious but awesome powers of a priest-king, whose rise and fall represents both the cycle of nature and the pattern of the presiding deity. Anthropologists soon learned to treat these ideas with caution, but modernist writers and critics continued to embrace them enthusiastically.

Yeats was among the most enthusiastic of those who gathered Parnell into the myth of the sacrificial king, and his views – particularly those expressed in his lecture 'Modern Ireland' – were taken up and amplified by Herbert Howarth in *The Irish Writers: Literature under Parnell's Star*:

> Irish writers slowly recognized Parnell's death as the source of the creation of the Irish Republic. Out of the public passions and the ignominy that caused his death a myth flared up that produced the Rising of 1916 and the quick subsequent events: revolution, civil war, and the Republic. . . . The Irish committed the crucial act of killing their prophet and the guilt, the desire to purify the guilt, the belief that his sacrifice sanctified, the belief that sacrifice assures rebirth, gave them irresistible vigour in the next generation. . . . Parnell was reborn in the intransigent underground from which he had by class, temperament, and policy, stood apart.[2]

Yet the very aptness of Parnell to Frazer's typology should give us pause, and Howarth's book, while judicious in many of its literary judgements, leaves important questions unanswered. He has little to say, for example, about the mechanisms whereby the myth was translated into action, or about the relative potency of other political and cultural models available to the Insurrectionaries. It is also clear that those writers who took Parnell as a theme differed fundamentally in their perception of his role in history.

The complexity of these questions becomes evident when we try to track Yeats's various responses to Parnell, for he did not begin to see him as 'that sacrificial victim' until the 1930s. In 1891 Parnell's fall induced 'a moment of supernatural insight', the 'sudden certainty that Ireland was to be like soft wax for years to come'. Ten years later he was still confident that it had released a wholesome and perhaps supernaturally inspired vitality: 'a new kind of Ireland, as full of energy as a boiling pot, was rising up amid the wreck of the old kind', the national life 'was finding new utterance' as if it 'obeyed some impulse from beyond its wild and capricious will'. By 1907 this optimism has evaporated, for the supernatural moment has been appropriated by a new sociological grouping that is all too much of this world, and Yeats laments his inability to foresee that a new class, which had begun to rise into power under the shadow of Parnell, would change the nature of the Irish movement, which needing no longer great sacrifices . . . could do without exceptional men, and those activities of the mind that are founded on the exceptional moment.

In his Nobel speech of December 1923, he returned to the notion that the fall of Parnell began a process that was to have political issue, although he is circumspect in identifying precisely what constituted that process: 'A disillusioned and embittered Ireland turned from parliamentary politics; an event was conceived; and the race began, as I think, to be troubled by that event's long gestation.'[3] To confound the issue further, critics such as John Kelleher argue that Parnell's fall resulted in Celtic melancholy rather than the vibrant messianism identified by Howarth, while Malcolm Brown doubts whether it had any effect at all on the progress of Irish literature.[4]

Any attempt to make sense of these conflicting assertions should begin by teasing out three recurrent but distinct elements of the myth: that the fall and death of Parnell effected a profound shift in Irish cultural consciousness (although there are fundamental disagreements as to what this shift constituted); that the personality of Parnell and the manner of his death generated a messianic myth that was eagerly endorsed by influential writers; that this shift in consciousness, or the literary myth of Parnell, or both together, led to the 1916 Rising and the Irish Republic. However, if we examine each of these contentions in turn, we soon discover that the shift in consciousness after Parnell had as strong a political as cultural dynamic, that the literary myths constructed around him were inspired far more by class and social imperatives than by messianic aspirations, and that the treatment of Parnell changed over time in response to precise rather than mythological historical pressures.

II

I have argued elsewhere that the fall and death of Parnell did have a palpable influence on the cultural history of Ireland, but that it was not the transcendent mystery intuited by Yeats, or the Celtic melancholy described by Kelleher, or the messianic reaction celebrated by Howarth.[5] What occurred was a coalescence of men, mood, moment and method. The men and women were already in place, the shift in mood after the fall of Parnell gave them their moment, and they devised methods and institutions to prolong the moment into a movement.

The first architects of the Irish cultural awakening – Yeats, Hyde, O'Grady, Tynan and Rolleston – had begun writing before 1890, but they found that a literary career in Ireland was frustrating and unrewarding. Yeats's first book, like those by Tynan and O'Grady, had to be published by private subscription; various attempts to found literary periodicals quickly foundered; and repeated efforts to establish networks of literary societies (to circumvent the lack of Irish publishers, journals and critical standards) had come to nothing because the young men to whom they appealed were preoccupied with politics. Nor did attempts to foster Gaelic culture fare better: by the end of the 1880s both the Gaelic Union and the Society for the Preservation of Irish were recognized to be in terminal decline.

The atmosphere, so uncongenial to cultural enterprises in the 1880s, suddenly altered after the fall of Parnell, and this change was self-conscious from its beginning: contemporaries were astonished at the speed with which cultural awareness developed after the split, and as early as 1892 the terms 'Irish literary revival' and 'Irish Renaissance' were in frequent use. This new mood is caught in an article written in June of that year, which expatiated upon the energy and abruptness of the new cultural situation: 'Eighteen months ago there was no man so poor as to do Irish national intellectual life reverence' whereas 'today – why, today . . . it promises to stand against the world'.[6] Significantly, this observation was made in a Parnellite journal, for the Parnellite press first and most enthusiastically took up the cause of an independent Irish culture.

The suddenness with which interest in Irish literature and culture revived may appear to corroborate Yeats's view that the Irish Revival was an almost miraculous outcome of the political upheaval of 1891, attendant upon a 'moment of supernatural insight', but this is not so. It had long been taken for granted that a lull in politics would lead to renewed vigour in cultural life, but neither Yeats nor others who held this opinion could foresee that the lull would come about not as expected through the success of the home rule movement but through the abrupt fall of Parnell and political disunion. And political disunion and failure were key factors in shaping the new response to cultural identity.

After his defeat in Committee Room 15, Parnell's strategy was to distance himself from the Liberal alliance, to smash the 'Union of Hearts', and to play upon traditional Irish mistrust of England

and English politicians. Gladstone, hailed by the Parnellite press only a short while before as the 'great English statesman', was now blamed for the split in the Irish party, and represented as an English Machiavelli who had divided honest – or gullible – Irishmen against themselves. Politically this was a shrewd if desperate tactic. It also had a cultural dimension that the Parnellite papers were quick to exploit. Even before 1891 *United Ireland*, under the literary editorship of John M'Grath, had begun to publish articles, reviews and verse by Irish writers, and now, as the political news became daily more dismal, it devoted an increasing amount of space to literature. But it was not simply a question of quantity: more significant was the change in tone. The two years following the events in Committee Room 15 saw a spectacular reversal in the value attached to the relative merits of literature and politics in defining an Irish identity. This reversal was grounded in the conviction that Irish culture, like Irish politics, must free itself from English influence. The perceived cultural desolation of the 1880s, no longer complaisantly accepted but now regarded as a matter of national shame, is ascribed not as hitherto merely to the syphoning of intellectual energies into politics, but to the fact that, as *United Ireland* claimed in February 1891, '*We do not work in our own material*'.[7] The leader of the anti-Parnellites provided an irresistible example of this process of Anglicization, and throughout the spring of 1891 the paper held him up as an awful warning: 'Mr. Justin McCarthy was asked a few years ago why he did not write an Irish novel. Because, he replied, he could not; he had been too long living in England; he had lost touch with the people.' And a few weeks later it asserted that had he 'lived all his life in Ireland, and followed the bent of his own young, fresh, and original Celtic intellect, he could have been a much greater novelist than he is'.[8] The narrow political animus here is transparent, but the debate soon widened to embrace not merely political enemies but all Irish artists. The contrast between English cultural decrepitude and decadence and native wholesomeness, nature and spirituality becomes a recurrent theme, an opposition that was to harden into a cliché of Irish criticism in the later 1890s, and to cause Irish dramatists a good deal of trouble at the beginning of the new century.

It was bad enough when potentially fine Irish writers squandered their talents in a vain attempt to be English, but it was far worse when they succeeded; when, that is, Irish elements were assimilated into the literature of the enemy, and *United Ireland* insisted:

We want our own literature made known to our own people, so that their genius may be bent into its natural and true groove. We want furthermore to let the world know that intellectually and artistically, the Irish are a distinct, and a distinguished race with their own laws and literature.[9]

Literature is no longer merely 'ornamentation' but an essential ingredient of national identity. There is now no question of disregarding it until after home rule. On the contrary, Irish critics began to look back upon the literary barrenness of previous decades with distress and shame. Culture was no longer regarded as peripheral to the political struggle but, at first, as of a more or less equal importance: 'We do not see why it should not be possible to establish a standard of patriotism in Irish art and literature as well as in Irish politics',[10] and later, significantly, as more important. In 1891 *United Ireland* argued 'that a mere Parliament alone would not make Ireland the nation we longed to see her' and maintained 'that all true and thinking Nationalists are striving not alone for independence in politics, but for independence in literature and art . . . that without these we could never become the independent people we hoped one day to be', and in April 1892 it went even further, expressing what only two years earlier would have been the heretical view that

an Irish Parliament is only one means to the end we have in view; we are convinced that, in comparison with literature and art – and especially literature – its influence would be small in creating the sturdy *Irishism* amongst our people which will be the ultimate guardian of our National liberties.[11]

III

United Ireland supposed it could create an Irish Literary Revival by its own fiat: 'But won't we have some literature in the future', it asked in March 1891, contemplating the sorry state of contemporary Irish letters, and answered its own question with blithe assurance, 'Certainly if we make up our minds to have it.'[12] Yet, for all its propaganda, it could do no more than establish a new mood for cultural initiatives, and the second wave of the literary awakening is the history of its cultural institutions – particularly the National Literary Society, the New Irish Library and the Gaelic League – that were founded in the immediate aftermath of Parnell. The mood had produced the moment and the men produced the methods to prolong the inspiration of that moment.

A detailed account of these institutions does not concern us here, but it is worth emphasizing how crucial the mood established by the fall of Parnell was to their success. In attempting to foster an Irish literature in the 1880s Yeats had lamented the lack of a critical public, the lack of Irish publishers and the lack of Irish periodicals to create the taste whereby new native literary talent was to be relished. *United Ireland* had now taken on the role the *Nation* had played in the 1840s, and he set about reviving his other cultural plans. During the late 1880s his attempts to establish a Young Ireland League, a network of literary clubs and reading rooms that would provide cultural centres and a new audience for Irish literature, had failed utterly because political excitement absorbed the energies and interest of the young men to whom they were supposed to appeal. But a campaign to inaugurate a literary society in 1892, which took its energy precisely from the Parnellite aesthetic that had been developing since the split in the Irish party, proved a success. An article in the London *Daily Telegraph*, arguing that any Irish literary society must have its headquarters in London since London was the cultural and political capital of Ireland, provoked a correspondence in *United Ireland* which culminated in the announcement that a National Literary Society, based in Dublin, was to be set up.[13] The objects and organization of this society closely resembled those proposed at meetings of the Young Ireland League in 1885 and 1891. What was new, in the mood following Parnell, was both the wide support enjoyed by the new society and the importance which Irish literature had now assumed in the popular press and the public mind.

The National Literary Society did not establish the country branches that Yeats had hoped for, but it survived into the new century as a centre for Irish cultural enterprises, and most of the leading Irish writers, historians, scholars and journalists lectured to it in due course. It was the first link in a chain of cultural initiatives that exerted a seminal influence on Irish life, for it became the sponsor of the New Irish Library and later of the Irish Literary Theatre. It also acted as midwife to the Gaelic League, whose history provides another illustration of the fundamental change in cultural attitudes at this time. Before its foundation in 1893 the two organizations dedicated to the revival of the Irish language, the Gaelic Union and the Society for the Preservation of the Irish Language (SPIL), had both experienced the greatest difficulty in reaching an audience dominated by political issues. SPIL's *Annual Report* in March 1887 ruefully acknowledged that 'owing to the unsettled state of the public mind, and its being preoccupied with political and social questions of serious import, the progress made in the movement is not such as its friends might otherwise be led to expect'.[14] In July 1889 Michael Cusack, founder of the Gaelic Athletic Association, declared in the *Nation*: 'No man now living can recall a period . . . during which the nationality that is based upon the national tongue was at so low an ebb in Ireland.'[15] His letter initiated a long exchange, in the course of which one contributor, suggesting that the Gaelic Union and SPIL should amalgamate to form a 'Celtic League', detailed a plan for such a body that is almost identical with the constitution adopted by the Gaelic League in 1893.[16] If we ask why this proposal had to wait three years to generate active support, we again discover that political preoccupations were stifling cultural initiatives. The imminence of a general election, the prospect that the constitutional agitation of a decade was coming to fruition, pushed cultural discussions to one side and the debate in the *Nation* petered out with no result.

The new mood, attendant upon the fall and death of Parnell, the wish to 'stop the Anglicising process', changed all this. In December 1892 Douglas Hyde, catching the new spirit, first delivered his influential lecture to the National Literary Society on 'The necessity for de-Anglicising Ireland', and the following July he and some fellow members of the society took the (by now) logical step of setting up the Gaelic League. The *Gaelic Journal* congratulated them on their perspicacity: 'In the noted Bismarckian phrase, it is abundantly clear that the founders of the Gaelic League have "seized the psychological moment".'[17] Once in their grasp they did not let the initiative go. They were conscious that what they had won from politics might be lost to politics. The 1895 general election, following the Lords' rejection of the second Home Rule Bill, threatened to entice the minds of Ireland once again towards Westminster, but the *Gaelic Journal*, now the organ of the league, warned against this: 'Those engaged in the Irish language movement . . . will not allow even the excitement of a great political crisis to divert them from their aim or from their work.'[18]

Nor did they, at this time. In fact, all the cultural institutions founded in the aftermath of Parnell insisted on political neutrality. This apparent harmony was, however, deceptive. Although Yeats was to use a metaphor of passivity to describe the Irish mind after Parnell ('like soft wax'), it not only had the very definite political imprints we have traced, but it also proved to be a palimpsest of competing cultural impressions. Within a few years the Gaelic League was to scorn the notion that 'Irish' literature could be written in English, and from the first, even among those who seemed his allies, Yeats found significantly different views as to what constituted Irish culture. Excited by the sudden awakening, he had entertained high Romantic ambitions of restoring Ireland to what he termed 'Unity of Being' through 'Unity of Culture', calling upon Ireland's mythological tradition, her Celtic sensibility and a symbolist aesthetic. As the decade progressed these ideas perplexed the journalists on *United Ireland* and frightened the more orthodox members of the National Literary Society. A signal failure of these years was his inability to keep control of the New Irish Library, a scheme for a series of inexpensive books that would bring the new Irish literature to a wider audience. His project was appropriated by Sir Charles Gavan Duffy, the former Young Irelander, who had recently offered himself as an anti-Parnellite candidate and who used – so Yeats alleged – clerical influence to oust Yeats from the enterprise. Furious debates raged in the committee room of the National Literary Society in early 1893, and it was perhaps at this time that Yeats began to appreciate his affinities with Parnell: like him he was fighting an anti-Parnellite, clerically backed foe, who took the majority with him. Duffy won, and instead of inaugurating the series with one of the original and imaginative works Yeats advocated, published an arid historical work by Thomas Davis and so lost the project prestige and popularity.

In his *Autobiographies* Yeats imagines Duffy's deprived cultural background,[19] and portrays him as representing the philistine tendencies of an emergent Catholic middle class, whose power he and others of his social position found increasingly threatening. For the new literary institutions brought Yeats into contact, and into conflict, with people and classes little known to him hitherto. As a letter of 1894 reveals, these encounters had the unforeseen consequence of profoundly altering his outlook: 'Ireland is greatly demoralised in all things,' he wrote:

> My experience of Ireland during the last three years has changed my views very greatly, & now I feel that the work of an Irish man of letters must be not so much to awaken or quicken or preserve the national ideal among the mass of the people but to convert the educated classes to it on the one hand to the best of his ability, & on the other – & this is the more important – to

fight for moderation, dignity, and the rights of the intellect among his fellow nationalists.[20]

So it was that in looking back he was to describe the events of the early 1890s as 'the failure of our first attempts to create a modern Irish literature'.[21] These words, written in a period of discouragement, are too absolute and too pessimistic, for Parnell's fall had made possible an influential and energetic cultural movement. Until the end of the decade he was still able to describe the situation as a 'boiling pot', but the pot held, it seemed, some indigestible ingredients. And, when Yeats took the lid off, he found most indigestible of all the 'new class, which had begun to rise into power under the shadow of Parnell' and which 'would change the nature of the Irish movement'.[22] Parnell, a gentleman and landlord, had kept that class in order until it turned upon him, and as the decade progressed the attention of those I shall loosely call 'Ascendancy'[23] writers became less concerned with the cultural repercussions of his fall and more and more fascinated by his personality and authority. In this they were animated not by the large anthropological and millennial possibilities celebrated by Howarth, but rather by a more precise sense of their class and its historical predicament.

IV

A crucial difference between the 'Ascendancy' (and largely Protestant) treatment of Parnell and that of the (largely Catholic) 'middle class' is that the former interpreted his fall and death as a personal sacrifice; the latter as a betrayal by his followers. Moreover, while both present him as a ghost, the 'Ascendancy' writers – until 1916 – see him as a model for possible surrogates, but the middle class regard him as a minatory absence. The title of the poem Yeats wrote in immediate response to his death, 'Mourn and then onwards', catches that Ascendancy sentiment, its allusions to Moses and the wandering in the desert implying ultimate success under a new leadership.[24] The nature of that new leadership, and the kind of promised land to which it might lead, were to become of increasing concern to the writers of Yeats's class.

In his final year Parnell faced two enemies – Gladstone and the agrarian wing of his own party – in whom the Ascendancy recognized their own class enemies. Until his fall few Ascendancy writers cared much for Parnell: he is hardly mentioned in Yeats's writings, published or unpublished; he was suspect to Rolleston, Lady Gregory and O'Grady because of his association with agrarian agitation and boycotting; and in the month of his death Douglas Hyde confessed 'with shame I never valued Mr. Parnell till we had lost him'.[25] What begins after the final year and death is an astonishing transformation of Parnell from class enemy into class (although they said 'national') hero.

Writing soon after the split and before Parnell's death, William O'Brien noted the

> incontrovertible fact that every landlord, agent, removable magistrate, emergencyman, or landgrabber in the country . . . has suddenly blossomed into an ardent Parnellite. In any first-class carriage you are sure to meet a squire who has discovered Mr. Parnell to be a man of genius.[26]

O'Brien's characteristic penchant for rhetorical hyperbole has been heightened by the intensified political struggle, and his purpose is to show that Parnell's support comes from those most inimical to home rule. But even qualifying his 'incontrovertible' facts, there is a truth in what he says. Over the course of the next decade Parnell's reputation among certain sections of Protestant opinion underwent an astounding change.

The causes of that change are not hard to seek. Although the second Home Rule Bill was defeated, and although the Liberal administration was swept away in the general election of 1895, it was evident to thinking members of the Ascendancy that their days of political hegemony were drawing to a close, and their place in a new Ireland was unresolved. In reviewing their situation they were oppressed by certain grievances: that they were a people who had served Ireland and England and did not deserve to be put to the wall; that they had been used and betrayed by English politicians; that their enemies in Ireland were the unscrupulous political representatives of a rising Catholic middle class eager to usurp their traditional powers through yet more radical reforms in land tenure and local government.

Parnell, although a landlord, had demeaned himself to lead their Irish enemies and allied himself with the English betrayers, but had been betrayed in his turn by both. He stood up to this treachery with energy and fortitude which could not fail to stir the heart. But more than the heart was stirred. Here was a man who, although apparently on the wrong side, was of the right stock and the right stuff. He was a man who if times had been a little different – and times were now a good deal different – might indeed have been an Ascendancy champion.

Ascendancy admiration for Parnell resided mainly in three perceptions. In the first place he was 'one of us', a gentleman with the qualities that O'Grady, Yeats, Martyn and Lady Gregory wanted to find in their class: courteous, remote, solitary, passionate and yet utterly self-controlled, high principled and intelligent. And although one of Yeats's very few pre–1891 references described him as a 'famous agitator',[27] it was now taken as axiomatic that Parnell had always been opposed to land agitation, that there was nothing of the revolutionary and little of the radical in him. Deep down, in fact, he was a friend of the landlords. This led on to a second source of admiration: Parnell had kept the unruly natives in awe and order. He commanded his party through force of personality and authority of caste; stopped their scheming, and prevented their excesses. But he had done more than overawe the Irish members; he had also (and this was the third ground for admiration) put fear and respect into perfidious and patronizing English politicians who were given to take their Irish garrison too much for granted. In doing so he had asserted an Anglo-Irish identity that was perpetually in question.

Constructing a myth of Parnell was greatly facilitated by the fact that little was known of the real man. Few of the writers had met him, and until his final months he had kept a low profile through ill-health and his sexual intrigue. Thus the myth was constructed from hearsay, anecdotes and chance encounters, and took much of its power from a reading of his personality rather than his policies. One of the first sustained Ascendancy attempts to come to terms with him occurred in 1894, when Standish James O'Grady, mythologist and apologist for landlordism, devoted the final two chapters of *The Story of Ireland* to him. Although 'no friend to his politics', O'Grady confessed that he liked Parnell 'extremely', and liked him for qualities that were to become familiar in Ascendancy writing: 'the singular "withdrawnness" of the man, something suggestive of a mind remote and solitary. Fastidiously polite and courteous himself, I fancy he was one with whom it was impossible to take a liberty . . .'.[28] In other words, a regular gent, and one who, as such, was a good deal less hostile to his fellow landlords than might have been supposed, for he 'did not regard landlords as coroneted ghouls. . . . Parnell was nothing of a fanatic. Classes, interests, parties . . . were . . . means of the making of an Irish nation'.[29] Even during the bitter land campaign of 1880–1 Parnell 'spoke not like a modern politician, but like a man who had work to do, and meant to do it'. O'Grady wished that the landlords would produce just such a man on their side but they ran 'to England for shelter, and of course . . . the statesmen of England betrayed them'.[30] The sad irony was that Parnell could have been their champion, since

> born and bred an aristocrat he knew that his class were the possessors of certain moral and intellectual qualities without which Ireland as a nation would be the poorer. I think he had planned out ways and means for preserving the Irish gentry.[31]

As a mythologist and classicist O'Grady cannot resist recounting the stories of elemental disturbances at Parnell's funeral, 'the sky was bright with strange lights and flames', but the cosmic fireworks are of less significance than the earthly potentialities that a contemplation of Parnell's career suggest. For O'Grady derived many of his ideas on society from Carlyle and his politics from the Tory democracy espoused by Lord Randolph Churchill. Like both, he saw modern society in desperate need of a responsible and ruling aristocracy, and much of his writing is directed to urging the Irish landlords to take up, or rather resume, that role. In this book he acknowledges that the economic power of the landlords was broken in 1881, but the memory of Parnell persists as an example of how a landlord endowed with the right spirit might yet wield political influence in Ireland.

The careers of two Irish Protestant writers who were to write on Parnell, Lady Gregory and W. B. Yeats, enable us to see how O'Grady's perceptions of Parnell became more widely current. Lady Gregory was widowed in 1892, only six months after Parnell's death, and from a life based largely on London and foreign travel, she returned to the west of Ireland and a life largely concerned with paying off the mortgage on the estate that was her young son's inheritance. At this time she was implacably opposed to home rule and in 1893 published a pamphlet to warn of its evils. Entitled *A Phantom's Pilgrimage, or Home Ruin*, it imagines the ghost of one who had been foremost in the campaign revisiting Ireland ten years after independence has been introduced. Instead of the anticipated land of contentment and plenty, he finds it run-down, gripped by famine and terrorized by corner-boy nationalists who rule without the encumbrance of law. But the disappointed revenant is not Parnell, as one might expect given his recent demise, but Gladstone, who in 1893 still had five years of his earthly course to run. In other words, this is a document concerned less with Irish agitation

than with English betrayal. Parnell does not appear, but his shade
hovers just off stage, for during an assault by a disgruntled Dublin
mob on the Irish Parliament 'a sallow, black-haired individual . . .
appeared at a window. He was greeted with howls of "Traitor!"
"Judas!" "Who killed his master! . . . Hold on to the tribute!" '[32]
The sallow man who killed his master will be associated with Zimri
by Yeats, and identified by him, and by Lady Gregory in her
Journals, as John Dillon, her particular *bête noire*.[33] And a particular *bête noire* because he was a leader of agrarian agitation, the
class and economic enemy whom she feared and despised as a
representative of a rising Catholic middle class.

Like O'Grady, Lady Gregory understood that Ascendancy power
had been deeply undermined, and that the lull in the Land War
was no more than a temporary respite. Even the defeat of the
home rule parties in the 1895 election could not hide the fact that
the British connection was no longer to be relied upon. At a dinner
party in London James Lowell had cheerfully informed her that
'we landlords must make up our minds to the spread of democracy
in the nineteenth century and be the Jonah thrown to the whales'.[34]
Back in Ireland, her work on her husband's memoirs, and the
editing of *Mr. Gregory's Letter-Box*, deepened her critique of political structures, as did her reading of Froude, 'which has opened my
eyes to the failings of the landlords, & I may say of *all* classes in
Ireland in the past, & makes me very anxious to do my duty'.[35]
But by April 1894 she acknowledged that time was running out:

> I feel that this Land Bill is the last of 'Dobson's Three Warnings'
> & am thankful that we land-owners have been given even a little
> time to prepare & to work while it is day. It is necessary that as
> democracy gains power, our power should go.[36]

The problem perhaps was not one of 'as' but 'how' democracy
gained power. Was it to be an orderly movement to a new order,
or, as she had pictured in *A Phantom's Pilgrimage*, a downward
spiral into impoverished anarchy led by treacherous and incompetent rabble-rousers like Dillon? While Yeats was evolving an
aesthetic which depended upon the cultural interaction between the
'educated classes' and the peasantry, to the exclusion of the middle
classes and their so-called 'popular' literature, she was coming to
the conclusion that the future of Ireland depended upon an alliance
between an enlightened gentry and the people, to the exclusion of
middle-class politicians.

Parnell was emerging as an example of someone who had bridled the democratic movement and not only kept his aristocratic code, but used it as an instrument in that bridling. Her reappraisal of his career was aided not only by *The Story of Ireland* but, more influentially, by her friendship with Barry O'Brien, Parnell's biographer, whom she met in 1897. Although not of the Ascendancy, O'Brien, a barrister and journalist, was strongly influenced by Fenian views on Parnell and emphasized the strength of his personality, his hatred of England, and his dislike of agrarian agitation. Central to the discussions about Parnell that took place between O'Brien, Lady Gregory, Yeats, Horace Plunkett, George Moore and others in 1897 and 1898 is the question of identity. In the days of more certain Unionist hegemony the Ascendancy had preserved its sense of social and racial identity by insisting upon its differences from a stereotype of the 'mere Irish'; as that hegemony weakened, the more far-sighted sought a rapprochement with the people and tried to authenticate their Irishness by defining it against a stereotype of Englishness. 'The people', Lady Gregory noted, 'have grown to hate England through their love for Ireland – Our class is now through dislike of England growing to care for their own country.'[37] This was straight Parnellism, as she learned from O'Brien who quoted his remark: 'These English despise us because we are Irish; but we must stand up to them. That's the way to treat the Englishman – stand up to him.'[38]

Hatred of England might be one definition of Irish identity but, as O'Brien's biography amply illustrates, many of those who knew Parnell thought his personality and characteristics completely unIrish.[39] This was a problem for Ascendancy writers like Lady Gregory and Yeats: in seeking an Irish identity they had no wish to imitate those they despised, but to outsiders the Anglo-Irish code of behaviour seemed indistinguishable from that of patrician Englishmen. And racial definitions were unconvincing. Sir Richard Burton, weary of Lady Gregory's perpetual references to her Irishness, told her bluntly that she had no Irish blood at all, and James Joyce was to maintain that 'there was not even a drop of Celtic blood' in Parnell.[40] Yeats would have none of this. When Horace Plunkett told him Parnell was 'quite unlike an Irishman', he immediately retorted that it was 'quite Celtic to have that strong will', and on another occasion that 'Parnell was a representative Irishman – he lived for an idea – Englishmen will only live for an institution'.[41] He used the example of Parnell to discriminate between apparent similarities in English and Anglo-Irish reserve, maintaining that an Englishman 'is reserved because of his want of sensibility – Parnell was reserved in spite of it', and to draw larger political and racial conclusions: 'The Irish are a feminine nation with masculine ideals – The English are a masculine nation with feminine ideals. . . . But England would never take a masculine ruler, Napoleon or Parnell as Ireland would do.'[42]

Here is the beginning of Yeats's myth of the Anglo-Irish, in which his reading of Parnell was to play a major role, but at this period he wishes to give the qualities a more general Irish application. Moreover, public events held hope that a 'masculine' Ascendancy leader might yet be able to unite Ireland and undermine the power of the anti-Parnellites. The report of the commission into financial relations between Ireland and Britain led to an all-party Irish convention. Horace Plunkett, who had set up the Recess Committee, was active in this agitation, as was another Unionist, Lord Castletown. In other quarters Irish politicians seemed to be hopelessly divided: the three-way quarrel between Dillon, Healy and Redmond dragged on, and Yeats found that even the more radical '98 Committees on which he served were riven by jealousies and spite.[43] The time seemed ripe for a leader to arise, who should be untainted by factional dogma and attitudes.

On 21 March 1897 Lady Gregory arranged a dinner party so that she and Yeats could introduce Barry O'Brien to Horace Plunkett, and her report of the evening reveals how far Parnell was being appropriated as a model for Anglo-Irish political aspirations and behaviour. O'Brien was, she notes, eager to meet Plunkett 'as all sections of Nationalists of late have been agreeing that he is the only possible leader to unite all parties'. When Plunkett arrived the conversation soon turned to Parnell. Plunkett thought he over-dominated his followers, but O'Brien, taking up a position that he argues vigorously in his biography, said 'it was necessary he should dominate for the campaign, & that he was a great general'. Asked what he would do at this moment in Ireland if he had power there, O'Brien replied, ' "I would make Mr Horace Plunkett our leader & follow him" – Yeats agrees enthusiastically & says "we all want it" '. Over coffee they urged Plunkett to make a powerful speech on the financial relations question, O'Brien insisting 'that it ought to be rubbed into the Govt that it was their own Protestant colony they destroyed in destroying trade'. Lady Gregory chimed in with the observation

that the Liberals, & indeed the Govt, have confessed already the enormity of England's conduct in the past – & by way of making up, gave liberally of the landlords' money, the Church [of Ireland] money or anything they could get at the expense of others – but as soon as it comes to their own money . . . they say – oh now, we must have another commission, & button up their pockets.

And she pleased her guests by pointing out that it 'is not the money that is the important thing – it is getting all Ireland into line'.[44]

The pattern recognizable from O'Grady's history onwards is emerging. Ireland should be led by a moderate Ascendancy figure (Plunkett was a Dunsany) against the exploitation of England, and the divisive policies of her own populist politicians. For, characteristically, none of them had 'a good word for Dillon – I ask B O'B what he thinks of him, & he says "What Parnell did – that it is a wonder the Irish people haven't found out what a consummate fool he is" ', and Plunkett reported himself 'much disgusted with Dillon's behaviour on the financial committee, upsetting the whole coach by his silly amendments'. When Plunkett had left O'Brien said, 'We could go fast with that man as a leader', and Lady Gregory agreed:

> His courteous restrained manner – good looks & some quality in his voice are all in his favour – & he must have some magnetic influence to have got over the suspicions of the farmers & induced them to co-operate.[45]

These were precisely Parnell's qualities as identified by O'Grady, O'Brien and the Ascendancy, but in the event Plunkett turned out not to be Parnell's heir; his opposition to home rule, his absorption in the Co-operative Movement and the Department of Agriculture and Technical Instruction meant that he did not take up the cause with the passion and energy it required. One man who temporarily did seem to have the requisite commitment was Lord Castletown. He was already a pan-Celtic enthusiast, and made a number of rousing speeches on the iniquity of imperial taxation, but he failed to reproduce these in Westminster. Nevertheless, in April 1897 Lady Gregory sounded him out and 'had some financial talk with him – He says he is no Home Ruler but is a Nationalist'. She contented herself with telling him that she was sorry he toned down his speech on the financial relations in the Lords.[46]

V

The first literary manifestation of these Ascendancy attitudes is to be found in the plays produced by the Irish Literary Theatre. Although Parnell appears in none of the plays by name, the sentiments now associated with him are constantly felt. The theatre itself operated under the sponsorship of the National Literary Society and might therefore be seen as another institutional by-product of the Parnell split. It was underwritten by Edward Martyn, a landlord, and most of its guarantors were of the Ascendancy. The plays presented during its three-year existence were, with one exception, Ascendancy in authorship, and all (apart from a one-act piece in Irish by Hyde) have striking similarities of theme and outlook: they are written from an aristocratic viewpoint, and the leading characters are without exception landlords, or of a superior caste, even when the source is mythical or pseudo-mythical: Yeats's Countess Cathleen is an aristocrat and a wealthy landowner, and in her magnificent sacrifice of her soul for her tenants' wellbeing *noblesse oblige* is carried to sublime heights. *Diarmuid and Grania*, written in collaboration with George Moore, celebrates aristocratic ideals and behaviour at the expense of the common people.[47] Carden Tyrrell, hero of Edward Martyn's *The Heather Field*, is also a landlord, while the eponymous heroine of his *Maeve*, a full if impoverished Gaelic princess, rejects marriage into the British plutocracy.

But the play which expresses most fully the search for a new Parnell is *The Bending of the Bough*, a five-act political drama written by George Moore with the not inconsiderable assistance of Yeats and based on Martyn's *The Tale of a Town*. In *Hail and Farewell* Moore parodies the idea of messianic succession, moving to Ireland after hearing a ghostly voice 'on the road to Chelsea', and, once resident in Dublin, discovering himself in a mock-Wagnerian climax to be the true heir to Parnell.[48] This revelation was still in the future when he set about rewriting Martyn's crude and ill-constructed play, a rewriting that 'awakened the Irishman that was dormant in me'.[49] Both versions have the same theme: a dispute between two towns, Northhaven and Southhaven, over the ownership of a line of steamers. Southhaven – industrialized, commercial and materialistic – clearly represents England, while the spiritual, idealistic, but hopelessly divided Celtic Northhaven stands for Ireland. Northhaven desperately needs a leader and in the course of the play one arises: Jasper Dean, a well-connected, Oxford-educated young man under the influence of the Celtic idealist, Ralf Kirwan, unites the political factions on the town council to form a common front against the commercial exploitation of Southhaven. Then, just as victory seems assured, he renounces the struggle to please his Southhaven fiancée, Millicent Fell.

Although the Oxbridge educated hero, with his established position in Irish life, his appeal to 'the mountainy men' and his final political failure through a relationship with an Englishwoman, may echo aspects of Parnell's career, this is less a Parnellite than a post-Parnellite play, embodying Ascendancy attitudes that we have seen evolving over the years following Parnell's fall, and given a further push by Moore's habitual over-exuberance. Three familiar themes run through the play. On one level it is a satire on the bitterness and triviality of contemporary Irish politics; at another it explores Anglo-Irish political and financial relations; while at a third it is an exploration of Irish – or Celtic – identity.

The quarrel over the steamers is clearly an allegory for the quarrel over financial relations in 1896–7, and the members of the Northhaven council are based on contemporary figures in Irish politics. The astringent Celtic mystic, Kirwan, owes much to Standish James O'Grady, whose *All Ireland*, written in response to the Financial Relations question, is echoed throughout the play. Jasper Dean is a more composite figure. He is obviously based on Castletown, has traces of Parnell, and perhaps owes something to Horace Plunkett and T. W. Rolleston.

But above all Dean is the projection of an ideal Ascendancy leader. He dominates and unites the squabbling factions in Northhaven, and beats the politicians of Southhaven at their own game. As in the case of Parnell, a wide social gulf exists between him and the people, but Kirwan assures him that it is this which ensures his success: 'your appeal is stronger because you are not of the people',[50] and, as with Parnell, this appeal is particularly effective with the hillside men, so achieving the looked-for alliance between the Ascendancy and the peasantry. The play's problem is to define his political programme. The financial dispute with Southhaven is clear-cut, but this is only one issue and, although there is more than enough about Celtic spirituality, we gain little information about further policies. Kirwan regards Dean not as an individual but as articulating a moment of racial destiny, and Dean resolves to 'believe in self-sufficiency and in the destiny of the race'.[51] Under Kirwan's tutelage he is able to assure Millicent that Southhaven is 'soulless', but that 'because of its spiritual inheritance' 'the spiritual destiny of the Celtic race . . . is greater than any other'.[52] As so often in the case of Ascendancy heroes, there is the little difficulty of blood in ascribing this racial identity, but Dean explains that blood has, in fact, very little to do with race: 'it is not a question of race, it is the land itself that makes the Celt . . .'.[53] This was a view that for obvious reasons appealed to the Anglo-Irish Ascendancy.

But the myth of Parnell as an Ascendancy gentleman with a mysterious power of inspiring loyalty is beginning to exact its price. In Jasper Dean, his supposed successor, the leader is becoming divorced from the politician, and hard political thinking disperses itself in the soft green mists of a vague Celtic dawn. The charisma of caste and personality, the odd speech in the mountains, these are apparently enough to regain a lost hegemony.

VI

Jasper Dean fails to be the successor to Parnell. So, too, did Moore; after a ten-year sojourn he left Ireland to return to London. In that decade most of the Ascendancy writers found themselves increasingly at odds with new forces in Irish life. As Yeats's impatience with popular opinion grew, he discovered a relationship between his developing literary views and the aristocratic, social and authoritarian qualities which had impressed him in Parnell. In the 1890s he had identified these qualities as characteristically 'Irish' or 'Celtic', but now he narrowed their application to one class. The people could only be 'conquered by an ideal of life upheld by authority', and he took to defining literary style as 'but high breeding in words and in argument'.[54] 'Protestant social prejudice', deplored in the previous decade, he now praised for keeping 'our ablest men from levelling passions',[55] and, in associating Parnell with this code of behaviour, he began to contrast him with O'Connell:

> The sense of form, whether that of Parnell or Grattan or Davis, of form in active life, has always been Protestant in Ireland. O'Connell, the one great Catholic figure, was formless. The power of self-conquest, of elevation has been Protestant, and more or less a thing of class. All the tragedians were Protestant – O'Connell was a comedian. He had the gifts of the market place, of the clown at the fair.[56]

In 1908 the Abbey produced Norreys Connell's *The Piper* which, in dramatizing the squabbles of a group of 1798 rebels, seemed to epitomize the situation in Ireland after Parnell. Yeats interpreted it as 'a satire on those dreadful years of the Parnellite split – those years of endless talk, of endless rhetoric, of drivelling folly',[57] but found in the character of the play's hero, Black Mike, 'a figure which had deeply impressed my boyhood . . . Charles Stewart Parnell. I see that angry, heroic man once again as I saw him in my boyhood face to face with Irish futility'.[58] Yeats is misremembering either his age or his attitudes, for as we have seen there was no evidence of any admiration for Parnell before the split, by which time he was 25, but this very forgetfulness is an indication of how far he had come to identify Parnell's fight with his own struggle against 'Irish futility'. Parnell becomes an example of correct Irish attitudes, embodying controlled passion, Nietzschean distance, Castiglionean manners.

Lady Gregory shared these views, and gave them expression in many of her plays. A recurrent theme, as in *The White Cockade*, is the need for a strong man, an aristocratic hero, who will unite a people confused by false bourgeois compromises and lead them to dignity and national self-consciousness. Even more pervasive is her attack on middle-class values and their political consequences in disrupting her vision of an Ireland organized from the top into an orderly, benevolent and harmonious society.

These themes are central to *The Deliverer*, a play ostensibly about Moses, but in fact about Parnell, produced in January 1911. The play takes up an association with Moses first used by Parnell himself, implicit in Yeats's poem 'Mourn: and Then Onwards!', and repeated by Joyce, but Lady Gregory's play soon deviates from Exodus. Moses kills the overseer, as in the biblical account, but immediately begins to arrange the Israelites' escape. Plans are almost complete when they turn against him, at first because of sexual jealousy (their wives praise him), and then because the king's priest (a crafty amalgam of a Liberal politician and an Irish bishop) suggests that his methods and morals are suspect. Dan and Ard (Dillon and Healy) begin to fight among themselves as to who should succeed him as leader, and in trying to separate them Moses/Parnell antagonizes the mob who stone him to death and feed him to the king's cats (the Liberal party). The king's officer sentences the Israelites to prison, and while they await incarceration the ghost of Moses/Parnell is seen, and his only faithful follower prophesies that he will wander through a score and through two score years. . . . A strange thing to get the goal, and the lad of the goal being dead. (*Another screech of the cats. He laughs*) I wouldn't wonder at all he to bring back cross money to shoot the cats. He will get satisfaction of the cats.[59]

The play follows in allegorical form the standard Ascendancy view of Parnell. Egypto-Jewish Moses stands up to the Egyptians as Anglo-Irish Parnell stood up to the English; Moses, nurtured in a palace, is the only one of his nation with the authority and personality to lead them out of bondage as Parnell, nurtured in the Big House, had the qualities to lead the Irish. Parnell took a divided nation, united it, and brought it to the brink of freedom only to be betrayed by his former followers and allies: Moses plans to liberate 'a crushed and miserable race' but (and here there is a significant swerve from Exodus) on the point of departure they turn on him and quarrel among themselves. This rewriting of Exodus is an ideological rather than a dramatic imperative, for Lady Gregory's treatment of the Israelites is conspicuously hostile, and it is difficult to comprehend how this demoralized, querulous, priest-ridden, sexually anxious and bickering people could reach the Promised Land without him. The timing of the play's composition is significant here, for the third Home Rule Bill constituted an apparently achieved Promised Land to those for whom Lady Gregory entertained the greatest dislike: for Dillon, O'Brien, the Irish bourgeois politicians and the English Liberals. These, as often in her works, are the target of the play's satire – especially the Liberals. At the play's end Parnell's shade is foreseen as exacting revenge not upon the Irish turncoats, but upon those who had deserted Lady Gregory and her class. As in *A Phantom's Pilgrimage*, the 'king's cats', the English politicians and particularly Gladstone, remain the real enemy.

After 1916 it became less easy to conceive of Parnell, or a successor to Parnell, exercising any influence in Irish politics. Henceforward plays and novels tend to treat him as a purely historical figure, but there was one last Ascendancy attempt to summon his ghost as a potential political force. Lennox Robinson's *The Lost Leader*, produced in 1917, addresses the question of succession by the ingenious device of making Parnell his own successor, for the play proposes that he did not die in 1891, but was spirited away to Connemara where he has lived on peacefully as Lucius Lenehan. However, the events of 1916 and their aftermath begin to disturb him, and when he is accidentally hypnotized by a visiting psychologist he reveals his identity. He arranges to meet representatives of the major parties to confirm his identity and to divulge his solution to the post-Rising political situation, but, before he can do either, he is accidentally killed by his most fervent admirer, an old ballad-singer significantly named Houlihan.

The play has two main themes: the question of whether Lucius is Parnell, and the nature of his message to Ireland. Robinson evades both issues, and the evasion is symptomatic of the unresolved contradictions (between personality and politician) in the Ascendancy portrayal of Parnell. At his fatal last meeting Lucius/Parnell reviews the three main Irish parties – the Unionists, the Parliamentarians and Sinn Fein – and finds them wanting because they lack a plan. He does have a plan, 'so simple, it could be told in twenty words. . . . It only needed to be told to Ireland by a man with personality, a man who was loved and feared, and the problem was solved for ever'.[60] Unfortunately he never gets round to divulging this twenty-word spell that 'solves everything' and is 'so simple a child could understand it',[61] but from his remarks we gather that he is preaching spirituality, 'the spiritual side of Sinn Fein, the only side that matters, the side that's pure gold'.[62] In the 1880s, he explains, this had not been possible, but even then he recognized 'this greater fight, a fight not with a landlord or government, not for the possession of a few acres of land, but a fight between each man and his lower self, a fight for possession of the nation's soul'.[63]

Lucius's speeches complete a process begun in 1894 by O'Grady, the subsuming of the historical Parnell's acute sense of political and economic realities into the articulation of an idealized and ill-defined national destiny. As in many Ascendancy treatments of the theme, the enemy in this play is not the Unionist landlord, nor even the rival Sinn Fein politician, but Long John Favin, a representative of the upwardly mobile Catholic middle class whom Lucius must extirpate: 'Bribe-taker, gombeen man, seller of justice, liar, thief. I shall break you and your sort, I shall grind you to powder.'[64] Gombeen man and Ascendancy bogy man, Long John is the latest in a line of grasping and unscrupulous natives familiar in the works of Yeats, Lady Gregory, Martyn and O'Grady. But in trying to beat him off, the honest, loyal and, alas, blind Houlihan strikes Lucius by mistake, and once again Ireland destroys Parnell through misprision brought on by a treacherous middle class.

Earlier Ascendancy attempts to revive Parnell in the guise of Plunkett or Castletown had been fanciful enough, and Jasper

Dean's Celticism clouded the more tangible political and financial issues facing him, but Robinson's Parnell ('a nation must be noble and beautiful before it can be free . . . when we speak of parliaments and republics we speak of shadows of a shadow')[65] has almost refined himself out of political existence. It is hard to reconcile this portrayal with the Parnell in whom Morley found the least discursive mind he had ever known. *The Lost Leader* represents the last Ascendancy attempt to explore the possibility of a revived Parnell exerting a direct influence on Irish political history by force of personality, by his ability to speak to a wide spectrum of Irish society, and by his ability to keep crooked upstarts in their place. But, like his predecessors, Robinson's Parnell is too abstracted from contemporary political realities to do more than voice the vague transcendenta hopes of a politically defeated class.

VII

If the literary consequences of the fall of Parnell were more intricately bound up with politics than Yeats and other Ascendancy writers wanted to admit, their literary presentation of him also had a more precise focus than is often realized. Howarth suggested that this presentation set in motion further political consequences, including the Easter Rising and the declaration of an Irish Republic, but in turning to these claims it is as well to discriminate between the treatment of Parnell by the landowning classes and by the middle classes.

In fact, the influence of Parnell among middle-class nationalists quickly waned. The anti-Parnellites dismissed him as irrelevant to the developing situation, and the Parnellites were so busy holding on that, in spite of Ivy Day and lip service, there was little real engagement with his memory. For the more advanced nationalists Parnell became at best part of a series and at worst almost eclipsed by more potent sacrificial victims. On 5 January 1901 Arthur Griffith, the architect of Sinn Fein and a vigorous Parnellite in the early 1890s, noted in his *United Irishman* that 'Grattan is dead and O'Connell is dead and Parnell is dead, but Emmet and Davis, Mitchel and the Fenian men are living still'.[66] Pearse's bible was Wolfe Tone's *Autobiography*, and if Parnell's was not the last name on the minds of the men of 1916, he was a very long way from being the first.

Catholic nationalists called up Parnell's shade to berate the veniality of the parliamentarians: for such writers he is an accusing absence which defines a venial present. In both 'Ghosts' and 'The Separatist Idea' Pearse names 'Tone and Davis and Lalor and Mitchel as the four among us moderns who have chiefly developed the conception of an Irish nation'.[67] These are 'the Fathers', the others 'are just their commentarists' and, although he mentions Parnell 'tentatively' as a possible addition to the major quartet, it is as a poor fifth. The essay 'Ghosts' begins uncompromisingly:

> There has been nothing more terrible in Irish history than the failure of the last generation. . . . One finds oneself wondering what sin these men have been guilty of that so great a shame should come upon them. . . . Does the ghost of Parnell hunt them to their damnation?

Yet, he goes on, even if these men had been less base, their failure was inevitable for they 'conceived of nationality as a material thing, whereas it is a spiritual thing'.[68] By selective quotation he corrals Parnell into the separatist camp, but thought the policy of home rule led his followers to surrender the national position, and in subsequent pamphlets Parnell is not mentioned with the other four: 'Tone is the intellectual ancestor of the whole modern movement of Irish nationalism'[69] is the crux of Pearse's view of Irish political history.

The invocation of Parnell as a ghost, hunting or rebuking his traitorous followers, dominates Catholic middle-class treatments of him. The theme was still going strong in the 1920s and 1930s,[70] and the greatest writer to articulate it was James Joyce. Unlike the Ascendancy writers, his family's allegiance to Parnell went back some way. His father was one of the first 'to greet the rising star of Parnell', and developed a 'fanatical life-long devotion which he handed on to his son'.[71] There was even talk of John Joyce standing as a Parnellite candidate, and at the time of the split he travelled to Cork to urge his tenants to vote for Parnell. One of the 'most successful' of young Joyce's early works was a poem on the death of Parnell, 'Et tu, Healy', described by his brother (all copies are now lost) as:

> a diatribe against the supposed traitor, Tim Healy, who had ratted at the bidding of the Catholic bishops and become a virulent enemy of Parnell, and so the piece was an echo of those political rancours that formed the theme of my father's nightly, half-drunken rantings to the accompaniment of vigorous table-thumping. . . . At the end of the piece the dead Chief is likened

to an eagle, looking down on the grovelling mass of Irish politicians from

His quaint-perched aerie on the crags of Time
Where the rude din of this . . . century
Can trouble him no more.[72]

It is significant that the young Joyce's first awareness of Parnell is not as leader but as rejected leader. From the very outset his interest is more in the act of betrayal and the betrayers than The Chief himself. Significantly Joyce thought the betrayal more complete than it was, and habitually gave the vote in Committee Room 15 as 83 to 8, not 44 to 27. Parnell for Joyce, as for many of his class and religion, is a negative force in that his memory throws into relief the pusillanimity of the present. But in Joyce's case this was to have more far-reaching effects. As his brother says, during childhood

the vaguely understood drama of Parnell had not stirred any feelings of patriotism or nationalism in his heart; rather, under his father's influence, it had implanted there an early spirit of revolt against hypocrisy and clerical authority and popular servility to it.[73]

This revolt was to lead him to try to throw off the 'nightmare' of history altogether, and seek an art which, while drawing upon various historically based discourses, would subvert the authority of their historicity in a radical play of language, association and irony. It is not too fanciful to see this process at work even in this juvenile piece. The title already gathers Parnell into a recurrent pattern of noble victims – Brutus implies Caesar – and Joyce will go on to associate Parnell with Moses and Christ. Historical specificity is already becoming but one component in a universal recurrence, as Bloom will be associated with Ulysses, Stephen with Hamlet and Earwicker with everyone. To achieve this purchase upon history Joyce found it necessary to abscond from history, and, like the betrayed Parnell, frequent 'the crags of Time', far above the 'rude din' of the century. Once there he took up the discordancies of history's 'rude din' and recomposed them in multi-layered fictions, a series of overlapping harmonies that are so resonant with linguistic and associative possibilities that they perpetually defy any fixed or absolute signification.

Parnell achieved his 'quaint-perched aerie' as a direct consequence of Healy's treachery, and Joyce was to make the fear of betrayal crucial to his strategy of maintaining artistic freedom from the otherwise entangling nets of religion and politics that threatened to hold him back from flight. It may be that this perception came to him as he wrote 'Et tu, Healy', but certainly by the time of his early fiction and his articles on Parnell, it is the theme of betrayal that dominates his attention. In his essays 'Home rule comes of age' and 'The shade of Parnell' he attacks the 'self-seeking politician' Gladstone for deserting Parnell, but reserves the greatest blame for the party and the priests as exemplifying an Irish appetite for treachery that he sees going back to the Anglo-Norman invasion and extending through every subsequent incident in Irish politics. His most withering attack is on the 'bankrupt' Irish party, portrayed as incompetent place-seekers, who 'have given proof of their altruism only in 1891, when they sold their leader, Parnell, to the pharisaical conscience of the English Dissenters without exacting the thirty pieces of silver'.[74] In both essays the key and culminating element in the story is the betrayal of Parnell by the Irish. Irish treachery is the abiding and exemplary fact, for Joyce denies Parnell 'any original political talent' and insists that his political achievements have come to seem 'stale', his methods no longer of practical interest to Ireland. Indeed, as his brother reminds us, by the time Joyce entered the university, eleven years before these essays were written, 'Parnell's story had become a memory of the dead'.[75] As such that memory becomes part of a series. With Griffith and Pearse this was a political series; for Joyce it was a mytho-poetical series.

By *Ulysses* this process is well under way. But in the early works Parnell exerts a more precise historical and moral role. In the *Portrait* an awareness of politics is thrust upon Stephen Dedalus by the Parnell dispute, echoes of which reach him in Clongowes:

> That was called politics. There were two sides in it: Dante was on one side and his father and Mr Casey were on the other side but his mother and uncle Charles were on no side. . . . It pained him that he did not know well what politics meant and that he did not know where the universe ended.[76]

Politics are a component in an endless universe, a component that cannot be ignored, although he will later try to entrap and neutralize it in a perception of the universe as endlessly recurrent. Feverish in the school sanatorium in October 1891, an hallucinatory dream of his own death merges with the death of Parnell and the return of his body to Ireland.

This episode leads in immediately to the Christmas dinner scene. Here again, the central concern is betrayal and death. From the beginning the cheerfulness of the 'great banked fire' is dampened by the Christmas decorations that this year take on an unspoken symbolic significance: 'the ivytwined branches of the chandelier' hint at an absent presence. A stonily negative presence is Dante Riordan, silently seething with fury against Parnell and his supporters. For the first third of the episode she says nothing but 'no' and 'no thank you', but as soon as the conversation turns to the political situation she flares out in support of the priests, and refuses to be suppressed. Under her goading the argument rises to its emotional climax, the desertion of Parnell by the priests and people: 'Sons of bitches! cried Mr Dedalus. When he was down they turned on him to betray him and rend him like rats in a sewer. Lowlived dogs! And they look it! By Christ, they look it!'[77] Mr Casey recalls the violent abuse of 'a drunken old harridan' at one of Parnell's meetings in Arklow, and how, when she called Kitty O'Shea an unrepeatable name, he leant down and spat his tobacco juice into her eye. In *Ulysses* Joyce is to symbolize Ireland as an ignorant, superstitious and patronized old milkwoman; here, an anonymous, foul-mouthed Arklow woman represents Cathleen ni Houlihan as vindictive crone, a symbolic kinswoman of the red-eyed superstitious peasant with whom Stephen imagines himself struggling to the death at the end of the novel. Mr Casey achieved a temporary tactical advantage over her by his ballistic skill with tobacco juice, but the quicklime flung in Parnell's eye was to do more lasting damage, and the final victory belongs to Dante and the priests:

> At the door Dante turned round violently and shouted down the room, her cheeks flushed and quivering with rage: –
> Devil out of hell! We won! We crushed him to death! Fiend!
> The door slammed behind her.
> Mr Casey, freeing his arms from his holders, suddenly bowed his head on his hands with a sob of pain.
> –Poor Parnell! he cried loudly. My dead king!
> He sobbed loudly and bitterly.
> Stephen, raising his terrorstricken face, saw that his father's eyes were full of tears.[78]

This episode is crucial in distancing Stephen from any further political involvement. Later he recalls his feverish dream of Parnell's death and remarks, 'But he had not died then, Parnell had died'.[79] That Parnell is dead is central to Joyce's thinking about Irish politics and about his own role in Irish life. If he is to live on in Parnell's place, it is as a free artist, not as a politician. As surely as Irish politics had killed Parnell so they would shackle and destroy his own creative gift. He cultivates the memory of Parnell's betrayal like a scratched itch to keep alert his own resistance to political engagement. In a famous passage Stephen rebuts Davin's political propaganda:

> No honourable and sincere man, said Stephen, has given up to you his life and his youth and his affections from the days of Tone to those of Parnell but you sold him to the enemy or failed him in need or reviled him and left him for another. And you invite me to be one of you. I'd see you damned first[80]

and he goes on to speak of his Dedalian role in escaping the labyrinths of Irish intrigue: 'When the soul of a man is born in this country there are nets flung at it to hold it back from flight. You talk to me of nationality, language, religion. I shall try to fly by those nets.'[81]

It was shortly after first flying those nets, in the late summer of 1905, that Joyce wrote his most extended treatment of the Parnell theme, a story called 'Ivy Day in the committee room'. The action takes place on 6 October 1902, eleven years to the day since Parnell's death, and, as always in *Dubliners*, far more is going on than the apparently desultory conversations between a group of hard-up election canvassers waiting to be paid by their employer, 'Tricky Dicky Tierney', a slippery candidate for municipal office. Each detail in the story contributes to a contrast between the soulless mediocrity of contemporary Ireland and the idealistic authority of the Parnellite era. If the Ascendancy treatment of Parnell had two major themes, his betrayal by unworthy enemies and the possibility of a worthy successor, the two major themes of this story are the betrayal of Parnell by unworthy enemies and the impossibility of a worthy successor.

Although he has been dead for over a decade, Parnell's silent absence is more potent than the words of the living. His memory is inescapable: one of the canvassers is wearing an ivy leaf, the committee room is situated in Wicklow Street, and the election is taking place in the Royal Exchange Ward. The name of the ward is significant, for it is likely that once elected the ostensibly 'nationalist' Tierney will support a municipal address of welcome to King Edward VII during a forthcoming royal visit. In the Royal Exchange, allegiance to the essentially monogamous uncrowned king of Ireland is being bartered for allegiance to the notoriously promiscuous crowned king of England.

This theme finds its fullest expression in a discussion between O'Connor, the bustling trimmer, Henchy, and a 'frail young man' called Lyons. Henchy defends the royal visit on wholly materialistic grounds: what the country needs is capital and the 'King's coming here will mean an influx of money into this country'.

> 'But look here, John,' said Mr O'Connor. 'Why should we welcome the King of England? Didn't Parnell himself . . .'
> 'Parnell,' said Mr Henchy, 'is dead'.[82]

When Lyons objects that Edward's life is immoral he is waved aside:

> 'Let bygones be bygones,' said Mr Henchy. 'I admire the man personally. He's just an ordinary knockabout like you and me . . .'
> 'That's all very fine,' said Mr Lyons. 'But look at the case of Parnell now.'
> 'In the name of God,' said Mr Henchy, 'where's the analogy between the two cases?'
> 'What I mean,' said Mr Lyons, 'is we have our ideals. Why, now, would we welcome a man like that? Do you think now after what he did Parnell was a fit man to lead us? And why, then, would we do it for Edward the Seventh?'
> 'This is Parnell's anniversary,' said Mr O'Connor, 'and don't let us stir up any bad blood. We all respect him now that he's dead and gone – even the Conservatives,' he added, turning to Mr Crofton.[83]

'Parnell . . . is dead', and in that safe and fixed situation can be respected by all, but the betrayal of him and his ideals continues unabated. There is no evidence in this story that his memory can have any effect on the venial age that has succeeded him. Old Jack looks back to the days of Parnell (when, as another character points out, there would have been no talk of an address of welcome) as to a more vibrant age: ' "Musha, God be with the times!" said the old man. "There was some life in them." ' Those were days when Parnell kept the backbiting transacting Irish politicians in control: 'he was the only man that could keep that bag of cats in order', recalls Mr Henchy; ' "Down, ye dogs! lie down, ye curs!" That's the way he treated them'.[84] Without this discipline veniality and self-interest hold dreary sway. Only lucre holds the canvassers to

Tricky Dicky, whom they despise and habitually describe in diminutive terms, a 'little hop-of-my-thumb' who is 'as tricky as they make them'. But this physical and moral dwarf is the contemporary representative of Parnell's party. His metier is backroom intrigue, with strong implications of financial chicanery, and his nationalist sentiments are so feeble that the Unionists have no qualms about supporting him. Nor is this the most sinister of his alliances, for besides enlisting the influential Father Burke as his nominator, he has dealings with the dubious Father Keon, a spoiled priest of ambiguous manner, who hob-nobs with notorious political fixers. Burke and Keon, the representatives of the priests who crushed Parnell, are now hand in glove with his corrupt successors.

If the present breed of politicians are bad, Joyce seems at pains to indicate that there is scant hope in future generations. Tierney himself is in appropriate succession as the son of a hand-me-down bootlegger. The son of Old Jack, the caretaker, is a drunken wastrel; Joe Hynes's father was a 'decent, respectable man' but Hynes himself 'is not nineteen carat', and may be spying for the rival candidate or even the Castle, like another patriot who is 'a lineal descendant of Major Sirr . . . a fellow now that'd sell his country for fourpence – ay – and go down on his bended knees and thank the Almighty Christ he had a country to sell'.[85]

The theme of betrayal permeates the elegy, 'The death of Parnell', that Hynes is persuaded to recite at the end of the story. The poem is a brilliant *tour de force* by Joyce, a doggerel poem in the vein of the effusions that filled the pages of the *United Ireland* in October 1891, but which is so exact that it escapes mere parody. Nine of its eleven stanzas iterate that fact that Parnell is dead. More narrowly, over half of the poem is devoted to a denunciation of his treacherous followers, 'the fell gang/Of modern hypocrites', the 'coward caitiff hands' who betrayed him to 'the rabble-rout/Of fawning priests', and, taking up a comparison Joyce was to make in a later essay, makes a connection between Parnell and Christ: his Judas-like followers 'smote their Lord or with a kiss/Betrayed him'.

The last two stanzas make tentative gestures towards the future:

They had their way: they laid him low.
    But Erin, list, his spirit may
Rise, like the Phoenix from the flames,
    When breaks the dawning of the day,

The day that brings us Freedom's reign.

And on that day may Erin well
 Pledge in the cup she lifts to Joy
  One grief – the memory of Parnell.[86]

It 'may' (not 'will') be that Parnell's spirit will rise phoenix-like, but no one reading this story would take any bets on that. The phoenix flames (the image also glances at the Fenian tradition) have guttered down to Old Jack's miserable fire, and while Tricky Dicky buys his way into power and the younger generation take disconsolately to drink, the dawning of the day of Freedom's reign seems light years away. The 'pok' of a cork from a stout bottle provides an ironic comment on these proceedings: the canvassers have been lifted for a moment out of their shabby, compromised world, but to no purpose.

That Hynes has no illusions about Parnell's return becomes clear in *Ulysses*. At Dignam's funeral in Glasnevin, Leopold Bloom reflects on the fading of Ivy Day and Parnell's memory, and Hynes, a fellow mourner, suggests they go round 'by the chief's grave'. John Wyse Power repeats the legend that 'he is not in that grave at all. That the coffin was filled with stones. That one day he will come again.'

Hynes shook his head.
–Parnell will never come again, he said. He's there, all that was mortal of him. Peace to his ashes.[87]

In *Ulysses*, set in 1904 but written between 1914 and 1921, there are signs that Joyce's attitude towards Parnell's politics was hardening. Bloom acknowledges his 'fascination' but goes on to observe that he 'used men as pawns. Let them all go to pot. Afraid to pass a remark on him. Freeze them up with that eye of his. That's the fascination of the name'.[88] The fascination here seems to depend upon an autocratic manner and manipulation that is finally destructive of democratic processes which (in so far as he ever committed himself on such subjects) Joyce endorsed. By 1920 he was telling Djuna Barnes that the Irish 'have produced one skeleton – Parnell – never a man'.[89]

But whatever qualifications Joyce may have had about his politics, Parnell's significance remained as the betrayed leader amid his enemies both abroad (*The Times* Commission and Pigott's misspelling 'hesitency' provide *Finnegans Wake* with one of its motifs) and at home. Joyce, with his poor eyesight, found the incident at Castlecomer particularly horrific and typically Irish. Empathizing with Parnell in that smart enabled him to keep his own divorce from Ireland absolute. Writing in 1939 he asserted that he had not and would not return to Ireland:

> Having a vivid memory of the incident at Castlecomer when quicklime was flung into the eyes of their dying leader, Parnell, by a chivalrous Irish mob, he did not wish a similar unfortunate occurrence to interfere with the composition of the book he was trying to write.[90]

As always, the example of the politician justifies the ways of the artist, not only in his stance of isolation, but also in the nature of his art. The 'book he was trying to write' was *Finnegans Wake*, the culminating achievement of his attempts to fly by the nets of politics, and to find a language and discourse that would free him from the authority of history.

VIII

'Ivy Day in the committee room' appeared in *Dubliners* in the same year as Yeats's poem 'To a Shade' was published in *Responsibilities*, and a comparison of the two indicates the differences in their treatment of Parnell. Both story and poem register anger and dismay at the venial state of Ireland. Both invoke the memory of Parnell as a figure from a more passionate and authentic past to stand in silent reproach of the present. But in writing of Ireland's debasement Yeats makes a significant selection. As Parnell revisits his old haunts in 'To a shade', he is associated with other values, close to the Irish Protestant ethic that Yeats now thought of crucial value to modern Ireland. In 'Ivy Day in the committee room' Parnell is heirless; in Yeats's poem he has a successor:

>   A man
> Of your own passionate serving kind who had brought
> In his full hands what, had they only known,
> Had given their children's children loftier thought,
> Sweeter emotion, working in their veins
> Like gentle blood, has been driven from the place,
> And insult heaped upon him for his pains,
> And for his open-handedness, disgrace;
> Your enemy, an old foul mouth, had set
> The pack upon him.[91]

In Joyce's story Parnell is 'dead and gone'; in Yeats's poem his shade is certainly directed back to his 'Glasnevin coverlet' (where Yeats will revisit him in 'Parnell's Funeral' in twenty years' time), but it is intimated that this will be a temporary sojourn:

> The time for you to taste of that salt breath
> And listen at the corners has not come. . . . [92]

'Has not come . . .', but the poem holds out the unspoken expectation that it will come, one day. Unlike Joyce's absent presence, Yeats's Parnell seems to be an abiding presence. This may appear to be merely part of a messianic job-description – the hero who waits his call to return – but there is a closer engagement with the actual processes of history in this poem. Parnell is associated with Hugh Lane, one who stands in an apparently apostolic succession to him, and who, like him, wished to confer upon the Irish gifts that they rejected. Parnell wanted to give home rule; Lane wanted to present distinguished pictures at knock-down prices. But Yeats's interest is less in the gifts as such as in their consequences and the nature of the opposition to them. Lane's pictures are seen as offering the grandchildren of those who reject them 'loftier thought' and 'Sweeter emotion', qualities that are otherwise seen as the prerogatives of class and breeding ('gentle blood'), and which are conspicuously absent from the 'old foul mouth' leaders of Irish opinion. In a note to the poem Yeats also set Lane in Parnell's tradition, the failure to establish his Municipal Gallery being one of the 'three public controversies [that] have stirred my imagination', the first of which had been the fall of Parnell.[93]

XI

Lady Gregory, belatedly reading Katharine O'Shea's *Life of Parnell* in April 1932, observed it was 'such an old story now . . . that touched us so nearly then'.[94] This is how it would have appeared to most Irishmen and women. But not to Yeats. Yeats had already been building his particular version of the Parnell myth before 1916. In the 1890s he had wanted to associate the characteristics he discerned in Parnell – cold passion, solitary self-confidence, utter self-control and determination of purpose – with the 'true' Celtic and Irish nature. After the turn of the century, when he was opposed by a very different sort of Irish mind, he began to conceive Irish character in Manichaean terms. The aloof, proud, tragic, Protestant Parnell against the gregarious, vain, comic, Catholic O'Connell. This distinction continued to convince him, and in his address at the Thomas Davis centenary celebration in November 1914 he blamed O'Connell not only for preparing 'Committee Room No. 15 and all that followed' but as being 'the chief cause of our social and political divisions'.[95]

His reading of Katharine O'Shea's biography did not qualify his view of Parnell. Rather than seeing something banal in her version of the relationships he picked out the Nietzschean aspects in her account of Parnell's refusal to apologize or explain, and his holding her out over the waves on Brighton pier. Morley's *Recollections* furnished him with more traits of this kind and earned Parnell one of the few modern places in Yeats's eighteenth-century Anglo-Irish pantheon. By now he had completely divorced him from any involvement in agrarian and social reform:

> Parnell was a nationalist and that only; some of his party were agrarian agitators and that only. So long as Parnell had his party about him the Fenians distrusted him because they were National-ists and that only. When Parnell was in prison agrarianism broke into extremes. . . . Parnell [was] a pure Nationalist throughout, seeing the whole nation where others saw a class.[96]

This is the Parnell of 'The Great Day', 'Parnell' and 'What Was Lost', a conservative leader with no belief in the social or economic benefits of revolution. But if Parnell had seen Ireland where others saw class, those class divisions still remained, and, if anything, accentuated themselves after Independence. In the Senate debate on the abolition of divorce, Yeats again used the O'Connell-Parnell dichotomy to make a social and political point, contrasting the bishops' condemnation of Parnell's marriage (an act which in 'the opinion of every Irish Protestant gentleman' was 'essential as a man of honour') with what 'was said about O'Connell . . . that you could not throw a stick over a workhouse wall without hitting one of his children, but he believed in the indissolubility of marriage, and when he died his heart was very properly preserved in Rome'. Honour is contrasted with hypocrisy, Irish Protestant form with Irish Catholic spawning formlessness, a distinction that also finds expression in a defiant articulation of the Anglo-Irish tradition:

> We against whom you have done this thing are no petty people. We are one of the great stocks of Europe. We are the people of Burke; we are the people of Grattan; we are the people of Swift, the people of Emmet, the people of Parnell. We have created

the most of the modern literature of this country. We have created the best of its political intelligence.[97]

He returned to this tradition in October 1930, maintaining that it was distinguished by what Blake had called 'naked beauty displayed': 'The great men of the eighteenth century were that beauty; Parnell had something of it, O'Leary something, but what have O'Connell and all his seed, breed, and generation but a roaring machine?'[98]

But somehow that seed and breed seemed to have inherited Ireland. Parnell, the perfect example of Anglo-Ireland, the last national leader, and a man whose qualities of mind and personality contemporary Ireland should have been crying out to imitate, had failed politically and had almost faded from the popular mind. Travelling from Limerick, a priest in Yeats's compartment began to question a girl about Irish history and 'When he asked about Parnell and the Land bill found that she had heard of neither'.[99] Yeats was aghast at this neglect, and at the same time unwilling to accept it. Other Ascendancy writers had explored the possibility of Parnell's political influence being resuscitated, and he, too, had thought such a resuscitation might issue in a 'spiritualization' of Irish politics. But now he saw Parnell's importance as lying not in any political formula, but in his embodiment of a myth. He was shortly to write that 'man cannot know truth, but he can embody it', and for him Parnell now came to embody the myth of the sacrificial victim.

Yeats's chief condemnation of the 'new class' who rose to power in the shadow of Parnell was that they were incapable of 'great sacrifices'.[100] The writings of O'Grady and the example of Lady Gregory had persuaded him that the Anglo-Irish destiny was not merely to command but to serve, even – or especially – if such service entailed sacrifice. The Countess Cathleen sacrifices herself for her tenants; Jasper Dean is supposed to sacrifice a comfortable and conventional life for his nation: and now Yeats begins to find in Parnell an imperative for sacrifice. In *A Vision* this is seen as self-sacrifice. As a representative of Phase 10, Parnell is said to have had 'a kind of burning restraint, a something that suggests a savage statue to which one offers sacrifice'. This sacrifice 'is code, personality no longer perceived as power only', but which can never completely escape from mass emotion, so that 'the life remains troubled, a conflict between pride and race, and passes from crisis to crisis'. He 'sees all his life as a stage play where there is only one good acting part', but he is not a stage player, for he wears a stony mask and resembles that Norse god who made a sacrifice of himself.[101]

As Yeats contemplated the Free State with a jaundiced but still passionate eye, Parnell's sacrifice came to seem less self-immolation than a public, tribal, 'mass-emotion' event. His most powerful articulation of this theme is in his poem 'Parnell's Funeral'. The falling star seen at the funeral is absorbed into Cretan myth and one of Yeats's own visions to transform Parnell's death into a public ritual. Fated Parnell is buried under the tomb of the casual Great Comedian, O'Connell, a star falls, and the animal blood of the mourners shudders as with a sense of a sacrifice accepted. The public ritual is also a rite of passage from one sort of Ireland to its antithesis:

> An age is the reversal of an age;
> When strangers murdered Emmet, Fitzgerald, Tone,
> We lived like men that watch a painted stage.
> What matter for the scene, the scene once gone:
> It had not touched our lives. But popular rage,
> *Hysterica passio*, dragged this quarry down.
> None shared our guilt; nor did we play a part
> Upon a painted stage when we devoured his heart.[102]

But who had 'devoured his heart'? Not Jasper Dean, as we know; nor it seems more recent politicians, for in the second part of the poem, entitled 'Forty years later', he finds the 'loose-lipped demagogue' de Valera, the pedestrian Cosgrave and the disappointing O'Duffy unworthy successors: had they eaten Parnell's heart things would be different.

Where Joyce saw betrayal, Yeats saw sacrifice. Ascendancy *noblesse oblige* charged with mythical and anthropological reverberations has irrevocably altered Ireland – whether girls on trains are aware of it or not. In a lecture on 'Modern Ireland' of this time he associated the fall and death of Parnell with the sacrificial victims of ancient Rome and went on: 'From that national humiliation, from the resolution to destroy all that made the humiliation possible, from that sacrificial victim I derive almost all that is living in the imagination of Ireland today.'[103] And so at last Yeats proposes a myth of Parnell, which, derived from the intellectual traditions that produced *The Golden Bough*, is the one that has been most enthusiastically endorsed by the cultural critics. But we should note that Yeats uses the first person singular: 'I derive'. Joseph Holloway who heard the first version of this lecture thought it irrelevant to contemporary Ireland,[104] and the idea that the deaths of Emmet and Tone had 'not touched our lives' indicates a very partial reading of Pearse and the other 1916 Insurrectionaries. But Tone, Emmet and Fitzgerald had been inspired by the Jacobin ideas underlying the French Revolution, ideas that Yeats, like most of his class, detested. Parnell, now conceived of as securely conservative, non-revolutionary and non-agrarian, was a far more congenial hero. Although his ostensible political programme had failed, Yeats snatches victory from this very defeat. In his sacrificial death Parnell makes possible a deepening of Irish consciousness; his example, not his policies or possible successors, have exerted an Ascendancy force on modern Irish history, despite all superficial appearances to the contrary.

X

Yeats was to write a further ballad on Parnell after reading Henry Harrison's book on his relationship with the O'Sheas,[105] but 'Parnell's funeral' is his most powerful treatment of the Parnell myth, and the one that has been accepted as the most authentic. In reality, it was just one of many competing views, and like the others owes a great deal to a historical perspective that was much influenced by class perceptions.

This myth depends upon a number of questionable assumptions. The first is that the fall of Parnell initiated a change in consciousness *ab novo*. While the 1890s did see a cultural revival that articulated an altered Irish consciousness, that revival owed much of its dynamic initially to political factors, and it drew its prevailing aesthetic from the example and writing of the Young Irelanders, an influence which Yeats found himself obliged to fight during the 1890s and, in the criticism of Arthur Griffith, well into the twentieth century. In other words, what we now term the 'Irish Literary Revival' was a far more complex and even contradictory phenomenon than the purity of Yeats's and Howarth's myth of Parnell will allow.

A second component in the myth is that the personality of Parnell and the manner of his death generated a messianism that was eagerly endorsed by influential writers. Once again, the situation is rather more complicated. For both middle-class and Ascendancy writers Parnell's ghost was minatory and offered an alternative set of values to those prevailing in contemporary Ireland. For Catholics such as Joyce, this disparity was purely negative and ironic in its effect. For the Ascendancy writers Parnell became not merely a minatory ghost but a potential model, a symbol of a possible political authority that might just still be open to their class. When this was no longer historically feasible, he became a mythical embodiment of those qualities which they considered modern Ireland sorely missed. Parnell was at first a blank cheque; as more became known about him, writers continued to pillage the biographies for those details or anecdotes which suited their picture of him, but that picture was already coloured by social and religious attitudes. Parnell became a myth to support other myths.

A third and even more dubious strand of the myth is that there was a messianic relationship between Parnell, the events of 1916 and the later manifestations of Irish republicanism. In reality those who led the 1916 Rising were far more interested in Tone and an older tradition of separatist action than that espoused by Parnell. Nor could fictional representation be said to have compensated for this political lacuna. None of the literary treatments of Parnell is revolutionary in tendency, their messianism, such as it is, is ambiguous, and, in any case, few of them were widely available in Ireland before 1916. *The Bending of the Bough* was not revived after 1900, and audiences found Lady Gregory's *The Deliverer* badly constructed, vaguely absurd in its adoption of 'Kiltartanese', and perplexing as to its political aspect.[106] *Dubliners* was not published until 1914, and was then virtually ignored. It was not until Yeats, as the representative of a disestablished class, began to find in Parnell's sacrifice the key to modern Irish history that he became associated with messianic republicanism, and that rereading (which is more illuminating about Yeats's political imagination than about Irish history) did not occur until long after Easter 1916.

NOTES

1 William O'Brien, *Recollections*, London, 1905, p. 400.
2 Herbert Howarth, *The Irish Writers: Literature under Parnell's Star*, London, 1958, p. 5.
3 See W. B. Yeats, *Autobiographies*, London, 1955, p. 199; Lady Augusta Gregory (ed.), *Ideals in Ireland*, London, 1901, p. 88; W. B. Yeats, *Essays and Introductions*, London, 1961, p. 259; *Autobiographies*, p. 559.
4 Malcolm Brown, *The Politics of Irish Literature*, London, 1972.
5 See John S. Kelly, 'Parnell and the rise of Irish literature', *Anglo-Irish Studies*, II, 1976, pp. 1–23.
6 *United Ireland*, 4 June 1892.
7 Ibid., 14 February 1891.

8 Ibid., 24 January 1891, 14 February 1891.
9 Ibid., 14 April 1894.
10 Ibid., 14 April 1894.
11 Ibid., 9 April 1892.
12 Ibid., 14 March 1891.
13 *Daily Telegraph*, 7 March 1892; *United Ireland*, 4 June 1892.
14 *Eighth Annual Report of the Society for the Preservation of the Irish Language*, Dublin, 1887, p. 1.
15 *Nation*, 6 July 1889.
16 Ibid., 11 January 1890.
17 *Gaelic Journal*, November 1893, p. 228.
18 Ibid., July 1895, pp. 63–4.
19 Yeats, *Autobiographies*, p. 225.
20 John Kelly and Eric Domville (eds), *The Collected Letters of W. B. Yeats*, Oxford, 1986, vol. I, p. 399.
21 Yeats, *Autobiographies*, p. 218.
22 Ibid., p. 259.
23 These categories are used in a broad sense, and by 'Ascendancy' I understand not only those like Lady Gregory, George Moore and Edward Martyn who were extensive landowners, but also Standish James O'Grady, W. B. Yeats and Lennox Robinson, who had Ascendancy affiliations or who made themselves Ascendancy by adoption.
24 *The Variorum Edition of the Poems of W. B. Yeats*, ed. Peter Allt and Russell K. Alspach, London, 1971, pp. 737–8.
25 Unpublished letter to John O'Leary, National Library of Ireland.
26 William O'Brien, *Irish Ideas*, London, 1895, pp. 204–5.
27 *Uncollected Prose by W. B. Yeats*, ed. John P. Frayne, London, 1970, vol. I, pp. 145–6.
28 Standish James O'Grady, *The Story of Ireland*, London, 1895, pp. 204–5.
29 Ibid., p. 207.
30 Ibid., p. 209.
31 Ibid., p. 210.
32 Lady Augusta Gregory, *A Phantom's Pilgrimage, or Home Ruin*, published anonymously, London, 1893, pp. 10–12.
33 See Yeats, *Autobiographies*, p. 366, and Lady Augusta Gregory, *Journals*, Gerrards Cross, 1978, vol. I, p. 338.
34 Lady Augusta Gregory, *Diary*, Berg Collection, New York Public Library.
35 Ibid.
36 Ibid.
37 Ibid.
38 R. Barry O'Brien, *Life of Parnell*, London, 1898, vol. I, pp. 41. 48.
39 See, for example, R. Barry O'Brien, *Life of Parnell*, vol. I, pp. 248–9, 295–6, 352.
40 Gregory, *Diary* (Berg); and *The Critical Writings of James Joyce*, ed. Ellsworth Mason and Richard Ellmann, London, 1959, p. 162.
41 Gregory, *Diary* (Berg).
42 Ibid.
43 Ibid.

44 Ibid.
45 Ibid.
46 Ibid.
47 See, for example, Act III (*The Variorum Edition of the Plays of W. B. Yeats*, ed. Russell K. Alspach, London, 1966, p. 1209).
48 George Moore, *Hail and Farewell: Ave*, Uniform Edition, London, 1947, pp. 281–3.
49 Ibid., p. 282.
50 George Moore, *The Bending of the Bough*; revised edn, London, 1900, p. 56.
51 Ibid., p. 64.
52 Ibid., p. 65.
53 Ibid., pp. 94, 124.
54 Yeats, *Essays and Introductions*, p. 253.
55 Yeats, *Autobiographies*, p. 317.
56 W. B. Yeats, *Memoirs*, ed. Denis Donoghue, London, 1972, pp. 212–13.
57 *Uncollected Prose of W. B. Yeats*, ed. John P. Frayne and Colton Johnson, London, 1975, vol. II, p. 362.
58 Ibid.
59 Lady Augusta Gregory, *Collected Plays*, Gerrards Cross, 1970, vol. III, p. 277.
60 Lennox Robinson, *The Lost Leader*, Dublin, 1918, p. 56.
61 Ibid., p. 97.
62 Ibid., p. 96.
63 Ibid., pp. 96–7.
64 Ibid., pp. 100–1.
65 Ibid., p. 99.
66 *United Irishman*, 5 July 1901.
67 Padraic Pearse, *Political Writings and Speeches*, Dublin, 1962, p. 263. See also pp. 240, 246.
68 Ibid., p. 224.
69 Ibid., pp. 265, 284.
70 See, for example, *An Phoblacht*, 21 August 1925, p. 3.
71 Stanislaus Joyce, *My Brother's Keeper*, London, 1958, p. 49.
72 Ibid., p. 65.
73 Ibid., pp. 172–3.
74 *The Critical Writings of James Joyce*, p. 196.
75 Stanislaus Joyce, *My Brother's Keeper*, p. 173.
76 James Joyce, *A Portrait of the Artist as a Young Man*, definitive text, ed. Chester Anderson and R. Ellmann, London, 1964, p. 17.
77 Ibid., p. 35.
78 Ibid., p. 41.
79 Ibid., p. 96.
80 Ibid., p. 207.
81 Ibid.
82 James Joyce, *Dubliners*, Harmondsworth, 1956, p. 129.
83 Ibid., pp. 129–30.
84 Ibid., p. 130.
85 Ibid., pp. 122–3.

86 Ibid., p. 132.
87 James Joyce, *Ulysses: A Critical and Synoptic Edition*, New York and London, 1984, vol. I, p. 231.
88 Ibid., p. 135.
89 Djuna Barnes, 'James Joyce', *Vanity Fair*, April 1922, pp. 65, 104; quoted in R. Ellmann's *James Joyce*, London, new and revised edn, 1982, p. 320.
90 Quoted in Ellmann, *James Joyce*, p. 338.
91 Yeats, *Variorum Poems*, p. 292.
92 Ibid., p. 293.
93 Ibid., p. 818.
94 Gregory, *Journals*, vol. II, p. 607.
95 W. B. Yeats, 'Thomas Davis', in *Davis, Mangan, Ferguson? Tradition and the Irish Writer*, Dublin, 1970, pp. 16–17.
96 Unpublished reader's report on an unproduced play, *The Red Petticoat*, submitted to the Abbey Theatre (Michael Yeats).
97 *The Senate Speeches of W. B. Yeats*, ed. Donald R. Pearce, London, 1960, pp. 97–9.
98 W. B. Yeats, *Explorations*, London, 1962, p. 336.
99 Ibid., pp. 411–12.
100 Yeats, *Essays and Introductions*, p. 259; see above, p. 243.
101 W. B. Yeats, *A Vision*, London, 1962, pp. 121–4.
102 Yeats, *Variorum Poems*, pp. 541–2.
103 W. B. Yeats, 'Modern Ireland', *Massachusetts Review*, 5 (1), 1964, pp. 256–8.
104 *Joseph Holloway's Irish Theatre*, ed. Robert Hogan and Michael O'Neill, Dixon, Cal., 1969, vol. II, pp. 17–18.
105 Yeats, 'Come Gather Round Me, Parnellites', *Variorum Poems*, pp. 586–7.
106 *Irish Times*, 14 January 1911.

12 'The portrait of the King is the King'[1]

The biographers of Charles Stewart Parnell

D. George Boyce

A search for Parnell must end with his biographers. It was they who shaped and hewed a recognizable personality and public figure from what they knew, or thought they knew, about the man, his background, his style and political beliefs. Parnell was a Victorian; and so were his early, and formative, biographers. Victorian biography as an art form reflected Victorian sensibility. It was discreet; it presented 'great' (and not so great) lives as examples for the age, as exemplifying virtues, both private and public, in a society where the standards for judging characters were agreed. As John Gibson Lockhart put it, 'England expects every driveller to do his Memorabilia'.[2]

Parnell was different; and so, therefore, were his biographers. He was an Irish nationalist; his private life became the subject of an unsavoury divorce scandal; his untimely death provoked recrimination instead of the comfortable regrets reminiscent of those cut off in their prime. Yet his biographers had at least one trait in common with that of their sober Victorian contemporaries; they wanted to give Parnell a form of commemoration, for, as Sidney Lee, editor of the *Dictionary of National Biography* put it,

> In its absence the commemorative purpose, the personal significance, of a surviving portrait, or statue, or monument, or foundation lacks any certain guarantee of long life.

> Vain was the chief's, the sage's pride,
> They had no memoir and they died.[3]

Parnell's 'commemoration' was very different from that envisaged by Lee; but since Parnell left no substantial, or even meagre, private materials from which a life could be reconstructed (apart from his public utterances), his contemporary biographers were of central importance in transmitting to posterity what Lee defined as the 'history of a human being who by virtue of a combination of character and exploit has arrested contemporary attention and is likely to excite the curiosity or interest of a future generation'.[4]

The life of Parnell did excite future generations. Parnell's earliest biographers were nationalist journalists like Thomas Sherlock and R. Barry O'Brien; Irish parliamentary party MPs such as T. P. O'Connor (also a considerable journalist) and T. M. Healy; members of his family such as J. H. Parnell, his brother, and Emily M. Dickinson his sister; the woman who stood at the centre of his personal and political life, Katharine O'Shea; literary biographers like St John Ervine. And then, representing the 'future generation', a line of distinguished professional historians, including Conor Cruise O'Brien, F. S. L. Lyons, R. F. Foster and Paul Bew. The biographies themselves fall into three distinct groups. There were a handful written as interim reports, and published when he was a coming man; then came a series of formative lives, published (sometimes hurriedly) after his fall, and constituting a kind of running argument about Parnell's life and legacy. This debate began with the appearance of T. P. O'Connor's *Charles Stewart Parnell: a Memory* in 1891 and ended, neatly, with the same author's *Letters and Leaders of my Day* in 1929. Thus the bulk of Parnell's biographical writing for some forty years reflected the changing and volatile politics of Ireland as she moved from political division to political unity, then back to division (and partition), and civil war.[5] This writing was overshadowed by the question: could the bloodshed, the enmity, the factions have been prevented by the leadership of Parnell, had not fate (or his foes) brought him down? Closely tied to this debate was the argument over Parnell's fall, the circumstances of the O'Shea divorce case, the role of the British press and political establishment, and especially of Joseph Chamberlain: Parnell must, in the eyes of some, be 'vindicated'. Finally Parnell's personality and career became subjected to the scrutiny arising from the revolution in Irish historical scholarship begun in the 1930s, and now, in the 1950s, extending to the most controversial episodes in modern Irish history.

This chapter is not concerned with the presentation of Parnell in the press, or the making and manufacturing of Parnell artifacts. Nor with Parnell as a figure in literature. These, though of vital importance to an understanding of Parnell's significance, are the subject of other essays. The purpose here is to explore how Parnell biography was influenced by the conventions of the age; how it broke or advanced these conventions; and how successful the biographical method has been in portraying the uncrowned king of Ireland.

There were various slight sketches of the coming man in the early 1880s, of which the most significant were by Thomas Sherlock and J. S. Mahoney. Sherlock was a journalist who contributed to the group of newspapers owned by T. D. Sullivan and controlled from the offices of the *Nation* in Lower Abbey Street, Dublin. These included the weekly *Nation*, and *Young Ireland*. Sherlock wrote a series of articles on Parnell's ancestry and early political career up to 1882, the year the series ended, and published his *Charles Stewart Parnell: his Youth and Development*. He continued to support Parnell at the split and beyond.[6]

Sherlock's study is important because it was not – as of course were all biographies published after 1891 – influenced by the knowledge of the O'Shea divorce case and the dramatic events of 1890–91; nor was it even able to anticipate the first Home Rule Bill, which placed Parnell at the very centre of British politics. Sherlock spent some time on Parnell's early life, stressing his 'distinguished ancestry' (which all subsequent writers followed) and supplementing his own version of the Parnell family background with an appendix incorporating some details of Parnell's early career, written by his mother – another literary device much resorted to by subsequent writers.[7] But the bulk of the book was concerned with Parnell's rise to power; and on the essentially moderating influence, and rational political choices, of the leader of the home rule party. When he discussed the Land League and Parnell's role in that agitation, he emphasized Parnell's advice and teaching and above all his 'practicable plan which, while compensating the landlords for the relinquishment of their proprietorial privilege, would inevitably transfer to the tillers the ownership of the soil'.[8]

This picture, of a triumphant but essentially practical politician, was reiterated throughout the book. The most controversial aspect of Parnell's career up to 1882, as controversial even as his involvement with the Land League, was his policy of obstruction, of defying the House of Commons by manipulating its rules to delay and destroy its normal functioning. Sherlock reminded his readers that

> here it may be remarked that the essence of what is now commonly called the Parnell policy consists in having, on every occasion, when it is brought into play, a distinct, appreciable, and reasonable purpose. Its strength lies in the fact that, while every form of Parliament is to be availed of, nothing is to be

done blindly, or without an object readily comprehensible by at least the leaders of the House. It is elastic as well as strong, for it can be employed on every variety of topic that can come before the Commons at Westminster.[9]

Thus, from the policy of obstructionism, was won a concession on Irish university education.[10]

This plain portrait was typical of early Parnell biographical writing. J. S. Mahoney, in his *Life of Charles Stewart Parnell* (published in New York in 1885) argued that the people saw Parnell as 'essentially Irish', and that they knew he was 'a disinterested and capable leader, who has a thorough acquaintance with the ills from which their country languishes and who has the will and – with their help – the ability to remedy them'. He had great parliamentary knowledge; he was a 'cold, clear, logical speaker'. And the men who followed him were 'cool-headed, intelligent and calculating', and not the peasants delineated by Charles Lever and Samuel Lover. Would he succeed? 'Mr. Parnell himself, than whom no statesman of modern times has more conspicuously shown the possession of tact, ability, sound judgement and unerring political foresight, firmly believes that he will.'[11] R. Johnston, in his *Parnell and the Parnells* (London and Dublin, 1888) traced the history of the Parnell family, revealing them as holding a traditionally liberal attitude towards the Roman Catholics which Parnell simply inherited and developed.[12] T. P. O'Connor, in his *The Parnell Movement* (London, 1886), traced the Parnell political ancestry to the same roots, and, while admitting that it was 'particularly difficult to follow the mental history of a man that is neither introspective nor expansive', offered a few suggestions about the origins of Parnell's political beliefs, which he tentatively attributed to the memories of the 1798 rebellion in County Wicklow, and the Fenian uprising of 1867; but he also stressed that the revolutionary movement, of which Parnell placed himself at the head – the Land League – must not obscure the fact that 'in every one of the speeches in which he spoke of peasant propriety, he definitely laid down the doctrine that peasant propriety was to be obtained not by violence, but by the payment of reasonable compensation to the landlords'.[13]

These early sketches, though necessarily incomplete, intimated that Parnell was well on the way to becoming a typical creation of nineteenth-century biographical writing: an exemplary figure, a sober statesman, the centre of a moral earnestness: a man of 'tact, ability, sound judgement and unerring political foresight'.[14]

Parnell's fall shifted the whole perspective of his biographical treatment. The emphasis shifted from the sober statesmanship of the early writing to drama and tragedy; and it was for this reason that the life written by T. P. O'Connor was of central importance in the history of Parnell's biography.

O'Connor was a journalist and Irish home rule MP, and a biographer of characters as diverse as Disraeli, Napoleon and Sir Henry Campbell-Bannerman. Moreover, he was a close observer of Parnell, and was a significant operator in Irish politics in Great Britain, for which Parnell paid him handsome compliments in public. O'Connor was greatly anguished by the O'Shea divorce case and its unwelcome publicity for his leader. And, as a journalist and biographer, he saw the importance of personality, of dramatic events, of tragedy, in the lives of men and also of nations.[15] The O'Shea case was slow at first to exercise any kind of impact on the Irish party; since the divorce petition was filed on 24 December 1889, it ran concurrently with *The Times*'s 'Parnellism and Crime' trial and the exposure of the Pigott forgeries; thus it was not unreasonable to think that Parnell would ride out this storm as he had the last; and anyway the home rule cause seemed so nearly on the verge of success that it would have been folly to push the issue too hard. It was better to wait and see. But when on 15 and 17 November the verdict of the divorce case was announced, and Parnell was proclaimed an adulterer, the issue could no longer be avoided. O'Connor opposed Parnell, mainly because Parnell now seemed bent on repudiating the Liberal alliance which O'Connor, and the bulk of the Irish party, regarded as an essential part of the whole parliamentary strategy.[16]

Parnell died on 6 October 1891. Within possibly as little as a week O'Connor published his *Charles Stewart Parnell: a Memory*. The *Freeman's Journal* on Friday, 16 October, carried an advertisement announcing that the book was 'Just Ready at all Booksellers and railway bookstalls', available for two shillings, or one shilling in a paper wrapper.[17] O'Connor used portions of his 1886 study of the Parnell movement. Now he was anxious to vindicate his anti-Parnellite stance. But the book was much more than a personal self-justification, though that was an important element of O'Connor's determined defence of the Liberal alliance. It set the trend for all Parnell biographies before the modern historians of the 1950s.

O'Connor was, after all, a founder of the 'new journalism', as it came to be called, of the 1880s and 1890s which thrived not so much on sensationalism as on a 'human interest' style of writing.

O'Connor drew his reader into Parnell the man in a way that previous writers, such as Sherlock (and for that matter the early O'Connor), failed to do. The young Parnell was, it seemed, destined for the life of a country gentleman, with his English accent, his cricketing prowess, his membership of the Wicklow militia; yet there were hints of the tragedy to come. There Parnell stood in his portrait, wearing his militia uniform, with 'the face of a typical young Englishman of the aristocratic classes; shy, commonplace, *gauche*, proud and undistinguished'. But even here there is a premonition: 'There is infinite pity in its hope of youth in its fulness, when one thinks of the prematurely worn-out man whose thin and haggard remains have just been returned to earth at what should have been life's prime.'[18]

As well as this O'Connor created the portrait of the solitary figure. Parnell hung around Westminster 'with the air of a man who had no other place to go'.

> This awful loneliness of the life of the Irish Member . . . this untold fact in his life must always be steadily borne in mind when one considers the terrible event which darkened and destroyed his life and ultimately brought it to an untimely end.[19]

O'Connor had much to say about the politics of Parnellism: and much to disagree with. But it was not his criticism of Parnell that was the most influential part of O'Connor's book; it was his account of the personal side of the man, and the kind of impact that O'Connor discerned Parnell had, and would have, on Irish politics. The chapter headings of O'Connor's book plotted the course for subsequent writers: 'The opening of the tragedy'; 'Reaching the zenith'; 'Black ruin'.

The most important chapter in O'Connor's book was his section 'Characteristics and estimate'. For here it might be said that O'Connor set the agenda for subsequent biographers of Parnell. The chapter was written in a vivid, simple style. First 'as to Mr. Parnell's appearance. As he was, so he looked. The iron resolution, the impenetrable reserve, the frigid fanaticism were written in his lithe figure, and still more in the strange, striking, unique countenance'. Parnell's face was 'one of the handsomest in the House of Commons'; his voice was 'clear, sure and penetrating, and, when he was excited could be thrilling'; but his most arresting features were his eyes.

> They were the most meaning eyes I have ever seen. They were

of the hard dark sort, which you see in the Red Indian – red-brown, like flint; but who can describe their varying lights and expressions? Sometimes you thought they never changed, for they certainly never revealed anything; at others they seemed to flash and burn; and they always had a strange glow in them that arrested your attention.[20]

O'Connor listed some of Parnell's characteristics: his lack of care for his creature comforts; his meanness with money; his fits of abstraction. But O'Connor also directed future biographers to what was, in the end, a central part of their concern: Parnell the enigma.

Parnell's political failures could not take away the central drama, mystery and fascination of the leader of nationalist Ireland: a feeling captured in another quickly published posthumous account of the 'uncrowned king'. This book – hardly worthy of the name, for it was a compilation rather than a coherent account, published under the name of Robert MacWade and including pieces by O'Connor and by Parnell's mother, Delia Parnell – offered a single, reverberating sentence that caught the essence of the Parnell story as it was now to develop: ' "I was at Parnell's funeral" shall be a proud yet melancholy boast in days to come'[21] (a quotation lifted from the *Freeman's Journal* of 17 October 1891).

O'Connor caught something of the magic of Parnell's personality, which has so baffled later historians. But it was R. Barry O'Brien who produced a breakthrough, not only in Parnell biography, but in the art of Victorian biography itself.[22] Any Victorian writer would have found it difficult to assess a subject whose private life had been the occasion of such public scandal; and O'Brien's reaction was simply to avoid the issue, which he did with great dignity. He quoted from Mrs O'Shea's diary for 7 October 1891: 'We mean to forget all the last year. I shall always think of him as a fine man, and be proud to have known him', adding 'with these words I shall pass lightly over the proceedings in the Divorce Court, and consider only their effect on the public life of Parnell.[23] But this was the only way in which it might be said that Barry O'Brien conformed to contemporary taste. His contribution to Parnell biography, and to biographical writing as an art, lay in his rediscovery of what Harold Nicolson described as the Boswellian formula: that of 'invented actuality'. Boswell

discovered and perfected a biographical formula in which the narrative could be fused with the pictorial, in which the pictorial in its turn could be rendered in a series of photographs so vividly, and above all so rapidly, projected as to convey an impression of continuity, or progression – in a word, of life.

Boswell's method was 'that of the cinematograph'.[24] O'Brien, too, allowed his readers to accompany Parnell; 'and, as it were, see each scene as it happened'. He collected and recorded Parnell's conversation – and that of others – in such a way as to create the sense of listening in to actual speech; he handled Parnell's death scene with delicacy by tactfully withdrawing from it: there were no famous last words or agonizing farewells.

Barry O'Brien's Boswellian method was unique; no later biographer could emulate it, for it required not only Barry O'Brien's skills but his personal shadowing of his subject. In a real sense, then, Barry O'Brien created Parnell, giving flesh and blood to the exciting and authentic, but somehow elusive portrait of T. P. O'Connor. O'Brien noted what others before him had remarked: Parnell's handsome form, his capacity for silence, his mastery of men. But he portrayed something else, that perhaps gets the reader closer than any other biographer to the mystery of Parnell. There was at its heart a combination of opposites: on the one hand the sense of the theatrical that Parnell possessed, which he displayed on the occasion of departing from New York after his 1880 tour. Barry O'Brien offered T. M. Healy's description of the event:

As soon as I got on board the tender I turned towards the cabin to get under shelter from the driving sleet. Parnell stood on the bridge the whole time until the tender left with head uncovered; and it was a fine sight to see the 69th [regiment – a Fenian unit] salute as we sailed off, and Parnell wave his hand in response, looking like a king.[25]

Yet there was also a sense of cordiality mixed with vulnerability, which Parnell's Cork friend, M. J. Horgan, conveyed. Horgan asked Parnell to attend his wedding as his best man and after the ceremony 'I thought he would dash off, glad to be rid of us. Not a bit of it. He came to the luncheon, entered quite into the spirit of business, and did not leave until my wife and I drove away'. On another occasion Parnell had made a speech, showing a 'majesty . . . which fascinated and awed you'. But afterwards, when Parnell returned to spend the night at Horgan's home, the other side of Parnell's nature was revealed.

Coming home he was as simple and as proud as a child of the whole performance. 'I think', he said, 'I got through very well'.

He did not seem to have the faintest notion that people looked up to him, not only as the greatest man in Ireland, but one of the most remarkable men in England. He spoke like a young man making his debut at a debating society. I can see him now walking upstairs to bed with a candle in his hand, and stepping so quietly and lightly as to disturb no one. He was like a young fellow who has come home late and was afraid to wake 'the governor'.[26]

O'Brien created Parnell; did he also create Parnellism? Whereas T. P. O'Connor, to whom the Liberal alliance was all, played down the more combative aspects of Parnellite tactics, Barry O'Brien observed no such niceties. Parnell simply declared 'War'. His policy was

To combine all Irishmen in solid mass and hurl them at the Saxon, that was his policy. In the ensuing pages we shall find him pursuing that policy, steadily, skilfully. We shall find him gradually winning the confidence of the Church and of the Fenians – the two great forces, be it said, in Irish politics – and ultimately obtaining an ascendancy over both. We shall find him forming and dominating a strictly disciplined parliamentary party, and at length reaching that position of eminence well described by the title which the people gave him – the 'uncrowned king of Ireland'.[27]

Barry O'Brien traced how Parnell forged a great political instrument, combining Fenians, church, tenant-farmer and home ruler in one great movement under his leadership. The rest of his book was a study of how that instrument broke in Parnell's hands. For Barry O'Brien, this was entirely because of the divorce case; he had no doubt that otherwise Parnell was on the edge of victory. Again and again he stressed the central point of Parnell's leadership: that it was above all essential to hold together the 'Irish people' in their conflict with the Saxon. Parnell's success was portrayed as due to his hatred of England, 'English ways English modes of thought';[28] it was also shown as vital to prevent Ireland falling into what she fell into in the winter of 1881–2 when Parnell was imprisoned in Kilmainham jail: with Parnell in prison 'every turbulent spirit in the country' was let loose.

The accounts from the west filled him with alarm. Ireland was passing out of his hands and into the hands of an irresponsible jacquerie. His first thought was to leave jail, to crush the jacqueries, and to stamp his own authority once more upon the people.[29]

O'Brien, then, interpreted Parnell in terms of the necessary strong, anti-English, yet disciplined leader, the only figure who could bind together a factious people and mobilize them for success. The consequences for Irish nationalism, of the party split, were fragmentation and impotence. Parnell in his prime was depicted as the one man who could settle the problem of Anglo-Irish relations, and who could hold anarchy in check.[30] But Barry O'Brien distanced Parnell from the Liberals even though he had been the leader who took his party into the Liberal alliance. The English people would 'do, what we can make them do'; home rulers had implicit faith in the Liberals and cultivated the friendliest relations with them, but

> Parnell stood apart. He disliked going on English platforms and shunned English society. He believed only in his own strength. . . . His reliance was always on the 'mailed hand', soft though the covering in which it might be encased. 'I do not object', he said to me in later years, 'to an English alliance which we can control; I object to an English alliance which the English control.'[31]

How, then, did Barry O'Brien justify the closer and closer alliance between home rulers and Liberals in the years immediately preceding the split? He did this by concentrating on the role of Gladstone in Irish politics, and in particular on Gladstone's radicalism when it came to Irish affairs. 'The ex-Minister became an agitator; the agitator a circumspect statesman.' Gladstone's speeches were full of 'fire and energy'.

> Had he been an Irishman they would have been called violent, perhaps lawless. He had in truth, caught the spirit of Irish agitation. Had he been born under the shadow of the Galtee mountains his denunciations of English rule could not have been more racy of the soil.[32]

Gladstone's radicalism and Parnell's balanced each other; and the way was paved for Parnell the leader, and Gladstone the statesman to combine Irish and English radicalism. Barry O'Brien sympathized with Parnell in his last campaign, and even went so far as to say that he thought the too close alliance between the home rulers and the Liberals was a 'mistake'. But his concluding sections were a masterpiece of political ambiguity. He was able to engage Parnell with English Liberalism, in that he co-opted Gladstone to assess Parnell's life and achievements; or near achievements; yet he distanced Parnell from England by describing Gladstone as 'the only Englishman who was worthy of his steel' and thus allowing Gladstone to 'bear witness to his greatness'.[33] He declared that Parnell had 'brought Ireland within sight of the Promised Land', adding that 'The triumph of the national cause awaits other times, and another Man'.[34] Yet he put Parnell's final resting place 'under the shadow of the tower which marks the spot where the greatest Irishman of the century – O'Connell – sleeps'. It was significant that W. B. Yeats tried to wrest Parnell from the constitutional tradition assigned to it, posthumously, by Barry O'Brien, when the 'greatest Irishman' became the 'great comedian'.[35]

Parnell's life remained an obsession for his contemporaries. It was still a matter of great dispute, especially on the question of the split, and Parnell's conduct. But whether like his sister, Emily Dickinson, or his brother, J. H. Parnell, he was regarded as a hero brought down by wolves ('The vulgar onslaught of the common scheming herd');[36] or as the necessary deposition of a 'Dictator' (M. M. O'Hara: 'Davitt was the one prominent Irish politician who saw clearly from the very beginning that a guilty Parnell was an impossible Irish leader'),[37] Parnell was still presented as the one leader who could have delivered a solution to the Irish question. Parnell's mother, Delia, in her contribution to Robert MacWade's *The Uncrowned King*, published in 1891, recorded that

> Whatever else I have done in life in giving such a son as this to the Irish poor, I feel that I have contributed to humanity a blessing and to Ireland a boon, that the lapse of coming years can never efface. If he has planted in the hearts of the Irish people the ideas of liberty and of union, which shall lead them finally from under the thraldom which has cursed them for the centuries gone by, I shall only be happy and satisfied to have paid the cost which has wrung from my heart many bitter tears and taken from me the pride of my life in the prime and glory of his manhood.[38]

When Katharine O'Shea published her memoir of Parnell in 1914, she claimed that Ireland still 'hugs her chains, and will hug them, for she killed the subtle brain and steadfast heart that alone could free her'.[39] In his memoir of his brother published in 1916, John Howard Parnell recounted, in a somewhat bizarre passage, a visitation by Parnell's ghost in 1897, at Avondale. Charles was sitting at his bedside, with the collar of his greatcoat turned up, at 2 o'clock (when he was used to visit for a chat).

> He was talking about politics, a subject which he very rarely discussed. I remember asking him what were the prospects of Unity. He replied that the parties would unite under John Redmond. Then he got quite angry, and cried out that Harrington was standing in the way.[40]

This prediction of future troubles created by a disunited party, by 1916, hardly needed a visitation from the other side to authenticate it; but it reinforced the idea that Parnell, and Parnell alone, had created the national unity, the essential unity that moved Ireland towards the goal of independence.[41]

This kind of belief made Parnell, as his old follower William O'Brien put it, 'an even more powerful factor of contemporary history than he was when a more or less remorseful nation saw his coffin pass a generation ago'.[42] O'Brien's remarks must be seen against the political conditions of his own day, when Ireland had just passed through an exhausting and bitterly divisive struggle which ended in dominion status for twenty-six counties and partition for the remaining six. St John Ervine, an Ulsterman, and scion of the Literary Revival, while making some acerbic asides on Parnell and his relationship to his followers ('Parnell was of Anglo-Saxon blood, the blood of authority and leadership, while his followers were Celts, in whose veins flowed only the blood of obedience and submission'),[43] saw him as a man who fell 'not before the English wolves, but before the wolves of Ireland', and yet who was 'the cornerstone of the Irish arch'. 'And as it was five hundred years ago, so it is now, and so it will remain until another chieftain comes, as Parnell came, and beats the Irish into a unity that will endure'.[44]

St John Ervine depicted Parnell, then, as a kind of Irish, or rather Anglo-Irish, King Arthur; a kind of role-reversal, for while Arthur, the British Celtic king, was in due course to be seen as the great leader of the English nation, Parnell, the 'Englishman', was the leader of the Celtic Irish nation. William O'Brien responded to this portrait by asserting that Parnell's actions were those of the weak; and the weak must be cunning. Parnell, the leader of a weak nation, had to practise opportunism. The maintenance of the Liberal alliance was 'the fixed point of his policy . . . a truism'.[45] He ended with an assessment of Parnell, not as the hero of some tragedian romance, but as an honest and pertinacious statesman, whose fall was due to the lack of frankness on John Morley's part,[46] and to the blunders of Irish politicians, who were unable to heal the split. Thus the fall of Parnell and his defeat was not some great act of tragedy, or the consequence of 'Irish wolves', but was reducible to 'two blunders of not more than half a dozen politicians working upon an organized popular ignorance'. The lesson from Parnell's life was not one of betrayal, of downfall, of the loss of the dead king, but was found in the politics of contemporary Ireland. Of the two cardinal errors, the first was 'the want of foresight that proclaimed it an unforgivable treason for us to make any attempt to prevent the fate of Parnell from becoming a settled poison in the blood of the country'. The second was committed when, after the reunification of the parliamentary party, and the successes of the 1903 land conference, and Ireland was still 'undarkened by the faintest suggestion of a cleavage into two Irelands', certain 'ill-advised politicians' set out to 'devastate the newly-established unity of an all-but-unanimous country, and did so, of all sardonic ironies, as the high priests of National Unity and Majority Rule'. The result was the destruction of the policy of conciliation, and

> the substitution for the broad and tolerant Nationality of Wolfe Tone of a ubiquitous secret society, restricted to an exclusively Catholic membership, under the sanction of a Catholic sacramental test, with the result of alarming the Protestants of Ulster into preparations for an appalling civil war; and the final panic-stricken bargain made by the dregs of Parnell's denationalised and sectarianised Party, to buy off Sir Edward Carson with the Partition of Ulster, as part of the Home Rule Bill of 1916, to be followed two years afterwards by the deep disgrace and political execution of the entire body who had first consented to the mutilation.[47]

O'Brien was here venting his anger at what he regarded as the folly of Redmond's, and more especially Dillon's, leadership of the Irish parliamentary party: leadership which he believed placed party solidarity before a genuine national unity. O'Brien had nothing but contempt for what he called 'the Hibernian Partitionists'.[48] From this sad history O'Brien concluded that Ireland needed another Parnell, combining as the original did a 'mixture of the magic of the idealist with the firmness of the ruler of men', and doing so with 'a moderation which would long ago have made his English (and Irish) revilers blush for their silliness'. He alleged that it would be a 'sin of national despondency to suggest that this can never be again'. O'Brien, writing before the report of the boundary commission of 1925, had no doubt that the notion entertained by Collins and Griffith at the treaty negotiations that a boundary commission would reduce Northern Ireland to an unviable fragment was unrealistic. And he saw only one way of preventing Ireland from demanding secession, and that was to return to 'those other methods of winning the assent of Ulster which were nearer to success than is generally suspected before the Northern Protestants were goaded to arms and an unendurable wound given to our national pride by the Partition bargain of the IPP in 1916'. A second Parnell might avoid the separatist demand altogether, or would exercise the right of secession 'without a shadow of menace to the safety of England or to the sensibilities of Ulster'.[49]

Writings about Parnell reflected the politics of Ireland after Parnell. But his early biographers, between his fall and 1929, were valuable, not only for their personal accounts of Parnell, but because they were in a sense jockeying for a place beside Parnell's political lying-in-state, rather like Soviet leaders whose political future could be assessed by their proximity to the departed leader. This necessity – to absolve themselves from blame, and to establish their own political credentials for posterity – obliged them to break through the bounds of Victorian biographical propriety.[50]

This mass of detail, some of it of a most personal and intimate nature, marked out Parnell's biographers from those of most Victorian eminences. The fact was that, as Sir Shane Leslie remarked in his *Studies in Sublime Failure*, published in 1932, 'In the case of Parnell, almost everybody, who knew him well, has recorded memories and *without the restraint* which attends general biography'.[51] The personal reticence about Parnell and Mrs O'Shea, noticeable in O'Connor's and Barry O'Brien's books, was swept away by Mrs O'Shea's own revelations, and especially the publication of Parnell's love letters. The fact that Parnell remained a figure of controversy, even after the apparent settlement of the Irish question in 1925, ensured that the revelations and material would continue to be released. Henry Harrison, in particular, in his *Parnell Vindicated* (1931), *Parnell, Joseph Chamberlain and Mr. Garvin* (1938) and *Parnell, Joseph Chamberlain and The Times* (1953) continued to offer voluminous material dealing with the complexity of Parnell's career: the divorce court story; *The Times* forgeries; for, as Harrison wrote:

The dividing line between public career and private life was strictly drawn and rigorously preserved by Parnell himself. In this he was well within his rights, and the general usage of the day completely justified him. But history requires broader effects and the breaking down of the minor obstacles to a comprehensive vision. It wants to judge the man in all his aspects. For good or evil, the privacy of Parnell's private affairs has long since been violated. Is it not better, then, that the discussion of it in history should be furnished with the maximum possible equipment of truth? For Ireland's sake? For the sake of the Ireland that was torn asunder by the feud that sprang from an incomplete revelation?[52]

The generation which wrote these books was disappearing just at the time when the historiographical revolution of modern Ireland was being launched, and was about to produce its first major results. It was both ironic and appropriate that one of the chief founders of this revolution, T. W. Moody, should give his imprimatur to one of the last of the books written about Parnell by one of his contemporaries. When in 1953 Henry Harrison published that last of his Parnell trilogy, *Parnell, Joseph Chamberlain and The Times*, T. W. Moody wrote an introduction, in which he referred to the 'campaign of calumny and falsehood that darkened Parnell's last days', and which

did not close with his death, but from time to time has been reopened under new forms and with new resonances. All such attempts have encountered in Captain Harrison a challenger in whom the audacity, the steadfastness, the chivalry of a crusader are matched by the patience, the critical acumen, the passion for accuracy and the religious respect for documentary evidence that are at once the heavy responsibility and the highest glory of the historian.

The present publication was 'the record of Captain Harrison's crowning victory in a long and arduous struggle'.[53] Moody was, as it happened, the supervisor of the first of the new historians who tackled the subject of Parnell, not as contemporary history, but as history; this was Conor Cruise O'Brien, whose doctoral thesis was the origin of his book *Parnell and his Party, 1880–1890*, first published in 1957,[54] and – appropriately enough – dedicated to the memory of the anti-Parnellite David Sheehy and the Parnellite Henry Harrison, thus symbolizing the beginning of a process by which Parnell historiography and biography would be uncoupled from the rancour of the past.

Cruise O'Brien's book was not a biographical study, but an analysis of party politics and political behaviour. But it was not unlike modern historical biography, which tended to reject the Great Man theory of history, and argue that the hour produced the man, and not the man the hour.[55] Cruise O'Brien believed that biographical writing set a man apart, thus making him appear more of an isolated and self-sufficient phenomenon.[56] Parnell had to be explained; but the question lay in deciding how to formulate the questions. This might mean moving the focus away from the personality and character of Parnell, to a consideration of the kind of social, political and economic forces that made Parnell and Parnellism possible. This, in turn, would require a different approach to historical methodology, one that was not merely a 'life and times' approach, but which would explain Ireland, Britain and the kind of stage their relationship had reached by the 1880s, when Parnell made his impact on the political world of the United Kingdom.

Thus when Cruise O'Brien set about his cool, professional analysis of Parnell and his party, he was able to correct the picture, either that Parnell was the colossus of his party, or that he was a hollow man, the creation of a well-tuned propaganda machine. Cruise O'Brien offered a quotation from T. M. Healy who alleged that

> we created Parnell and Parnell created us. We seized very early in the movement the idea of this man with his superb silences, his historic name, his determination, his self-control, his aloofness – we seized that as the canvas of a great national hero.

This, though an exaggeration, gave Cruise O'Brien his cue. Parnell was all too often seen as a figure separate from his party; Cruise O'Brien's trenchant study restored him to his party. His purpose was: 'To examine how the Irish party at Westminster in the eighties was made up; how it developed and what it did; how it was led, and how, finally, it and its leader destroyed each other.'[57] His first chapter dealt not with Parnell at all, but with the membership of the party in 1880; and he showed that, if ever Parnell was tempted to give up the constitutional and parliamentary game, as for example in February 1881 when the government decided on coercion, then the bulk of his party was certainly not tempted to follow this course.[58] In pursuing this theme, O'Brien was able to show that the outcome of the heated and passionate discussion in Committee

Room 15 had a by no means surprising outcome: the fact was that Parnell's party was firmly committed to the Liberal alliance strategy, and to the parliamentary way; and that its decision to reject its chief was not some kind of Judas Iscariot behaviour, but the logical outcome of the leadership which Parnell had given it over the past decade, and of the core beliefs of the party itself.

Cruise O'Brien's study was not primarily concerned with the relationship between the British and Irish parties. But again he showed that the position, the strengths and weaknesses of the Irish party depended very much on the nature of British politics at any given time. This shifted the focus away from Parnell the maker of events to Parnell the man who must of necessity wait upon the turn of events. The value of placing Parnell firmly in the British political setting opened up new perspectives in interpreting Parnell: not as a kind of sworn enemy of the English, 'not as a magnetic extremist . . . but as the centre of a political complex'.[59] This opened up possibilities for British politicians, Joseph Chamberlain as well as Gladstone, the Conservatives as much as the Liberals, of seeking to move Parnell away from the extremist forces with which his movement had undoubtedly associated, to a more moderate arrangement which might allow of a compromise between the home rulers and the British constitution; an event made more likely by Parnell's closer association with the Roman Catholic church from 1884. This in turn threw new light on Gladstone's conversion to home rule in 1885–6 which was more of a recognition that all other avenues of Irish policy had been tried and failed than a sudden and either idealistic or, on the other hand, cynical expedient. It also pointed future research in the direction followed by scholars such as O'Day and Lubenow:[60] in seeing the home rule party and its leader, not as alien irruptions into the British political system, but as a kind of wing of the British radical political spectrum, as indeed an integral part of the British party system. This, in turn, threw more light on Parnell's ambivalent behaviour in 1891. What had seemed a brave and determined defiance of the 'English' political world, with all its dire consequences for Irish nationality, was given a new subtlety. The careful phrasing of Parnell's last speeches, his profoundly inconsequential words about what might have to be done if parliamentary methods failed, could now be seen as a surer indication of his political ideas than the appeals (always carefully guarded) to the 'hillside men'.

By the 1970s, it was clear that modern, professional historiography had reclaimed Parnell for the Irish constitutional tradition. This was most clearly stated by Cruise O'Brien in his analysis of Parnell's dislike of the Plan of Campaign and his speeches – especially his speech to the Eighty Club on 8 May 1888[61] – which, again, had been noted by earlier biographers,[62] but the significance of which had escaped them, locked as they were in their strategy of presenting Parnell as the wronged party on the one hand, or as the wilful destroyer of the Liberal alliance after the split on the other. Cruise O'Brien's masterly analysis was influenced by his understanding of the nature of political activity itself; he wrote:

> A certain repose and economy characterised his leadership: when he spoke there was a weight of silence behind his words. He acted, in his sparse way, as one who knew that a leader does not just shape events: he must watch, often for long periods, to see how they would shape themselves if left alone.[63]

This choice of words – 'does not *just* shape events' – reflected Cruise O'Brien's own predilection for Burkean political principles: for Burke was always at pains to stress (as conservative thinkers after him expressed) the idea that the political leader rarely shaped events. More, he should not even try to do so: for the best leadership was that which listened for intimations, which uncovered the wishes and needs of his people, which chose carefully the moment when they might be given political articulation.

It was the strength of Cruise O'Brien's analysis that he demonstrated that there was no antithesis, no contradiction, between Parnell the Burkean politician and Parnell the romantic hero. This made the point that there was, perhaps, no essential Parnell, no core of personality or character, of a political or private kind, that excluded any other. The Parnell of Cruise O'Brien's study was a figure at the centre of a complex of politics, a complex created not only by himself, but by the circumstances in Ireland and Great Britain between 1879 and 1886 – and beyond. Thus the man whose policy was 'the very antithesis of Tone's' could take his place in the pantheon of Irish heroes, because of the political needs of Ireland, and the exigencies of British politics: what began as a technique of power, and an adaptation to personal circumstances 'grew upon Parnell in such a way that he finished as the servant, instead of the master, of his own legend'. The British Tory and Irish nationalist press created Parnell in their own image: as hero and demon. Parnell played to both, and in so doing held together in alliance the Fenians, the church, the nationalist electorate, the party and the Liberal alliance, not to break the Union but 'to make it more flexible, more efficient, and more acceptable'.[64]

Conor Cruise O'Brien's study of Parnell and the parliamentary party, however accomplished, left the field open for a modern biography which would reflect not only the Irish historiographical revolution of the 1930s, but also modern biographical writing. The field was taken in 1977 with the publication of F. S. L. Lyons's study[65] which he made, to use Cruise O'Brien's phrase, having spent many years 'casing the joint'.[66] Lyons was a graduate of the modern school of Irish history founded by T. W. Moody. He was a meticulous scholar; and his papers reveal a historian dedicated to tracking down every significant reference in public and private archives. He had indeed cased the joint: a book on the *Irish Parliamentary Party* published in 1951 was followed by a spate of books in the 1960s and 1970s: *The Fall of Parnell* (1960), *John Dillon* (1968), *Ireland since the Famine* (1971).

And yet Lyons found some difficulty in coming to grips with Parnell in a biographical sense. It was as if the context had now overwhelmed the man; indeed, the context produced not one Parnell, but four: the country gentleman, the political genius, the engaging companion, the 'man of passion, driven by demonic pride'.[67] Lyons's difficulty in portraying his subject in a biographical sense is perhaps deducible from his handwritten drafts, where he referred to T. P. O'Connor's description of Parnell in his manhood:[68] 'here is T.P.'s portrait of him, overdone as was T.P.'s [habit] custom, but [nea nea close, lurid] penetrating enough [to other descriptions] [reality] to bear reproduction'. His final published draft read: 'Here is T. P. O'Connor's portrait of him, overdone as was "T.P.'s" habit, but also perceptive.'[69]

Lyons's biography marked the dissolution of that link between the Anglo-Irish and Parnell, which even the scientific historian, T. W. Moody, represented. The Anglo-Irish – Yeats, Lady Gregory – had helped create Parnell as a mythical figure. Now that link was broken, and broken by a historian from that tradition; but this seemed to make it more, not less, difficult to answer the question which Parnell invariably raised. What was it about him that fascinated his contemporaries; more, that fascinated also later generations? When Lyons attempted to sum up Parnell's place in Irish history, he could do no more than offer a fairly traditional (but not necessarily misleading) theme: 'He gave his people back their self respect.'[70] But this left unanswered important questions: was this why Parnell entered politics? And who were Parnell's people?

This question was addressed by two students of Parnell, using very different contexts for their research. R. F. Foster's *Charles Stewart Parnell: the Man and his Family* was published while Lyons's book was in the press. His purpose was to avoid discussing Parnell's political life, and instead to analyse Parnell and not only Parnell but his family, in the context of their social background: nineteenth-century Wicklow, the Anglo-Irish ascendancy of Wicklow, and the location of Parnell's place in this context. This involved him in a form of micro-history, and in the search for the unknown Parnells, in the course of which he discovered 'the neglected figure of his paternal grandfather, a radical pamphleteer and improving landlord'. Foster's hope was that this 'necessarily limited view of his background and personal life' would shed light 'on the "traditionally enigmatic figure he became" '.[71]

The second biography was a contrast, both in method and purpose. Paul Bew's *Charles Stewart Parnell* was a volume in the Gill's Irish Lives series, and as such it was, necessarily, brief, and also based on secondary material (though Bew also employed a wide range of newspaper material to place Parnell in the political life of the Ireland of his day). More significantly, Bew approached his subject from the opposite end of the historical spectrum. He defined

> three great epochs of crisis in Anglo-Irish relations since the Great Famine. These were the agrarian revolution and Home Rule crises of the 1880s; the period from the Easter Rising of 1916 to the Anglo-Irish Treaty of 1921; and the Ulster 'troubles' which erupted in 1968 and are still prevalent.

Yet only one of these was dominated by a single Irish politician – 'The nationalist leader of the 1880s, C. S. Parnell, whose fall in 1891 significantly altered the content of the "Irish question" as it existed in his time.'[72]

Foster saw Parnell in his intimate family context; Bew allocated him his place in a great broad national political crisis – and crises. But despite their different approaches – or perhaps because of them – they offered a convincing portrait of Parnell's motives. They did so because they saw Parnell, not as some strange, odd, isolated figure, not as a 'king', placed at the head of a Catholic nationalist movement, but as a man typical of a certain kind of people, and by no means unrepresentative of them: the Anglo-Irish gentry, somewhat impoverished by the mid nineteenth century; ambivalent in their attitude to the country from which they traced their origin; and with their outlook and political career shaped by their special predicament. Parnell's outlook was by no means unusual in the context of County Wicklow, in that it embraced, as Foster pointed out and Bew endorsed, a liberal patriotism, liberal towards Roman Catholics and critical of the ascendancy tradition that held that its only safety lay in maintaining the British connection inviolate and in distancing itself from Roman Catholic political ambitions and activity. The way forward, Bew wrote, was for Parnell to fight for his class to play their rightful part in Irish politics, as they had done in the time of Henry Grattan. This involved, not the maintenance of their privileges (such as they were) as landlords, but the abandonment of their opposition to land reform, and thus the removal of the barrier to their association with the home rule movement: 'Parnell felt that Ireland should be governed by men of substance *who lived in it.* In this sense he was indeed perhaps the last representative of the Protestant gentlemen who had appealed for an autonomous Ireland in the age of Grattan.'[73] These two works, however different in scope and method, removed the mystery and enigma from Parnell. They showed him in his political tradition; they revealed that the search for some key 'turning point' in his life (his sending down from Cambridge; the Fenian activity in Wicklow in 1867) was a chimera. They showed also that Parnell was no mere technician of political power, no mere manipulator of political strings for its own sake; but a man whose background, family and political outlook were perfectly compatible with his own career, outlook and purpose. This placed Parnell more firmly in the Irish political context: his aims, it might be said, were 'domestic' rather than 'foreign' in their centrality.[74] His motive was less to create, as Cruise O'Brien believed, an Anglo-Irish rapprochement for its own sake[75] than to create it for the sake of saving the landlord class as the natural political leaders of their nation. The modern historians showed how the idea of 'mystery' and 'enigma' were misdirecting signposts: and that there were, after all, rational explanations for Parnell's political career.

It might seem, therefore, that a century after Parnell's death there was little more to be said about him in any biographical sense. His assessment had indeed covered the whole range of biographical writing, revealing a kind of geological stratum of the art of biography itself. And yet modern Ireland, and modern Irish history, remained in a sense under Parnell's star.[76] Even the professional historians of the 1950s onwards could not resist speculating on the impact that Parnell might have had, had he lived, on Ireland and on Anglo-Irish relations. In 1957 Cruise O'Brien mused,

Whether that policy, backed as it was by a great English party, and a great Irish party, and by the combined prestige of Gladstone and Parnell, could have succeeded in bringing all Ulster without serious bloodshed, within the framework of home rule, can obviously never be known. It may be said, however, that no subsequent policy, and no subsequent combination of leaders, offered such good grounds for hope of a united and self-governing Ireland – or of real and well-founded friendship between England and Ireland.

By 1978, however, the same writer, as Bew noted, commented on Parnell in a very different tone:

He could not . . . ever have 'won Home Rule' because Home Rule was simply not winnable. Parnell, though a Protestant, was speaking for the Catholics of Ireland, not – as he and his followers appeared to take for granted – for an Irish nation that included the Ulster Protestants.[77]

F. S. L. Lyons, who in his biography of John Dillon remarked that 'The obstinate . . . resistance of Ulster and English Unionists to the extremely moderate self-government which Parnell, Redmond, and Dillon were originally prepared to accept will always remain one of the strangest mysteries of politics',[78] by 1977 acknowledged that Parnell 'never seems to have asked himself what he meant by the "Irish nation" or "Irish race" which he claimed to lead, and the idea that Ireland might possibly contain two nations, not one, apparently never entered his head'.[79]

In 1933 Harold Nicolson, in his *Development of English Biography*, argued that biography had its origins in the 'commemorative instinct' and the 'didactic temptation';[80] and certainly Parnell's early biographers, including the great Boswellian, R. B. O'Brien, displayed these characteristics. Since the 1950s, Parnell biographical writing has been influenced by the rise of history as a professional subject and the search for historical truth. But modern biography has not reduced Parnell's importance: on the contrary, by investigating Parnell's sins of omission as well as commission, modern biographers have made him an even more pivotal figure in the history and politics of modern Ireland. And yet a comparison between Parnell's early and his modern biographers reveals that, if Parnell was no longer surrounded by myth, then, deprived of myth, his extraordinary power over his contemporaries remains something of a mystery.

Parnell thus poses a problem which modern historical biography, by its very nature, cannot resolve. Modern historical biography is concerned with reality, not image. Political figures live three lives: a private life; a public life; and another kind of public life, which is largely conducted in a private way, as they make the necessary compromises, engage in brokerage, act as fixers. Parnell in perspective fused the last two, so that brokerage became elevated into an even more enhanced image: home rule, a necessary compromise, became the prophet leading his people into the promised land. The reason is that Parnell's most influential early biographers created a world in which 'image' and 'reality' were blended into a kind of Yeatsian 'Unity'; even those who disapproved of his last campaign left a memory of an incarnate myth, and the biographer of Parnell needs to uncover the means by which the memory of the king was produced, and come to grips with the reality that the portrait of the king is the king. It is perhaps appropriate to leave the last word with Yeats, who in his poem 'Among School Children' explored the heartbreaking contrast between 'image' and 'reality': and reaffirmed that these opposites need not be so. For it can be said of Parnell that life helped art, and art assisted life. And when history and symbol converge

How can we know the dancer from the dance?[81]

NOTES

1 Jacques de Goff, *Times Literary Supplement*, 14–20 April 1988, p. 405, quoting Louis Marin.
2 Quoted in Joseph W. Reed, jr, *English Biography in the Early Nineteenth Century*, New York and London, 1966, p. 3.
3 Sir Sidney Lee, *The Perspective of Biography*, English Association Pamphlet 41, London, 1918, p. 7.
4 Ibid.
5 William Michael Murphy, *The Parnell Myth and Irish Politics, 1891–1956*, New York, 1986, ch. 7.
6 Lorcan Sherlock, Preface to the London 1945 edition of T. Sherlock, *Charles Stewart Parnell*, first published 1882.
7 T. Sherlock, *Charles Stewart Parnell*, London, 1945 edn, pp. 5–30 and app. 1.
8 Ibid., pp. 79–80.
9 Ibid., p. 79.
10 Ibid., p. 48.
11 J. S. Mahoney, *The Life of Charles Stewart Parnell*, New York, 1885, pp. 88–9, 93–4, 140.
12 R. Johnston, *Parnell and the Parnells: a Historical Sketch*, London and Dublin, 1888, pp. 12–19.

13 T. P. O'Connor, *The Parnell Movement*, London, 1886, pp. 253–9, 390.
14 Mahoney, *Life of Parnell*, p. 140. See also T. P. O'Connor and Robert MacWade, *Gladstone–Parnell and the Great Irish Struggle*, Sydney, 1886.
15 L. W. Brady, *T. P. O'Connor and the Liverpool Irish*, London, 1983, pp. 123–5.
16 Ibid., p. 122.
17 Murphy, *The Parnell Myth*, p. 22.
18 T. P. O'Connor, *Charles Stewart Parnell: a Memory*, London, 1891, pp. 27–8.
19 Ibid., p. 53.
20 Ibid., pp. 213–14.
21 Robert MacWade, *The Uncrowned King: the Life and Public Services of Charles Stewart Parnell*, 1891, p. 42.
22 R. Barry O'Brien, *The Life of Charles Stewart Parnell*, London, 1898: all page references cited here are to the London, 1910 edition.
23 Ibid., p. 465.
24 Harold Nicolson, *The Development of English Biography*, London, 1933, ch. IV.
25 R. Barry O'Brien, *Life of Parnell*, p. 163.
26 Ibid., pp. 206, 319.
27 Ibid., pp. 86–7.
28 Ibid., p. 177.
29 Ibid., p. 413.
30 Ibid., p. 420.
31 Ibid., pp. 419–20.
32 Ibid., pp. 425–6.
33 Ibid., p. 552.
34 Ibid., p. 563.
35 Ibid., pp. 551–2; W. B. Yeats, 'Parnell's funeral', in *Collected Poems*, London, 1950 edn, pp. 319–20.
36 Emily M. Dickinson, *A Patriot's Mistake: being Personal Recollections of the Parnell Family by a Daughter of the House*, Dublin and London, 1905, p. 189.
37 M. M. O'Hara, *Chief and Tribune: Parnell and Davitt*, Dublin and London, 1919, p. 314.
38 MacWade, *The Uncrowned King*, pp. 68–9.
39 Katharine O'Shea, *Charles Stewart Parnell: his Love Story and Political Life*, 2 vols, London, 1914, vol. I, pp. ix-x.
40 J. H. Parnell, *Charles Stewart Parnell: a Memoir*, London, 1916, pp. 259–60.
41 O'Hara, *Chief and Tribune*, p. 328; see also p. 71: 'without Parnell, the Irish citizen would still be a political Ishmael'.
42 William O'Brien, *The Parnell of Real Life*, London, 1926, p. 209.
43 St John Ervine, *Parnell*, London, 1925; Penguin, 1944 edn, p. 111.
44 W. O. O'Brien, *Parnell*, p. 244.
45 Ibid., p. 135.
46 Ibid., pp. 147–9, 174–8.
47 Ibid., pp. 205–8.
48 Ibid., p. 207.

49 Ibid., pp. 209–13.
50 For a convenient summary of these biographies see Murphy, *The Parnell Myth*, pp. 22–32. There is an interesting review of Katharine O'Shea's book by Darrell Figgis in *Nineteenth Century*, 19–20, July-December 1914, pp. 217–27.
51 Shane Leslie, *Studies in Sublime Failure*, London, 1932, p. 296.
52 Henry Harrison, *Parnell Vindicated*, London, 1931, p. 15.
53 T. W. Moody, Introduction to Henry Harrison, *Parnell, Joseph Chamberlain and The Times: a Documentary Record*, Belfast and Dublin, 1953.
54 Conor Cruise O'Brien, *Parnell and his Party, 1880–1890*, Oxford, 1957.
55 Robert Skidelsky, 'Only connect: biography and truth', in Eric Homberger and John Charmley (eds), *The Troubled Face of Biography*, London, 1988, p. 2.
56 Cruise O'Brien, *Parnell and his Party*, p. 10.
57 Ibid., p. 10.
58 Ibid., pp. 59–61.
59 Ibid., p. 93.
60 Alan O'Day, *The English Face of Irish Nationalism*, Dublin, 1977; W. C. Lubenow, *Parliamentary Politics and the Home Rule Crisis*, Oxford, 1988.
61 Cruise O'Brien, *Parnell and his Party*, pp. 219–20.
62 R. Barry O'Brien, *Life of Parnell*, p. 461.
63 Cruise O'Brien, *Parnell and his Party*, p. 245.
64 Ibid., pp. 349–51.
65 F. S. L. Lyons, *Charles Stewart Parnell*, London, 1977; all references are to the Fontana, 1978 edition.
66 Cruise O'Brien, reviewing Lyons's *Parnell, Irish Historical Studies*, 20, 1976–77, p. 516.
67 Lyons, *Parnell*, p. 51.
68 F. S. L. Lyons MSS, TCD MS 10337/3/B; final MS Draft, p. 80. Words in square brackets indicate Lyons's deletions. Quotation from F. S. L. Lyons's MSS is given with the kind permission of Mrs Jennifer Lyons.
69 Lyons, *Parnell*, p. 51.
70 Lyons, *Parnell*, p. 616. As Murphy, *The Parnell Myth*, pp. 119, 177, remarks, this verdict is consistent with the Parnell myth in his own day and afterwards.
71 R. F. Foster, *Charles Stewart Parnell: the Man and his Family*, Sussex, 1976, pp. ix-x.
72 Paul Bew, *Charles Stewart Parnell*, Dublin, 1980, pp. 1–3.
73 Ibid., pp. 13–15, 138, 142–3.
74 Foster, *Parnell*, pp. 308–9.
75 'He and his party accepted Gladstonian Home Rule – essentially a compromise between Irish national and English imperial traditions – as a final settlement, and they obtained the approval of the Irish people for this acceptance'; Cruise O'Brien, *Parnell and his Party*, p. 349.
76 See the reviews of Lyons's *Parnell* in TCD MS 1033/D/2/8, 13, 18, 21, 22.
77 Bew, *Parnell*, p. 141.
78 F. S. L. Lyons, *John Dillon: a Biography*, London, 1968, p. 483.

79 Lyons, *Parnell*, p. 623.
80 Nicolson, *Development of English Biography*, p. 17.
81 W. B. Yeats, 'Among school children', in *Collected Poems*, London, 1971 edn, p. 245.

I am grateful to Mr Owen Dudley Edwards for commenting on an earlier draft of this chapter.

Index

Note. Most references are to Parnell and his influence

formed (1879) 10, 43; Land War and O'Brien 52–76: and political thought of Parnell 161–4; and press 221–2, 225–6, 229, 231; *see also* Irish National League

Land League of Mayo 11

Land Purchase Act (1885) 95; *see also* Ashbourne Act

Land Purchase Migration Company 61–2, 182

Land War *see* Land League

landlords and rent 253–4; economic thought of Parnell 174–8, 189, 190; *see also* Land League

Lane, Hugh 275

language, Irish 245, 248–9; *see also* Gaelic

Larkin, Emmet 21, 26

Lee, Sir Sidney 284

legislative independence 154, 161

Leinster 23, 210

Leitrim, Lord 162

Leo XIII, Pope 17

Leonard, Hugh 3

Leslie, Sir Shane 297

Lever, Charles 287

Liberal alliance 25, 62, 65, 70, 86, 96, 98, 208, 245–6, 304: biographers on 293–4, 299–300; and fall of Parnell 129–47 *passim*; formation of 120, 124–6

Liberals 24, 26–7, 45, 46, 53, 61–2, 109, 113–21; and nationalism 81–2, 84, 86, 90, 93, 95–6; and 'Union of Hearts' 65, 70, 97; *see also* Gladstone: Liberal alliance

Limerick 13, 210

literature, Irish 243–83

Liverpool, Lord 91

Lockart, John Gibson 284

Louden, John James 10, 23

Loughlin, James xii, 217; on Parnell, press and national leadership 221–41

Louth 234

Lover, Samuel 287

Lowell, James 255

Lubenow, W. C. 121, 135, 300

Lucas 228

Lynch, Bishop 29

Lynch, Michael 96

Lynch, Thomas 13

Lyons, F. S. L. 2, 5; as biographer 285, 302, 303, 305; on Catholic church 19; on fall of Parnell 129, 131, 133, 138, 145; on landlords 42; on methodology 151

Maamtrasna affair 20

MacAllister, Patrick 29

McCabe, Archbishop Edward 15, 16, 19, 22

McCarthy, Denis 14

McCarthy, Justin 84, 246

McCarthy, M. J. F. 225, 229, 232

MacDonagh, Oliver 151

McEvilly, Archbishop John 16–17, 20, 21

McGettigan, Bishop Daniel 19

MacHale, Archbishop John 10–11, 12

MacHale, Thomas 11

Machiavelli, Nicoló 246

MacWade, Robert 290, 294

Mahoney, J. S. 286, 287

'Manchester martyrs' 10, 18, 110, 222

Manning, Cardinal Henry Edward 20

Martyn, Edward 253, 259, 264

Marx, Karl 46, 222

Maryborough 190

mass agitation 10, 224–51

Mayo 10, 11, 17, 20

Meath 2, 109, 152, 205; bishop of *see* Nulty

M'Grath, John 246

Migration Company: *see* Land Purchase Migration Company

militia disbanded 159

Mitchel, John 265, 266

Monaghan 39, 210

Moody, T. W. 39, 40, 43–4, 45, 46, 298, 302

Moore, George 246, 259, 260, 261

Moore, Thomas 122

Moran, Bishop 16